ISBN 978-0-259-96040-9
PIBN 10838320

1 MONTH OF
FREE
READING

at

www.ForgottenBooks.com

By purchasing this book you are eligible for one month membership to ForgottenBooks.com, giving you unlimited access to our entire collection of over 700,000 titles via our web site and mobile apps.

To claim your free month visit:
www.forgottenbooks.com/free838320

English
Français
Deutsche
Italiano
Español
Português

www.forgottenbooks.com

Mythology Photography **Fiction**
Fishing Christianity **Art** Cooking
Essays Buddhism Freemasonry
Medicine **Biology** Music **Ancient
Egypt** Evolution Carpentry Physics
Dance Geology **Mathematics** Fitness
Shakespeare **Folklore** Yoga Marketing
Confidence Immortality Biographies
Poetry **Psychology** Witchcraft
Electronics Chemistry History **Law**
Accounting **Philosophy** Anthropology
Alchemy Drama Quantum Mechanics
Atheism Sexual Health **Ancient History**
Entrepreneurship Languages Sport
Paleontology Needlework Islam
Metaphysics Investment Archaeology
Parenting Statistics Criminology
Motivational

THE

𝕸𝖊𝖎𝖘𝖙𝖊𝖗𝖘𝖈𝖍𝖆𝖋𝖙 𝕾𝖞𝖘𝖙𝖊𝖒.

A SIMPLE AND PRACTICAL METHOD,

ENABLING

ANY ONE TO LEARN, WITH SLIGHT EFFORT, TO SPEAK
FLUENTLY AND CORRECTLY

𝕱𝖗𝖊𝖓𝖈𝖍, 𝕲𝖊𝖗𝖒𝖆𝖓, 𝕾𝖕𝖆𝖓𝖎𝖘𝖍, 𝖆𝖓𝖉 𝕴𝖙𝖆𝖑𝖎𝖆𝖓,

BY

TERMS.

WE have arranged with Dr. ROSENTHAL, the author of the "Meisterschaft System," for its introduction in America under his own supervision, and he has opened

The Meisterschaft School of Practical Linguistry

FOR NON-RESIDENTS.

The student does not need to leave his home. The lessons of each language are prepared by the Professor, and printed and sent in pamphlet shape to each member of the School wherever he may reside.

The course of study for each language—German, French, Italian, or Spanish—makes fifteen pamphlets of three lessons each.

All members of the School have

THE PRIVILEGE

of asking, by letter, questions concerning each lesson, or consulting on any difficulty which may have occurred to them. All exercises corrected and all questions answered by return post by Dr. ROSENTHAL or one of his assistants.

TERMS OF MEMBERSHIP.

Five Dollars is the price for membership in the school for each language. This amount ($5.) entitles the member to receive the fifteen books or pamphlets containing the lessons, also answers to his questions. Return postage for the answer must accompany the question.

State distinctly which language, or languages, you desire to study There are *no extra charges*. The price, **Five Dollars**, pays for one language; **Ten Dollars** for two languages, etc. All exercises and questions must be written on a separate sheet of paper, and must state full address of the pupil.

Remittances must be made in Post-Office Order or registered letter addressed to

I. K. FUNK & CO.,

10 and 12 Dey Street, New York.

THE MEISTERSCHAFT SYSTEM HAS BEEN UNIVERSALLY SUCCESSFUL IN GERMANY AND ENGLAND, AND IS ENTHUSIASTICALLY ENDORSED BY EDUCATORS, STATESMEN, EDITORS, AND BUSINESS MEN.

FROM THE MASS OF TESTIMONIALS WE SELECT THE FOLLOWING:

DR. BERNH. SCHMITZ, *Professor of Modern Philology at the Royal University, Greifswald, Prussia, author of the "Encyclopædie des Philologischen Studiums der neueren Sprachen:"* "Having carefully studied Dr. Rosenthal's '*Meisterschaft System*' I can bear testimony to its *great superiority over the older methods* so far as *conversation* is concerned. The acquisition of the grammar is also considerably simplified. Of course there is no royal road to learning, but the pupil who will give a fair amount of time to study will, under this system, be rewarded with *most astonishing results*." . . .

DR. CARL PLOETZ, *author of numerous French Standard Grammars and Manuals, all of which are used in the Prussian schools:* . . . "Dr. Rosenthal aims, in the first place, at *the ability of conversation*, and he is the first linguist who has properly defined the extent of every-day speech. . . . The difference between the language of literature and that used in every-day life is so marked, that even the talented and educated philologist on coming to a foreign country finds himself at a loss for those ordinary terms most necessary to him on all occasions. The '*Meisterschaft System*' in giving only the necessary '*stock vocabulary*' of speech, and in teaching the learner to think in the foreign language from the very start, is certainly the *most practical method* I know, and *recommends itself especially to adults*."

DR. HEINRICH SCHLIEMANN, *the celebrated explorer of Greek antiquities:* "The '*Meisterschaft System*' is simply a scientific adaptation of the natural method by which all persons, whether children or adults, educated or otherwise, rapidly and correctly acquire the language which they constantly hear, and which they are instinctively impelled to imitate when resident in a foreign country. . . . It is the best system for all practical purposes." . . .

THE LATE HOFRATH LUDWIG SCHNEIDER, *Private Court Councillor and Reader to His Majesty the Emperor William of Germany:* . . . "Dr. Rosenthal's ideas coincide entirely with my own. . . . This is the way in which I myself have mastered half-a-dozen European languages so thoroughly that I can speak them fluently." . . .

THE HON. HUGH CHILDERS, Secretary of War, England: "I hope to see your *excellent and most practical system* used by all candidates who present themselves for the army examinations, none of whom can express themselves in French or German." . . .

literal translation, being, in my opinion, the great secret of its success. As one of your pupils, I have much pleasure in bearing testimony to its efficacy, and *feel confident that the results, in my own case, could not have been attained by any other system in so short a time.*"

FROM DR SCHWARTZ, *Professor of Modern Languages' Berlin :* " Having used the ' *Meisterschaft System* ' for about two years, I can conscientiously recommend it to all who wish to make *rapid progress in acquiring a language conversationally and idiomatically.* There is, in my opinion, *no doubt that it is the easiest and most certain way of acquiring perfect mastery over any foreign language.*"

FROM HER EXCELLENCY, COUNTESS TAAFFE, *sister of the Austrian Prime Minister :* " After having studied the Spanish language under you for a short period, I find that I have made such rapid progress that I can safely bear witness to the wonderful excellence and practical simplicity of your system. . . . It is the most natural way of acquiring fluency of speech in a foreign tongue." . . .

FROM THE BARONESS DE KAISERSTEIN, *first Lady in Waiting to Her Imperial Highness, Archduchess Isabella of Austria :* " I can confidently state that, so far as my experience goes, *the ' Meisterschaft System' is astonishingly efficacious, and not overrated. . . . After but six lessons I find myself frequently forming sentences in Spanish mentally ; I can already translate easily in writing ; and fluency in speaking the language*—an acquisition so much desired—*cannot fail to be the result of the daily practice recommended.*" . . .

FROM HIS EXCELLENCY, DR. LEONHARDT, *late Justiz Minister* " Lord Chancellor " to *His Imperial Majesty, the Emperor of Germany :* . . . " I have much pleasure in bearing witness to the " *Meisterschaft System* ' as taught by you. My son *only had seven lessons* from you in English, *and he can not only speak and write it with a fluency that I never expected him to attain in so short a time, but I am sure he has a much more complete knowledge of the language than he could have obtained under any other system.*"

FROM COUNT THASSILO FESTETICS, *Magnate of Hungary :* Having studied the Spanish language for upward of two years by the old system with indifferent results, I resolved to make a trial of the ' *Meisterschaft System.*' My eyes had for some time been opened to the fact that I had been learning to talk about Spanish in lieu of learning to speak the language itself. . . . *In my very first lesson I was enabled,* to my extreme delight, to utter a Spanish sentence containing 21 words as fluently and accurately as its German equivalent—a feat which I had never been able to accomplish hitherto. From this sentence an innumerable variety of new sentences were extracted, all of which were mastered at once with like precision. In conclusion, I have only to state that the result of three weeks' tuition has far exceeded my highest anticipation, and I can therefore confidently recommend the method to those who are desirous of becoming acquainted with modern languages."

What the CHRISTIAN WORLD, LONDON, England, says : " Many of our readers must have contended, in some form or another, with the difficulties of learning a foreign language ; and not a few have regretted the pains they have taken and the money they have spent to procure an acquaintance with French or German, so as to be able to understand it easily when spoken, and speak it for themselves. WE ARE, THEREFORE, GLAD TO CALL SPECIAL ATTENTION TO SOME VERY SENSIBLE AND VIGOROUS EFFORTS WHICH ARE NOW BEING MADE BY WAY OF PROMOTING THE STUDY OF THE FRENCH AND GERMAN LANGUAGES IN THIS COUNTRY. DR. RICHARD S. ROSENTHAL, late director of the Academy for Foreign Languages in Berlin and Leipzig, is *now issuing two separate works for these languages respectively*, entitled "The Meisterschaft System," which is *a method perfected for* THE PRACTICAL AND NATURAL LEARNING *of these languages for business and conversation. His aim is to promote fluency in speaking rather than the grammatical learning which so commonly takes its place.* He properly insists upon the necessity, which every day becomes more apparent, of increasing our facilities for communication with other people by acquiring a *practical acquaintance* with their language, and not merely a theoretical knowledge of their respective grammars. His method involves frequent and persistent utterances of French and German phrases, so that the ear may become accustomed to the sound as the eye to the written word."

What the OXFORD JOURNAL, OXFORD, England, says : "*This system overcomes the greatest of all difficulties* hitherto found in teaching and acquiring a language, viz., FLUENCY OF SPEECH. . . . ITS WONDERFUL SIMPLICITY SAVES MUCH TIME, as CONTINUOUS STUDY IS NOT REQUIRED, while the *pronunciation* is so *clearly shown* that even the most uneducated can master it. . . . Dr. Rosenthal's method is based upon a sound and natural principle. . . . IT IS THE MOST PRACTICAL METHOD WE KNOW, and certainly does much to simplify the task of learning a foreign language." . . .

What the LITERARY WORLD, LONDON, England, says : "We can by no means express satisfaction with the method of teaching generally prevalent in our English schools. An enormous amount of time, strength, and money is expended by parents, pupils, and teachers upon the principal continental languages with most unsatisfactory results. Any one, therefore, who introduces a real improvement of method is entitled to hearty thanks. . . . Dr. Rosenthal's method of instruction aims in the first place at THE ABILITY OF CONVERSATION, and he has worked out his theory WITH A SKILL, THOROUGHNESS, AND ADHERENCE TO SOUND SCIENTIFIC PRINCIPLES WHICH WE HAVE NOT FOUND ELSEWHERE." . . .

What the BRADFORD OBSERVER, BRADFORD, England, says : "This is a French instruction book on a novel method, or at least novel to this country, for it has been adopted for three years past in different German institutions, and, as we understand, with most surprising results. . . . The principle of the system is to imitate the method by which children learn their mother tongue, and by which all persons pick up a language they constantly hear spoken. . . . The art of speaking French is to be acquired by the constant repetition of sound, and this naturally will soon be followed by thinking in French. THE PLAN IS MOST INGENIOUS AND PRACTICAL, AND WE ARE BOUND TO SAY THAT A CAREFUL EXAMINATION OF THE

LESSONS IMPRESSES US MOST FAVORABLY. . . .. We recommend the work most earnestly to all who wish to speak French and German." . . .

What the SCOTSMAN, EDINBURGH, Scotland, says : "Although we have several excellent works for the improvement of our method of teaching languages, WE HAVE NO HESITATION IN DECLARING THE ONE BEFORE US — 'Dr. Rosenthal's Meisterschaft System'—TO BE THE VERY BEST ; because, in the first place, it is so simple that every one can use it without interfering with business, or interruption of other studies ; and next, because *it has never been known to fail in what it professes*, viz., *to give a complete mastery over a foreign language in a wonderfully short time.*"

What the ACADEMY, LONDON, England, says : "We have heard continually from our correspondents in Berlin and Leipzig of the celebrated teacher, Dr. Rosenthal, and his 'Meisterschaft System,' and can only say, after a careful examination of his work, that *their success is well deserved.* A pupil cannot fail, be he ever so stupid or disinclined to study, to master a knowledge of French from the *wonderfully simple and ingenious method.* . . . Dr. Rosenthal has certainly devised a plan by which study is rendered comfortable and natural." -

What the SHEFFIELD INDEPENDENT, SHEFFIELD, England, says : "The system of Dr. Rosenthal is WONDERFULLY adapted for a RAPID MASTERY OF THE LANGUAGE. *The pronunciation of each* WORD IS GIVEN and WITH FIRST-RATE SUCCESS. . . . Perhaps the greatest recommendation of all is that every subscriber becomes a pupil of Dr. Rosenthal's, and all exercises are received, corrected, and returned by him. The author's system is certainly French and German made easy." . . .

What the EASTBOURNE GAZETTE, EASTBOURNE, England, says : "The portion of this system that lies before us is devoted to the French language, and will be completed in 15 parts, at 1 s. each. The introduction to the work is one of the most practical essays on the subject of languages that has come under our notice. The author states many truths concerning the learning of foreign languages which will at once commend themselves to the reader. Thus we are told 'the speaking of foreign tongues is not a matter of the intellect, but a trick of the ear and tongue, as proved by the fact that children acquire a foreign language much more rapidly than grown persons ; they speak, in fact, without thinking at all.' For this reason the Meisterschaft System is 'simply a scientific imitation of the natural method' of speaking. Instead of dry grammatical rules, the author makes a feature of conversations, for, as he very pithily observes, 'of what use is a perfect knowledge of all the regular and irregular verbs to the tourist who fails to understand the rapid utterances of even a railway porter, and who can scarcely ask for his common necessities?' The conversations given are those that are most likely to be useful, and they are arranged in such a way as to give but a nominal amount of labor in mastering ; and we should say that the study of French under these conditions becomes an agreeable pastime rather than a labor. To dwell upon the advantage of a knowledge of French is unnecessary. Firstly, its possessor has an immense advantage in the battle of life, for by its aid many lucrative situations are open to him ; and abroad it is invaluable in facilitating his social intercourse. Dr. Rosenthal will correct the exercises of every subscriber to the entire work, who thus virtually becomes a pupil of the Doctor's. WE FULLY ANTICIPATE THAT THE 'MEISTERSCHAFT SYSTEM' WILL DO FOR THE ACQUIREMENT OF THE FRENCH AND GERMAN LANGUAGES WHAT PHONOGRAPHY HAS DONE FOR THE ACQUIREMENT OF SHORTHAND."

What the EASTERN MORNING NEWS, HULL, England, says: "WE HAVE NO HESITATION AT ALL TO SAY THAT FLUENCY OF SPEECH IS TO BE ACQUIRED BY THIS SYSTEM ONLY OR BY RESIDENCE ABROAD. . . . . Besides this, Dr. Rosenthal's method recommends itself by its simplicity, especially to time-pressed business men, because the time for study is at intervals, and is not required to be continuous. Last, but perhaps most important of all, is the exceedingly plain and exact method of pronunciation, which admits of no mistakes on the part of even the most uneducated."

What the DOVER CHRONICLE, DOVER, England says : "This system is a great improvement on the mastery series of Prendergast, as adapted to the French language. It is an adaptation of one of Locke's precepts for the improvement of memory, namely, by constant repetition, or rather the iteration of the same idea under different aspects. Starting with the simplest elements of conversation, it aims at obviating that greatest of all difficulties in teaching—fluency of speech. It is admirably adapted for business men, and there are familiar precepts for obtaining an exact pronunciation, as far as it can be acquired without residence in a foreign land. . . . IT IS CERTAINLY THE BEST AND MOST PRACTICAL WORK WE HAVE THUS FAR SEEN." . . .

What the NORTHERN WHIG, BELFAST, Ireland, says : "This method has already proved most successful in several instances we know of. . . . The method does not deal with mere grammatical rules and long lists of words, but it commences at once with sentences, giving the pronunciation and meaning. These sentences refer to subjects necessary to the pupil, whether for business purposes or a pleasure trip. . . . The student learns thus from the very first lesson to speak. . . . This may be aptly called the natural system of linguistry, as distinct from philology. . . . THE SYSTEM IS REALLY WONDERFUL IN ITS RESULTS." . . .

Among the patrons of the " Meisterschaft System " are : His Imperial Highness Archduke Frederic of Austria ; Archduchess Elisabeth of Austria ; Archduchess Isabella of Austria ; Prince Windischgräz ; Duke of Coburg ; Count Taaffe ; Countess Taaffe ; Countess Festeticz ; Baron Rothschild ; Count Bismarck, Jr. ; General Fransecky ; Colonel Bigot, etc., etc.,—many members of the German and Austrian Parliament ; of the Prussian Cabinet ; over 300 German teachers, etc., etc.

THE

𝕸𝖊𝖎𝖘𝖙𝖊𝖗𝖘𝖈𝖍𝖆𝖋𝖙 𝕾𝖞𝖘𝖙𝖊𝖒.

A SIMPLE AND PRACTICAL METHOD,

ENABLING

ANY ONE TO LEARN, WITH SLIGHT EFFORT, TO SPEAK FLUENTLY AND CORRECTLY

𝕱𝖗𝖊𝖓𝖈𝖍, 𝕲𝖊𝖗𝖒𝖆𝖓, 𝕾𝖕𝖆𝖓𝖎𝖘𝖍, 𝖆𝖓𝖉 𝕴𝖙𝖆𝖑𝖎𝖆𝖓.

BY

DR. RICHARD S. ROSENTHAL,

Late Director of the "Akademie für fremde Sprachen" in Berlin and Leipzig, of the "Meisterschaft College" in London, and Principal of the "Meisterschaft School of Practical Linguistry" in New York.

FRENCH.

IN FIFTEEN PARTS, EACH CONTAINING THREE LESSONS.

NEW YORK:

I. K. FUNK & CO., PUBLISHERS,

10 AND 12 DEY STREET.

It is a widely known and acknowledged fact that, although our young men and women study German and French for years, frequently under the tuition of able native masters, they very rarely attain any degree of

PRACTICAL FLUENCY IN SPEAKING THESE TONGUES.

In our times, when international commerce and intercourse is so constantly increasing, our schools and colleges must aim at other and more practical results than heretofore were considered necessary.

It is no longer sufficient to teach the student the grammatical peculiarities of French and German, and to introduce him into the classic literature of these languages; but *the true end and aim of our linguistic education must be to actually speak the modern tongues, and to really be able to converse in them fluently and idiomatically.*

"The usual mistake," says the New York *World*, in an able editorial on the study of modern languages, "in America, throughout the majority of schools, is that in studying a foreign tongue more actual study is put upon English and a formation of a smooth translation than in building up and acquiring the language in question. But whatever the faults of teachers or of the system, of one fact the parents and public are painfully assured, and that is that after years of study the scholars are still unable to speak and write the language, and with difficulty can even read it. Everybody knows how he has been able to repeat pages of grammatical rules and foreign words, and then, amid his congratulations on mastering so much, how some day he has found himself stranded in a foreign land only to discover that he has no use for the rules and words he has learned—that somehow and strangely enough the people have quite a different stock of language.''

For two, three, and frequently five years the pupils —according to our present false and unnatural systems —study different French and German grammars, manuals, and vocabularies ; they learn to conjugate and to decline, to parse and to analyze, etc.

If a boy will learn how to build a chair his master does not give him chairs to break asunder ; but rather wood to build them with. He does not tear apart, but builds up. So, if one would learn French, or any foreign speech, his work must not consist of taking a certain amount of French, tearing it into bits, and then building it up into good English, which he already knows, but it must be just the reverse.

In our preparatory schools, our seminaries, the best of all our colleges and universities—indeed throughout our whole land, the greater part of the time is spent in this false and absurd way—and the student who takes a piece of Latin, Greek, French; or German, and renders it into the smoothest English, stands first and best above his fellows.

It is an utter deception ; for the same student would be quite unable to reverse the process and render the same amount of English into even a passable foreign phrase. In one word, our schools educate philologists and grammarians, but only in rare instances do they turn out practical linguists.

Of what use, however, is a perfect knowledge of all grammatical French rules to the tourist who fails to understand the simple utterances of even a railway porter, and who after five years' study of the best French grammars, can scarcely ask for his common necessities ?

To understand the grammar of a language is desirable, but it is by no means so important as being able to speak the language.

As we can never become painters by the critical study of pictures, so we can never hope to make ourselves practical linguists by the mere study of grammar.

Or to use a still clearer illustration : We may understand perfectly the theory of swimming, but this theoretical knowledge will be of little practical help when we are obliged to take the first actual plunge.

These are *incontrovertible facts*, felt and acknowledged not only by almost all learners, but even by the majority of our teachers.

THE TASK OF LEARNING A FOREIGN LANGUAGE

has hitherto been so difficult, so wearisome and productive of so little efficiency, that few persons of mature age have attempted it, however great their need of it either for business purposes or for cultivation.

"These difficulties," writes *Dr. Heinrich Schliemann*, the celebrated explorer of Greek antiquities, " have now been happily obviated by the

'MEISTERSCHAFT SYSTEM,'

which is simply a scientific adaptation of the natural method by which all persons, whether children or adults, educated or otherwise, rapidly and correctly acquire the language which they constantly hear, and which they are instinctively impelled to imitate when resident in a foreign country."

HOW THE MEISTERSCHAFT SYSTEM TEACHES.

Jacotot, Prendergast, Bayard Taylor, and others proved years ago that

the Speaking of Foreign Tongues

is *not* a matter of the *intellect*, as shown by the fact that *children* acquire a foreign language much more rapidly than grown persons.

They have neither teacher, book, nor interpreter ; they are frequently too young to read or write in their own tongue ; they understand nothing about the principles of grammar ; they do not think about this or that method of acquiring the language ; yet without thinking at all, in coming either to Calcutta or Paris— they rapidly enunciate the foreign sounds correctly, and in a few short weeks chatter like natives with their foreign attendants.

It must have been observed by every intelligent traveller how the ignorant donkey boys in Alexandria— native Egyptians mostly, who never went to any school —express themselves clearly and sometimes very

-fluently in both English, French, and Italian ; sometimes even in Greek and Turkish. In spite of their uncultivated intelligence, the natural and wonderfully subtle power of imitation does for them what a longcourse of grammatical study fails to do for the educated and refined.

These facts must show to the most casual observer that some natural laws exist governing the mode by which foreign languages are acquired, and which should be scientifically considered and made useful for practical purposes.

ALL SCIENCE IS BUT THE SEARCHING OUT OF NATURAL LAWS.

The greatest scientific results have originated by the careful observation of some very simple and commonplace occurrence, which has itself directly illustrated some great unchangeable natural law.

The fall of an apple, the steam of a boiling kettle, have conferred untold blessings upon mankind, and yet apples innumerable had fallen before Newton's time.

" The careful observation of ' the lisp of children and their earliest words'—or rather the common and natural process by which human beings master the powers of speech, has"—to quote the language of the celebrated philologist *Professor Bernhard Schmitz*— " produced a system by which we can rapidly acquire other tongues, and which has really created a new science—that of *Linguistry*, which must not be confounded with Philology."

Now in what way do children—and we might add adults —learn to master a foreign language when resident in a foreign country ?

At first, the mind gets entirely confused by the multiplicity of foreign sounds which it hears continually uttered without possessing the ability of grasping what is said. In the course of a few weeks, however, the ear becomes accustomed to some of these sounds, and we begin to utter *that sentence* (not a single noun, for *unconnected words are not language*), which we have heard most frequently used by the persons about us.

This sentence is usually relative to our most urgent necessity ; a common object, water, food, towels, or a railway ticket.

In a little while a new necessity arises. We use again the same sentence—not knowing any other—altered only by the substitution or addition of a new noun, adjective, or adverb. For instance, the water or food required may be asked for either hot or cold, at once or later, etc. ; and the sentence is then altered or enlarged by a new word which the attendant—understanding us—suggests.

This new word may have some remote or close affinity of ideas with some other word we know, and after a few repetitions, the ear is so accustomed to it that it becomes a part of ourselves, and is uttered by the tongue *unconsciously* whenever the necessity occurs.

This is the process by which *sound* becomes a matter of language. Foreign words at first convey no ideas to us, and it is only by constant repetition and use of them that we are led directly to think in them. They are then no longer foreign, but have become part of ourselves, and suggest to us the same ideas as do the words of our native tongue.

It is clear that the *intelligence* has at first but little to do in the acquirement of foreign languages. The truth of this observation will very likely be doubted, for it seems as if *all* study *must* appeal to our faculties of reason. Yet the experience of any one who has studied the modern languages in our colleges will verify my statement. A college graduate will undoubtedly understand the peculiarities of the French or German grammar; he will be able to read the literature to a certain extent; he may even be capable of writing a letter faultlessly and grammatically in these languages, and yet as soon as he tries to converse in them he gets utterly confused and is unable to express himself.

How is this to be accounted for? He can read French and cannot speak it. He can write French letters and yet cannot express himself orally. He understands French grammar better than a native, and still he cannot give utterance to his simplest thoughts in that language.

It is just here where our school-systems are at fault. They appeal to the reasoning-power, instead of to the *memory*.

The ear, the tongue, and the memory are almost solely employed in mastering the foreign sounds, and our *intelligence*, though it superintends the whole process, can only really be said to come into action when the foreign sounds have become our mental and bodily property so fully and entirely that we begin to think in them just as readily as in our own vernacular.

And this brings me to

THE PRINCIPAL MISTAKE OF OUR PRESENT METHODS AND SYSTEMS.

Every observer of human nature must be aware of the existence of an *unconscious process of thought* which is entirely apart from and independent of will power, and which—in speaking our mother tongue—is mainly instrumental in expressing our wants and desires. For instance, we go into a shop to purchase a pair of gloves. Our *conscious thought* is occupied in the *size, color,* and *quality of the gloves* we wish to purchase. All these different points *we readily express without one thought of the words to be used.* At the very moment of uttering these expressions, our thoughts are often occupied with some care or sorrow which is far removed from our bodily necessities. Still, in this *absent-minded* condition we buy our gloves, pay for them, and probably exchange some civilities with the attendant.

This *unconscious power* of thinking and speaking has so far never been touched upon by philologists and teachers, and only Schopenhauer and Hartmann among modern philosophers have alluded to it. Yet I am fully convinced, by practical experience and by close study of the human mind, that in acquiring a foreign tongue it is the mainspring of all proficiency.

Our own tongue is of course flesh and blood to us. We express our thoughts distinctly and clearly without being aware of any mental activity. I allude, of course, only to common, every-day experiences, and NOT to subjects which require conscious and concentrated thought.

Now let any one who has studied a foreign tongue for years according to the prevailing methods try to express such a simple sentence as, " *I should like to purchase some goods this morning. Would you be kind enough to accompany me?*"

It surely cannot be said, when we utter such a trite and commonplace phrase in our own tongue, that we even for a moment realize that any activity of thought is going on in our minds ; but in the very instant we have this thought the tongue unconsciously utters it.

Yet, I say, let the graduate of any college try to give this sentence as rapidly in French as in English, and not one in a thousand will be able to do it.

He has to think about each single word ; he searches the recesses of his memory for the proper equivalents ; he weighs the different grammatical-rules which may or may not govern this construction. In one word, he thinks *about* his French instead of thinking *in* French.

This is one of the greatest fundamental errors in the present grammatical systems, and the chief cause of failure in learning to speak ; and to this alone it is to be attributed that *Latin* is no longer spoken by our scholars.

I choose this seemingly far-fetched illustration on purpose, as it will give me an occasion to show HOW AND SINCE WHEN OUR UNNATURAL METHODS HAVE COME IN VOGUE.

It is an undeniable fact that up to the middle of the sixteenth century *Latin* was the language *spoken*, like a *living tongue*, in all cultivated and refined society throug out Europe.

· And how was it taught? Undoubtedly by word of mouth, since the art of printing was almost unknown, and the old manuscripts were only within the reach of a very wealthy and privileged few.

With the birth of the press died the practice of oral teaching.. The teacher gave the living tangible word over to the dumb book ; the frequent repetition of *sound*, so vital to the learning of a foreign tongue, was lost, and the scholars remained dumb, like the book which they had been studying. For how could linguistic results be expected from the *intelligence*, instead of— as by the natural process—from the *ear* and the *tongue* ?

Latin is more generally studied in our times than in the past ; yet who is able to *speak* it ?

It may be argued that, in taking Latin for an example, I overlook the fact that it is a *dead language*. But was it not equally dead five hundred years ago ? And yet it was *spoken* because it was studied in a *common-sense, natural manner*.

And for the same reason—though they are *living tongues—French and German are not now spoken in our schools, because they are taught in a false, unreasonable, and unnatural way.*

The observation of these facts caused me to investigate the subject fully, and to determine in the first place THE SIZE AND CHARACTER OF THE VOCAB-ULARY OF EVERY-DAY CONVERSATION.

It is well known to philologists that the ordinary vocabularies of men are quite small ; that children, who are able to express nearly every physical wish, are nevertheless armed with oftentimes less than 500, and seldom over 1000 words. Nature provides the child with some subtle instinct by which he selects no word which is not of absolute and immediate importance. From the first uttered syllables on through his whole little life, not a moment is wasted in learning superfluous words.

Similar it is with the vocabulary of every-day life. It has occurred to more than one scholar that if he could only actually determine the extent and nature of these words he would be able to make the acquisition of modern languages a very easy matter.

Bayard Taylor, in his "Views Afoot," has declared himself able to acquire a *working knowledge of almost any language in less than a month*, and he goes on to show the character of the words he would learn. He naturally hit upon this idea; it was suggested by the very wide experience which he had, and the demand that his travels made upon him for acquiring a great many languages.

My own rather extended experience as a traveller and linguist coincides exactly with Bayard Taylor's.

In *all* languages there is what might be called

A STOCK VOCABULARY,

a quantity of words necessary in all walks of life, understood by all, learned first by all, needed and used by all, and with the great mass of people never increasing above a certain number, put variously by scholars at from one to three thousand. The nature of these words is about the same with all civilized nations.

The observation of many scholars has done much to determine this. The results of these studies are now beginning to be felt in Germany especially, where a visit to the public schools will convince any one that school-children are no longer learning the interesting facts given in a well-known American grammar, that "*the Italian shoemaker has purchased an Egyptian antelope*," or that "*the shoes of the Spanish peasant have a golden heel*," or that "*the shepherds rested, and the swine and sows grazed*." German text-books begin to be formed on a more sensible basis. Efforts have been made to select the words of every-day speech, and the results are such that, although still •hampered by the influence of the old methods, the German schools are certainly producing the best linguists in the world.

The study of foreign languages has been made hitherto as difficult as possible, the memory in addition to the numerous abstruse rules being taxed with many words unnecessary for conversation in its initiatory stage.

An examination of most American grammars, manuals, conversation books and all the labored aids to this study, will show that the vocabularies are crammed with promiscuous words, which seem to have been drawn out of the dictionaries by some novel system of "legalized lottery"—not so much with a view to provide a *necessary vocabulary* as to do reverence to the dictionary, and give every word a fair chance of representation.

I hold that *a few idiomatic sentences, containing the most necessary words, should be learned in the commencement, enabling the student to at once begin conversation.* It is astonishing how naturally and rapidly other words will then be learned, while at the same time the ear is becoming accustomed to the sounds, and the mind begins to *think* in them.

Lepsius, the celebrated scholar on Egyptian antiquities, limits

THE NUMBER OF WORDS NECESSARY FOR CONVERSATION ON ALL GENERAL TOPICS to six hundred. I take about four times that number, *i.e.*, 2,000–2,500, founding my estimate upon the fluency of speech usually attained by young men of between 15 and 18 years of age.

This number of words appears at first sight absurdly small, but if we remember that with 40 words we can construct 1,024,000 sentences of twenty words each, it will be seen that my estimate is strictly correct.

For persons interested in mathematical calculations, I give the following table :

From 6 words we can form 8 combinations of 3 words each ; from

WORDS.	COMBINATIONS.	WORDS.
8	16	4
10	32	5
12	64	6
14	128	7
16	256	8
18	512	9
20	1024	10
40	1,024,000	20

It is therefore self-evident what an enormous number of sentences may be formed with 2000 words, and that the knowledge of them is absolutely sufficient for the common occurrences of every-day life.

It must also be remembered that if we really *know* 2000 words, we will *recognize* at least five to ten times as many more which are either derived from or closely related to them.

Aided and assisted by the works and the help of many teachers, I have made all possible efforts to select only those words which are and must be always employed in all transactions of our daily life.

Certainly, if a man in common life is able to do with 2000 words, it will *not* be a difficult matter to acquire his language, provided only these words are rightly selected. Nature never fails to select the proper ones. Men can only do it by long and extensive study.

The proper selection of the vocabulary of common life is the first distinguishing feature of the 'Meisterschaft System.'

But, highly important as this part of the work is, it must not be forgotten that ·

UNCONNECTED WORDS ARE NOT LANGUAGE,

and that in acquiring a foreign tongue we must have a framework, or rather a series of formulæ which contain the *peculiar constructions* of the language in question.

This is a very important point, as each and every language has

CERTAIN FORMS OF EXPRESSION, OR IDIOMS,

which are entirely and peculiarly its own, and which cannot be literally translated into any other tongue. For example, we all say, "*How do you do?*" **Do** what?.. What are we supposed- to be doing that we should be asked ¡' *how we do it* "? This mode of salutation is just as peculiarly English as the German greeting, " *Wie geht es ?*" or, literally, '' *How goes it ?*'' is intrinsically German.

Yet, in order to master either of these, or any other language, we must learn their peculiar idioms almost mechanically. *We must free ourselves from that most misleading habit of translating literally from one language into another*, and must accustom ourselves from the very start to the foreign idioms and constructions.

This seems at first exceedingly difficult, and yet it is the only practical way in which real mastery of the foreign forms of speech can be reached. Grammatical rules will certainly assist us in so far as to give us a more or less lucid explanation of peculiar constructions and modes of expression, but only in rare instances can they give a *logical reason* for these peculiarities of language. For who can explain the involved constructions of the German tongue in a logical manner? Or who can give a logical reason for the way in which the French handle their pronouns? Such peculiarities of speech must be received as *facts*, and all we can do is *to practice these idioms and constructions* so fully that they become *natural* to us, and are uttered just as glibly as the English equivalents.

We all know that most grammars plunge the scholar directly into dry grammatical rules, and syntax, and long, tedious, ill-arranged vocabularies. The bulk of the ordinary scholar's time is consumed in learning hundreds of unconnected words, which, though of literary and etymological importance, are **proven to be** outside of daily or yearly wants, and learned only to be forgotten.

"This," says a highly accomplished American scholar in a letter to the *Evening Post*, "is the complaint of teachers and students everywhere. But now that in the '*Meisterschaft System*' *a method has been devised, grounded on the laws actually governing the nature of 'volk' vocabularies, giving at once sentences formed of these words instead of silly phrases and useless vocabularies, introducing a scholar into an idiomatic, and not a literal study of the foreign tongue, its benefit and value can hardly be estimated.* . . . I believe this is the method to be adopted throughout our schools. We study French, but the soul of our work is in English. We study German, but strive only to make good English from it. And so with Latin and Greek. And any one who has observed the results in our highest and our best institutions feels like hiding for shame. It is the wickedest sham that ever lurked about our life. I believe it will be bettered ; and as I see the '*Meisterschaft System*' applied so sensibly to self-study it seems to me practical that *if its author can only be induced to visit America, it will be possible for him to carry on this work so far that it shall root up our wretched methods and work a reform straight through our schools.*"

It is an old established maxim that
WHOEVER WISHES TO SPEAK A FOREIGN
LANGUAGE MUST THINK IN IT;
but, incontrovertible and true as this principle undoubtedly is, *the difficulty of thinking in the language itself is almost insurmountable.* When resident in a foreign country

among persons who speak nothing but their own vernacular, we gradually and imperceptibly catch their
meaning, and in time become—as we have shown—so
accustomed to the foreign sounds that we at last begin
to think in them.

But *how* can this be accomplished in our *own* land?
How is this *possible* when we are continually surrounded
by our own countrymen, and are perpetually obliged to
use our mother tongue?

We know that the study of grammar as practiced in
our schools does not give us this ability. Oral teaching
so called has also been tried, but with very indifferent
success. *Robertson, Ollendorff, Otto, Prendergast*, and *Jacotot*
attempted to solve the difficulty, and though the two
last-named scholars started undoubtedly with correct
ideas, they all failed to give us facility of speech.
Prendergast, perhaps the most original mind among
modern philologists, worked out a most able theory;
but being himself no linguist, and unfortunately being
totally blind, he was obliged to leave the practical part
of his work to his assistants, who made—as he acknowledged himself to me—a most miserable failure in the
compilation of his text-books.

My system, though far from being entirely original,
combines the good features of *all* modern methods, and
follows at the same time *nature's own way* as closely as
possible. While *some grammars teach nothing but theory*, *I
lay the greatest stress on practical mastery.* While others
give nothing but a *number of ill-arranged French or German conversations*, and sneer at any grammatical study, *I
give the English equivalent, and as much of the grammar as*

must be known for all practical purposes. While others,
again, do not distinguish between the *language of literature and that of every-day life, I give the common vocabulary
first,* and leave other less necessary words for *after-studies.*

In one word, *my system is,* to use *Dr. Schliemann's* expression, " *a scientific adaptation of the natural mode of mastering foreign tongues ;*" and while I gratefully acknowledge my obligation to the works of many grammarians,
and especially to those of *Lehmann, Prendergast,* and
Jacotot, I claim that " *the Meisterschaft System,*" so far as
any scientific work can be original, is my own, and has
been thoroughly tried by myself for more than 14 years,
and most successfully used by teachers and scholars all
over the Continent of Europe for the last three years.

A glance at the first few pages of the lessons will
show

HOW I TEACH THE STUDENT TO THINK IN THE FOREIGN LANGUAGES THEMSELVES.

I give first what I call a *foundation sentence,* which contains a number of idiomatic peculiarities, and is com-
posed of about 20 words most necessary for ordinary
conversation. *As a native teacher* is not always accessible,
I have given the *exact pronunciation of each word so clearly
and distinctly that no mistake can possibly be made.*

The student must *not* attempt to learn the foundation sentence by heart, but read and repeat it aloud
until it sounds perfectly familiar to his ear, and flows
smoothly from the tongue without effort or mistake.

Of course he must read the *English* equivalent of
the phrase first so that he may have a *general* idea of its
meaning.

The *foundation sentence* is next divided into different parts, and having *perfectly* mastered the *pronunciation* the pupil may proceed to study the *meaning of each word*, so that he can follow the different transpositions and variations intelligently.

For in order *to accustom* the pupil to the *peculiar foreign constructions*, and to make him *familiar* with their *modes of thought and expression*, I form new and similar sentences, repeating the same constructions and some of the words learned. By introducing some nouns, adverbs, adjectives, or conjunctions, the sentences are continually altered and enlarged.

Short grammatical rules, or rather *hints*, are constantly given in the foot-notes, so that the student may understand what he is learning, and not simply work mechanically, as *Prendergast* erroneously recommends. *Practice and theory must be united.*

STUDY NEVER TO EXCEED TEN MINUTES AT A TIME.

After the learner has intelligently gone through the variations of Part I. he must *read and re-read them aloud for about 3-5 minutes.*

This done, the pupil will turn to the *English*, which, as will be observed, is printed on the *opposite* page, *repeating aloud from it the foreign equivalent as fluently and quickly as possible.*

He must, however,

NEVER TRUST TO HIS MEMORY.

If he cannot remember a word, or if he is not quite sure that he has given the foreign phrase correctly, he must immediately re-read the French or.. Germán, and then give it once more from the English.

This exercise also must never be continued for more than five minutes, so that the *whole time of reading and translating is not to exceed ten minutes at a time ; but this must be repeated at intervals during the day, as often as the convenience of the pupil permits, but in no case less than three times a day. Always read and translate aloud.*

By these frequent repetitions the pupil not only masters the pronunciation thoroughly, but gets also perfectly familiar with the foreign sounds, which imperceptibly impress themselves so indelibly on his memory that after a few days he will find himself able to utter the foreign equivalents as fluently and unconsciously as his native English.

At the same time he has become so familiar with the foreign constructions and modes of thought that he will begin to form other similar sentences for himself, without making the slightest grammatical mistake. For this purpose the vocabulary must be used and the exercises translated.

The student must never begin a new division before he has gained perfect command and mastery over all the preceding sentences.

My rules strictly followed will undoubtedly lead to the most perfect success, as proved by the experience of thousands of my pupils.

THE AUTHOR.

NEW YORK.

PRONUNCIATION.

A correct pronunciation is the first and most essential consideration in speaking a foreign tongue.

Learn the pronunciation—if possible—from a native. Any person, however, who can read French may easily guide you, if you should experience difficulties in pronouncing a word.

Observe that :

a is always pronounced like our **a** in **father.**

e when short = ĕ is pronounced like **e** in met; when accented = é, or è, or ê, it is pronounced like **ai** in **air.**

i sounds like ee in **green.**

o is pronounced like our **o.**

u is very hard to pronounce, as there is no equivalent in the English language for this sound. It is so utterly different from anything in our tongue that the nearest approach we find to it is in "*u,*" in the word "*gude,*" in the Scotch dialect. To pronounce a French "**u,**" it is necessary to round the lips as if going to whistle and then sound an ēē.

As a native teacher is not always accessible, and in order to make the lessons thoroughly useful for self-instruction, I have given the exact pronunciation after.

Directions for Private Study.

As all fluency of speech in a foreign language is mainly attained through the repetition of the different sounds, the pupil must not simply read, *but repeat aloud the sentences given, so that he can hear the sound of his own voice.*

He must begin with the **Foundation Sentence,** and read and repeat it *aloud,* until it sounds perfectly familiar to his ear, and flows smoothly from the tongue without effort or hesitation.

This, it will be observed, is *not* study, but *an exercise of the tongue and the ear.*

The pupil will naturally read the English equivalent of each sentence, so that he will have a *general* idea of its meaning, but *literal translation — word for word — is in this system strictly forbidden.*

He must *not* attempt to learn the Foundation Sentence by heart. By reading it often, it will unconsciously impress itself so indelibly on his memory that he cannot possibly forget it again.

Having perfectly mastered the *pronunciation* of the *Foundation Sentence,* the pupil may proceed to study *the meaning of each word of Division I.,* so that he may be able to follow the different transpositions and variations intelligently.

All the French variations of the first division must then be read and re-read aloud.

This exercise should last from three to five minutes only, so that no fatigue whatever is felt. After a correct and fluent pronunciation has been attained, the pupil will then turn to the English, giving aloud from it the

French equivalent without looking at the French pages.

He must, however, never trust to his memory. If he cannot remember a word instantly, or if he is not quite sure that he has given the French phrase correctly, he must immediately re-read the French, and then repeat it once more from the English.

This exercise also should never exceed five minutes, so that all in all about *ten minutes* may be given to the reading of the French, and the translating from the English into the French.

These short exercises must be repeated at intervals during the day as often as the convenience of the pupil permits, **but in no case less than three or four times a day.**

By these frequent repetitions, the pupil not only masters *the pronunciation thoroughly, but secures the French sentences and idioms so accurately, that after a few days he will find himself able to utter the French phrases as fluently and unconsciously as those of his native tongue.*

He will thus gradually and imperceptibly learn *to think* in French, and must for that purpose translate the *Exercises,* and learn the words of the vocabulary by heart.

The student must **never begin a new sentence** before he has gained *perfect command and absolute mastery over all the preceding ones.*

These rules must be **strictly** *followed, since it is only by constant repetition that real success can be attained.*

These books are issued in a form intended expressly for the convenience of learners, and should not be bound, but kept in the soft cover so that the book can be doubled back. It is not a book intended to be preserved for binding or show, but should be always carried in the pocket and made a constant companion so that the spirit of the language shall impress itself thoroughly upon the mind of the student.

CORRESPONDENCE WITH THE TEACHER.

At the end of each lesson will be found Exercises for translation — French into English, and English into French.

These should be examined by a teacher.

-At great personal inconvenience Dr. Rosenthal has established himself for a time in New York, thus placing himself in direct postal communication with every Subscriber in the United States, to answer all inquiries relative to study, and to correct all exercises sent to him.

THE GRAMMATICAL REMARKS.

Pupils who wish to study for colloquial purposes only, need not study them. They will be found useful however, and should be studied after all the sentences have been mastered.

The Meisterschaft System.

FRENCH.

PART I.

I.

· FOUNDATION SENTENCE.[1]

— I should like to make some purchases this

morning; will you have the kindness to come

with me to the French tailor's?

1.

**I should like to make some purchases this
morning.**

I '

should like (*or,* would like)

---

1) The student must—if possible under the guidance of a refined native Frenchman — read the "Foundation Sentence" until he can pronounce it smoothly and without the slightest hesitation. He must always read aloud, so that both his ear and tongue may get accustomed to the foreign sounds. The French intonation is peculiar; there is always a *slight rising* accent on the last syllable. The voice does not fall at the end of a sentence as in English, but rises slightly.

2) '*è*' is pronounced like '*e*' in our English word '*met.*'

I.

FOUNDATION SENTENCE.[1]

Je voudrais faire des emplettes ce matin;
jĕ[2] voū[3]-dray fair day[4] zăng[5]-plĕt sĕ mă-taing

voulez - vous avoir l'obligeance de venir avec
voū-lĕh voū zăv'woar[6] lŏ-blĕĕ-jăngs dĕ vĕ-nĕĕr ă-vĕk

moi chez le tailleur français?
m'woăh[6] shay lĕ tă-yeūr[7] frăng-say.

1.

Je voudrais faire des emplettes ce matin.
jĕ voū-dray fair day zăng-plĕt sĕ mă-taing.

Je *(jĕ)*

voudrais *(voū-dray)*

---

3) '*ou*' is pronounced like '*u*' in '*rude*,' only somewhat shorter.

4) *If one word ends* with *s, z, x, t, d, n,* and the *next begins* with *a vowel* or *h mute*, the two are for euphony's sake joined together, so as to form one word, as : veut-il = veū-tĕĕl ; voulez-vous aller = vou-lĕh-voū-zah-lay ; les hommes = lay-zom. The small arch (⌒) denotes this joining of words.

5) '*a*' in French has always the sound of '*a*' in '*father.*'

6) woăh is to be melted into one sound.

7) '*eu*' is pronounced like '*ea*' in '*early*,' only longer.

to do (*or* to make)
some
shopping; purchases
this
morning.

1. I should like to make some purchases.
2. I should like to do my (*mes*) shopping.
3. I should not like (*je ne voudrais pas*) to make my purchases.
4. I should not like to make my purchases this morning.

5. Would you like (*voudriez-vous*) to make your purchases (*vos emplettes*)?
6. Would you not like to make your purchases this morning (*ce matin*)?
7. Why (*pourquoi*) would you not like to make your purchases this forenoon?
8. Would you like to make your purchases at (*dans*) this store (*ce magasin*)?
9. Why would you not like to make your purchases at this store?
10. I should like to do my shopping at this store.
11. I should not like to do my shopping at this store.

12. I should not like to do it (=*it to do, le faire*) [1].

---

1) The English word '*not*' must always be expressed by *two* negative words in French, viz. : '*ne—pas*,' the first of which is placed before the simple verb, the other after it, as : *Je voudrais*, I should like ; je *ne* voudrais *pas*, I should not like.

faire (*fair*)

dès (*day*)

emplettes (*ăng-plĕt*)

ce (*sĕ*)

matin (*mă-taing*).

1. Je voudrais faire des emplettes (*day zăng-plĕt*).
2. Je voudrais faire mes emplettes (*may zăng-plĕt*).
3. Je ne voudrais pas[1] (*jĕ nĕ voŭ-dray păh*) faire mes emplettes.
4. Je ne voudrais pas faire mes emplettes ce matin (*sĕ mă-taing*).
5. Voudriez-vous (*voŭ-drĕē-ēh voŭ*) faire vos emplettes (*vō-zăng-plĕt*)?
6. Ne voudriez-vous pas faire vos emplettes ce matin?

7. Pourquoi (*poŭr-quo-ăh*) ne voudriez-vous pas (*nĕ voŭ-drĕē-ēh voŭ păh*) faire vos emplettes ce matin?
8. Voudriez-vous faire vos emplettes dans ce magasin (*dāng sĕ mă-gă-zaing*)?
9. Pourquoi ne voudriez-vous pas faire vos emplettes dans ce magasin?
10. Je voudrais faire mes emplettes dans ce magasin.
11. Je ne voudrais pas faire mes emplettes dans ce magasin.
12. Je ne voudrais pas le[2] faire (*lĕ fair*).

---

2) The so-called *Conjunctive Personol Pronouns*, ' me, thee, him, her, it, us, you, them,' are always placed immediately before the verb. The French conjunctive personal pronouns are :

me (*mĕ*), me	la (*lă*), her	nous (*noŭ*), us.
te (*tĕ*), thee	le (*lĕ*), it	vous (*voŭ*), you.
le (*lĕ*), him		les (*lay*), them.

32

13. I should like to do it (=it to do) this forenoon (*matin*).

14. Would you like (*voudriez-vous*) to do it?

15. Why (*pourquoi*) would you not like to do so (*le*)?

16. Would you like to go (*aller*) to (*à*)[1] this establishment (*or* to this store)?

17. I should not like to go (*aller*) to this store.

18. Would you not like to go to the (*au* = to the) theatre?

19. He (*il*) would like to go to the theatre.

20. He would not like to go to the French theatre (*literally*: to the theatre French[2]).

21. My brother (*mon frère*) would not like to go to the French theatre.

22. Why would he not like to go to the French theatre?

23. To which (*au quel*) store would he like to go?

24. Would you not like to go to Paris (*à Paris*)?

25. I should very much (*bien*) like to go to Paris.

26. She (*elle*) would not like to make her (*ses*) purchases in (*dans*) this establishment.

---

1) We have three accents in French, viz: 1. *The acute accent* which is only placed over *e*, as été.—2. *The grave accent*, which is placed over the vowels *a, e, u=à, è, ù.*—3. *The circumflex accent*, which may be placed upon any of the vowels, as *âme, rêve.*

2) Under *c* we see a peculiar little hook which is called a cedilla (une cédille), and gives to *c* the sound of *s* before *a, o,* and *u*.

The French place the adjective mostly after the noun, *i.e., the theatre French.*

13. Je voudrais le faire ce matin.

14. Voudriez-vous le faire (*voŭ-drēē-ĕh voŭ lĕ fair*)?

15. Pourquoi (*poŭr-quo͞o-ăh*) ne voudriez-vous pas le faire?

16. Voudriez-vous aller (*voŭ-drēē-ĕh voŭ zăh-lay*) à [1] ce magasin (*āh sĕ mă-gă-zaing*)?

17. Je ne voudrais pas aller (*păh zăh-lĕh*) à ce magasin.

18. Ne voudriez-vous pas aller au spectacle (*ŏh spēc-tāh-kl*)?

19. Il voudrait aller (*eel voŭ-dray-tăh-lĕh*) au spectacle.

20. Il ne voudrait pas aller au spectacle français [2] (*frăng-say*).

21. Mon frère (*mong frair*) ne voudrait pas aller au spectacle français.

22. Pourquoi (*poŭr-quo͞o-ăh*) ne voudrait-il pas aller (*nĕ-voŭ-dray tēēl păh zăh-lĕh*) au spectacle français?

23. A quel (*ă kĕll*) magasin voudrait-il aller?

24. Ne voudriez-vous pas aller à Paris (*nĕ voŭ-drēē-ĕh voŭ păh zăh-lĕh āh Pă-rēē*)?

25. Je voudrais bien (*byaing*) aller à Paris.

26. Elle (*ĕll*) ne voudrait [3] pas faire ses emplettes (*say zăng-plĕt*) dans (*dăng*) ce magasin.

---

3) *Je voudrais*, I should like, *or* I would like is conjugated thus :
je voudrais (*jĕ voŭ-dray*), I would like.
tu voudrais (*tŭ voŭ-dray*), thou wouldst like.
il voudrait (*ēĕl voŭ-dray*), he would like.
elle voudrait (*ĕll voŭ-dray*), she would like.
nous voudrions (*noŭ voŭ-drēē-ong*), we would like.
vous voudriez (*voŭ voŭ-drēē-ĕh*), you would like.
ils voudraient (*ēĕl voŭ-dray*), they would like (*masc.*).
elles voudraient (*ĕll voŭ-dray*), they would like (*fem.*).

Will you have the kindness to come with.

me ?

will

you

will you ? (*or*, are you *willing?* do you wish? do you
want to ?)

to have

the kindness

to

come (*or* to come)

with

me. [The student must well distinguish between 'me' and 'moi' ;
the first is always placed *before* the verb ; the second stands
after prepositions and such affirming imperative forms as
donnez-moi, give me ; *apportez-moi*, bring me].

---

1) *Final consonants* are generally silent. A final consonant,
however, *followed by a word that begins with a vowel* or a *silent h*, is
pronounced with the next syllable, as if the two formed but one word,
as : *veut-il*=veŭ-teēl ; *mes emplettes*=may zăng-plĕt ; *voulez-vous écrire*
=voŭ-lay-voŭ zay-kreēr.

Voulez - vous avoir l'obligeance de venir
voŭ-lĕh voŭ ză-v'wŏār [1] lŏ-blĕĕ-jăngs dĕ vĕ-nĕĕr

avec moi?
ă-vek m'wŏăh

voulez (*voŭ-lĕh*)

vous (*voŭ*)

voulez-vous?

avoir (*ă-v'wŏār*)

l'obligeance (*lŏ-blĕĕ-jăngs*)

de (*dĕ*) [*de* before the infinitive of verbs means ' *to*,' but as a preposition, ' *of*' or '*from*'].

venir (*vĕ-nĕĕr*)

avec (*ă-vĕk*)

moi (*m'wŏăh*) [It would lead us too far if we were to explain here all
the personal pronouns. The rules are given in the
4th, 5th, and 6th lesson.]

Final c, before a vowel, is sounded like k, as *du blanc au noir*=dŭ
blăng-kŏh n'wŏăhr.

    d,   ::   ,,   t, as *quand il est* = kăng
tĕĕl-lay.

    s or x   ,,   ,,   z, as *ils ont*=ĕĕl zŏng; *aux
oncles*=ŏh zŏng-kl'.

1. Will you have the kindness to go (*d'aller*) with me?

2. Why will you not have the kindness to come with me to the French store (= store French)?
3. I will (*or*, I am willing).
4. I am not willing (*or*, I do not wish to).
5. I want (*je veux*) to do my shopping this forenoon (*matin*).
6. When (*quand*) do you want to make your purchases?
7. I wish (*je veux*) to make my purchases to-morrow (*demain*) morning. Will you have the kindness to go with me?
8. I should very much (*bien*) like to go with you, but I have no time (*Literally :* I have not [*je n'ai pas*] the time [*le temps*]).
9. Why (*pourquoi*) will you not go to the theatre with my brother (*mon frère*)?
10. I should very much (*bien*) like to go to the theatre with him (*lui*),but I have no time (*je n'ai pas le temps*).

11. Will you do it (*le*) for (*pour*) me?
12. I do not want (*je ne veux pas*) to do it for him.

13. Will you have it done (*or*, order it = *le faire faire*)?

---

1) *de* is apostrophed before words commencing with a vowel, as *de aller*=d'aller ; *de écrire*=d'écrire.

2) '*eu*' is pronounced like '*ea*' in '*early*,' only much longer.

Je veux means am willing, *or* I wish, *or* I want, *or* I will, and is conjugated thus :

> je veux (*jĕ veŭ*), I am willing.
> tu veux (*tü veŭ*), thou art willing.
> il veut (*ĕel veŭ*), he is willing.
> elle veut (*ĕll veŭ*), she is willing.

1. Voulez-vous avoir l'obligeance d'aller[1] (*dăh-lēh*) avec moi ?

2. Pourquoi ne voulez-vous pas avoir l'obligeance de venir avec moi au (*ōh*) magasin français ?

3. Je veux (*veū*)[2].

4. Je ne veux pas (*jĕ nĕ veū pāh*).

5. Je veux faire mes emplettes ce matin.

6. Quand (*kāng*) *voulez-vous* faire vos emplettes ?

7. Je veux (*veū*) faire mes emplettes demain (*dĕ-maing*) matin. Voulez-vous avoir l'obligeance d'aller (*dăh-lēh*) avec moi ?

8. Je voudrais bien (*byaing*) aller avec vous, mais je n'ai pas le temps (*may jĕ nay pāh lĕ tāng*).

9. Pourquoi (*poŭr-quo-āh*) ne voulez-vous pas aller au spectacle avec mon frère (*mong frair*) ?

10. Je voudrais bien (*byaing*) aller au spectacle avec lui (*l'wēē*), mais je n'ai pas le temps (*may jĕ nay pāh lĕ tāng*).

11. Voulez-vous le faire pour (*poŭr*) moi.

12. Je ne veux pas (*jĕ nĕ veū pāh*) le faire pour lui (*poŭr l'wēē*).

13. Voulez vous le faire faire ?

---

nous voulons (*noū voū-long*), we are willing.
vous voulez (*voū voū-lēh*), you are willing.
ils veulent (*ēēl veūl*), they are willing (*masc.*).
elles veulent (*ĕll veūl*), they are willing (*fem.*)

3) In English we use in *questions* and *negations* the auxiliary verb *to do*, as : *do you* want to go ? *I do not* want to go. In French we have no corresponding auxiliary, and cannot express it. We simply say instead of ' *do you want to go* ' ?=want you to go; *voulez-vous* aller ? Instead of ' *I do not want to go* '=I not want to go; *je ne veux pas aller*.

14. He does not want (*il ne veut pas*) to have it done..
15. Why will he not have it done for you?

16. Where (*où*) will you have it done?
17. Where will you have your (*votre*) coat (*habit*) done (*or*, your dress made)?
18. Will you order (*faire faire*) your coat at (*chez*) my (*mon*) tailor's (*tailleur*)?
19. Your tailor won't make my coat.
20. Why will he not have his (*son*) coat done at the French tailor's?
21. The French tailor will not make my black (*noir*) waistcoat (*gilet*).
22. Where will you have your black coat done?

23. Why will you not buy (*acheter*) your black coat at the French tailor's?
24. Will you have your luggage (*bagage*) booked (*enregistrer*)?
25. I will not have my luggage booked (*or* checked).
26. Why are you unwilling to have your luggage booked (*or* checked)?
27. What (*que*) will you do?
28. What will you do this evening (*or*, to-night = *ce soir*)?
29. Will you go to the theatre to-night?
30. No, sir, this evening I'll write a letter (*une lettre*) to my uncle in London (*Londres*).

---

1) '*ü*' There is no equivalent in the English language for this sound. It is so utterly different from anything in our tongue, that the nearest approach we find to it is in 'u' in the word 'gude' in the

14. Il ne veut pas (*ēēl ně veū păh*) le faire faire.

15. Pourquoi ne veut-il pas (*ně veū-tēēl păh*) le faire faire pour vous?

16. Où (*oū*) voulez-vous le faire faire?

17. Où voulez-vous faire faire votre habit (*vōt-rā-bēē*)?

18. Voulez-vous faire faire votre habit chez (*shay*) mon tailleur (*mong tă-yeŭr*)?

19. Votre tailleur ne veut pas faire mon habit (*mŏn-nă-bēē*).

20. Pourquoi ne veut-il pas faire faire son habit chez le tailleur français (*frăng-say*)?

21. Le tailleur français ne veut pas faire mon gilet noir (*jēē-lay n'wo-ār*).

22. Où voulez-vous faire faire votre habit noir (*vŏt-rā-bēē-n'wo-ār*)?

23. Pourquoi ne voulez-vous pas acheter (*pāh-zăsh-tay*) votre habit noir chez le tailleur français?

24. Voulez-vous faire enregistrer (*ăng-r*⬛*-gĭs-tray*) votre bagage (*bă-gāhjĕ*)?

25. Je ne veux pas faire enregistrer mon bagage.

26. Pourquoi ne voulez-vous pas faire enregistrer votre bagage?

27. Que (*kĕ*) voulez-vous faire?

28. Que voulez-vous faire ce soir (*sĕ-s'wo-ār*)?

29. Voulez-vous aller ce soir au spectacle?

30. Non, monsieur (*mŏ-syeū*), ce soir je veux écrire (*jĕ veū zay-krēēr*) une[1] lettre à mon oncle à Londres (*ŭhn lĕt-rā mŏn nong-kl' āh lōng-dr'*).

31. What will he do to-night?

32. What will you do with (*de*) this (*cette*) letter?

33. What is to be done? (*Literally*: What do)?

34. What's to be done in regard to (*de*) your luggage (*vos bagages*)?

35. What is to be done? He will not have his luggage (*ses bagages*) checked.

36. What do you want of me? (*Literally*: What me will you?*)

37. What does he want of you?

38. He does not want to buy this black waistcoat.

39. Will you bring (*apporter*) my dinner (*dîner*)?

40. Bring (*apportez*) my dinner immediately (*or*, at once = *tout de suite*).

41. Bring my dinner at once, if you please (*s'il vous plaît*).

3

to the French tailor's?

to (by; at the house of; at the store of)

the [Definite article. Compare the Grammatical Remarks. As conjunctive personal pronoun, '*le*' means 'him' or 'it.']

tailor

French [The French place the adjective *after* the noun—*i.e.*, the French].

---

1. Why will he not come (*venir*) to-day (*aujourd'hui*

31. Que veut-il faire ce soir ?

32. Que voulez-vous faire de cette lettre (*sĕt lĕtt'r*) ?

33. Que faire ?

34. Que faire de vos (*vōh*) bagages? (*Bagages* is mostly used in the plural).

35. Que faire ?- Il ne veut pas faire enregistrer ses (*say*) bagages.

36. Que me voulez-vous ?

37. Que vous veut-il ?

38. Il ne veut pas acheter ce gilet noir (*ēēl nĕ veŭ pāh zăshtay sĕ jēē-lay n'wo-ār*).

39. Voulez-vous apporter mon dîner (*voŭ-lēh voŭ zăp-portēh mong dēē-nay*) ?

40. Apportez (*ăp-por-tēh*) mon dîner tout de suite (*toŭ-d's'wēet*).

41. Apportez mon dîner tout de suite, s'il vous plaît (*sēē-veŭ play*).

3

chez le tailleur français?
shay lĕ tă-yeŭr frăng-say

chez (*shay*).

le (*lĕ*) [There exists only one form for the definite masculine article '*the*' and the personal pronoun 'him' or 'it,' viz. '*le.*']

tailleur (*tă-yeŭr*)

français (*frăng-say*) [The adjective is, mostly placed *after* the noun].

---

1. Pourquoi ne veut-il pas venir aujourd'hui (*vĕ-nēēr ŏh-joŭr-dŭ-ēē or d'wēē*) ?

2. He won't come to-day, but (*mais*) he says (*il dit*) that (*que*) he will come to-morrow (*demain*).

3. Will you do me the favour (*le plaisir*) of coming with me ?

4. Where to (*où*) (then = *donc?*) [The French are very fond of adding this '*donc*' which cannot be translated into English].

5. I should like (*je voudrais*) to go to the English (*anglaise*) church (*l'église*).

6. I should like to buy (*je voudrais acheter*) a black (*noir*) waistcoat and a pair (*une paire*) of boots. Won't you do me the favour to accompany me (*de m'accompagner*, instead of *de me accompagner*) ?

7. I should like very much (*bien*) to go with you, but (*mais*) I have no time. (*Literally :* I have not the time = *je n'ai pas le temps*).

8. Have you (*avez-vous*) time (= the time) to go with me ?

9. No, sir, I have no time.

10. What have you to do ? (The French '*donc*' cannot always be translated. Compare phrase 4.)

11. I have much (*beaucoup*) to do.

12. I should like to accompany you, but I have no time.

---

1) '*Que*,' what, must be *apostrophed* before words commencing with a *vowel*, as : *qu'avez vous* instead of *que avez-vous?*

2) The auxiliary verb *j'ai*, I have, is thus conjugated :
j'ai (*jay*), I have.
tu as (*tü äh*), thou hast.

2 Il ne veut pas venir aujourd'hui, mais il dit (*may zĕĕĺ dĕĕ*) qu'il (*kĕĕl*) veut venir demain (*dĕ-maing*).

3. Voulez-vous me faire le plaisir (*play-zĕĕr*) de venir avec moi ?

4. Où donc (*dong*)? (*Donc* can in this phrase not be translated).

5. Je voudrais aller (*jĕ voū-dray-zăh-lēh*) à l'église anglaise (*lay-glēēse āng-glayse*).

6. Je voudrais acheter (*jĕ voū-dray-zāsh-tay*) un gilet noir et une paire de bottes (*ün pair dĕ bot*). Ne voulez-vous pas me faire le plaisir de m'accompagner (*mă-kong-păn-yēh*) ?

7. Je voudrais bien (*byaing*) aller avec vous, mais (*may*) je n'ai pas (*jĕ nay păh*) le temps (*tăng*).

8. Avez-vous (*ăvēh voū*) le temps d'aller avec moi ?

9. Non, monsieur, je n'ai pas le temps.

10. *Qu'avez-vous*[1] donc à faire (*kă-vēh-voū dong āh fair*)?

11. *J'ai*[2] beaucoup (*bōh-koū*) à faire.

12. Je voudrais bien vous accompagner (*voū-ză-kong-păn-yēh*), mais (*may*) je n'ai pas le temps.

---

il a (*ēĕl lăh*), he has.
elle a (*ĕll lăh*), she has.
nous avons (*noū ză-vong*), we have.
vous avez (*voū zăvēh*), you have.
ils ont (*ēĕl zōng*), they have (*masc.*).
elles ont (*ĕll zōng*), they have (*fem.*).

13. I have a great deal (= much, *beaucoup*) to do at my office (*bureau*).

14. Are you going to your office?

15. Go to my office at once (*tout de suite*).

16. Will you do me the favor to go to my office for me?

17. When (*quand*) will he come?

18. What in the world (*donc*=then) has he to do that he is unwilling to come to-day?

19. Will you do me the favor to call (*passer*) at the French shoemaker's (*cordoñnier*)?

20. Do you pass (*passez-vous*) my office?

21. I am passing (*je passe*) by the station (*gare* = *depot, terminus*).

22. When you pass the station to-morrow, will you oblige me by calling on my uncle (= will you do me the favor of calling on my uncle)?

23. Pass me the bread (*le pain*).

24. Waiter (*garçon*), pass me the bread and the butter (*le beurre*).

25. Will you please (*veuillez*) pass me the bread and the butter? my little son (*mon petit fils*) is very hungry. (*Literally*: has great hunger = *a grand'faim*.)

26. Are you hungry? (*Literally*: Have you hunger=*avez-vous faim?*) No; but I am very thirsty (= I have much thirst=*j'ai bien soif*).

27. Will you please bring me a cup (*une tasse*) of coffee (*de café*)?

28. I should like very much to pass several (*quelques*) days (*jours*) with you, but I have no time.

13. J'ai beaucoup à faire à mon bureau (*āh mong bü-rōh*).

14. Allez-vous à votre bureau ?

15. Allez tout de suite (*toū-d'swēēt*) à mon bureau.

16. Voulez-vous me faire le plaisir d'aller à mon bureau pour moi (*poūr m'woāh*) ?

17. Quand (*kāng*) veut-il venir ?

18. Qu'a-t-il donc (*kă-tēēl dong*) à faire qu'il ne veut pas venir aujourd'hui (*ōh-joūr-d'wēē*) ?

19. Voulez-vous me faire le plaisir de passer (*păs-sēh*) chez le cordonnier (*kor-don-yēh*) français ?

20. Passez-vous (*păs-sēh voū*) mon bureau ?

21. Je passe (*jē pass*) la gare (*gār*).

22. Quand vous passez la gare demain (*dē-maing*), voulez-vous me faire le plaisir de passer chez mon oncle ?

23. Passez-moi le pain (*paing*).

24. Garçon (*găr-song*), passez-moi le pain et le beurre (*ay lĕ beūr*).

25. Veuillez (*veū-yēh*) me passer le pain et le beurre; mon petit fils a grand faim (*mong p'tēē fēĕs āh grāng faing*).

26. Avez-vous faim ? Non, mais j'ai bien soif (*s'woāf*).

27. Veuillez m'apporter une tasse de café (*ün tăs d'kăh fay*).

28. Je voudrais bien passer quelques jours (*kĕl-kē joūr*) avec vous, mais je n'ai pas le temps.

29. He does not pass by your sister-in-law's garden (=by the garden of Mrs. (*Madame*) your sister-in-law (*votre belle-sœur*).

30. Let us pass (*passons*) on the other side (*de l'autre côté*).

31. Will you please tell (*dire*) me, sir, where one (*on*) takes (*prend*) the tickets (*billets*) for Paris?

32. The tickets for Paris are taken on the other side (= one takes the tickets, &c.).

33. Will you please pass me your tickets, gentlemen (*messieurs*)?

34. Will you please take (*prendre*) your ticket at the ticket-office (*au guichet*), and pass into the waiting-room (*la salle d'attente*)?

35. Will you please tell me, sir, where the waiting-room is?

36. Will you please come with me?

37. Why have you no time to call on him (*lui*)?

38. Will you do me the favor of calling to-morrow morning (*matin*) at his house (=on him)?

39. Is he at home? (*Literally :* Is he [*est-il*] at him?)

40. Is she (*est-elle*) at home (*or*, in)?

41. Mr. B. is not at home, but Mrs. B. is within.

42. Is Mr. B. at home? (*Literally :* Mr. B., is he at home?)

---

1) *Passons, let us pass*, is the plural of the so-called *imperative*.

2) *Est-il*, is he, is the 3rd person of the singular of the auxiliary verb *to be*, which is thus conjugated :

je suis (*jᵉ sw-ĕe*), I am.
tu es (*tü ay*), thou art.

29. Il ne passe pas le jardin (*jăr-daing*) de Madame votre belle-sœur (*mădăm vot bell-seŭr*).

30. Passons[1] de l'autre côté (*pās-song de lōt-koh-tay*).

31. Veuillez me dire (*dēĕr*), monsieur, où l'on prend (*oŭ long prăng*) les billets pour Paris (*lay bĕĕ-yēh poŭr Pārēē*)?

32. On prend les billets pour Paris de l'autre côté.

33. Veuillez me passer les billets, messieurs (*mĕs-yeŭ*)?

34. Veuillez prendre (*prăng-dr*) votre billet au guichet (*ghēē-shay*) et passer à la salle d'attente (*sāhl-dāt-tăngt*).

35. Veuillez me dire, monsieur, où est la salle d'attente?
36. Veuillez venir avec moi?
37. Pourquoi n'avez-vous pas le temps de passer chez lui (*lŭ-ēē*)?
38. Voulez-vous me faire le plaisir de passer demain matin (*mă-taing*) chez lui?
39. Est-il[2] (*ay-tēĕl*) chez lui?
40. Est-elle (*ay-tĕll*) chez elle?
41. Monsieur B. n'est pas (*nay păh*) chez lui, mais madame est chez elle (*ay shay zēll*).
42. Monsieur B. est-il chez lui? [The subject of every question if a noun is placed at the beginning of the phrase].

---

il est (*ēĕl lay*), he is.
elle est (*ĕll lay*), she is.
nous sommes (*noŭ sŏm*), we are.
vous êtes (*voŭ zayt*), you are.
ils sont (*ēĕl song*), they are (*masc.*).
elles sont (*ĕll song*), they are (*fem.*).

43. Is Mrs. B. within?

44. I am very sorry (*je regrette bien*), Mr. B. is not at home.

45. Where is he gone to?

46. Master is gone to the office.

47. Are you going home? (*Literally :* Go you to you?)

48. The French shoemaker is not (*n'est pas*) at my house (=at me), he is at yours.

43. Madame B. est-elle chez elle?

44. Je regrette (*rĕ-grĕt*) bien, monsieur B. n'est pas chez lui.

45. Où est-il allé (*oŭ ay-tēēl ăh-lēh*)?

46. Monsieur est allé au bureau (*ay-tăh-lēh ōh bü-rōh*).

47. Allez-vous chez vous?

48. Le cordonnier français n'est pas (*nay păh*) chez moi, il est chez vous.

GRAMMATICAL REMARKS.

Exercises and Words used in Common Conversation.

1

Of the definite article.

There are but *two* genders in the French language, viz.: the *masculine* and *feminine*.

This distinction applies not only to persons, but also to *inanimate objects*.

In order to indicate this distinction of gender, the *definite article* is *prefixed* to substantives.

There are *two forms* for the definite article—viz., *le (lĕ)* for the *masculine,* and *la (lăh)* for the *feminine* form.

Examples.[1]

Masculine.	*Feminine.*
le père (*payr*), the father.	*la* mère (*mayr*) the mother.
le fils (*fees*), the son.	*la* fille(*fee-yĕ*[2]),the daughter.
le frère (*frayr*), the brother.	*la* sœur (*seūr* [3]), the sister.

---

1) As I have only given words which every one *must* know, I beg that students will commit them to memory.

2) The liquid sounds are the most difficult ones in the French language. They are very sweet sounds. But it is almost impossible —even with physical demonstration—to show how they are produced. In the above word the ' yĕ ' has a soft lingering sound.

3) '*eū*' has the sound of the English '*ea*' in the word '*early*,' only much longer.

Masculine.	Feminine.
le cousin (*coŭzaing*), the cousin.	*la* cousine (*coŭ-zēēn*), the cousin.
le beau-frère (*bōh-frayr*), the brother-in-law.	*la* belle-sœur (*bell-seŭr*), the sister-in-law.
le beau-père (*bōh-payr*), the father-in-law.	*la* belle-mère (*bell-mayr*), the mother-in-law.
le neveu(*nĕ-veŭ³*),the nephew	*la* nièce (*nēē-ayse*), the niece.
le grand-père(*lĕ grāng-payr*), the grand-father.	*la* grand'mère (*lă grāng-mayr*),the grand-mother
le petit-fils (*lĕ p'tēē-fēēs*), the grand-child.	*la* petite-fille (*lă p'tēēt-fēē-yĕ*), the grand-child.

Rūlĕ : Before *nouns* beginning with a *vowel* or an *unaspirated* (*i.e.*, mute) *h*, *le* and *la* are changed into *l'*, thus forming but one word with the noun.

Examples.

Masculine.	Feminine.
*l'*oncle (*lōng-kl*), the uncle.	*l'*amie (*lăh-mēē*), the friend.
*l'*ami (*lăh-mēē*), the friend.	*l'*assiette (*lă-syet*), the plate.
*l'*homme (*lŏm*), the man.	*l'*habitude (*lă-bēē-tüd*), the custom, habit.
*l'*état (*lay-tāh*), the state.	

Exercise.

1) Why will you not write to (*à*) my (*mon*) brother-in-law? — 2) My (*mon*) father-in-law will not go to the theatre. — 3) My son-in-law will not go to (*à*) Paris. — 4) My (*mon*) friend will write a French letter to (*à*) your (*votre*) brother-in-law. — 5) Why will he not buy (*ache-*

(*ma*) sister-in-law will buy this waiscoat for (*pour*) my (*mon*) friend Charles. — 7) When will you dine (*diner* = dēē-nay))? — 8) Will you please (*veuillez*) pass me this newspaper (*ce journal*=joūr-nāhl). — 9) Why will you read (*lire*=lēēr) this letter (*cette lettre*)?—10) I should like to read your friend's letter (=the letter of your friend). — 11) When will you do your shopping? — 12) I should like to make my purchases to-day; will you be kind enough to accompany me to the shop?

Exercise.

1) Mon beau-frère ne veut pas aller à Londres (*London*). — 2) Votre amie veut aller au (*to the*) concert (*concert*; pronounce : cōng-sair). — 3) Pourquoi ne voulez-vous pas écrire une lettre française à notre (*our*) agent (āh-jāng) à Marseille (Mār-zĕ-yĕ')? — 4) Je ne veux pas acheter ce gilet. — 5) Quoi! il ne veut pas acheter ce gilet? — 6) Ma (*my*) tante (tāngt=aunt) ne veut pas acheter cette assiette (ās-syĕt).—7) N'avez-vous pas le temps d'aller au spectacle ce soir (s'wo-āhr)?—8) Qu'avez-vous donc à faire que vous n'avez pas le temps d'aller à l'église avec moi ?—6) Veuillez me dire (dēēr), monsieur, si (*if*) l'on prend (long-prāng) les billets à Paris au guichet de ce côté? — 10) Non, Monsieur, de l'autre côté. — 11) Veuillez lui dire de faire l'habit de madame tout de suite. — 12) Avez-vous faim? Non, monsieur, je n'ai pas faim, mais j'ai grand' soif (*or*, bien soif).

---

1) Observe the liquid sound. Compare Note 2, page 50.

Of Declension (Cases).

There are four cases in the French declension, viz :

The Nominative (le nominatif).
The Genitive or Possessive (le génitif).
The Dative (le-datif).
The Accusative or Objective case (l'accusatif).

1) There is only *one form* for the *nominative* and *objective* cases, both in singular and plural. They can only be distinguished by their *position* in the sentence. In order to *find* the *nominative*, we must ask '*Who*'?; for the *objective* '*Whom*' or '*What*'? Ex. :

Le tailleur (tă-yeūr) *fait* (fay) *le gilet ; the tailor makes the waistcoat.*

Who makes the waistcoat ? The answer is : *the tailor.* Therefore *le tailleur* is the *nominative case,* or the *subject* of the sentence. *What* does the tailor make? Answer : *the waistcoat.* Consequently *le gilet* is the *accusative* or the *object.* The construction of French phrases is, therefore, very simple — viz., *subject, verb, object.* The subject or nominative *precedes* the verb, the object or accusative *follows* it.

2) The *genitive* or *possessive case* replies to the question '*Whose,*' '*of whom,*' or '*of which*'? It is known by the preposition **de** (*of*) which appears either *unchanged* or *contracted with the article.* The *contraction* takes place whenever *de* occurs *before the masculine article le* or the

plural-form (for both genders exists only *one* form, viz.:
les). Ex. :

Singular : **du** père (instead of *de le père*), of the father
or the father's.

   du tailleur (instead of *de le tailleur*), of the
   tailor *or* the tailor's.

Plural : **des** frères (instead of *de les frères*), of the brothers *or* the brothers'.

   des sœurs (instead of *de les sœurs*), of the sisters
   or the *sisters'*.

 3) Before the *feminine article* **la,** however, or before
l', **de** remains unchanged, as :

  de la mère, of the mother *or* the mother's.
  de la sœur, of the sister *or* the sister's.
  de l'homme, of the man *or* the man's.
  de l'ami, of the friend *or* the friend's.

 4) The *dative case* answers to the question ' *to whom,*'
and is formed by putting the preposition **à** (*to*) before the
article, as :

   à la mère, to the mother.
   à l'homme, to the man.

 Before the *masculine article* **le,** and before the *plural
form* **les,** the dative *à le* is changed into **au** (singular
masculine) and *à les* into **aux** (plural, both masculine and
feminine). Ex. :

  au (ōh) père (instead of *à le père*), to the father.
  aux (ōh) frères (instead of *à les frères*), to the brothers.
  aux (ōh) tantes (instead of *à les tantes*), to the aunts.

Singular.

Masculine.	*Feminine.*	*With the apostrophe.*	
Nom. le (*lĕ*)	la (*lă*)	l'	the
Gen. du (*dü*)	de la (*dĕ lă*)	de l'	of the
Dat. au (*ŏh*)	à la (*ā lă*)	à l'	to the
Acc. le (*lĕ*)	la (*lă*)	l'	the

Plural.

Nom. les (*lay*) the	Only *one* form both for
Gen. des (*day*) of the	the masculine, feminine
Dat. aux (*ŏh*) to the	and apostrophe.
Acc. les (*lay*) the	

Declension of Nouns.

Nouns remain *unchanged* in the *singular.*

The *plural* is generally formed as in English, by an *addition* of *a silent* s to the singular—viz., le père, the father, les pères, the fathers; l'ami, the friend, les amis, the friends; la cousine, the (female) cousin, les cousines, the (female) cousins.

T a b l e.

With the definite article.

Singular.	*Singular.*
Nom. le père, the father.	la mère, the mother.
Gen. du père, of the father or the father's.	de la mère, of the mother or the mother's.
Dat. au père, to the father.	à la mère, to the mother.
Acc. le père, the father.	la mère, the mother.

Plural.	*Plural.*
Nom. les pères, the fathers.	les mères, the mothers.
Gen. des pères, of the fathers *or* the fathers'.	des mères, of the mothers *or* the mothers'.
Dat. aux pères, to the fathers.	aux mères, to the mothers.
Acc. les pères, the fathers.	les mères, the mothers.

With the apostrophe.

Singular.	*Plural.*
Nom. l'ami, the friend.	les amis[1], the friends.
Gen. de l'ami, of the friend *or* the friend's.	des amis, of the friends *or* the friends'.
Dat. à l'ami, to the friend.	aux amis, to the friends.
Acc. l'ami, the friend.	les amis, the friends.

The indefinite article.

Besides the definite article, there is also an *indefinite one* for the singular, answering to the English *a* or *an*, viz. : **un** (eūng) for the masculine, and **une** (ün) for the feminine. Ex.: un oncle (eūn-nong-kl),' an uncle; un gilet, a waistcoat; une lettre, a letter.

· The indefinite article is thus declined :

Singular (masc.).	*Singular* (fem.).
Nom. un (eūng[2]).	une (ün) a.
Gen. d'un (deūng).	d'une (dün) of a.
Dat. à un (ah eūng).	à une (āh ün) to a.
Acc. un (eūng).	une (üne) a.

---

1) Pronounce : lay-zā-mēē ; day-zā-mēē ; ōh-zā-mēē ; lay-zā-mēē.

2) '*eū*' is pronounced like our '*ea*' in '*early*,' only longer.

Singular.	Singular.
Nom. un frère, a brother.	une lettre, a letter.
Gen. d'un frère, of a brother or a brother's.	d'une lettre, of a letter or a letter's
Dat. à un frère, to a brother.	à une lettre, to a letter.
Acc. un frère, a brother.	une lettre, a letter.

General Rules.

1) The *definite article* must be employed in French before all nouns which are used in a *general sense* or which designate a *whole species of objects.* The definite article in such cases is not used in English, but must be employed in French, as:

L'homme (lŏm), man; *la nature* (nă-tür), nature; *la fortune* (for-tün), fortune; le *dîner* (dēē-nēh), dinner.

2) The *definite article* must be *repeated* before *each* substantive in a sentence, as:

Bring the salt, pepper and vinegar, *Apportez* le *sel*, le *poivre et* le *vinaigre* (ăp-por-tēh lĕ sĕl, lĕ po-āvr ēh lĕ vēē-nay-gr). The men, women, and children, Les *hommes*, les *femmes et* les *enfants* (lay zŏm, lay fām ay lay zāng-fāng).

3) The possessor *follows* the objects possessed, and must be *preceded* by the definite article; for instance, *the brother's coat*, must be inverted = the coat of the brother, *l'habit du frère* ; *my uncle's letter* = the letter of (*or* from) my uncle, *la lettre de mon oncle.*

Words.

Decline (and learn by heart) the following words:

Habillement (m.).	Dress.
(ă-bēē-yĕ-māng)	
la redingote (_rĕ-daing-gŏt_)	the overcoat.
l'habit (m.) (_lă-bēē_)	the coat _or_ the dress.
le gilet (_jēē-lay_)	the waistcoat.
le pantalon (_păng-tāh-long_) _only used in the singular._	the trowsers.
le chapeau (_shā-pŏh_) plural: _les chapeaux (lay shā-pŏh)_	the hat _or_ bonnet.
la cravate (_crāvāt_)	the necktie.
le faux-col (_fōh-cŏl_)·	the collar.
la chemise (_shĕ-mēēse_)	the shirt.
le mouchoir (_moŭ-shwoar_)	the pocket-handkerchief.
les bretelles (f.) (_bray-tell_) _only used in the plural_	the suspenders.
les bas (m.) (_bāh_)	the stockings
les bottes (f.) (_bŏt_)	the boots.
le caleçon (_kă-lĕ-song_)	the drawers.
le gilet de flanelle (_flă-nel_)	the flannel waistcoat.
le bouton (_boŭ-tong_)	the button.
la boutonnière (_boŭ-tŏn-yair_)	the buttonhole.
les gants (m.) (_gāng_)	the gloves.
les pantoufles (f.) (_păng-toŭfl_)	the slippers.
la robe	the dress.
la robe de chambre (_shāng-br'_)	the morning-dress.
le jupon (_jü-pong_)	the petticoat.
le peignoir (_pĕn-yoar_)	the wrapper.

Exercise.

1) Why will you not have your coat done at (*chez*) my tailor's?—2) Will you please write an English (*anglaise*) letter (=letter English) to our agent in (*à*) London? — 3) Why will he not buy these (*ces*) collars and pocket-handkerchiefs?—4) What will you do with (*de*) this (*cette*) letter? — 5) Why will he not make these trousers and this black vest (= vest black)? — 6) Will you please (*veuillez*) bring me (*m'apporter*) my dinner at (*à*) one o'clock (*une heure*=eūr)?

Exercise.

1) Pourquoi ne voulez-vous pas aller avec moi (*with me*) chez (*to*) mon oncle? — 2) Montez (mong-tay=*bring up*) mon bagage, s'il vous plaît, à ma chambre (shăng-br =*my room*).—3) Apportez ce pantalon à mon tailleur, s'il vous plaît.—4) Pourquoi ne voulez-vous pas me faire le plaisir d'aller avec ma sœur chez notre blanchisseuse (blăng-shĭ-seūse=*washerwoman*)? — 5) Que faire? Il ne veut pas monter votre bagage.

3

Of the regular verb parler, to speak.

There are in French *three regular conjugations* of which

the *first* ends in **er**, as parl**er**, to speak.
„ *second* „ **ir**, „ ven**ir**, to come.
„ *third* „ **re**, „ vend**re**, to sell.

The *infinitive mood* is the. *ground-form* of the verb, on which its conjugation depends.

What *precedes* the terminations *er, ir* and *re* is the *root* which remains always *unaltered* in regular verbs.

To the *root*, different terminations are added, by which *persons, tenses* and *moods* are distinguished, and which are common to all the verbs of the same conjugation. .

All the *variable terminations* of the regular verbs are printed in *large* italics.

First Conjugation: parler, to speak.

Indicative Mood.

Present Tense.

Je parle (*jĕ pārl*), I speak.	nous parlo*ns* (*noŭ pār-long*), we speak.
tu parl*es* (*tŭ pārl*), thou speakst.	vous parl*ez* (*voŭ pār-lĕh*), you speak.
il parle (*ēĕl pārl*), he speaks.	ils parl*ent*[1] (*ēĕl pārl*), they speak.
elle parle (*ĕll pārl*), she speaks.	elles parl*ent* (*ĕll pārl*), they speak.

Imperfect.

Je parl*ais* (*jē pār-lay*), I spoke.	nous parl*ions* (*noŭ pār-lyong*), we spoke.
tu parl*ais* (*tŭ pār-lay*), thou spokst.	vous parl*iez* (*voŭ pārl-yĕh*), you spoke.
il parl*ait* (*ēĕl pārlay*), he spoke.	ils parl*aient* (*ēĕl pār-lay*), they spoke.
elle parl*ait* (*ĕll pār-lay*), she spoke.	elles parl*aient* (*ĕll pār-lay*), they spoke.

---

1) The termination *ent* in the Present tense of all verbs is *silent*, as : ils donn*ent* (don), ils pens*ent* (pāngs), ils trouv*ent* (troŭv), etc.

Preterite.

Je parlai (_jĕ pār-lay_), I spoke.	nous- parlâmes (_noŭ' pār-lāhm_), we spoke.
tu parlas (_tü pār lāh,_), thou spokst.	vous parlâtes (_voŭ pār-lāht_), you spoke.
il parla (_ēĕl pār-lāh_), he spoke.	ils parlèrent (_ēĕl pār-layr_), they spoke.
elle parla (_ĕll pār-lāh_), she spoke.	elles parlèrent (_ĕll pār-layr_), they spoke.

There is _but one way_ of rendering the expréssions :

I speak, I am speaking, I do speak, viz.: je parle.
I spoke, I was speaking, I did speak, I used to speak, viz.: je parlais, etc.

In the _interrogative_ and _negative forms_, the auxiliary _to do_ cannot be expressed, as : 'Did he speak?' parlait-il? 'Will you not?' ne voulez-vous pas ? 'Does he not speak?' ne parle-t-il pas? 'He does not pass,' il ne passe pas.

Present.

Interrogative form.

Est-ce que je parle ?[1]) do I speak?
parles-tu ? dost thou speak?
parle-t-il ?[2]) does he speak?
parlons-nous ? do we speak?
parlez-vous ? do you speak?
parlent-ils (_pārl-tēĕl_)? do they speak?

· 1) This form is nowadays always emplóyed instead of the obsolete parlè-je? and is pronounced : ays-kĕ jĕ`pārl.
2) The _t_ is inserted for euphony.

Negative form.

Je ne parle pas, I do not speak.

tu ne parles pas, thou dost not speak.

Il ne parle pas, he does not speak.

nous ne parlons pas, we do not speak.

vous ne parlez pas, you do not speak.

ils ne parlent pas (*ēēl nĕ pārl pāh*), they do not speak.

Negative-interrogative form.

Est-ce que je ne parle pas (*ays kĕ jĕ nĕ pārl pāh*)? do
I not speak?

ne parles-tu pas? dost thou not speak?

ne parle-t-il pas? does he not speak?

ne parlons-nous pas? do we not speak?

ne parlez-vous pas? do you not speak?

ne parlent-ils pas (*nĕ pārl tēēl pāh*)? do they not speak?

The *Preterite* is but rarely used in *ordinary conversation,*
while it occurs frequently in narrative, anecdote, and in
historical and other compositions.

The *Imperfect* is used in *description* of persons and
things, and must be employed whenever in English the
Imperfect '*I was*' with the *present participle* is used, as
'*I was speaking*'=je parlais. For the other tenses, see
Part III.

Conjugate in the same manner : aimer[1] (*ay-mēh*), to
love *or* to like; penser (*pāng-sēh*), to think; donner (*don-
nēh*), to give; arriver[1] (*ā-rēē-vēh*), to arrive; trouver (*troū-*

---

1) *Je* is apostrophed before a *vowel*, as j'aime ; j'arrive ; j'appor-
tais, etc.

vēh), to find; apporter[1] (*ap-por-tēh*), to bring; chercher (*shĕr-shēh*), to seek ; prier (*prēē-ēh*), to pray *or* to beg ; tomber (*tong-bēh*), to fall.

Words.

Chemin de fer (m.).	**Railroad.**
(*shĕ-maing dĕ fair*).	
la gare (*gār*),	the station, terminus, depôt.
le billet (*bēē-yēh*),	the ticket.
le guichet (*ghēē-shay*),	the ticket *or* booking-office.
le surpoids (*sür-pwoāh*),	the surplus, overweight.
le bagage ⎫ (*bā-gāhje*),	the luggage.
les bagages ⎭	
le bulletin (*bül-taing*) de bagage,	the luggage-cheque.—
la salle d'attente (*sāhl dāt-tāngt*),	the waiting-room.
le quai (*kay*),	the platform.
le waggon (*vāh-gong*),	the railway-carriage.
le compartiment (*kong-par-tēē-māng*),	the railway-compartment.
le coin (*cŏ-aing*),	the corner, corner-seat.
le train (*traing*),	the train.
le train express (*ex-pray*),	the fast-train.
le train omnibus (*ong-nēē-büs*),	the parliamentary train, slow train.
le conducteur (*kong-dük-teūr*),	the conductor.
le facteur (*fāk-teūr*),	the commissioner, porter.
la station (*stă-syong*),	the station.

le buffet (*bü-fay*),   the buffet.
le départ (*day-pār*),   the departure.
le signal (*sin-yăhl*) du dé-   the starting-bell.
    part,
côté des hommes (*kō-tay   for gentlemen.
    day zom*).
côté des dames (*kō-tay day   for ladies.
    dāhm*),

Repas (*rĕh-pāh*).   Meals.

le déjeuner (*dāy-jeū-nēh*),   the breakfast.
le dîner (*dēē-nēh*),   the dinner.
le souper (*soū-pēh*),   the supper.
le café (*kāh-fay*),   the coffee.
le lait (*lay*),   the milk.
une tasse (*ün tās*),   a cup.
une tasse de café au lait (*ōh   a cup of coffee (with milk).
    lay*),
le thé (*tày*),   the tea.
une tasse de thé.   a cup of tea.
la serviette (*sĕr-vyĕtt*),   the napkin.
le plat (*plāh*),   the dish.
une assiette (*ās-syĕtt*),   a plate.
le couteau (*coū-tōh*)   the knife.
les couteaux (*coū-toh*),   the knives.
la fourchette (*foūr-shĕtt*),   the fork.
la cuillér (*kwēē-yēh*),   the spoon.
la carte du jour,   the bill of fare.
le couvert (*coū-vayr*),   the cover (the knife, fork,
                        plate, spoon, and napkin).
le pain (*paing*),   the bread.

le beurre (*beür*),	the butter.
le verre (*vĕrr*),	the glass.
un verre d'eau (*doh*),	a glass of water.
le sel (*sĕll*),	the salt.
le poivre (*poāvr*),	the pepper.
le vinaigre (*vēē-naygr*),	the vinegar.
l'huile (*lwēēl*),	the oil.

Exercise.

1) I should like (*je voudrais bien*) to go to the theatre with you this evening, but I have no time. — 2) Have you no time to go to church (*à l'église*) with me?—3) Why have you no time to call at my tailor's? — 4) Will you please do me the favor to call at my friend's uncle when you pass by the post-office (*le bureau de poste*)?—5) Speak [1] French to my sister-in-law; she does not understand (*elle ne comprend pas=*ĕll nĕ kong-prāng pāh) English (*anglais* =āng-glay). — 6) How do you call........ in French (*Que veut dire* (say) *en français=*āng frāng-say)?—7) Waiter, bring me (*apportez-moi*) a cup of coffee (with milk) and an English paper (*un journal anglais=*joūr-nāhl āng-glay). — 8) He arrives by (*par*) this train. — 9) When will you do your shopping (*vos emplettes=*vo-zāng-plett)? — 10) I should like to do my (*mes*) shopping this forenoon (*ce matin*); will you do me the favor to accompany me (*de m'accompagner*)? — 11) Will you please tell me, Sir (*veuillez me dire, monsieur*), if the tickets to B. are taken at

---

1) Parlez; the imperative form.

the (*au*) ticket-office on (*de*) this side (*ce côté*) (=if one takes (*si l'on prend*). the tickets at the ticket-office, etc.)? —12) The tickets to B. are taken at the ticket-office on the other side (*de l'autre côté*)=(one takes [*on prend*] the tickets, etc.)

Exercise.

1. Parlez-vous français? — Je le parle un peu (eūng peū=*a little*).—Je le parle assez (ās-say=*sufficiently*) pour me faire comprendre (kong-prāng-dr=*to understand*). — 2) Ne parlez pas si (*so*) vit (vēēt=*quick*, *fast*).—3) Parlez-moi français. — J'ai beaucoup de peine (payne=*much difficulty*) à parler français. — Mais vous prononcez (prō-nong-sēh=*pronounce*) bien. — 4) Allez déjeuner. Le déjeuner est prêt (pray=*ready*). — J'ai grand faim. — J'ai bon appétit (ăp-pay-tēē=*a good appetite*). — 5) Qu'avons-nous (*what have we*) à déjeuner? Voulez-vous déjeuner avec nous? Voulez-vous du café ou (*or*) aimez-vous mieux (m'yeū=*do you prefer*) du chocolat (*chocolat*)? Voulez-vous du jambon (jāng-bong = *some ham*) pour votre déjeuner? — 6) Il est temps de dîner.—A quelle heure (āh kell eūr=*at what o'clock*) dînez-vous aujourd'hui? — Où sont ('song' = *are*) les couteaux, les fourchettes, les cuillers, les verres et le tire-bouchon (tēēr-boū-shong = *cork-screw*)?

THE TEACHER'S EDITION

OF THE

REVISED NEW TESTAMENT

With New Concordance and Index, Harmony of the Gospels, Maps,
Historical and Chronological Tables, Parallel Passages printed
in full, Blank Pages Interleaved for manuscript notes, and
many other New and Indispensable Helps to the Study
of the Revised Version.

After the excitement connected with the sale of the first copies of the new
revision, which lack the usual indexing headlines and marginal references
to parallel passages, and also the appendixes of tables, maps, etc.—all of
which helps preachers, teachers and Bible students have come to consider as
absolutely essential to a working copy of the Bible—there arises an imperative
demand for an edition of the Revised New Testament, containing all the
marginal and appendix helps of former TEACHERS' AND REFERENCE BIBLES,
adapted carefully and accurately to the Revised Version. We are, therefore, preparing, as rapidly as is consistent with accuracy, such an edition of
the Revised New Testament. The work is under the supervision of well-
known Bible scholars, with numerous helpers, and will be issued as early as
it can be done with thoroughness. In style and size the book will resemble
the Bagster Bible, "Fac-simile large edition," known as "the Moody Bible,"
being the same width and length and size of type. It will be supplied at
prices *within the reach of all*.

This "Teachers' Edition of the Revised New Testament" will be an exact,
certified reproduction of the entire Oxford and Cambridge Edition, including
the Preface and all the marginal readings and explanations. It will contain
the appendix notes of the American Revisers, printed in the margin of each
page by the side of the passages referred to. The parallel passages, to which
reference is m de in the "Bagster Bibles," with numerous others, so far as
appropriate, will be PRINTED IN FULL in the margin. The running headings,
usually printed at the tops of pages of the King James version, will be here
supplied. A small black mark will be inserted below the last letter of each
verse to facilitate reference, and aid in RESPONSIVE READING of the Revised
Version. The second half of the volume will consist of the most carefully
prepared HELPS TO THE STUDY OF THE REVISED NEW TESTAMENT, gleaned
from the best Teachers' Editions of the authorized version, and supplied
from various original sources—all being revised and adapted to harmonize
with the Revised Version. We shall introduce many other important features,
making this the most valuable edition of the New Testament ever issued.

Popular Cloth Edition—Ready in July—Price, Postage Free, $1.00.
Send for prospectus giving full description and prices of finer Bindings.

I. K. FUNK & CO., Publishers, 10 and 12 Dey St., New York.

COMPANION TO THE
Revised Version of the New Testament.

Explaining the Reasons for the Changes Made on the Authorized Version.

BY ALEXANDER ROBERTS, D.D.,
Member of the English Revision Committee.

WITH SUPPLEMENT BY A MEMBER OF THE AMERICAN COMMITTEE.

Containing a Brief History of the Revision of the Work and Co-operation of the New Testament Companies, of the Points of Agreement and Difference, and an Explanation of the Appendix to the Revised New Testament.

ALSO, A FULL TEXTUAL INDEX,

Being a Key to Passages in which Important Changes have been Made.

This book, having been carefully prepared by Members of both Revision Committees, carries official weight. It shows what changes have been made, and also the reasons which influenced the revisers in making them. It will be difficult to judge of the merits of the revision without the aid of this Companion volume. Our edition is printed by special arrangement with the English publishers. It is well known that, by an arrangement between the two Committees of Revision, the changes suggested by the American Committee, but which were not adopted by the English Revisers, are published as an Appendix to the Revised New Testament. The *Companion* volume is an explanation of *all* the changes adopted by both committees, and of those suggested by the American Committee, but not assented to by the English Committee, in their final revision. The book will be indispensable to a right understanding of the revision. This cheap edition of the combined books, although authorized and copyrighted, will be sold for 25 cents in paper, and 75 cents in cloth—sent postage free.

TESTIMONIALS.

T. W. CHAMBERS, D.D., a Member of the American Committee of Revision, says of this book: "Many persons have expressed a desire that, simultaneously with the issue of the Revised New Testament, there should appear an authentic explanation of the reasons for such changes as will be found in its pages. The work of Dr. Roberts is exactly fitted to meet this desire....Nowhere else in print can be found a statement so full and exact. It gives all needed information, and does it in an unexceptional way."

C. F. DEEMS, D.D., Pastor of the Church of the Strangers, New York, writes: "The Companion to the Revised Version seems to me almost indispensable. Even scholars who were not at the meeting of the Revisers would have a wearisome work in seeking to discover all the changes made, and to ordinary readers very much of the labor would be lost. ....All this is set forth by Dr. Roberts with admirable perspicuity. Those who have any intelligent interest in the Holy Scriptures, will find this little book absorbingly interesting. I shall urge every member of the church of which I am pastor to give it a careful reading, and purpose to introduce it as a text-book in our Bible-classes."

"So valuable, interesting and useful is this publication, that we advise every one who wishes to know the why and wherefore of the revision, to obtain it immediately."—*New York Observer.*

Paper, 8vo size, 25 cents; Cloth, 16mo, 75 cents.

*** For Sale by Booksellers and Newsdealers, or sent postage-paid, on receipt of price, by

I. K. FUNK & CO., Publishers, 10 & 12 Dey St., N. Y.

THE

𝕸𝖊𝖎𝖘𝖙𝖊𝖗𝖘𝖈𝖍𝖆𝖋𝖙 𝕾𝖞𝖘𝖙𝖊𝖒.

A SIMPLE AND PRACTICAL METHOD,

ENABLING

ANY ONE TO LEARN, WITH SLIGHT EFFORT, TO SPEAK
FLUENTLY AND CORRECTLY

𝕱𝖗𝖊𝖓𝖈𝖍, 𝕲𝖊𝖗𝖒𝖆𝖓, 𝕾𝖕𝖆𝖓𝖎𝖘𝖍, 𝖆𝖓𝖉 𝕴𝖙𝖆𝖑𝖎𝖆𝖓.

BY
DR. RICHARD S. ROSENTHAL,

*Late Director of the "Akademie für fremde Sprachen" in Berlin and Leipzig,
of the "Meisterschaft College" in London, and Principal of the
"Meisterschaft School of Practical Linguistry" in New York.*

FRENCH.

IN FIFTEEN PARTS, EACH CONTAINING THREE LESSONS.

PART II.

NEW YORK:
I. K. FUNK & CO., Publishers,
10 AND 12 Dey Street.

TERMS.

WE have arranged with Dr. ROSENTHAL, the author of the "Meisterschaft System," for its introduction in America under his own supervision, and he has opened

FOR NON-RESIDENTS.

The student does not need to leave his home. The lessons of each language are prepared by the Professor, and printed and sent in pamphlet shape to each member of the School wherever he may reside.

The course of study for each language—German, French, Italian, or Spanish—makes fifteen pamphlets of three lessons each.

All members of the School have

THE PRIVILEGE

of asking, by letter, questions concerning each lesson, or consulting on any difficulty which may have occurred to them. All exercises corrected and all questions answered by return post by Dr. ROSENTHAL or one of his assistants.

TERMS OF MEMBERSHIP.

Five Dollars is the price for membership in the school for each language. This amount ($5.) entitles the member to receive the fifteen books or pamphlets containing the lessons, also answers to his questions. Return postage for the answer must accompany the question.

State distinctly which language, or languages, you desire to study There are *no extra charges*. The price, **Five Dollars,** pays for one language ; **Ten Dollars** for two languages, etc. All exercises and questions must be written on a separate sheet of paper, and must state full address of the pupil.

Remittances must be made in Post-Office Order or registered letter addressed to

I. K. FUNK & CO,

10 and 12 Dey Street, New York.

The Meisterschaft System.

FRENCH.

PART II.

II.

FOUNDATION SENTENCE.

Did not the physician whom we saw in the waiting-room of the Northern Railway-station tell him, that the persons with whom your sister-in-law came here from Cologne, bought a house in Church Street?

1.

The physician whom we have seen at the waiting-room of the Northern Railway-station.

---

1) oû is to be pronounced like 'u' in 'rude', only somewhat shorter.

2) ā like 'a' in 'father'; ă is pronounced a little shorter.

3) ú-ēē is to be pronounced like *one* sound.

4) eû is pronounced like 'ea' in 'early', only much longer.

FOUNDATION SENTENCE.

Le médecin que nous avons vu à la salle
lĕ maid-saing kĕ noū[1]) zăvong vü āh[2]) lă săhl

d'attente de la gare du Nord, ne lui a-t-il pas dit
dăt-tăngt dĕ lă gār dü nōr nĕ lü-ēē[3])āh tēēl pāh dēē

que les personnes avec lesquelles madame votre
kĕ lay pĕr-sŏn ā-vĕk lay-kĕll mă-dăm vŏt

belle-sœur est venue ici de Cologne, ont acheté
bĕll - seūr[4]) ay vĕ-nü ēē-sēē dĕ kō lŏn-yĕ[5]) ōng tăsh-tay

une maison dans la rue de l'église?
ün may-zong dāng lāh rü dĕ lay-glēēze

1.

Le médecin que nous avons vu à la salle
lĕ maid-saing kĕ noū zăvong vü āh lă săhl

d'attente de la gare du Nord.
dăt-tăngt dĕ lă gār dü nōr

---

5) The so-called liquid sounds are the most difficult ones in the French language. They are very sweet sounds. But it is almost impossible to show how they are produced. In the above word the 'yĕ' has a soft lingering sound.

The physician

whom (or *which, what*)

we have	I have	we have
	thou hast	you have
	he has	they have, *masc.*
	she has	they have, *fem.*

(Compare the table of *avoir, to have,* in the Grammatical Remarks.)

seen

whom we have seen

in the waiting-room of

the Northern Railway-station. (*Literally :* the station of the North.)

---

1. Did you not see my sister-in-law? (*or,* Have you not seen, etc. ?)
2. Has he not seen Mr. D. at the waiting-room?
3. I saw (*or,* I have seen) the English physician.
4. What (*que*) have you seen?
5. What did you (*or,* What have you) seen at his office (*à son bureau*) ?
6. What did he say? (*or,* What has he said [*dit*]) ?
7. What did you buy? (*or,* What have you bought [*acheté*]) ?
8. Why have you not written (*écrit*) to the French physician?
9. When did you speak to Mrs. D. about (*de*) this affair (*cette affaire*) ?

Le médecin (*lè maid-saing*)

que (*kĕ*) ('There is only one form, viz. : *que*, for our relative pronouns *whom*, *which* and *what*.)

nous avons (*noŭ-ză-vong*). 1st person plural of :

J'ai (*jay*)	nous avons (*noŭ-ză-vong*)
tu as (*tŭ āh*)	vous avez (*voŭ-ză-vēh*)
il a (*ēĕl āh*)	ils ont (*ēĕl zong*), *masc.*
elle a (*ĕll āh*)	elles ont (*ĕll zong*), *fem.*

vu (*vŭ*)

que nous avons vu

à la salle d'attente de (*āh lā săhl dăt-tăngt dĕ*)

la gare du Nord (*lă gār dŭ Nôr*).

---

1. N'avez-vous pas vu ma belle-sœur (*bĕll-seŭr*) ?

2. N'a-t-il pas vu monsieur-D. (*day*) à la salle d'attente ?
3. J'ai vu le médecin anglais (*āng-lay*).
4. Qu'avez-vous vu (*kā-vēh voŭ vŭ*) ?
5. Qu'avez-vous vu à son bureau (*āh song bŭ-roh*) ?

6. Qu'a-t-il dit (*kā-tēēl dēē*) ?
7. Qu'avez-vous acheté (*kā-vēh voŭ zāsh-tay*) ?

8. Pourquoi n'avez-vous pas écrit (*pāh zay-crēē*) au médecin français ?
9. Quand avez-vous parlé (*quăng tā-vēh voŭ pār-lày*) à madame B. (*bay*) de cette affaire (*sĕt-tāf-fair*)?

10. What have you done (*fait*); waiter (*garçon*)?

11. You have checked (*or* booked, *fait enregistrer*) my travelling-rug (*ma couverture de voyage*).

12. What is the matter with you? (*Literally :* What have you)?

13. What is the matter with him? (*or*, **What ails him?** = what has he)?

14. What is the matter with her? (*or*, **What ails her**)?

15. What is the matter with your sister-in-law?

16. *Nothing* [1] is the matter with me (=**I have nothing**).

17 I don't know (*je ne sais pas*) what (*ce que*) is **the matter** with me (=what I have).

18. What is the matter with you? **You do not look well.** (*Literally :* You have not good look, *bonne mine.*)

19. What in the world (*donc*) is **the matter with your** brother-in-law? He does not look well.

20. You are right. (*Literally :* You *have* right, *raison*). He looks badly. (*Literally :* he has bad look, *mauvaise mine*).

21. Your friend does not look well. Is he ill (*malade*)?

22. I have a (*or* the) headache (*mal à la tête*).

23. He has a headache and is obliged (*obligé*) **to keep** (*garder*) his room (= the room, *la chambre*).

24. Is she not pale (*pâle*)? Yes, Sir, she is looking ill.

25. Waiter, this fillet (*or* steak) does not look **nice.**

---

1) *Nothing* is always expressed by two words in French, viz.: ne—rien, the first of which, 'ne,' must always be placed *before* the

10. Qu'avez-vous fait, garçon (*fay gȧr-song*) ?

11. Vous avez fait enregistrer ma couverture de voyage (*voū zā-vēh fay tāng-ray-jĭs-tray māh coū-vĕr-tür de voāh-jāsh*) ?

12. Qu avez-vous (*kā-vēh-voū*)?

13. Qu'a-t-il (*kā-tēēl*) ?

14. Qu'a-t-elle (*kā-tĕll*) ?

15. Madame votre belle-sœur qu'a-t-elle donc (*kā-tĕll dong*) ?

16. Je *n'*ai *rien*[1] (*rēē-āing*).

17. Je ne sais pas ce que j'ai (*jĕ nĕ say pāh s'kĕ jay*).

18. Qu'avez-vous? Vous n'avez pas bonne mine (*bŏn mēēn*).

19. Monsieur votre beau frère qu'a-t-il donc ? Il n'a pas bonne mine (*bŏn mēēn*).

20. Vous avez raison (*ray-song*). Il a mauvaise mine (*mŏ-vayz mēēn*).

21. Votre ami n'a pas bonne mine. Est-il malade (*ay-tēēl māh-lāhd*) ?

22. J'ai mal à la tête (*măhl ā lā tait*).

23. Il a mal à la tête, et est obligé de garder la chambre (*ay tŏ-blēē-jay dĕ gar-dēh lāh shāng-br*).

24. N'est-elle pas pâle (*pāhl*)? Oui (*oū-ēē*) monsieur, elle a mauvaise mine (*mŏ-vayz mēēn*).

25. Garçon, ce filet (*fēē-lay*) n'a pas bonne mine (*mēēn*).

---

verb, as : *il* n' *a dit rien*, he said nothing, *or* he did not say any-thing.

26. Waiter, take this steak away (*ôtez* = take off ; away);
it does not look nice.

27. *Why ; what is the matter with you?* [1] I am suffering
with the tooth-ache. (*Literally :* What have you then?
I have pain [*mal*] in the teeth [*aux dents*].)

28. My brother is obliged to keep his room (*la chambre*);
he is suffering with the tooth-ache.

29. My throat pains me. (*Literally :* I have pain [*mal*] in
the throat [*à la gorge*].)

30. I should like to go to bed (*aller au lit*); my throat
pains me.

31. Why? what is the matter with him?

32. He has the stomach-ache; he wants to go to bed.
(*Literally :* He has pain in the stomach [*au ventre*];
he will go to bed.)

33. She feels sick (=She has pain *at the heart* [*au cœur*]).

34. *I don't know* (*je ne sais*) [2] what is the matter with
me; but I do not feel well (= I am ill [*mal*] at my
ease [*à mon aise*].)

35. I feel sleepy (=I have sleep [*sommeil*]); I want to go
to bed.

36. I am very thirsty (= I have great thirst [*bien soif*]);
waiter, give me a glass of water (*un verre d'eau*).

1) All these *idiomatic expressions* with *avoir, to have,* must be
very thoroughly studied. The French *cannot* say : *I am* hungry, but
I have hunger, &c. I have given the most common idioms of *avoir,
to have,* in the above sentences. The following list will be found useful :

j'ai faim (*faing*), *I am* hungry.	*qu'avez-vous,* what is the matter
j'ai soif (*s'woaf*), *I am* thirsty.	with you ?
j'ai raison (*ray-zong*), *I am* right.	*je n'ai rien,* nothing is the matter
j'ai tort (*tore*), *I am* wrong.	with me.
j'ai sommeil (*sòm-mĕ-yĕ*), *I feel*	*j'ai* mal à la tête, I have the head-
sleepy.	ache.

26. Garçon, ôtez (*ō-tày*) ce filet, il n'a pas bonne mine.

27. *Qu'avez-vous*[1] donc ? J'ai mal aux dents (*măll oh dāng*).

28. Mon frère est obligé de garder la chambre (*shāng-br*) ; il a mal aux dents (*măll oh dāng*).

29. J'ai mal à la gorge.

30. Je voudrais bien aller au lit (*ōh lēē*) ; j'ai mal à la gorge.

31. Qu'a-t-il donc ?

32. Il a mal au ventre (*ōh vāng-tr*), il veut aller au lit (*ōh lēē*).

33. Elle a mal au cœur (*ōh keūr*).

34. Je ne sais ce que j'ai, mais je suis mal à mon aise (*jĕ s'wēē măll āh .mon-naize*).

35. J'ai sommeil (*som-mĕ-yĕ*) ; je veux aller au lit (*jĕ veū zā-lay ōh lēē*).

36. J'ai bien soif, garçon ; donnez-moi un verre d'eau (*eūng vĕrr dōh*).

---

j'ai mal aux dents (*dāng*), I have the tooth-ache.
j'ai mal à la gorge, my throat pains me.

j'ai mal au ventre (*vāng-tr'*), I have the stomach-ache.
j'ai mal aux yeux (*oh z'yeūh*), my eyes pain me.

j'ai mal aux oreilles (*oh zō-rĕyĕ*), my ears pain me.

Compare the *grammatical remarks* on the ' *idiomatic expressions of avoir.*'

2) *I do not know* is given either by : *je ne sais pas*, or oftener by : *je ne sais* (*jĕ nĕ say*).

37. Give me the bill of fare (*la carte du jour*) waiter; I am very hungry (= I have great hunger [*grand' faim*]).

38 The tailor has not yet (*encore*) brought (*apporté*) your coat.

39. Has not the laundress (*la blanchisseuse*) brought (*rapporté*) my linen (*linge*) yet?

40. Yes, sir, she has brought it and I have put it on (*sur*) your bed (*lit*). (*Literally:* She *it*[1] has brought and I *it*[1] have put, &c.)

41. Did you speak to her when she brought my linen? (*Literally:* To *her* [*lui*] have you spoken, &c.?)

42. Did you see him last evening? (= *Him*[1] have you seen, &c.?)

43. We saw him (= *We him*[1] *have seen*) this morning when he was going (*il est allé*) to the post office (*au bureau de poste*).

44. Did you understand me? (*Literally:* *Me*[1] have you understood?)

45. No, sir, I did not understand you (= I not you have understood).

---

1) The difficulty in the use of the '*conjunctive personal pronouns*' is in their proper position. We give a table of them on page 102. Observe the following rules:

a) The nominative cases '*je, tu, il, elle, nous, vous, ils, elles*' precede the verb, as in English, as: '*I speak*, je parle;' 'we go, nous allons,' &c.

b) In *interrogative sentences* they are placed *immediately after* the verb, as *parlez-vous? voulez-vous? donne-t-il?* &c., while the auxiliary *do you, does he?* &c., is never expressed.

37. Donnez-moi la carte du jour, garçon (*lā cart dü jour, gār-song*); j'ai grand' faim (*grāng faing*).

38. Le tailleur n'a pas encore (*pāh-zăng-kōr*) apporté votre habit (*vŏt-rā-bēē*).

39. La blanchisseuse (*blāng-shĭ-seūze*) n'a-t-elle pas encore rapporté mon linge (*pāh-zăng-kōr rāp-por-tay mong laingsh*)?

40. Oui monsieur, elle *l'a*[1] apporté et je *l'ai*[1] mis (*mēē*) sur (*sür*) votre lit (*lēē*).

41. *Lui avez-vous parlé*[1] quand elle a apporté mon linge (*kāng tĕll-lā āp-por-tay mong laingsh*)?

42. *L'avez-vous vu*[1] hier soir (*yair swoār*)?

43. Nous *l'avons vu*[1] ce matin (*sĕ mătaing*) quand il est allé au bureau de poste.

44. *M'avez-vous compris*[1] (*cong-prēē*)?

45. Non, monsieur; je ne *vous*[1] ai pas compris (*jĕ nĕ voū zay pāh cong-prēē*).

---

c) The *dative* and *accusative cases, me te, lui, le, la, nous, vous, leur, les,* are placed *immediately before* the verb in a *simple tense,* and before its *auxiliary* in a *compound one,* as: Je *vous* donne, I give you; il *me* comprend, he understands me; je *vous* ai compris, I have understood you; il *m*'a vu, he has seen me; je *leur* ai dit, I have told them.

d) In negative sentences *ne* is placed directly *after the subject* and *before the governed pronoun,* as: il ne *m*'a pas vu; vous ne *m*'avez pas compris; je ne *vous* ai pas vu; ne *lui* a-t-il pas donné? je ne *leur* ai pas dit; ne *lui* a-t-il pas dit?

46. I did not understand you. You are speaking too (*trop*) fast (*vite*). (*Literally :* I not *you* have understood, &c.)

47. My brother understood him; he speaks English (*anglais*) pretty well (*passablement*).

48. She is wrong (=She has wrong '*tort*').

49. Your friend is (=has) wrong; Mr. N. has passed (*or* spent, lived) three (*trois*) years (*ans*) in Paris.

50. What do you think of the French language (*la langue*)? Do you not find it (=her[1]) very difficult (*difficile*)?

51. Why did you not brush (*brossé*) my clothes, waiter?

52. Waiter, brush my clothes and black (*cirez*) my boots.

53. Why did you not bring me my breakfast? (= Why not *me* have you brought, &c.)

2

Did he not tell him?

Not

to him (*or* to her). There is only *one* form for both pronouns, viz. : '*lui*'

has he

---

1) *her*, because it refers to '*la*' langue, fem.

46. *Je ne vous* ai pas compris; vous parlez trop vite (*trŏ vēēt*).

47. Mon frère *l'a* compris; il parle passablement anglais (*pă-sā-blĕ-măng tăng-glay*).

48. Elle a tort (*tŏr*).

49. Votre ami a tort; monsieur N. a passé trois ans (*trŏ-āh zăng*) à Paris.

50. Que pensez-vous de la langue (*lăng*) française? Ne *la*[1] trouvez-vous pas bien difficile (*dĭ-fēē-sēēl*)?

51. Pourquoi n'avez-vous pas brossé mes habits, garçon (*may zā-bēē gar-song*)?

52. Garçon, brossez mes habits et cirez (*sēē-ray*) mes bottes.

53. Pourquoi ne m'avez-vous pas apporté mon déjeuner (*nē mā-vay voŭ pāh zăp-por-tay mong·day-jeŭ-nay*)?

2

Ne lui a-t-il pas dit?

nĕ lú-ēē a-tēēl pāh dēē

ne-pas (The English negation *not* is almost always expressed by *ne-pas*.)

lui

a-t-il (The "*t*" in questions is added for euphony, but only in the 3d person singular when the verb which precedes *il* or *elle* or *on* [one] ends in a vowel.)

has he not to him

said; told

has he not told him ; did he not tell him ?

---

1. Did he not tell you to go to the station?
2. Have I not told you to do it at once?

3. Why did you not tell him to write this letter?

4. I have told him so (= I *it to him*[1] have told), but he will not do it.
5. Why did he not give you the kniyes (*les couteaux*)?
6. Why did you give him my friend's address? (= the address of my friend)?
7. Why did you not tell him that I did not understand him?
8. Did you not understand me?
9. Why have you not told him that we have no time to lose (*à perdre*)?
10. Have I not told you that he will not send (*envoyer*) your coat?
11. Why did you not tell him *not*[2] to go to his office?

---

1) When a verb governs *two* pronouns, they are both placed *immediately before* the verb, so that the one in the *dative comes first* and the *accusative follows*.

This rule applies only to the following pronouns: *me le*, it me (*or* to me); *te le*, it thee (*or* to thee); *nous le*, it us (*or* to us); *vous*

ne lui a-t-il pas

dit

ne lui a-t-il pas dit ?

---

1. Ne vous a-t-il pas dit d'aller à la gare ?
2. Ne vous ai-je pas dit de le faire tout de suite (*tŏŏt-'swēĕt*)?
3. Pourquoi ne lui avez-vous pas dit d'écrire cette lettre ?
4. Je le lui[1] ai dit, mais il ne veut pas le faire.

5. Pourquoi ne vous a-t-il pas donné les couteaux (*koū-toh*)?
6. Pourquoi lui avez-vous donné l'adresse de mon ami (*dĕ mŏn nā-mēe*) ?
7. Pourquoi ne lui avez-vous pas dit que je ne l'ai pas compris (*cong-prēē*) ?
8. Ne m'avez-vous pas compris ?
9. Pourquoi ne lui avez-vous pas dit que nous n'avons pas de temps à perdre (*tāng āh pĕr-dr*) ?
10. Ne vous ai-je pas dit qu'il ne veut pas envoyer votre habit (*kēēl nĕ veū pāh zāng-voāh-yēh vot-rā-bēē*) ?
11. Pourquoi ne lui avez-vous pas dit de *ne pas*[2] aller à son bureau (*nĕ pāh zǎ-lay āh song bü-rōh*)?

---

le, it you (*or* to you). Ex. Il *me le* donne, he gives it to me. Je *vous l'*ai donné, I gave it you. *But observe that one always says :* le lui, it to him (*or* to her), and le leur, it to them.

2) Ne pas is always placed together *before the infinitive* and *not* separated.

12. ´Why has he done so (= it)?

13. He did not tell me that one (*que l'on*) takes (*prend*) the tickets at the ticket-office on (*de*) this side.

14. Did he not write to them (*leur*) that I wanted (*je veux*) a front room (*une chambre donnant sur la rue*) (= towards the street)?

15. Why did you not write to them that we refused (*re-fusé*) the draft (*la traite*)?

16. He wrote me about it (= he me it has written), but I forgot it (= I it have forgotten (*oublié*).

17. He has not brought me my breakfast.

18. Why did you not bring him his (*son*) dinner?

19. I told him so (=I it to him have said), but he will not do it.

20. My brother has commissioned (*chargé*) me to buy him three (*trois*) shirt-buttons (=buttons of shirt, *boutons de chemise*).

21. Did I not commission (*or* order) you to buy my gloves at the French glovemaker's (*le gantier*)?

22. Waiter, did you order (= have you made come) a cab (*un fiacre*)?

23. The servant (*le commissionaire*) told me, the carriage (*la voiture*) is at the door (*à la porte*).

24. Did you check my luggage (*mes effets*), and have you given him the check (*le bulletin*)?

25. I gave it to him last evening (*hier soir*), but he mis-laid it (= he it has mislaid, *égaré*).

---

1) **On** = one, they, people. For euphony's sake the **French say**

12. Pourquoi l'a-t-il fait (*lāh-tēēl-fay*)?

13. Il ne m'a pas dit que l'on[1] prend les billets au guichet de ce côté (*lŏng prāng lay bēē-yēh ŏh ghēē-shay dĕ sĕ kŏ-tay*).

14. Ne leur a-t-il pas écrit que je veux une chambre donnant (*dŏn-nāng*) sur la rue?

15. Pourquoi ne leur avez-vous pas écrit que nous avons refusé (*rĕfü-zay*) la traite (*trait*)?

16. Il me l'a écrit, mais je l'ai oublié (*oū-blēē-ay*).

17. Il ne m'a pas apporté mon déjeuner (*day-jeū-nay*).

18. Pourquoi ne lui avez-vous pas apporté son diner (*song dēē-nay*)?

19. Je le lui ai dit, mais il ne veut pas le faire.

20. Mon frère m'a chargé (*shăr-jay*) de lui acheter trois boutons de chemise (*boū-tong dĕ shĕ-mēēze*).

21 Ne vous ai-je pas chargé d'acheter mes gants (*gāng*) chez le gantier (*gāng-t'yay*) français?

22. Garçon, avez-vous fait venir un fiacre (*fēē-ăk'*)?

23. Le commissionaire (*cŏ-mĭss-yŏ-nayr*) m'a dit que la voiture (*voāh-tür*) est à la porte.

24. Avez-vous fait enregistrer mes effets, et lui avez-vous donné le bulletin (*bül-taing*)?

25. Je le lui ai donné hier soir, mais il l'a égaré (*ay-gā-ray*).

---

que l'on, that one ; *si l'on*, if one ; and *où l'on*, where one.

26. I saw you at the waiting-room.

27. Will you please tell them (viz. : it=*le*).

28. Of what (*de quoi*) did you speak to him when you saw him on the platform (*au quai*)?

29. I say yes.

30. He says no.

31. What did you say (*or*, I beg your pardon, what did you say)?

32. Why did you not write to them to send us a new (*une nouvelle*) collection (*collection*) of samples (*or* patterns, *d'échantillons*)?

33. My brother-in-law speaks French with our tailor.

34. Does he speak French? (*Parle-t-il;* the '*t*' is inserted for euphony).

35. Yes, sir, he speaks a little. (*Literally:* it a little = *un peu*).

3

that the persons with whom your sister-in-law came

here from Cologne, bought a house in Church

Street?

26. Je vous⌒ai vu à la salle d'attente (*dāt-tāngt*).

27. Veuillez le leur dire (*veū-yēh lě leūr dēēr*).

28. De quoi lui avez-vous parlé, quand vous l'avez vu au quai.(*ōh kay*) ?

29. Je dis *que* oui (*jě dēē kě oū-ēē*).

30. Il dit *que* non (*nong*).

31. Que disiez-vous (*kě dēē-syēh voŭ*) ?

32. Pourquoi ne leur avez-vous pas⌒écrit de nous⌒envoyer une nouvelle collection d'échantillons (*pāh zay-krēē dě noū zāng-voāh-yēh ün noū-věl col-lěk-syong dayshāng-tēē-yong*) ?

33. Mon beau-frère parle français à notre tailleur.

34. Parle-t-il français (*pārl-ţēēl frāng-say*) ?

35. Oui (*oū-ēē*), monsieur, il le parle un peu (*eŭng peŭ*).

3

que	les	personnes	avec	lesquelles	madame	votre
kě	lay	pěr-sŏn	ā-věk	lay-kěll	mădăm	vŏt

belle-soeur	est	venue	ici	de	Cologne,	ont	acheté
běll seūr	ay	vě-nü	ēē-sēē	dě	Kŏ-lon-yě	ōng	tăsh-tay

une	maison	dans	la	rue	de	l'église ?
ün	may-zong	dāng	lă	rü	dě	lay-glēēze

that

the persons, the parties

with

whom

Mistress ; Mrs.

your sister-in-law

is

come-

here

from

Cologne

have bought

a house

in

the street

of

---

1) When a verb is conjugated with the auxiliary être (as in the above sentence), the participle must agree with its subject. Votre *belle-soeur* est *venue,* your sister came. *La* Belle-soeur being the

que (*kĕ*)

les personnes (*lay pĕr-sŏn*)   [Singular : *la personne.*]

avec (*ā-vĕk*)

lesquelles, (*lay-kĕll*) [*Accusative Plural fem.* of *laquelle.*]

madame (*mā-dām*)

votre belle-sœur (*vŏt bĕll-seūr*)

est (*ay*)

venue[1] (*vĕ-nü*) [*Fem. of the Participle* of *venir*, to come ; the *masc. participle* is *venu* without the final *e.*]

ici (*ēē-sēē*)

de (*dĕ*)

Cologne (*kō-lŏn-yĕ*)

ont acheté (*ong tăsh-tay*) [*Participle* of *acheter*, to buy. The *participle of all verbs conjugated with the auxiliary 'avoir,'* is *never* changed, or rather inflected.]

une maison (*ün may-zong*)

dans (*dāng*)

la rue (*lăh rü*)

de (*dĕ*)

---

subject of the sentence, the past participle *venue* must be placed in the feminine singular.   But *Vos sœurs sont* venue*s*, it must be feminine plural. . Votre frère est venu (masculine singul.) Vos frères sont venu*s* (mascul. plur.)

connection.)

---

1. The chambermaid has told them that she saw the persons with whom your niece came from London the other day (*l'autre jour*).

2. What does your father say of the person with whom he was in the waiting-room?

3. Of what did he speak to the persons?

4. What did he give to the persons to whose house (*chez lesquelles*) you are going?

5. No one arrived (= is come) by (*par*) this train (*ce train*).

6. Why did you not tell to *any one*[1] that my brother did not come by this train?

7. No one told him to do it immediately (*tout de suite*).

8. It is not allowed (*permis*) to *any one*[1] to stand about (*stationner*) on (*sur*) the platform.

9. Did any one inquire (*demander*) for me during (*pendant*) my absence (*absence*)? (*Literally:* Is one come to inquire, &c.)

10. No one has inquired for you during your absence.

---

1) *No one, nobody, not any one, not anybody* is always given by personne which must in this sense always be accompanied by the negation ne which must be placed *before* the verb. Observe that only

l'église [*fem.*] (*lay-gléēze*)

la rue de l'église

---

1. La fille de. chambre (*lā fēē-yĕ de shāng-br*) leur a dit qu'elle (*kĕll*) a vu les personnes avec lesquelles votre nièce est venue l'autre jour (*lō-t joŭr*) de Londres (*long-dr*).

2. Que dit monsieur votre père de la personne avec laquelle il a été à la salle d'attente?

3. De quoi (*dĕ quoāh*) a-t-il parlé aux personnes?

4. Qu'a-t-il donné aux personnes chez lesquelles vous allez?

5. Personne n'est[1] venu par ce train (*traing*).

6. Pourquoi n'avez-vouz dit à personne que mon frère n'est pas arrivé par ce train?

7. Personne ne lui a dit de le faire tout de suite (*swēēt*).

8. Il n'est permis (*pĕr-mēē*) à personne de stationner (*stā-syŏn-nay*) sur le quai (*kay*).

9. Est-on venu me demander pendant mon absence (*dĕ-măng-day păng-dāng mŏn năb-sāngs*)?

10. Personne n'est venu vous demander pendant votre absence (*voŭ dĕ-măng-day păng-dāng vŏt-rāb-sāngs*).

---

[1] ne is used in this connection, while *pas* **cannot** be used, as : *No one* is here, *personne n'est ici.* — *Not any one* has spoken, *personne n'a parlé.*

11. Two of your compatriots (*or* countrymen = *compa-triotes*) came to pay you a call (*or* to call on you = *vous rendre visite*).

12. Didn't they tell (*or* give) you their (*leurs*) names (*noms*), porter (*concierge*)?

13. Didn't they leave their cards with you? (=Not to you have they left (*laissé*) their cards (*leurs cartes*)?

14. They told me their names, but upon my word! (*ma foi!*) I forgot them.

15. Did nobody call during my absence?

16. I must reproach you. (= I have reproaches [*des re-proches*] to you to make).

17. Why? Because (*parce que*) you did not come to see me (*me voir*), since (*depuis que*) I moved. (*Literally:* I am moved = *Je suis délogé.*)

18. Who called? (*Literally:* Who is it who is come?)

19. To whom does this portmanteau belong? (*Literally:* To whom is this portmanteau?)

20. This portmanteau belongs to me. Will you please pass it to me?

21. Don't speak to him, if he is there.

22. Do not speak to them of this matter (*affaire*).

23. Who told you so? (*Literally:* Who is it who to you it has said?)

24. Who awakened you? (= Who is it who you has awakened [*éveillé*]?)

---

1) We have already seen (compare page 87 *Note* to : '*ont acheté*') that the *past participle* does not, under any circumstances, agree with the *subject* of its sentence when the verb is conjugated with the auxiliary '*avoir*,' *to have*.

The *past participle* does, however, agree with the *object*, when the said object *comes before* it, which can *only* be the case when the object is a pronoun (*personal, relative,* or other), as : Je les ai oubliés,

11. Deux de vos compatriotes (*deū dě vōh cong-pă-trēē-ŏt*) sont venus vous rendre visite (*rặng-dr vee-zeet*).

12. Ne vous‿ont-ils pas dit leurs noms (*nong*) concierge (*cong-syěrsh*)?

13 Ne vous‿ont-ils pas laissé (*lays-say*) leurs cartes?

14. Ils m'ont dit leur noms, mais ma foi! je les‿ai oubliés [1] (*mă fŏâh jě lay zay oŭ-blēē-ay*).

15. N'est-on pas venu me demander pendant mon‿absence?

16. J'ai des reproches (*rě-prōsh*) à vous faire.

17. Pourquoi donc? Parce que (*pārsě-kě*) vous n'êtes pas‿encore (*náyt-pāh-zāng-kor*) venu me voir depuis que (*dě-pü-ēē-kě*) je suis délogé (*dē-lō-jay*).

18. Qui est-ce qui est venu [2] (*kēě ays kēē ay věnü*)?

19. A qui est (*āh kēē ay*) ce sac de voyage?

20. Ce sac de voyage est à moi, veuillez me le passer.

21. Ne lui parlez pas s'il est là.

22. Ne leur parlez pas de cette affaire.

23. *Qui est-ce qui* [2] vous l'a dit (*kēē ays kēē voŭ lāh dēē*)?

24. *Qui est-ce qui* [2] vous a éveillé (*kēē ays kēē voŭ zā ay-vě-yēh*) ?

I have forgotten them. The object of the sentence is ' *les*,' them. It *precedes* the past participle, consequently ' *oubliés*,' forgotten, must also be placed like ' *les* ' in the masculine plural.

2) Instead of the *simple interrogative pronoun* ' **qui**' who? the French frequently use a more complicated form, viz. : ' *qui est-ce qui ?*' (kēē ays kēē), *who?* This form is more emphatic than the simple '*qui?*' Similarly they employ instead of **que** the more complicated form, *qu'est-ce que* (*kays-kě*).

25. The waiter woke me (*or* called me) very early (*de très-bonne heure*).

26. What do you want? (= What is it which you want?)

27. This gentleman is quite (*bien*) indisposed (*indisposé*); that's the reason why (= that is why) he did not come to your office this morning.

28. You are late (*vous êtes en retard*). Why didn't you come early (*de bonne heure*)?

29. If the tailor should bring (= if the tailor brings) my coat, please tell him to call again (*revenir*) tomorrow, because I have no time to try it on (*de l'essayer*) to-day (*aujourd'hui*).

30. What did your friend answer you, when you spoke to him about going (*d'aller*) to Cologne with us? (= What is it what to you has answered [*répondu*] your friend? &c.)

31. Tell him that I have no time to write this English letter now (*maintenant*).

32. It is quite vain for you to talk, as he will not do it. (= You will have fine talk, but, &c.)

33. Have you (really) bought this house?

34. Always buy in (the) large stores (*magasins*).

35. Will you do me the favor of coming with me after breakfast to do some (*des*) shopping (*emplettes*)?

36. What will you (then) buy?

25. Le garçon m'a éveillé dé très-bonne heure (*dĕ tray bŏn neūr*).

26. *Qu'est-ce que* (*kays-kĕ*) vous voulez?

27. Ce monsieur est bien indisposé (*aing-dĭs-pō-zay*) ; c'est pourquoi il n'est pas venu à votre bureau ce matin (*sĕ mă-taing*).

28. Vous êtes en retard (*voū zayt āng rĕ-tār*). Pourquoi n'êtes-vous pas venu de bonne heure (*dĕ bŏn neūr*)?

29. Si (*sēē*) le tailleur m'apporte mon habit, dites-iui, s'il vous plaît, de revenir (*rĕvĕnēēr*) demain, parce que je n'ai pas le temps de l'essayer (*ĕs-say-yēh*) aujourd'hui (*oh-joūr-d'wēē*).

30. Qu'est-ce que vous a répondu (*kays-kĕ, voū zā ray-pong-dü*) votre ami quand vous lui avez parlé d'aller à Cologne avec nous?

31. Dites-lui que je n'ai pas le temps d'écrire maintenant (*day-krēēr maing-tĕ-nāng*) cette léttre anglaise.

32. Vous aurez beau (*voū zō-ray bŏ*) dire,[1] mais il ne veut pas le faire.

33. Est-ce que (*ays-kĕ*) vous avez acheté cette maison (*voū zā-vay zāsh-tay sĕt may-zong*)?

34. Achetez toujours dans les grands magasins (*ash-tay toū-joūr dāng lay grāng mă-gă-zaing*).

35. Voulez-vous me faire le plaisir de venir avec moi après (*ă-pray*) le déjeuner faire des emplettes (*day zāng-plĕt*)?

36. Que voulez-vous donc acheter?

---

1) Idiomatic phrase, which can only be given so.

GRAMMATICAL REMARKS.

The beginner may learn the following tenses *first*, leaving the others for after-study: *Present, Imperfect, Perfect, Pluperfect, Future, Conditional.*

1.

AUXILIARY VERBS.

I. Avoir (*ǎ-voăr*) to have.

INDICATIVE MOOD.

Present Tense (Présent).

J'ai (*jay*), I have
tu as (*tü ǎ*), thou hast

il ⎫
elle ⎬a ⎡*ĕĕl* ⎤ ⎫ he ⎫
on ⎭ ⎢*ĕll* ⎬*ǎ* she ⎬has
⎣*on* ⎦ ⎭ one ⎭

nous avons (*noŭ zǎ-vong*), we have
vous avez (*voŭ zǎ-vĕh*), you have

ils · ⎫ ⎡*ĕĕl* ⎫ ⎤ they have
elles⁻⎬ ont ⎢*ĕll* ⎬ *zong* ⎥

Imperfect (*Imparfait*).

J'avais (*jă-vay*), I had.

tu avais (*tü ă-vay*), thou hadst.

il avait (*ĕĕl ă-vay*), he had.

nous avions (*noū ză-vyong*), we had.

vous aviez (*voū ză-vyĕh*), you had.

ils avaient (*ēel ză-vay*), they had.

Preterite (*Défini*).

J'eus (*iü*), I had.

tu eus (*tü ü*), thou hadst.

il eut (*ēĕl ü*), he had.

nous eûmes (*noū züm*), we had.

vous eûtes (*voŭ züt*), you had.

ils eurent (*ēēl zür*), they had.

Future (*Futur*).

J'aurai (*jō-rēh*), I shall *or* will have.

tu auras (*tü ōrā*), thou wilt have.

il aura (*ēĕl ōrā*), he will have.

nous aurons (*noū zō-rong*), we shall have *or* will have.

vous aurez (*voū zō-rēh*), you will have.

ils auront (*ēĕl zō-rong*), they will have.

1st *Conditional* (*Conditionnel Présent*).

J'aurais (*jō-ray*), I should have *or* would have.

tu aurais (*tü ō-ray*), thou wouldst have.

il aurait (*ēĕl ō-ray*), he would have.

nous aurions (*noū zō ryong*), we should have *or* would have.

vous auriez (*voū zō-ryĕh*), you would have.

ils auraient (*ēĕl zō-ray*), they would have.

COMPOUND TENSES.

eu (*ü*) had.

Perfect (*Passé indéfini*).

J'ai eu (*jay ü*), I have had.
tu as eu (*tü ä-zü*), thou hast had.
il a eu (*ēēl ä ü*), he has had.
nous avons eu (*noū zǎ-vong-zü*), we have had.
vous avez eu (*voū zǎ-vēh zü*), you have had.
ils ont eu (*ēēl zong-tü*), they have had.

Pluperfect (*Plusqueparfait*).

J'avais eu (*jǎ-vay-zü*), I had had.
tu avais eu (*tü ǎ-vay-zü*), thou hadst had
il avait eu (*ēēl ǎ-vay-tü*), he had had.
nous avions eu (*noū zǎ-vyong-zü*), we had had.
vous aviez eu (*voū zǎ-vyēh-zü*), you had had.
ils avaient eu (*ēēl zǎ-vay tü*), they had had.

2nd Pluperfect (*Passé antérieur*).

J'eus eu (*jü zü*), I had had.
tu eus eu (*tü ü-zü*), thou hadst had.
il eut eu (*ēēl ü-tü*), he had had.
nous eûmes eu (*noū züm-zü*), we had had.
vous eûtes eu (*voū züt-zü*), you had had.
ils eurent eu (*ēēl zür-tü*) they had had.

2nd Future (*Fut. antérieur passé*).

J'aurai eu (*jō-rēh-ü*), I shall have had.
tu auras eu (*tü ō-rā-zü*), thou wilt have had.
il aura eu (*ēēl ō-rā-ü*), he will have had.

nous aurons eu (*noŭ zō-rong zŭ*), we shall have had.
vous aurez eu (*voŭ zō-rèh zŭ*), you will have had.
ils auront eu (*èel zō-rong-tu*), they will have had.

2nd Conditional (Cond. passé).

J'aurais eu (*jō-ray-zŭ*), I should have had.
tu aurais eu (*tŭ ōray-zŭ*) thou wouldst have had.
il aurait eu (*èel ō-ray-tŭ*), he would have had.
nous aurions eu (*noŭ zō-ryong-zŭ*) we should have had.
vous auriez eu (*voŭ zō-ryèh-zŭ*), you would have had.
ils auraient eu (*èel zō-ray-tŭ*), they would have had.

SUBJUNCTIVE MOOD (SUBJONCTIF).

Present.

Que j'aie (*kě jay*), that I may have.
que tu aies (*kě tŭ ay*), that thou mayest have.
qu'il ait (*kēēl ay*), that he may have.
que nous ayons (*kě noŭ zay-yong*), that we may have.
que vous ayez (*kě voŭ zay-yèh*), that you may have.
qu'ils aient (*kēēl zay*), that they may have.

Imperfect.

Que j'eusse (*kě jŭss*), that I might have.
que tu eusses (*kě tŭ ŭss*), that thou mightst have.
qu'il **eût** (*kēēl ŭ*), that he might have.
que nous eussions (*kě noŭ zŭs-yong*), that we might have.
que vous eussiez (*kě voŭ zŭs-yèh*), that you might have.
qu'ils eussent (*kēēl zŭss*), that they might have.

Perfect.

Que j'aie eu (*kĕ jay ü*), that I may have had.

que tu aies eu (*kĕ tü ay-zü*), that thou mayest have had.

qu'il ait eu (*kēēl ay-tü*), that he may have had.

que nous ayons eu (*kĕ noū zay-yong zü*),that we may have had.

que vous ayez eu (*kĕ voū zay-yēh-zü*), that you may have had.

qu'ils aient eu (*kēēl zay-tü*), that they may have had.

Pluperfect.

Que j'eusse eu (*kĕ jüss ü*), that I might have had.

que tu eusses eu (*kĕ tü süs-zü*), that thou mightst have had.

qu'il eût eu (*kēēl ü tü*), that he might have had.

que nous eussions eu (*kĕ noū züs-syong-zü*), that we might have had.

que vous eussiez eu (*kĕ voū züs-yēh-zü*), that you might have had.

qu'ils eussent eu (*kēēl züss-tü*), that they might have had.

IMPERATIVE MOOD (IMPÉRATIF).

aie (*ay*), have (*thou*).

(qu'il ait [*kēēl ay*], let him have.)

ayons (*ay-yong*), let us have.

ayez (*ay-yēh*), have (you).

INFINITIVE MOOD (INFINITIF).

Present.	*Past.*
avoir (*ā-voār*)	avoir eu (*ā-voār ü*)
d'avoir (*dā-voār*) } to have.	d'avoir eu (*dā-voār ü*) } to have had.
à avoir (*ā ā-voār*)	à avoir eu (*ā-ā-voār ü*)

PARTICIPLES (PARTICIPES).

Present. | *Past.*

ayant (*ay-yáng*), having. | eu (*ü*), *fem.* eue (*ü*), had.
ayant eu (*ay-yáng-tü*), hav-
ing had.

Idiomatical expressions with avoir.

There are a number of idiomatical expressions in connection with *avoir*, which cannot be translated literally and which the student should carefully commit to memory. I only mention the most important ones:

J'ai froid (*froāh*), I am cold. | J'ai peur (*peür*[1]), I am afraid.
J'ai froid aux mains (*ŏ maing*), my hands are cold. | J'ai faim (*faing*), I am hungry.
| J'ai soif (*swoāf*), I am thirsty.
J'ai chaud (*show*), I am warm. | Il a bonne mine, he looks well.
J'ai mal à la tête, I have the headache. | Il a mauvaise mine, he is looking ill.
J'ai besoin de (*bĕ zŏ-aing*[2]) I need. | J'ai envie de (*āng-vēē*), I desire I feel inclined to.
Il a cinq ans (*saing kāng*), he is five years old. | J'ai sommeil (*sŏmmĕ-yĕ*[3]), I am sleepy.

---

1) eü=ea in early.
2) bĕ-zŏ-aing has to be pronounced like two syllables only.
3) Observe the vanishing liquid sound.

The pupil must make himself acquainted with the

PERSONAL PRONOUNS.

We distinguish between the:

Personal Conjunctive Pronouns.

SINGULAR.

1st *Person.*

Nom. je (*jĕ*)   I[1])
Dat. me (*mĕ*) to me
Acc. me (*mĕ*) me

2nd *Person.*

Nom. tu (*tü*) thou
Dat. te (*tĕ*) to thee
Acc. te (*tĕ*) thee

3rd *Person.*

Masculine.

Nom. il (*ēēl*) he *or* it
Dat. lui (*lü̂ ēē*) to him *or*
　　　　　 to it
Acc. le (*lĕ*) him *or* it

Feminine.

Nom. elle (*ĕll*) she *or* it
Dat. lui (*lü̂ ēĕ*) to her *or* to it
Acc. la (*lā*) her *or* it

Personal Disjunctive Pronouns.

SINGULAR.

1st *Person.*

Nom. moi (*mwoāh*), I
Gen. de moi   of *or* from me
Dat. à moi   to me
Acc. moi   me

2nd *Person.*

Nom. toi (*twoāh*), thou
Gen. de toi   of *or* from thee
Dat. à toi   to thee
Acc. toi   thee

3rd *Person.*

			elle, she
Nom. lui (*lü̂·ĕĕ*[2]), he		elle,	she
Gen. de lui	of *or*	d'elle	of *or*
	from him		from her
Dat. à lui	to him	à elle	to her
Acc. lui	him	elle	her

---

1) The Genitive of the conjunctive pronouns is wanting, and is circumscribed by ' de moi, de toi,' &c.
2) The *ü·ĕĕ* must be pronounced as one sound only.

PLURAL.			PLURAL.		
1st Person.			*1st Person.*		
N. nous	we		*Nom.* nous	we	
D. nous	to us		*Gen.* de nous	of *or* from us	
A. nous	us		*Dat.* à nous	to us	
			Acc. nous	us	
2nd Person.			*2nd Person.*		
N. vous	you		*Nom.* vous	you	
D. vous	to you		*Gen.* de vous	of *or* from you	
A. vous	you		*Dat.* à vous	to you	
			Acc. vous	you	
3rd Person.			*3rd Person.*		
Masculine.			*N.* eux (*eü*[1]), they	elles (*ëli*) they (*masc.*)	
N. ils	they				
D. leur	to them		*G.* d'eux (*deü*) of *or* from them	d'elles of *or* from them	
A. les	them				
Feminine.			*D.* à eux to them	à elles to them	
N. elles	they				
D. leur	to them				
A. les	them		*A.* eux. them	elles them	

We have already explained (comp. page 76, 77, 80 & 81) when and how the *conjunctive personal pronouns* are to be used.

The disjunctive personal pronouns are to be used :

1) after prepositions, as :

avec moi, with me ;

sans (*sāng*) toi, without thee ;

pour lui, for him ;

par elle, by her ; -

pour nous, for us ;

de vous, of *or* from you ;

avec { eux (m.) / elles (f.) } with them.

---

1) eü is pronounced like *ea* in 'early,' only much longer.

2) With the *affirmative imperative*, as :

parlez-moi, speak to me ;	apportez-lui, bring to him :
donnez-moi, give me ; •	parlez-leur, speak to them ;
envoyez-lui, send him ;	envoyez-leur, send to them.

a) If, however, the *imperative* is used *negatively* then the *conjunctive pronouns must* be employed and placed before the verb; as :

> ne me donnez pas, do not give to me ;
> ne leur parlez pas ; do not speak to them ;
> ne lui apportez pas, do not bring to him ;
> ne leur envoyez pas, do not send to them.

b) Compare the rules on 'Two pronouns' (p. 77 & 81.)

3) *The disjunctive personal pronouns* must be used in answer to questions, as : Who will go with him ? I. Qui veut aller avec lui ? Moi. Who did it ? I, thou, he, &c. Qui l'a fait ? Moi, toi, lui, elle, &c.

4) When *a stress* is laid on the *personal pronoun*, as : *it is I, the disjunctives* used are preceded by *c'est, c'était* (instead of *ce est, ce était*) &c., or the *disjunctive personal pronoun* is first used, while the conjunctive is repeated; as :

C'est moi (*say moãh*) it is I	c'est nous	it is we
c'est toi	it is thou	c'est vous	it is you
		ce sont enx	
		(sĕ song teŭ)	
c'est lui	it is he		it is they
c'est elle	it is she	ce sont elles	
		(sĕ song tĕll)	

C'était nous (*say tay noŭ*), it was we; est-ce vous (*ays-voŭ*), is that you ?—**I** say so, c'est moi, qui le dis; *or* **moi**, je le dis.—**We** have not said so, **nous**, nous n'avons pas dit cela; *or* ce n'est pas nous qui avons dit cela. — **They** have done it, **ce sont eux** *qui l'ont* fait.

3.

TWO PRONOUNS.

The following table will show the order in which conjunctive personal pronouns are to be placed when two different cases are governed by the same verb.

SINGULAR.			PLURAL.		
1st Person	*2nd Person*	*3rd Person*	*1st Person*	*2nd Person*	*3d Person*
Dat. Acc.	*Dat. Acc.*	*Acc. Dat.*	*Dat. Acc.*	*Dat. Acc.*	*Acc. Dat.*
me { le / la / les	te { le / la / les	le / la / les } lui	nous { le / la / les	vous { le / la / les	le / la / les } leur

Acc. Dat. } le la } moi *les*	These forms are used in the affirmative imperative.	*Acc. Dat.* } le la } nous les	After the affirmative imperative.	

Examples :

I give it to thee (=I to thee it give), Je *te le* donne.—He brings it to us (= he to us it brings), il *nous l'*apporte.—He has not told it to me (= he not to me it has told), il ne *me l'*a pas dit.—I gave it to you, je *vous l'*ai donné.—I did not give it to you, je ne *vous l'*ai pas donné. — Did he write it to you, *vous l'*a-t-il écrit? — Did he not write it to you, ne *vous l'*a-t-il pas écrit?—Je *le leur* ai dit, I told it to them.— Ne *le leur* avez vous pas écrit, did you not write it to them.— *Le lui* a-t-il envoyĕ, did he send it to him (*or* to her)? — Je *le lui* ai donné, I gave it to him *or* to her).

We see therefore that the dative (of the person) precedes the accusative, so that we always construe : **me le,
te le, nous le, vous le.**

The exceptions to the foregoing remark are the two
datives **lui,** to him *or* to her, and **leur,** to them, which always follow the accusative, and are placed thus : **le lui,
le leur.** *Ex. :*

Je *le lui* donne, I give it to him. Pourquoi ne *le leur*
prêtez-vous pas? Why don't you lend it to them?

With the Imperative they are used thus :

a) with the *affirmative*, as : Donnez-*le-moi*, give it to
me; apportez-*le-lui* (*leur*), bring it . to him *or* her (to
them); prêtez -*le-nous*, lend it to us ; passez-*le-nous*, pass it
to us.

b) with the *negative*, as : ne *me le* donnez pas, don't
give it to me; ne *le* (*la*) *lui* apportez pas, don't bring it to
him; ne *les leur* envoyez pas (*nĕ lĕ leūr āng-voāh-yay păh*),
do not send them to them.

Words.

Objects á l'usage du voyageur.	Objects for a tourist's use.
ŏb·jay āh lū-zāhsh dü voāh·yă. jeūr.	
la malle (*măll*),	the trunk.
le sac de voyage (*săc dĕ voāh-yāsh*),	the portmanteau.

les bagages (*bă-gāsh*) ⎫ les effets (*lay-zay-fay*) ⎭	the luggage.
la boîte (*b'woāt*),	the box.
la boîte à chapeau, (*b'woāt āh shā-pō*),	the hatbox.
la couverture (*coū-vĕr-tür*).	the cover.
la couverture de voyage (*dĕ voāh-yāsh*),	the travelling-rug.
la brosse (*brŏs*),	the brush.
la brosse à chapeau (*shā-pŏ*),	the hat-brush.
la brosse à cheveux (*shĕ-veū* [1]),	the hair-brush.
la brosse à dents (*dāng*),	the tooth-brush.
la brosse à ongles, (*ongl*),	the nail-brush.
le démêloir (*day-may-l'woār*),	the large comb.
le peigne (*pĕn-yĕ* [2]),	the comb.
le morceau de savon (*mŏr-sō dĕ sāh-vong*),	the cake of soap.
le porte-monnaie (*port-mo-nêh*),	the purse.
le porte-feuille (*port-feū-ye²*),	the pocket-book.
le parapluie (*pāh-rāh-plü*),	the umbrella.
le parasol (*păh-răh-sol*),	the parasol.
la canne (*kăn*),	the cane.

---

1) eū like '*ea*' in *early*.
2) Observe the liquid sound in 'ye.' Compare page 50.

Exercise.[1]

1) W,aiter, did you[2] order a cab?—Have you brought all my luggage downstairs (brought downstairs, *descendu*=dĕ-sāng-dü=)? — 2) Your trunk is downstairs (*en bas*=āng-bāh), sir; I am taking now (*maintenant*) your portmanteau and travelling-rug down (I am taking down, *je descends*=jĕ dĕ-sāng). — 3) Cab (*cocher*=kō-shay), to the Northern railway-station.— Drive quick (*allez vite*), we have no time to lose (*à perdre*). — 4) Will you please pay the fare (*la course*=lă koūrs) now; it is forbidden (*defendu*) to stop (*de stationner*) at the entrance gate (*à l'entrée*) of the station. — 5) Have you any (*des*) luggage, sir?—I have a trunk, a portmanteau, and a hatbox.— Will you have the three pieces (*les trois colis*=lay troāh kōlee) checked, sir?— No, only (*seulement*=seūl-māng), the trunk, please. — 6) Is this (*est-ce ici*) the waiting-room? — Yes, sir, please take (*veuillez prendre*) your ticket and go into the waiting-room. — 7) One first class ticket to London (*une première*, *Londres*=üin prĕm-yĕhr, Long-dr). — 8) Have I any (*du*) overweight?—Yes sir, you have five francs worth of overweight (=you have for five (*cinq*) francs of (*de*) overweight). — 9) Is that there (*est-ce là*) our train? Yes, that is the express (*or* fast) train for Calais and London.

---

1) This exercise contains a dialogue of a traveller who is departing from Paris.
2) Take the perfect=Have you ordered?

COMPANION TO THE
Revised Version of the New Testament.

Explaining the Reasons for the Changes Made on the Authorized Version.

BY ALEXANDER ROBERTS, D.D.,
Member of the English Revision Committee.

WITH SUPPLEMENT BY A MEMBER OF THE AMERICAN COMMITTEE.

Containing a Brief History of the Revision of the Work and Co-operation of the New Testament Companies, of the Points of Agreement and Difference, and an Explanation of the Appendix to the Revised New Testament.

ALSO, A FULL TEXTUAL INDEX,

Being a Key to Passages in which Important Changes have been Made.

This book, having been carefully prepared by Members of both Revision Committees, carries official weight. It shows what changes have been made, and also the reasons which influenced the revisers in making them. It will be difficult to judge of the merits of the revision without the aid of this Companion volume. Our edition is printed by special arrangement with the English publishers. It is well known that, by an arrangement between the two Committees of Revision, the changes suggested by the American Committee, but which were not adopted by the English Revisers, are published as an Appendix to the Revised New Testament. The *Companion* volume is an explanation of *all* the changes adopted by both committees, and of those suggested by the American Committee, but not assented to by the English Committee, in their final revision. The book will be indispensable to a right understanding of the revision. This cheap edition of the combined books, although authorized and copyrighted, will be sold for 25 cents in paper, and 75 cents in cloth—sent postage free.

TESTIMONIALS.

T. W. CHAMBERS, D.D., a Member of the American Committee of Revision, says of this book: "Many persons have expressed a desire that, simultaneously with the issue of the Revised New Testament, there should appear an authentic explanation of the reasons for such changes as will be found in its pages. The work of Dr. Roberts is exactly fitted to meet this desire....Nowhere else in print can be found a statement so full and exact. It gives all needed information, and does it in an unexceptional way."

C. F. DEEMS, D.D., Pastor of the Church of the Strangers. New York, writes: "The Companion to the Revised Version seems to me almost indispensable. Even scholars who were not at the meeting of the Revisers would have a wearisome work in seeking to discover all the changes made, and to ordinary readers very much of the labor would be lost. ....All this is set forth by Dr. Roberts with admirable perspicuity. Those who have any intelligent interest in the Holy Scriptures, will find this little book absorbingly interesting. I shall urge every member of the church of which I am pastor to give it a careful reading, and purpose to introduce it as a text-book in our Bible-classes."

"So valuable, interesting and useful is this publication, that we advise every one who wishes to know the why and wherefore of the revision, to obtain it immediately."—*New York Observer*.

Paper, 8vo size, 25 cents ; Cloth, 16mo, 75 cents.

*** For Sale by Booksellers and Newsdealers, or sent postage-paid, on receipt of price, by

I. K. FUNK & CO., Publishers, 10 & 12 Dey St.; N. Y.

THE TEACHER'S EDITION

OF THE

REVISED NEW TESTAMENT

With New Concordance and Index, Harmony of the Gospels, Maps, Historical and Chronological Tables, Parallel Passages printed in full, Blank Pages Interleaved for manuscript notes, and many other New and Indispensable Helps to the Study of the Revised Version.

After the excitement connected with the sale of the first copies of the new revision, which lack the usual indexing headlines and marginal references to parallel passages, and also the appendixes of tables, maps, etc.—all of which helps preachers, teachers and Bible students have come to consider as absolutely essential to a working copy of the Bible—there arises an imperative demand for an edition of the Revised New Testament, containing all the marginal and appendix helps of former TEACHERS' AND REFERENCE BIBLES, adapted carefully and accurately to the Revised Version. We are, therefore, preparing, as rapidly as is consistent with accuracy, such an edition of the Revised New Testament. The work is under the supervision of well-known Bible scholars, with numerous helpers, and will be issued as early as it can be done with thoroughness. In style and size the book will resemble the Bagster Bible, "Fac-simile large edition," known as "the Moody Bible," being the same width and length and size of type. It will be supplied at prices *within the reach of all.*

Thi; "Teachers' Edition of the Revised New Testament" will be an exact, *certified reproduction* of the entire Oxford and Cambridge Edition, including the Preface and all the marginal readings and explanations. It will contain the appendix notes of the American Revisers, printed in the margin of each page by the side of the passages referred to. The parallel passages, to which reference is m de in the "Bagster Bibles," with numerous others, so far as appropriate, will be PRINTED IN FULL in the margin. The running headings, usually printed at the tops of pages of the King James version, will be here supplied. A small black mark will be inserted below the last letter of each verse to facilitate reference, and aid in RESPONSIVE READING of the Revised Version. The second half of the volume will consist of the most carefully prepared HELPS TO THE STUDY OF THE REVISED NEW TESTAMENT, gleaned from the best Teachers' Editions of the authorized version, and supplied from various original sources—all being revised and adapted to harmonize with the Revised Version. We shall introduce many other important features, making this the most valuable edition of the New Testament ever issued.

Popular Cloth Edition—Ready in July—Price, Postage Free, $1.00.

Send for prospectus giving full description and prices of finer Bindings.

I. K. FUNK & CO., Publishers, 10 and 12 Dey St., New York.

THE

Meisterschaft System.

A SIMPLE AND PRACTICAL METHOD,

ENABLING

ANY ONE TO LEARN, WITH SLIGHT EFFORT, TO SPEAK
FLUENTLY AND CORRECTLY

French, German, Spanish, and Italian.

BY

DR. RICHARD S. ROSENTHAL,

Late Director of the "Akademie für fremde Sprachen" in Berlin and Leipzig,
of the "Meisterschaft College" in London, and Principal of the
"Meisterschaft School of Practical Linguistry" in New York.

FRENCH.

IN FIFTEEN PARTS, EACH CONTAINING THREE LESSONS.

I.

PART III.

NEW YORK:

I. K. FUNK & CO., Publishers,

10 AND 12 DEY STREET.

TERMS.

WE have arranged with Dr. ROSENTHAL, the author of the "Meisterschaft System," for its introduction in America under his own supervision, and he has opened

The Meisterschaft School of Practical Linguistry

FOR NON-RESIDENTS.

The student does not need to leave his home. The lessons of each language are prepared by the Professor, and printed and sent in pamphlet shape to each member of the School wherever he may reside.

The course of study for each language—German, French, Italian, or Spanish—makes fifteen pamphlets of three lessons each.

All members of the School have

THE PRIVILEGE

of asking, by letter, questions concerning each lesson, or consulting on any difficulty which may have occurred to them. All exercises corrected and all questions answered by return post by Dr. ROSENTHAL or one of his assistants.

TERMS OF MEMBERSHIP.

Five Dollars is the price for membership in the school for each language. This amount ($5.) entitles the member to receive the fifteen books or pamphlets containing the lessons, also answers to his questions. Return postage for the answer must accompany the question.

State distinctly which language, or languages, you desire to study There are *no extra charges*. The price, **Five Dollars,** pays for one language; **Ten Dollars** for two languages, etc. All exercises and questions must be written on a separate sheet of paper, and must state full address of the pupil.

Remittances must be made in Post-Office Order or registered letter addressed to

I. K. FUNK & CO,
10 and 12 Dey Street, New York.

The Meisterschaft-System.

FRENCH.

PART III.

III.

FOUNDATION SENTENCE.

Do not forget to call me at a quarter to five to-morrow morning, or even earlier, if you can; and tell the waiter, if you please, to bring me, at five o'clock precisely, a cup of coffee with milk, some slices of bread and butter, and some soft-boiled eggs.

Do not forget to call me at a quarter to five to-morrow morning, or even earlier, if you can.

III.

FOUNDATION SENTENCE.

N'oubliez pas de me réveiller demain matin à
noū-blēē-ay pāh dĕ mĕ ray-vĕ-yĕh dĕ-maing mā-taing āh

cinq heures moins un quart, ou plus tôt si vous
saing keūr mo-aing zeūng kāhr, oū plü tō sēē voū

pouvez ; et dites au garçon, s'il vous plaît, de
poū-vĕh ; aẏ dēēt ōh gār-song, sēē voū play, dĕ

m'apporter à cinq heures précises une tasse de
mă-por-tĕh āh saing keūr pray-sēēze ūn tāss dĕ

café au lait, des tartines de beurre et des oeufs à
kāh-fay oh lay, day tăr-tēēn dĕ beūrr aẏ day zeū āh

la coque.
lă cock

1.

N'oubliez pas de me réveiller demain matin à
noū-blēē-ay pāh dĕ mĕ ray-vĕ-yĕh dĕ-maing mă-taing āh

cinq heures moins un quart, ou plus tôt si vous
saing keūr mo-aing zeūng kāhr, oū plü tō sēē voū

pouvez.
poū-vĕh.

110

Do not forget [to forget, *oublier*. Compare the table of '*donner*,'
page 59.]

to [*de* before the infinitive means *to*]

me

to wake

to-morrow

morning

at

five

hour

at five o'clock

less

a quarter

at a quarter to five [*Literally :* at five less a quarter.]

or [*où* means ' where,' and *ou* ' or ']

more

soon

sooner, earlier

if

you can [Irregular verb. It means 'I am able' *or* I can' ; I cannot,
' je ne *puis*,' *or* ' je ne peux pas.']

N'oubliez pas (*noū-blēē-ay pāh*) [Imperative of the regular verb 'oublier;' compare page 59.]

de (*dĕ*)

me (*mĕ*)

réveiller (*ray-vĕ-yēh*)

demain (*dĕ-maing*)

matin (*mă-taing*) [Le matin, the morning]

à (*āh*)

cinq (*saingk*)

heure (*eūr*) [une heure (*fem.*), an hour, *or* one o'clock]

à cinq heures (*āh saing keūr*)

moins (*moaing*)

un quart (*eūng kāhr*)

à cinq heures moins un quart

ou (*oū*) [The pupil must distinguish well between '*ou*,' *or*, and '*où*,' where, which is always written with an accent grave.]

plus (*plü*)

tôt (*tô*)

plus tôt

si

vous pouvez [Second person plural of je peux *or* je puis, tu peux, il peut, nous pouvons, vous pouvez, ils peuvent (*peūv*).]

1. Have you forgotten anything (*quelque chose*)?

2. You forgot to mail this letter. (*Literally:* to put [*mettre*] this letter into the post office.)

3. Who called you?

4. No one called me.

5. Did you wake (*or* call) your brother?

6. No, sir, not yet (*pas encore*).

7. Well (*eh bien*)! You will miss (*vous manquerez*) the train. Do you not know (*ne savez vous pas*) that the fast train leaves (*part*) at five o'clock?

8. Call me early, if you please.

9. What o'clock is it?

10. Tell me, please, what o'clock it is?

11. Do you know what o'clock it is?

12. What o'clock do you think (*or* fancy=*croyez-vous*) it is?

13. I cannot tell you; I have not got my watch (*ma montre*) with me (*sur moi*).

14. I forgot to wind up (*remonter*) my watch.

15. It is late (*tard*).

16. It is early (*de bonne heure*).

17. I fancied it was later; *or*, I thought it was later.

18. It is one o'clock.

19. It is two (*deux*) o'clock.

---

1) *Avez-vous oublié* would also be correct, but the French often

1. *Est-ce que vous avez oublié*[1] quelque chose (*ays'-kĕ voū zā-vēh zoū-blēē-ay kĕlkĕ shows*) ?

2. Vous avez oublié de mettre cette lettre à la poste.

3. Qui vous a réveillé? *or*, Qui est-ce qui vous a réveillé?

4. Personne ne m'a réveillé.

5. Avez vous réveillé votre frère?

6. Non monsieur, pas encore (*păh zăng-kor*).

7. Eh bien (*ay byaing*)! vous manquerez (*māng-kĕ-rēh*) le train. ·Ne savez-vous pas (*nĕ să-vēh voū păh*) que le train express part à cinq heures (*traing ex-prēh păr tah saing keūr*)?

8. Réveillez-moi de bonne heure, s'il vous plaît.

9. Quelle heure est-il (*kĕl leūr ay-tēēl*) ?.

10. Dites-moi, s'il vous plaît, quelle heure il est (*or* l'heure qu'il est)?

11. Savez-vous l'heure qu'il est?

12. Quelle heure croyez-vous qu'il soit (*kroāh-yēh voū kēēl s'woāh*)?

13. Je ne puis (*pü-ēē*) vous le dire; je n'ai pas ma montre sur moi (*māh mong-tr sür m'woāh*).

14. J'ai oublié de remonter (*rĕ-móng-tay*) ma montre.

15. Il est tard (*tār*).

16. Il est de bonne heure.

17. Je croyais (*kroāh-yēh*) qu'il était (*ay-tay*) plus tard.

18. Il est une heure (*ēēl ay tün neūr*).

19. Il est deux heures (*dŭū zeūr*).

---

employ the more complicated form of asking a question, introducing it by *est-ce que?*

20. It is three (*trois*) o'clock.
21. It is four (*quatre*) o'clock.
22. It is five (*cinq*) o'clock.
23. It is six (*six*) o'clock.
24. It is seven (*sept*) o'clock.
25. It is eight (*huit*) o'clock.
26. It is nine (*neuf*) o'clock.
27. It is ten (*dix*) o'clock.
28. It is eleven (*onze*) o'clock.
29. It is twelve o'clock (*midi*=noon ¹).
30. It is twelve o'clock (*minuit*=midnight ¹).

2.

1. Tell him to bring me my dinner at three o'clock pre-
   . cisely (*précises.*)
2. Come to me at eleven o'clock to-morrow morning.

3. If it is later than five (*or* past five) o'clock (*plus de
   cinq heures*), don't go to him.
4. It is one o'clock.
5. It is five minutes (*minutes*) past one.
6. It is ten (*dix*) minutes past one.
7. It is a quarter (*quart*) past one.
8. It is twenty (*vingt*) minutes past one.
9. It is twenty-five (*vingt-cinq*) minutes past one.
10. It is half-past one. (*Literally :* It is one o'clock and
    half [*demie*].)

---

1) The number *douze*, twelve, is never used in regard to the time of day. But instead of 12 A.M. they say '*midi*,' and 12 P.M. '*minuit*.'

20. Il est trois heures (*troăh zeŭr*).
21. Il est quatre heures (*kăt-reŭr*).
22. Il est cinq heures (*saing-keŭr.*).
23. Il est six heures (*sēē-zeŭr*).
24. Il est sept heures (*sĕt-teŭr*).
25. Il est huit heures (*wēē-teŭr*).
26. Il est neuf heures (*neŭ-veŭr.*).
27. Il est dix heures (*dēē-zeŭr*).
28. Il est onze heures (*ēĕl lay tong zeŭr*).
29. Il est midi (*mēē-dēē*):[1]
30. Il est minuit (*mēē-n'wēē*).[1]

2.

1. Dites-lui de m'apporter mon dîner à trois heures précises (*ăh troăh zeŭr pray-sees*).
2. Venez (*vĕ-nēh*) chez moi demain matin à onze heures (*ŏng-zeŭr*).
3. S'il est plus de cinq heures, n'allez pas chez lui.
4. Il est une heure (*ēĕl lay tŭn neŭr*).
5. Il est une heure cinq (minutes = *mēē-nŭt'*).[2]
6. Il est une heure dix (minutes).
7. Il est une heure et quart (*ay kār*).
8. Il est une heure vingt (*vaing*).
9. Il est une heure vingt-cinq (*vaing saing*).
10. Il est une heure et demie (*dĕ-mēē*).

---

2) *minutes* may be left off.

11. It is twenty-five minutes to two (= it is two o'clock less [*moins*] twenty-five).

12. It is twenty minutes to two.

13. It is a quarter to two.

14. It is ten minutes to two.

15. It is five minutes to two.

16. It is two o'clock exactly.

17. Will you have the kindness (*la bonté*) to tell me, sir, what o'clock it is? .

18. My watch (*ma montre*) is ten minutes slow (*is slow=retarde*).

19. Your watch is five minutes fast, sir (=You advance [*vous avancez*] five minutes). On the contrary (*au contraire*), it is three minutes slow.

20. Cab, drive (*allez*) quickly. We have no time to lose (*à perdre*). The train leaves (*part*) at half past 12.

21. Tell the tailor, if you please, to send me **my black** (*noir*) trousers about (*vers*) a quarter to seven at the latest (*au plus tard*).

22. The town-clock (*l'horloge*) is just now (*à présent*) striking (*sonne*).

23. The town-clock struck two; but I think it is rather slow (*retarde de beaucoup* = much).

24. My watch does not agree (*s'accorde*) with **your** clock.

25. Why can he not come earlier?

---

1) I beg that the student will go in the same manner through

11. Il est deux‿heures moins vingt‐cinq ‧ (*ēēl ay dĕū zeūr mo-aing vaing saing*).

12. Il est deux‿heures moins vingt.

13. Il est deux‿heures moins‿un quart (*or* moins *le* quart).

14. Il est deux‿heures moins dix.

15. Il est deux‿heures moins cinq.

16. Il est deux‿heures précises.[1]

17. Voulez-vous‿avoir· la bonté (*bong-tay*) de me dire, monsieur, quelle‿heure il est (*kĕl-leūr-ēēl-ay*) ?

18. { Ma montre retarde de dix minutes,
    { *or* Je retarde de dix minutes.

19. Vous‿avancez (*voū zāh-vāng-say*) de cinq minutes, monsieur. Au‑contraire (*ōh cong-trayr*) je retarde de trois.

20. Allez vite cocher (*ăh-lēh vēēt cō-shēh*); nous n'avons pas de temps à perdre. Le train part à midi et dèmie (*lĕ traing pār tāh mēē-dēē· ay dĕ-mēē*).

21. Dites au tailleur, s'il vous plaît, de m'envoyer mon pantalon noir vers sept‿heures moins‿un quart au plus tard (*dēēt tōh tā-yeūr, sēē voū play, dē māng·voāh-yĕh mong pāng-tāh-long n'woāhr vayr sĕt teūr mo-aing zeūng kār ōh plü tār.*)

22. L'horloge (*lŏr-lōhjĕ*) sonne à présent (*āh pray-zāng*).

23. L'horloge a sonné deux‿heures, mais je crois qu'elle retarde de beaucoup (*kĕll rĕ-tār dĕ bōh-coū*).

24. Ma montre ne s'accorde pas avec la pendule (*pāng-dül*).

25. Pourquoi ne peut-il venir plus tôt ?

---

the different .hours, so that he may become thoroughly familiar with the French way of expressing the time of day.

118

26. I cannot tell you, madam.
27. Can't you make it at once?
28. Waiter, can we have a private room (*un cabinet particulier*)?

3

And tell the waiter, if you please, to bring me, at five o'clock exactly, a cup of coffee with milk, some slices of bread and butter, and some soft-boiled eggs.

And

tell [Irregular imperative of the verb *dire*, to say]

to the waiter

if you please; please; pray.

pleases [Irregular present of the verb, *plaire*, to please]

to bring me

a cup of coffee

some slices of bread (*tartines*) and butter

and

some eggs

26. Je ne puis vous le dire, madame.

27. Ne pouvez-vous le faire tout de suite.(*toút s'wēēt*)?

28. Garçon, pouvons-nous avoir un cabinet particulier (*căh-bēē-nēh păr-tēē-kü-lyēh*)?

3

Et dites au garçon, s'il vous plait, de m'appor-
ăy dēēt tŏþ găr-song sēē voū play dĕ mă-por-.

ter à cinq heures précises une tasse de café au
tēh āh saing keūr pray-sēēze ün tāss dĕ kāh-fay ŏh

lait, des tartines de beurre et des oeufs à la coque.
lay day tāhr tēēn dĕ beūrr ay day zeū āh lā cock.

Et

dites (*dēēt*) [Irregular imperative of dire (*dēēr*), to say]

au garçon

s'il vous plaît (*or* je vous prie [=*prēē*]) -

plaît (*play*) [The present is conjugated thus : Je plais, tu plait, il
plaît, nous plaisons, vous plaisez, ils plaisent=*playze.*]

de m'apporter (*dĕ măp-por-tēh*)

une tasse de café (*ün tass dĕ kāh-fay*)

des tartines de beurre (*day tāhr-tēēn de beūrr*)

et

des oeufs (*day zeū*)

shell; egg-shell
soft-boiled eggs. _____

1. Can you give us lodging for to-night? (*Literally*: Can you lodge us [*nous loger*] for this night [*cette nuit*]?)

2. Do you want a double bed (=a bed for two persons), gentlemen?

3. No, we should like (*nous désirerions*) to have a room with two beds.

4. This room does not please me; *or*, I do not like this room.

5. Show me another room in the second story (*au second*), please.

6. What is the price of this room per day (= of which price [*de quel prix*] is this room a [*par*] day)?

7. Five francs.

8. Attendance (*le service*) included?

9. No, sir, attendance is charged (*se paye*) extra (*à part*).

10. How much (*combien*) a day?

11. One franc daily.

12. All right (*c'est bien*); I will take (*j'arrête*) the room.

13. Have my luggage brought up (*monter*) and pay the cab, please; I have no change (*monnaie*) with me (*sur moi*).

14. I have paid for it already (*déjà*); it was four francs.

15. What!? That cannot be! *or*, That is impossible!

16. Waiter, bring me in the first place (*avant tout*) a little warm water. I want to wash myself (*me laver*).

la coque (*lă cock*)

des͡œufs à la coque (*day zeū āh lă cock*).

---

1. Pouvez-vous nous loger (*lōh-jay*) pour cette nuit (*n'wēē*)?

2. Voulez-vous͡un lit (*zeūng lēē*) pour deux personnes, messieurs?

3. Non, nous désirerions͡avoir une chambre à deux lits (*noū day-zēē-rĕ-ryong zā-v'woār ün shāng-br āh deū lēē*).

4. Cette chambre ne me plaît pas.

5. Montrez-moi une autre chambre au second, s'il vous plaît (*ōh sĕ-cong sēē voū play*).

6. De quel prix (*prēē*) cette chambre est-elle par jour?

7. C'est de cinq francs (*say dĕ saing frāng*).

8. Le service compris (*lĕ sĕr-vēēs cong-prēē*)?

9. Non, monsieur, le service se paye (*pay*) à part (*āh pār*).

10. Combien (*kong-byaing*) par jour?

11. C'est͡un franc par jour (*say teūng frāng pār joūr*).

12. C'est bien (*byaing*); j'arrête la chambre.

13. Faites monter mes͡effets et veuillez payer (*pay-yēh*) le cocher; je n'ai pas de monnaie (*mŏ-nay*) sur moi.

14. Je l'ai déjà (*day-jāh*) payé; c'était quatre francs.

15. Comment!? Cela ne se peut pas (*com-māng! sĕ-lā nĕ sĕ peū pāh*)!

16. Garçon, apportez-moi avant tout (*āh-vāng toū*) un peu d'eau chaude (*eūng peū dōh shōhd*); je veux me laver (*lāh-vēh*). .

17. Bring me some [1] fresh (*fraîche*) water, some soap (*du savon*) and towels (*des serviettes*). Above all things (*avant tout*) I want to wash.

18. The chambermaid shall bring you (*vous apportera*) everything (*tout ça*) in an instant.

19. Take care (*ayez soin*) to give me clean (*blancs*) sheets (*draps*), and be sure they are well aired (=and very dry [*secs*]).

20. Any other orders, sir? (*Literally:* Have you yet something else (*autre chose*) to command (*à commander*)?

21. Yes; please give us two mattresses (*matelas*); we do not like feather-beds (*lits de plume*).

22. You shall have everything, gentlemen.

23. And do not forget to tell the boy to wake us early to-morrow.

24. Have you brought us some fresh water?

25. As (*aussi*) fresh as (*que*) one can have it in Paris where the water is not drinkable. (*Literally:* Where the wells [*puits*] do not give drinkable [*potable*] water.)

26. Are my boots blacked (*cirées*)?

27. Yes, sir; please give me your clothes; I am going (*je vais*) to brush them.

28. Don't forget to call me at half past six.

---

1) The French have a peculiar form of the *article*, *not* found in English. This is the so-called **partitive article**, in which **du, de la** and **des** are employed before nouns used in a *partitive sense*; that is to say, when only *a part* of *the thing or person* spoken of is referred to.

This explanation of the *partitive article* is strictly grammatical, but hardly lucid. The pupil will therefore observe that expressions in which we employ the words *some* or *any* are rendered in French by

17. Apportez-moi de [1] l'eau fraîche (*fraysh*), du savon (*sāh-vong*) et des serviettes (*sĕr-vyĕt*); avant tout je veux me laver.

18. La fille vous⁀apportera tout ça (*toū sāh*)‿ dans⁀un instant (*dāng zeūng aing-stāng*).

19· Ayez soing (*so-àing*) de me donner des draps blancs (*drāh blānk*) et bien secs (*sĕck*).

20. Avez-vous⁀encore autre chose (*ōht shows*) à commander (*com-māng-day*)?

21. Oui, veuillez nous donner deux matelas (*mă-tĕ-lāh*) ; nous n'aimons pas les lits de plume (*plüm*).

22. Vous⁀aurez tout cela, messieurs.

23. Et n'oubliez pas de dire au comissionaire de venir nous réveiller demain de bonne‿heure.

24. Nous⁀avez-vous déjà apporté de l'eau fraîche?

25. Aussi (*ōh-sēē*) fraîche qu'on peut l'avoir à Paris où les puits (*pü-ēē*) ne donnent pas (*nĕ don pāh*) de l'eau potable (*de lŏ pō-tāh-bl*).

26. Mes bottes sont-elles cirées (*sēē-ray*)?

27. Oui, monsieur ; donnez-moi vos⁀habits, s'il vous plaît ; je vais (*vay*) les brosser.

28. N'oubliez pas de me réveiller à six⁀heures et demie.

- du (for the masc. sing.) ; by **de la** (for the fem. sing.) and by **des** (for the plural of both genders).

Give me **some** bread	Donnez-moi **du** pain
Bring me **some** eggs,	Apportez-moi **des** oeufs
He is drinking beer (*or* some beer),	Il boit **de la** bière.
Have you **any** towels ?	Avez-vous **des** serviettes?
Has he written **any** letters ?	A-t-il écrit **des** lettres ?

GRAMMATICAL REMARKS.

Learn the following tenses first, leaving the others for after-study: *Present, Imperfect, Perfect, Pluperfect, Future,* and *Conditional.*

AUXILIARY VERBS.

II. Être (*ay-tr*), to be.

INDICATIVE MOOD.

Present.

Je suis (*jĕ s'w-ēē*), I am.
tu es (*tü ay*), thou art.
il est (*ēēl ay*), he is.
nous sommes (*noū sŏm*), we are.
v̦ous‿êtes (*voū zayt*), you are.
ils sont (*ēēl song*), they are.

Imperfect.

J'étais (*jai-tay*), I was
tu étais (*tü ay-tay*), thou wast.
il était (*ēēl ay-tay*), he was.
nous‿étions (*noū zay-tyong*), we were.
vous‿étiez (*voū zay-tyĕh*), you were.
ils‿étaient (*ēēl zay-tay*), they were.

Preterite.

· Je fus (*jĕ fü*), I was.
tu fus (*tü fü*), thou wast.
il fut (*ēēl fü*), he was.

nous fûmes (*noū füm*), we were.

vous fûtes (*voū füt*), you were.

ils furent (*ēēl für*), they were.

Future.

Je serai (*jĕ sĕ-rēh*), I shall *or* will be.

tu seras (*tü sĕ-rā*), thou wilt be.

il sera (*ēēl sĕ-rā*), he will be.

nous serons (*noū sĕ-rong*), we shall *or* will be.

vous serez (*voū sĕ-rēh*), you will be.

ils seront (*ēēl sĕ-rong*), they will be.

1*st Conditional.*

Je serais (*jĕ sĕ-ray*), I should be.

tu serais (*tü sĕ-ray*), thou wouldst be.

il serait (*ēēl sĕ-ray*), he would be.

nous serions (*noū sĕ-ryong*), we should be.

vous seriez (*voū sĕ-ryēh*), you would be.

ils seraient (*ēēl sĕ-ray*), they would be.

COMPOUND TENSES.

été (*ay-tay*), been.

Perfect.

J'ai été (*jay ay-tay*),	I have been.
tu as̑été,	thou hast been.
il a été,	he has been.
nous̑avons̑été,	we have been.
vous̑avez̑été,	you have been.
ils̑ont̑été,	they have been.

Pluperfect.

J'avais été (*jă-vay-zay-tay*),	I had been.
tu avais été,	thou hadst been.
il avait été,	he had been.
nous avions été,	we had been. .
vous aviez été,	you had been.
ils avaient été,	they had been.

2nd Pluperfect.

J'eus été (*jü zay-tay*),	I had been.
tu eus été,	&c.
il eut été,	&c.
nous eûmes été,	we had been.
vous eûtes été,	&c.
ils eurent été,	&c.

2nd Future.

J'aurai été (*jŏ-ray-ay-tay*),	I shall *or* will have been.
tu auras été,	&c.
il aura été,	&c.
nous aurons été,	we shall *or* will have been.
vous aurez été,	&c.
ils auront été,	&c.

2nd Conditional.

J'aurais été (*jŏ-ray-zay-tay*),	I should have been.
tu aurais été,	&c.
il aurait été,	&c.
nous aurions été,	we should have been.
vous auriez été,	&c.
ils auraient été,	&c.

SÚBJUNCTIVE MOOD.

Present.

Que je sois (*kě jě s'woáh*),   that I may be.

que tu sois (*kē tü s'woáh*),   &c.

qu'il soit (*kēēl s'woáh*),   &c.

que nous soyons (*kě noū s'woá-yong*), &c.

que vous soyez (*kě voū s'woá-yēh*),   &c.

qu'ils soient (*kēēl s'woáh*),   &c.

Imperfect.

Que je fusse (*kě jě füss*), that I might be.

que tu fusses (*kě tü füss*),   &c.

qu'il **fût** (*kēēl fü*),   &c.

que nous fussions (*füs-yong*),   &c.

que vous fussiez (*füs-yēh*),   &c.

qu'ils fussent (*füss*),.   &c.

Perfect.

Que j'aie été (*kě jay ay-tay*), that I may have been.

que tu aies été,   &c.

qu'il ait été,   &c.

que nous ayons été,   &c.

que vous ayez été,   &c.

qu'ils aient été,   &c.

Pluperfect.

Que j'eusse été (*kě jüs ay-tay*), that I might have been.

que tu eusses été,   &c.

qu'il eût été,   &c.

que nous eussions été,   &c.

que vous eussiez été,   &c.

qu'ils eussent été .(*kēēl züs tay-tay*),   &c.

IMPERATIVE MOOD.

sois (*s'woăh*) be.   soyons (*s'woăh-yong*) let us be.
qu'il soit let him be.   soyez (*s'woăh-yĕh*) be (you).

INFINITIVE MOOD.

Present.   *Past.*

être (*ay-tr*) ⎫   avoir été (*ă-voăr-ay-tay* ⎫   to
d'être(*day-tr*) ⎬ to be.   d'avoir été (*dă-voăr-ay-tay* ⎬ have
à être ⎭   à avoir été ⎭ been.

PARTICIPLES.

Present.   *Past.*

étant (*ay-tăng*) being.   été (*ay-tay*) been, [**fem. unchanged.**]
                                       ayant été (*ay-yăng tay-tay*) having
                                       been.

Words.

Hôtel (*ŏh-tell*).	**Hotel.**
le maître de l'hôtel (*may-tr*),	the landlord.
le concierge (*kong-syĕrsh*),	the porter (night-**porter**).
le garçon (*gar-song*),	the waiter.
le commissionnaire,	the boots, the commissioner
la bonne,	
la fille (de chambre),	the housemaid.
la salle à manger (*măng-jay*),	the dining-room.
la salle des voyageurs (*voă-yă-jeŭr*),	the coffee-room, the break-fast-room ; the parlor.
la chambre (*shăng-br*),	the room.
la chambre donnant sur la rue (*sür lă rü*),	the front-room.

la chambre donnant sur la cour (*coūr*),	the back-room.
la table d'hôte (*tăhbl dote*),	the ordinary, table d'hôte,
la note, l'addition (*ād-dēē-syong*),	the bill.
au premier (*prĕ-myēh*),	on the first floor.
au second (*sĕ-gong*),	on the second floor.
au troisième (*troāh-zyēhm*),	on the third floor.
le vestibule (*vĕ-stēē-būl*),	the hall.
l'escalier (*lĕs-kāh-lyēh*),	the staircase.
la marche (*marsh*),	the step.

Translate the following

Exercise

into English, and then again, without assistance of the book, into French.

LE DÎNER.

Bon jour, cher ami. Vous voilà (*beho.'d, then*), revenu (*returned*) de voyage? Depuis (*since*) quand êtes-vous à Paris? Depuis hier soir. Ma première visite est pour vous. C'est bien aimable (*amiable*) de votre part (*on your part=of you, in you*, &c.). J'espère que vous me ferez (*future of faire*) l'amitié (*friendship, favor*) de dîner avec moi.

Comment trouvez-vous ce potage (*soup*)? Excellent; je vois (*I see*) que votre cuisinier(*cook*, kwēē-zēē-nyēh), est un homme de goût. Permettez-moi (*permit, allow me*) de vous verser (*pour out*) un verre de Madère (*Madeira*). Un petit verre de madère après la soupe (*soup*) ne fait

jamais (*never*) de mal (*does never any harm*). Bien, au contraire.—Puis-je vous offrir (*offer*) une tranche de boeuf
(*beef*), ou préférez-vous un biftek (*beefsteak*, often called
chateaubriand)? J'aime bien le biftek cuit à point (*well
done*, kwee ah pō-aing). Veuillez donc vous servir (*to
help yourself*). Voici des pommes de terre (*potatoes*), des
épinards (*spinach*) et des choux-fleurs (*cauliflower*).
Aimez-vous les épinards? Non, monsieur, pas du tout
(*not at all*). Dans ce cas (*then, in that case*) prenez (*take*)
des choux-fleurs ou un autre légume (*vegetables*). Quel
magnifique (măn-yēē-fēēk = *magnificent*) saumon (*salmon*) on apporte là (*there*). C'est vraiment (*really*) une
belle pièce (pēē-ayse). Voici (*there is*) de la sauce aux
capres. Je l'aime mieux (mee-eū, *better*) à l'huile et au
vinaigre. N'oubliez pas que les poissons (*fish*) deman-
dent à nager (*swim*). Ne craignez rien (nĕ krĕn-yēh
rēē-aing, *don't be afraid, never fear!*); votre vieux bor-
deaux (*claret*) se recommande tout seul (*alone*). Jean
(*John*), passez-moi le sel et le poivre, l'huile et le
vinaigre.

COMPANION TO THE

Revised Version of the New Testament.

Explaining the Reasons for the Changes Made on the Authorized Version.

BY ALEXANDER ROBERTS, D.D.,

Member of the English Revision Committee.

WITH SUPPLEMENT BY A MEMBER OF THE AMERICAN COMMITTEE.

Containing a Brief History of the Revision of the Work and Co-operation of the New Testament Companies, of the Points of Agreement and Difference, and an Explanation of the Appendix' to the Revised New Testament.

ALSO, A FULL TEXTUAL INDEX,

Being a Key to Passages in which Important Changes have been Made.

This book, having been carefully prepared by Members of both Revision Committees, carries official weight. It shows what changes have been made, and also the reasons which influenced the revisers in making them. It will be difficult to judge of the merits of the revision without the aid of this Companion volume. Our edition is printed by special arrangement with the English publishers. It is well known that, by an arrangement between the two Committees of Revision, the changes suggested by the American Committee, but which were not adopted by the English Revisers, are published as an Appendix to the Revised New Testament. The *Companion* volume is an explanation of *all* the changes adopted by both committees, and of those suggested by the American Committee, but not assented to by the English Committee, in their final revision. The book will be indispensable to a right understanding of the revision. This cheap edition of the combined books, although authorized and copyrighted, will be sold for 25 cents in paper, and 75 cents in cloth—sent postage free.

TESTIMONIALS.

T. W. CHAMBERS, D.D., a Member of the American Committee of Revision, says of this book: "Many persons have expressed a desire that, simultaneously with the issue of the Revised New Testament, there should appear an authentic explanation of the reasons for such changes as will be found in its pages. The work of Dr. Roberts is exactly fitted to meet this desire....Nowhere else in print can be found a statement so full and exact. It gives all needed information, and does it in an unexceptional way."

C. F. DEEMS, D.D., Pastor of the Church of the Strangers, New York, writes: "The Companion to the Revised Version seems to me almost indispensable. Even scholars who were not at the meeting of the Revisers would have a wearisome work in seeking to discover all the changes made, and to ordinary readers very much of the labor would be lost. ....All this is set forth by Dr. Roberts with admirable perspicuity. Those who have any intelligent interest in the Holy Scriptures, will find this little book absorbingly interesting. I shall urge every member of the church of which I am pastor to give it a careful reading, and purpose to introduce it as a text-book in our Bible-classes."

"So valuable, interesting and useful is this publication, that we advise every one who wishes to know the why and wherefore of the revision, to obtain it immediately."—*New York Observer*.

Paper, 8vo size, 25 cents; Cloth, 16mo, 75 cents.

I. K. FUNK & CO., Publishers, 10 & 12 Dey St., N.Y.

THE TEACHER'S EDITION

OF THE

REVISED NEW TESTAMENT

With New Concordance and Index, Harmony of the Gospels, Maps,
Historical and Chronological Tables, Parallel Passages printed
in full, Blank Pages Interleaved for manuscript notes, and
many other New and Indispensable Helps to the Study
of the Revised Version.

After the excitement connected with the sale of the first copies of the new
revision, which lack the usual indexing headlines and marginal references
to parallel passages, and also the appendixes of tables, maps, etc.—all of
which helps preachers, teachers and Bible students have come to consider as
absolutely essential to a working copy of the Bible—there arises an imperative
demand for an edition of the Revised New Testament, containing all the
marginal and appendix helps of former TEACHERS' AND REFERENCE BIBLES,
adapted carefully and accurately to the Revised Version. We are, therefore, preparing, as rapidly as is consistent with accuracy, such an edition of
the Revised New Testament. The work is under the supervision of well-
known Bible scholars, with numerous helpers, and will be issued as early as
it can be done with thoroughness. In style and size the book will resemble
the Bagster Bible, "Fac-simile large edition," known as "the Moody Bible,"
being the same width and length and size of type. It will be supplied at
prices *within the reach of all.*

This "Teachers' Edition of the Revised New Testament" will be an exact,
certified reproduction of the entire Oxford and Cambridge Edition, including
the Preface and all the marginal readings and explanations. It will contain
the appendix notes of the American Revisers, printed in the margin of each
page by the side of the passages referred to. The parallel passages, to which
reference is m de in the "Bagster Bibles," with numerous others, so far as
appropriate, will be PRINTED IN FULL in the margin. The running headings,
usually printed at the tops of pages of the King James version, will be here
supplied. A small black mark will be inserted below the last letter of each
verse to facilitate reference, and aid in RESPONSIVE READING of the Revised
Version. The second half of the volume will consist of the most carefully
prepared HELPS TO THE STUDY OF THE REVISED NEW TESTAMENT, gleaned
from the best Teachers' Editions of the authorized version, and supplied
from various original sources—all being revised and adapted to harmonize
with the Revised Version. We shall introduce many other important features,
making this the most valuable edition of the New Testament ever issued.

Popular Cloth Edition—Ready in July—Price, Postage Free, $1.00.
Send for prospectus giving full description and prices of finer Bindings.
I. K. FUNK & CO., Publishers, 10 and 12 Dey St., New York.

THE

𝔐eisterschaft 𝔖ystem.

A SIMPLE AND PRACTICAL METHOD,

ENABLING

ANY ONE TO LEARN, WITH SLIGHT EFFORT, TO SPEAK
FLUENTLY AND CORRECTLY

𝔉rench, 𝔊erman, 𝔖panish, and 𝔍talian.

BY

DR. RICHARD S. ROSENTHAL,

*Late Director of the "Akademie für fremde Sprachen" in Berlin and Leipzig,
of the "Meisterschaft College" in London, and Principal of the
"Meisterschaft School of Practical Linguistry" in New York.*

FRENCH.

IN FIFTEEN PARTS, EACH CONTAINING THREE LESSONS.

PART IV.

NEW YORK:

I. K. FUNK & CO., PUBLISHERS,

10 AND 12 DEY STREET.

TERMS.

WE have arranged with Dr. ROSENTHAL, the author of the "Meisterschaft System," for its introduction in America under his own supervision, and he has opened

FOR NON-RESIDENTS.

The student does not need to leave his home. The lessons of each language are prepared by the Professor, and printed and sent in pamphlet shape to each member of the School wherever he may reside.

The course of study for each language—German, French, Italian, or Spanish—makes fifteen pamphlets of three lessons each.

All members of the School have

THE PRIVILEGE

of asking, by letter, questions concerning each lesson, or consulting on any difficulty which may have occurred to them. All exercises corrected and all questions answered by return post by Dr. ROSENTHAL or one of his assistants.

TERMS OF MEMBERSHIP.

Five Dollars is the price for membership in the school for each language. This amount ($5.) entitles the member. to receive the fifteen books or pamphlets containing the lessons, also answers to his questions. Return postage for the answer must accompany the question.

State distinctly which language, or languages, you desire to study There are *no extra charges.* The price, **Five Dollars,** pays for one language; **Ten Dollars** for two languages, etc. All exercises and questions must be written on a separate sheet of paper, and must state full address of the pupil.

Remittances must be made in Post-Office Order or registered letter addressed to

I. K. FUNK & CO.,

10 and 12 Dey Street, New York.

The Meisterschaft-System.

FRENCH.

PART IV.

IV.

(*Continuation.*)

29. You may depend (*compter*) on it (*y*).
30. Good morning, sir; how did you pass the first **night** (*la première nuit*) in our house?

31. Was the bed quite to your taste? (*Literally :* Was the bed arranged [*arrangé*] according to [*d'après*] your habits [*vos habitudes*]?)
32. Not quite (*pas tout à fait*), madam; I should like to have another pillow (*un oreiller de plus*).
33. Please put on (*mettez*) another blanket (*une couverture de plus*).
34. Pray, give me a bolster (*traversin*); I cannot sleep (*dormir*), when my head lies so low (= when I have the head too [*trop*] low [*basse*]).
35 This evening you will find everything arranged to your liking (*goût*).
36. To-morrow morning, precisely at eight o'clock, you will bring me some coffee with milk and some rolls.

37. Do you keep (*tenez-vous*) an ordinary (*table d'hôte*)?
38. At what o'clock is the table d'hote?

IV.

(*Continuation.*)

29. Vous pouvez͡y (*zēē*) compter (*cong-tēh*).

30. Bonjour (*bong-joūr*), monsieur ; comment͡avez-vous passé la première nuit (*prĕm-yēhr n'w͡ēē*) dans notre maison?

31. Le lit était-il arrangé (*ăr-rāng-jay*) d'après vos͜habi-tudes (*dāh-pray vo zāh-bee-tüd*)?

32. Pas tout͡à fait (*toū-tāh-fay*) madame ; je voudrais͡a-·oir un͡oreiller de plus (*eūn noh-rĕ-yĕh dĕ plü*).

33. Mettez-moi (*mĕ-tay-m'w͡oāh*), je vous prie, une couver-ture de plus (*ün coū-vĕr-tür dĕ plü*).

34. Donnez-moi, s'il vous plaît, un traversin (*tră vĕr-saing*) ; je ne puis dormir (*dor-mēēr*), quand j'ai la tête trop basse (*trŏh bāss*).

35. Ce soir (*sĕ s'w͡oār*) vous trouverez tout͜cela arrangé à votre goût (*goū*).

36. Demain matin à huit͡heures précises vous m'appor-terez du café au lait et des petits-pains (*day p'tēē paing*).

37. Tenez-vous table d'hôte (*tābl dŏt*)?

38. A quelle heure dîne-t·on à la table d'hôte (*dēēn-tong āh lā tābl dŏt*)?

39. You can have lunch (*déjeuner à la fourchette*) in the breakfast room (*la salle des voyageurs*).

40. Would you be kind enough to register (*or* enter) your name and profession (*profession*) in the traveller's book ?

41. Did you leave the key (*clef*) in your door, or have you got it with (*sur*) you ?

42. Will you please give it to me, so that the house-maid may (*puisse*) clean (*faire*) your room ?

43. Waiter, did you order a cab ?

44. Have you brought all my luggage downstairs (brought downstairs = *descendu*) ?

45. Is this the waiting-room ?

46. Yes, sir ; please take your ticket at the office and go into the waiting-room.

47. Is that our train ?

48. Yes, that is the express-train for London.

49. I beg your pardon, s.r ; which is the way to St. Honoré Street ? (*Literally:* Street St. Honoré, if you please ?)

50. I beg your pardon, sir ; which is the way to the opera-house ?

51. Go straight ahead (*tout droit*).

52. Pass (over) the bridge (*le pont*) and then (*puis*) go right ahead.

53. What do you want to buy ?

54. Different things (*différentes choses*) ; linen (*de la toile*) in the first place (*d'abord*), to make some chemises ; and then (*puis*) neckties, handkerchiefs, and stockings.

55. Does Mr. N. live (*or* dwell = *demeure-t-il*) in this house ?

39. Dans la salle des voyageurs vous pouvez déjeuner à la fourchette (*foûr-shĕt*).

40. Auriez-vous la bonté (*ŏr-yēh voū lā bong-tay*) d'écrire votre nom et votre profession (*proh-fĕs-yong*) sur le livre des voyageurs (*vo-āh-yā-jeūr*)?

41. Avez-vous laissé la clef (*klay*) de la chambre à votre porte, ou l'avez-vous sur vous?

42. Veuillez me la donner pour que la bonne puisse (*pü-ĭs*) faire votre chambre?

43. Garçon, avez-vous fait (*fay*) venir un fiacre (*fēē-ā-k'r*)?

44. Avez-vous descendu (*dĕ-sāng-dü*) tous mes effets (*may-zay-fay*)?

45. Est-ce ici (*ay-sēē-sēē*) la salle d'attente?

46. Oui, monsieur; veuillez prendre votre billet au guichet, et passez à la salle d'attente.

47. Est-ce là (*there*) notre train?

48. Oui, monsieur, c'est l'express (*lex-pray*) pour Londres.

49. Pardon (*par-dong*), monsieur; la rue St. Honoré, s'il vous plaît (*rü saing-to-no-ray, sēē voū play*)?

50. Pardon, monsieur; l'opéra, s'il vous plaît?

51. Allez tout droit (*toū droāh*).

52. Passez le pont et puis (*pü-eē*) allez tout droit.

53. Que voulez-vous acheter?

54. Différentes choses (*dif-fay-rāngt. shows*); de la toile (*twoāhl*) d'abord (*dă-bōr*) pour me faire des chemises, et puis (*pü-ēē*) des cravates, des mouchoirs (*moū-shwoār*) et des bas (*bāh*).

55. Monsièur N. demeure-t-il (*dĕ-meūr-tēĕl*) dans cette

ɔ

56. Is Mr. N. at home, porter?
57. Does Mr. B. live here? (*Literally :* Is it here at Mr. B.'s?)
58. Is Mr. N. at home (*i.e.* for callers)? (*Literally :* Is Mr. N. visible?)
59. Yes, sir, walk in (*entrez*), pray.

60. Have I the honor of speaking to Mr. D.?

61. I have the honor of addressing Mr. D. (I think)?
62. That's my name. (These last eight phrases are idiomatic expressions, and can be given only so.)

IV.

FOUNDATION SENTENCE.

Always make your purchases in Paris in the large stores, where everything is sold very cheap and at fixed prices. For instance, here is a ball-dress which I have just bought for less than fifty francs.

56. Monsieur N. est-il chez lui, concierge?
57. Est-ce ici (*ays-sēē-sēē*) chez Monsieur B. (*bay*)?

58. Monsieur N. est-il visible (*vēē-zēēbl*)?

59. Oui monsieur; entrez (*āng-tray*) s'il vous plaît (*sēē voŭ play*).
60. Est-ce à (*ays ā*) monsieur D. (*day*) que j'ai l'honneur (*lŏn-neūr*) de parler?
61. C'est à monsieur D. que j'ai l'honneur de parler?
62. (C'est) moi-même (*say mwoāh-maim*).

IV.

FOUNDATION SENTENCE.

À Paris faites vos emplettes toujours dans les
āh pā-rēē fate voh zāng-plĕt toŭ-joŭr dāng lay

grands magasins, où tout se vend très-bon marché
grāng mā-gā-zaing oŭ toŭ sĕ vāng tray bong mār-shay

et à prix fixe. Par exemple, voici une robe de bal
ay āh prēē fix. părr ĕg-zāng-pl voāh-sēē ŭn robe dĕ bāhl

que je viens d'acheter pour moins de cinquante
kĕ jĕ vyaing dāsh-tĕh poŭr mo-aing dĕ saing-kāng·

francs.
frāng

1.

Always do your shopping in Paris in the large stores, where everything is sold very cheap and at fixed prices.

At; in; to; [Distinguish between à (*with* accent) *at, in*, and a (*without* accent) *has.*]

Paris

make; do[1]

your[2]

purchases

always

in

the

---

1) **Faire,** *to make, to do,* is an irregular verb, of which the pupil may now learn the following tenses :

Present.	Imperfect.	Future.
Je fais (*fay*).	Je faisais.	Je ferai.
tu fais (*fay*).	tu faisais.	tu feras.
il fait (*fay*).	il faisait.	il fera.
nous **faisons**(*fay-zong*).	nous faisions.	nous ferons.
vous **faites** (*fate*).	vous faisiez.	vous ferez.
ils **font** (*fong*).	ils faisaient.	ils feront.

Perfect.	Pluperfect.	Imperative.
J'ai fait.	J'avais fait.	Fais.
tu as fait.	tu avais fait.	faisons.
&c.	&c.	faites.

2) **The so-called possessive pronouns or possessive adjectives**

1.

À Paris faites vos͡emplettes toujours dans
ăh pă-rēē fate voh zăng-plĕt toū-joūr dăng

les grands magasins, où tout se vend très-bon
lay grăng mă-gă-zaing͡ oū toū sĕ văng tray bong

marché et à prix fixe.
măr-shay ay ăh prēē fix

À (*ăh*) [The accent on capital letters is usually omitted.]

Paris (*pă-rēē*)

faites[1] (*fate*) [Imperative of the irregular verb *faire*, to make, to do.]

vos[2] (*voh*) [Plural of *votre*.]

emplettes (*ăng-plĕt*)

toujours (*toū-joūr*)

dans (*dăng*)

les (*lay*)

---

must always *agree in gender and number with the noun* they qualify. They are :

SINGULAR.		PLURAL.
Masculine.	*Feminine.*	*Both genders.*
Mon (*mong*).	Ma (*măh*).	Mes (*may*), my.
ton (*tong*).	ta (*tăh*).	tes (*tay*), thy.
son (*song*).	sa (*săh*).	ses (*say*), his, her.
notre (*nŏt*).	notre (*nŏt*).	nos (*nōh*), our.
votre (*vŏt*).	votre (*vŏt*).	vos (*vōh*), your.
leur (*leūr*).	leur (*leūr*).	leurs (*leūr*), their.

Examples : *Mon* livre (masc.), my book ; *ma* maison (fem.), my house ; *mes* emplettes, my-purchases.

Remark : For euphony *mon, ton,* and *son* are used before *feminine nouns beginning with a vowel or unaspirated ' h '*, as : mon͡ opinion (*non nŏ-pēē-ni ong*), my opinion ; son͡humeur, his humor.

large [1]

stores

where

all; everything

itself

sells

very

good

market; market-price

very cheap; at a very cheap price

and

at

price

fixed

1. What do you want to do this forenoon?
2. I should like to do my shopping; will you accompany me?
3. Why do you want to make your purchases in this small shop (*cette boutique*)?
4. Buy always in the large stores, where everything is sold at fixed rates.

---

1) The *adjective* must always agree in number and gender with the noun it relates to; i.e., *grand*. when it refers to a masculine noun;

grands [1] (*grāng*)

magasins (*mā-gā-zaing*)

où (*oŭ*) [Distinguish between où, where, and ou (*without* accent), or.]

tout (*toŭ*)

se (*sĕ*)

vend (*vāng*) [2]

très (*tray*)

bon (*bong*)

marché (*mār-shay*)

très-bon marché

et (*ay*)

à (*āh*)

prix (*prēē*)

fixe (*fix*)

1. Que voulez-vous faire ce matin?
2. Je voudrais faire mes emplettes· voulez-vous m'accompagner (*mă-cong-păn-yĕh*)?
3. Pourquoi voulez-vous faire vos emplettes dans cette boutique (*boŭ-tēēk*)?
4. Achetez toujours dans les grands magasins, où tout se vend à prix fixe.

---

grande, when referring to feminines; *grands*, when referring to several masculines, and *grandes*, when relating to several feminines.

2) See the conjugation of *vendre*, Grammatical Remarks in No. VI.

5. I should like to buy some cloth (*du drap*) to make a coat of (= of which [*de quoi*] to make a coat).

6. What sort (*quelle sorte*) of cloth do you wish, sir?

7. Have you got any samples (*or* patterns)?

8. Yes, sir; here are (*voici*) samples (*or* patterns) of all the pieces of cloth (*de tous les draps*) which we have in stock (*dans le magasin*).

9. What (*quel*) is the price of this one (*celui-ci*)?

10. That costs (*il est de*) eighteen (*dix-huit*) francs a meter (*le mètre*).

11. That (*ça*) seems (*semble*) very dear (*cher*) to me.

12. That seems rather (= a little, *un peu*) dear.

13. I beg your pardon, sir, this (*ce*) is not dear for the quality (*la qualité*); on the contrary (*au contraire*), it is very cheap.

14. How much does this cost?

15. That costs ten (*dix*) francs.

16. What (*quel*) is the price of this (= of this object [*de cet objet*])?

17. What is the price of these gloves (*ces gants*)?

18. What is the price of this silk dress (*cette robe de soie*)?

19. How (*combien*) do you sell this (*cela*)?

20. How (*or* at what price, *combien*) do you sell this silk?

21. How much do you charge for this? (*Literally:* How much this object?)

---

1) We have the following pronouns for our this, viz., ce (masc.); cette (fem.); ces (plural, both genders), as: *ce* train (*sé traing*) *this* train; cette couverture, this cover; ces enfants (*say sáng-fáng*) these children.

5. Je voudrais⌢acheter du, drap (*drāh*) de quoi faire un⌢habit.

6. Quelle sorte de drap désirez-vous, monsieur?

7. Avez-vous des⌢échantillons (*day zay-shāng-tēē-yong*)?

8. Oui, monsieur; voici (*voāh-sēē*) des⌢échantillons de tous les draps que nous⌢avons dans le magasin.

9. Quel est le prix de celui-ci (*kĕll ay lĕ prēē dĕ cĕ-lü⌢ēē-sēē*)?

10. Il est de dix-huit francs le mètre (*ēēl lay dĕ dēē zwēēt frāng lĕ maytr*).

11. Ça me semble très-cher (*să mĕ sāngbl tray shayr*).

12. Ça me semble un peu cher (*eūng peū shayr*).

13. Pardon, monsieur; pour la qualité (*kā-lēē-tay*), ce n'est pas cher, au contraire (*cong-trayr*), c'est très-bon marché.

14. { Combien cela coûte-t-il (*kong-byaing sĕ-lah coūt-tēēl*)?
    { Combien ça (*săh*) coûte-t-il?

15. { Cela coûte dix (*dēē*) francs.
    { C'est de dix francs.

16. Quel est le prix de cet¹⌢objet (*kĕll lay lĕ prēē dĕ sĕt tob-jĕh*)?

17. Quel est le prix de ces¹ gants?

18. Quel est le prix de cette¹ robe de soie (*robe dĕ s'woāh*)?

19. Combien vendez-vous cela (*kong-byaing vāng-dēh voū sĕ-lāh*)?

20. Combien vendez-vous cette soie?

21. Combien cet⌢objet (*kong-byaing sĕt tob-jĕh*)?

Remark : Instead of *ce,* this, we must write c t before masculine nouns beginning with a *vowel* or a *silent h*, as : *c* ⌢enfant (*sĕ-lāng-fāng*), this child ; cet⌢homme (*sĕ-tŏm*), this m·

GRAMMATICAL REMARKS.

Of the Negative and Interrogative forms of the Auxiliaries.

Whereas in English the *negation* is simply expressed by the particle *not*, the French use *two* negative words, viz. **ne** and **pas**, the first of which is placed before the simple verb, the other after it, as: *Je* **ne** *suis* **pas**, I am not.—In compound tenses, the participle *follows pas*, as: *Je* **n'***ai* **pas** *eu*, I have not had.

In interrogations, the pronoun which is the subject of the verb is placed after it, and they are joined by a hyphen, as: *as-tu? avez-vous?* — When the third person singular ends with a vowel, *-t-* is placed between the verb and *il, elle* or *on: a-t-il? a-t-elle? a-t-on? aura-t-on?*

The proper use of the French negation being somewhat difficult, the pupil will do well to study thoroughly the

I.   Negative Form of the Auxiliaries.

INDICATIVE MOOD.

Avoir, to have.   **Être,** to be.

Present Tense.

Je n'ai pas, I have not.	Je ne suis pas, I am not.
tu n'as pas, thou hast not.	tu n'es pas, thou art not.
il n'a pas, he *or* it has not.	il n'est pas, he *or* it is not.
elle n'a pas, she has not.	elle n'est pas, she is not.

nous n'avons pas, we have not.

nous ne sommes pas, we are not.

vous n'avez pas, you have not.

vous n'êtes pas, you are not.

ils n'ont pas, they have not.

ils ne sont pas, they are not.

Imperfect.

Je n'avais pas, I had not, &c.

Je n'étais pas, I was not, &c.

Preterite.

Je n'eus pas, I had not, &c.

Je ne fus pas, I was not, &c.

Future.

Je n'aurai pas, I shall not have, &c.

Je ne serai pas, I shall not be, &c.

1st Conditional.

Je n'aurais pas, I should not have, &c.

Je ne serais pas, I should not be, &c.

COMPOUND TENSES.

Perfect.

Je n'ai pas eu, I have not had, &c.

Je n'ai pas été, I have not been, &c.

Pluperfect.

Je n'avais pas eu, I had not had, &c.

Je n'avais pas été, I had not been, &c.

2nd Future.

Je n'aurai pas eu, I shall not have had, &c.

Je n'aurai pas été, I shall not have been, &c.

2nd Conditional.

Je n'aurais pas eu, I should not have had, &c.

Je n'aurais pas été, I should not have been, &c.

SUBJUNCTIVE MOOD.

Present.

Que je n'aie pas, that I (may) not have, &c.

Que je ne sois pas, that I (may) not be, &c.

Preterite.

Que je n'eusse pas, that I might not have, &c.

Que je ne fusse pas, that I were not, &c.

Perfect.

Que je n'aie pas⌒eu, that I (may) not have had, &c.

Que je n'aie pas⌒été, that I (may) not have been, &c.

Pluperfect.

Que je n'eusse pas⌒eu, that I (might) not have had, &c.

Que je n'eusse pas⌒été, that I (might) not have been, &c.

IMPERATIVE MOOD.

N'aie pas, have not.

Ne sois pas, be not, do not be.

n'ayons pas, let us not have.

ne soyons pas, let us not be.

n'ayez pas, have not.

ne soyez pas, be not.

INFINITIVE MOOD.

Present.

N'avoir pas,
ne pas avoir, } not to have.

N être pas,
ne pas être, } not to be.

Perfect.

N'avoir pas⌒eu, not to have had.

N'avoir pas⌒été, not to have been.

PARTICIPLES.

Present.

N'ayant pas, not having.   N'étant pas, not being.

Past.

N'ayant pas⌢eu, not having   N'ayant pas⌢été, not hav-
   had.   ing been.

II. Interrogative Form of the Two Auxiliaries.

INDICATIVE MOOD.

Present.

Ai-je, have I ?	Suis-je, am I ?
as-tu, hast thou ?	es-tu, art thou ?
a-t-il, has he ?	est-il, is he ?
a-t-elle, has she ?	est-elle, is she ?
avons-nous, have we ?	sommes-nous, are we ?
avez-vous, have you ?	êtes-vous, are you ?

ont-ils, ⎫
ont-elles, ⎬ have they ?

sont-ils, ⎫
sont-elles, ⎬ are they ?

Imperfect.

Avais-je, had I ? &c.   Etais-je, was I ? &c.

Preterite.

Eus-je, had I ? &c.   Fus-je, was I ? &c.

Future.

Aurai-je, shall I have ? &c.   Serai-je. shall I be ? &c.

1st Conditional.

Aurais-je, should I have?   Serais-je, should I be ? &c.
   &c.

Perfect.

Ai-je eu, have I had ? &c.   Ai-je été, have I been ? &c.

Pluperfect.

Avais-je eu, had I had? &c.   Avais-je été, had I been? &c.

2nd Future.

Aurai-je eu, shall I have   Aurai-je été, shail I have
had?   been?

2nd Conditional.

Aurais-je eu, should I have   Aurais-je été, should I have
had? &c.   been? &c.

III. Negative and Interrogative Form.

INDICATIVE MOOD.

Present.

N'ai-je pas, have I not?   Ne suis-je pas, am I not?
n'as-tu pas, hast thou not?   n'es-tu pas, art thou not?
n'a-t-il pas, has he not?   n'est-il pas, is he not?
n'avons-nous pas, have we   ne sommes-nous pas, are we
  not?   not?
n'avez-vous pas, have you   n'êtes-vous pas, are you not?
  not?   ne sont-ils pas, are they
n'ont-ils pas, have they not?   not?   .

Imperfect.

N'avais-je pas, had I not? &c.   N'étais-je pas, was I not? &c.

Preterite.

N'eus-je pas, had I not? &c.   Ne fus-je pas, was I not? &c.

1st Future.

N'aurai-je pas, shall I not   Ne serai-je pas, shall I not
have? &c.   be? &c.

1st Conditional.

N'aurais-je pas, should I not   Ne serais-je pas, should I
have? &c.   not be? &c.

COMPOUND TENSES.

Perfect.

N'ai-je pas‿eu, have I not   N'ai-je pas‿été, have I not
had? &e.   been? &c.

Pluperfect.

N'avais-je pas‿eu, had I not   N'avais-je pas‿été, had I not
had? &c.   been? &c.

2nd Future.

N'aurai-je.pas‿eu, shall I   N'aurai-je pas‿été, shall I
not have had? &c.   not have been? &c.

2nd Conditional.

N'aurais-je pas‿eu, should I   N'aurais-je pas‿été, should
not have had? &c.   I not have been? &c.

2.

The pupil must make himself now familiar with the principal tenses of the

FIRST CONJUGATION.

Donner, to give.

INDICATIVE MOOD.

Present.

Je donne (*dŏn*), I give.	nous donnons (*don-nong*), we give.
tu donnes (*dŏn*), thou givest.	vous donnez (*don-nēh*), you give.
il donne (*dŏn*), he gives.	ils donnent (*dŏn*), } they give.
elle donne, she gives.	elles donnent (*dŏn*), } give.

Imperfect.

Je donn*ais* (*don-nay*), I gave. nous donn*ions* (*don-nyong*), we gave.

tu donn*ais*, thou gavest. vous donn*iez* (*don-nyēh*), you gave.

il donn*ait* (*don-nay*), he gave. ils donn*aient* (*don-nay*), they gave.

Preterite.

Je donn*ai* (*don-nēh*), I gave. nous donn*âmes* (*don-nāhm*), we gave.

tu donn*as* (*don-nāh*), thou gavest. vous donn*âtes* (*don-nāht*), you gave.

il donn*a* (*don-nāh*), he gave. ils donn*èrent* (*don-nayr*) they gave.

1st Future.

Je donn*erai* (*dŏn'-ray*), I shall give. nous donn*erons* (*don-nĕ-rong*), we shall give.

tu donn*eras* (*dŏn'-rāh*), thou wilt give. vous donn*erez* (*don-nĕ-rēh*), you will give.

il donn*era* (*dŏn'-rāh*), he will give. ils donn*eront* (*don-nĕ-rong*), they will give.

1st Conditional.

Je donn*erais* (*don-nĕ-ray*), I should give. nous donn*erions* (*don-nĕ-ryong*). we should give.

tu donn*erais* (*don-nĕ-ray*), &c. vous donn*eriez* (*don-nĕr-yĕh*), &c.

il donn*erait* (*don-nĕ-ray*), &c. ils donn*eraient* (*don nĕ-ray*), &c.

IMPERATIVE MOOD.

Donne (*dŏn*), give.   donnons (*don-nong*), let us
             give.
             donnez (*don-nĕh*), give.

INFINITIVE MOOD.

Donner, to give.   de or à donner, to give.

SUBJUNCTIVE MOOD.

Present.

Que je donne (*dŏn*), that I que nous donnions (*dŏn-*
  (may) give.   *nyong*), that we (may) give.
que tu donnes (*dŏn*), &c.   que vous donniez (*don-nyēh*),
             &c.

qu'il donne (*dŏn*), &c.   qu'ils donnent (*dŏn*) &c.

Imperfect.

Que je donnasse (*dŏn-nāss*), que nous donnassions (*don-*
  that I might give.   *nās-syong*), we might give.
que tu donnasses (*dŏn-nāss*), que vous donnassiez (*dŏn-*
  &c.   *nās-syēh*), &c.
qu'il donnât (*don-nāh*), &c.   qu'ils donnassent (*dŏn-nāss*),
             &c.

PARTICIPLES.

Donnant (*don-nāng*), giving.   Donné (*don-nay*), f. donnée
en donnant, (*āng don-nāng*)   (*don-nay*), given.
  by giving.

COMPOUND TENSES.

In active verbs, these are formed with the Participle
past and the auxiliary *avoir*, to have.

INFINITIVE. MOOD.

Avoir donné, to have given.

INDICATIVE MOOD.

Perfect (*Compound of the Present*).

J'ai donné, I have given.
tu as donné, thou hast given.
il a donné, he has given.
nous‿avons donné, we have given.
vous‿avez donné, you have given,
ils‿ont donné, }
elles‿ont donné, } they have given.

Pluperfect (*Compound of the Imperfect*).

J'avais donné, I had given, &c.

Compound of the Preterite.

J'eus donné, I had given, &c.

2nd Future (*Compound of the Future*).

J'aurai donné, I shall have given, &c.

2nd Conditional.

J'aurais donné, I should have given.

SUBJUNCTIVE MOOD.

Perfect.

Que j'aie donné, that I (may) have given.
Que tu aies donné, that thou (mayst) have given, &c.

Pluperfect.

Que j'eusse donné, that I (might) have given, &c.

PARTICIPLE.

Ayant donné (*mas.*),- } having given.
ayant donnée (*fem.*), }

Remarks.

1. Remember that there is but **one** way to render the expressions: *I give*, *I do give*, and *I am giving*, viz., *je donne; I was giving* or *I used to give* = *je donnais*, &c.

2. Observe that *I gave*, *I have given*, &c., are, mostly expressed by *J'ai donné*, &c. The Preterite is only used in historical style, but hardly ever in conversation. Of course these remarks refer not only to *give* but to *all* verbs.

3. In the interrogative and negative form, *the auxiliary* **to do** is **never** expressed. Ex.:

Present.

INTERROGATIVELY.

Est-ce que je donne? do I give? donnons-nous? do we give?

donnes-tu? doest thou give? donnent-ils (*dŏn-tēēl*), do they give?
donne-*t*-il? does he give?
donne-*t*-elle? does she give? donnent-elles? do they give?

NEGATIVELY.

Je ne donne pas, I do not give.
tu ne donnes pas, thou doest not give.
il ne donne pas, he does not give, &c.

NEGATIVE-INTERROGATIVE.

Est-ce que je ne donne pas (*ays kĕ jĕ nĕ don pāh*)? do I not give?

ne donnes-tu pas? doest thou not give?
ne donne-*t*-il pas? does he not give? &c.

Perfect.

Ai-je donné? as-tu donné? a-*t*-il donné? &c.

Have I given *or* did I give?- &c.

Je n'ai *pas* donné, tu n'as pas donné, &c.

N'ai-je pas donné? n'as-tu pas donné? &c.

Conjugate in the same manner: *parler*, to speak; *porter*, to carry, to take; *admirer*, to admire; *aimer*, to love, &c.

N.B.—Je is apostrophed before a vowel, as : J'aime, j'admire.

Translate the following

Letter

into English and then render it again into French:

Monsieur Gustave Fournier à Paris. [1]

Londres, le treize (13) Juin (June), 1881.

Monsieur,

Nous avons l'honneur de vous remettre (*remit*) ci-inclus (*inclosed*) 5000 francs (cinq mille francs) sur (*on*) Paris, dont (*wherewith*) veuillez créditer (*credit*) notre compte[2] (*account*) et nous accuser réception[3] (*and inform us of receipt thereof*).

Nous avons l'honneur de vous saluer,[4]

(*Yours very respectfully*)

R. & C.

---

1) This exercise is a sample of a simple French business-letter.
2) Pronounce=*kray-dĕĕ-tĕh nŏt kongt.*
3) Pronounce=*noŭ ză-ku-zĕh ray-sĕps-yong.*
4) *Literally :* 'We have the honor to salute you.' This phrase corresponds to our: 'Very respectfully.' Pronounce=*noŭ ză-vong lŏn-neŭr dĕ voŭ să-lü-ĕh.*

COMPANION TO THE
Revised Version of the New Testament.

Explaining the Reasons for the Changes Made on the Authorized Version.

BY ALEXANDER ROBERTS, D.D.,
Member of the English Revision Committee.

WITH SUPPLEMENT BY A MEMBER OF THE AMERICAN COMMITTEE.

Containing a Brief History of the Revision of the Work and Co-operation of the New Testament Companies, of the Points of Agreement and Difference, and an Explanation of the Appendix to the Revised New Testament.

ALSO, A FULL TEXTUAL INDEX,

Being a Key to Passages in which Important Changes have been Made.

This book, having been carefully prepared by Members of both Revision Committees, carries official weight. It shows what changes have been made, and also the reasons which influenced the revisers in making them. It will be difficult to judge of the merits of the revision without the aid of this Companion volume. Our edition is printed by special arrangement with the English publishers. It is well known that, by an arrangement between the two Committees of Revision, the changes suggested by the American Committee, but which were not adopted by the English Revisers, are published as an Appendix to the Revised New Testament. The *Companion* volume is an explanation of *all* the changes adopted by both committees, and of those suggested by the American Committee, but not assented to by the English Committee, in their final revision. The book will be indispensable to a right understanding of the revision. This cheap edition of the combined books, although authorized and copyrighed, will be sold for 25 cents in paper, and 75 cents in cloth—sent postage free.

TESTIMONIALS.

T. W. CHAMBERS, D.D., a Member of the American Committee of Revision, says of this book: "Many persons have expressed a desire that, simultaneously with the issue of the Revised New Testament, there should appear an authentic explanation of the reasons for such changes as will be found in its pages. The work of Dr. Roberts is exactly fitted to meet this desire.... Nowhere else in print can be found a statement so full and exact. It gives all needed information, and does it in an unexceptional way."

C. F. DEEMS, D.D., Pastor of the Church of the Strangers. New York, writes: "The Companion to the Revised Version seems to me almost indispensable. Even scholars who were not at the meeting of the Revisers wou'd have a wearisome work in seeking to discover all the changes made, and to ordinary readers very much of the labor would be lost. ....All this is set forth by Dr. Roberts with admirable perspicuity. Those who have any intelligent interest in the Holy Scriptures, will find this little book absorbingly interesting. I shall urge every member of the church of which I am pastor to give it a careful reading, and purpose to introduce it as a text-book in our Bible-classes."

"So valuable, interesting and useful is this publication, that we advise every one who wishes to know the why and wherefore of the revision, to obtain it immediately."—*New York Observer.*

Paper, 8vo size, 25 cents; Cloth, 16mo, 75 cents.

*** For Sale by Booksellers and Newsdealers, or sent postage-paid, on receipt of price, by

I. K. FUNK & CO., Publishers, 10 & 12 Dey St., N.Y.

THE TEACHER'S EDITION

OF THE

REVISED NEW TESTAMENT

With New Concordance and Index, Harmony of the Gospels, Maps,
Historical and Chronological Tables, Parallel Passages printed
in full, Blank Pages Interleaved for manuscript notes, and
many other New and Indispensable Helps to the Study
of the Revised Version.

After the excitement connected with the sale of the first copies of the new
revision, which lack the usual indexing headlines and marginal references
to parallel passages, and also the appendixes of tables, maps, etc.—all of
which helps preachers, teachers and Bible students have come to consider as
absolutely essential to a working copy of the Bible—there arises an imperative
demand for an edition of the Revised New Testament, containing all the
marginal and appendix helps of former TEACHERS' AND REFERENCE BIBLES,
adapted carefully and accurately to the Revised Version. We are, therefore, preparing, as rapidly as is consistent with accuracy, such an edition of
the Revised New Testament. The work is under the supervision of well-
known Bible scholars, with numerous helpers, and will be issued as early as
it can be done with thoroughness. In style and size the book will resemble
the Bagster Bible, "Fac-simile large edition," known as "the Moody Bible,"
being the same width and length and size of type. It will be supplied at
prices *within the reach of all.*

This "Teachers' Edition of the Revised New Testament" will be an exact,
certified reproduction of the entire Oxford and Cambridge Edition, including
the Preface and all the marginal readings and explanations. It will contain
the appendix notes of the American Revisers, printed in the margin of each
page by the side of the passages referred to. The parallel passages, to which
reference is made in the "Bagster Bibles," with numerous others, so far as
appropriate, will be PRINTED IN FULL in the margin. The running headings,
usually printed at the tops of pages of the King James version, will be here
supplied. A small black mark will be inserted below the last letter of each
verse to facilitate reference, and aid in RESPONSIVE READING of the Revised
Version. The second half of the volume will consist of the most carefully
prepared HELPS TO THE STUDY OF THE REVISED NEW TESTAMENT, gleaned
from the best Teachers' Editions of the authorized version, and supplied
from various original sources—all being revised and adapted to harmonize
with the Revised Version. We shall introduce many other important features,
making this the most valuable edition of the New Testament ever issued.

Popular Cloth Edition—Ready in July—Price, Postage Free, $1.60.

Send for prospectus giving full description and prices of finer Bindings.

I. K. FUNK & CO., Publishers, 10 and 12 Dey St., New York.

THE

𝕸𝖊𝖎𝖘𝖙𝖊𝖗𝖘𝖈𝖍𝖆𝖋𝖙 𝕾𝖞𝖘𝖙𝖊𝖒.

A SIMPLE AND PRACTICAL METHOD

ENABLING

ANY ONE TO LEARN, WITH SLIGHT EFFORT, TO SPEAK
FLUENTLY AND CORRECTLY

𝕱𝖗𝖊𝖓𝖈𝖍, 𝕲𝖊𝖗𝖒𝖆𝖓, 𝕾𝖕𝖆𝖓𝖎𝖘𝖍, 𝖆𝖓𝖉 𝕴𝖙𝖆𝖑𝖎𝖆𝖓.

BY

DR. RICHARD S. ROSENTHAL,

*Late Director of the " Akademie für fremde Sprachen" in Berlin and Leipzig,
of the "Meisterschaft College" in London, and Principal of the
"Meisterschaft School of Practical Linguistry" in New York.*

FRENCH.

IN FIFTEEN PARTS, EACH CONTAINING THREE LESSONS.

PART- V.

NEW YORK:

I. K. FUNK & CO., PUBLISHERS,

10 AND 12 DEY STREET.

TERMS.

WE have arranged with Dr. ROSENTHAL, the author of the "Meisterschaft System," for its introduction in América under his own
supervision, and he has opened

The Meisterschaft School of Practical Linguistry

FOR NON-RESIDENTS.

The student does not need to leave his home. The lessons of
each language are prepared by the Professor, and printed and sent
in pamphlet shape to each member of the School wherever he may
reside.

The course of study for each language—German, French, Italian,
or Spanish—makes fifteen pamphlets of three lessons each.

All members of the School have

THE PRIVILEGE.

of asking, by letter, questions concerning each lesson, or consulting
on any difficulty which may have occurred to them. All exercises
corrected and all questions answered by return post by Dr. ROSEN-
THAL or one of his assistants.

TERMS OF MEMBERSHIP.

Five Dollars is the price for membership in the school for
each language. This amount ($5.) entitles the member to receive
the fifteen books or pamphlets containing the lessons, also answers
to his questions. Return postage for the answer must accompany
the question.

State distinctly which language, or languages, you desire to study
There are *no extra charges.* The price, **Five Dollars,** pays for
one language; **Ten Dollars** for two languages, etc. All exercise
and questions must be written on a separate sheet of paper, and
must state full address of the pupil.

Remittances must be made in Post-Office Order or registered
letter addressed to

I. K. FUNK & CO.,
10 and 12 Dey Street. New York.

The Meisterschaft-System.

FRENCH.

PART V.

V.

(*Continuation.*)

22. That is very dear (*cher*).

23. That's awfully dear (*horriblement cher*).

24. Quite the contrary (*au contraire*), madam, that's very cheap.

25. Why! take this article (*cet objet-ci*); that is cheaper (*meilleur marché*).

26. Tell me your lowest price, if you please (= tell me the last [*le dernier*] price, if you please).

27. I do not like to bargain with people (= I do not like to bargain [*à marchander*]).

28. Please, tell me your lowest price, sir, I do not like to bargain with people.

29. We have only (*ne-que*)[1] one price, madam.

30. I have only *one* price, madam.

31. I cannot give it you at a lower price (= for less [*à moins*]) I assure you (*je vous assure*), madam.

32. I can give it you cheaper (=less dear [*moins cher*]), but not in the same (*même*) quality (*qualité*).

33. Can't you give it to me any cheaper (*moins cher*), sir?

34. I can get it (*procurer*) cheaper somewhere else (*ailleurs*).

35. I beg your pardon, madam, you are mistaken (*vous*

---

1) *Only* is often expressed by **ne-que**. The construction is the same as *ne-pas*.

V.

(Continuation.)

22. C'est bien cher (*say byaing shayr*).
23. C'est⌢horriblement cher (*say tor-rēē-blĕ-māng shayr*).
24. Au contraire, madame, c'est très bon marché.

25. Prenez donc (*prĕ-nēh dong*) cet⌢objet-ci, c'est meilleur marché (*sĕ tob-jēh sēē, say mĕ-yeūr mar-shay*).
26. Dites-moi le dernier prix, s'il vous plaît (*or* je vous prie = *dēēt m'wo͆āh lē dĕr-nyēh prēē jĕ voū prēē*).
27. Je n'aime pas à marchander (*jĕ naym pāh āh mār-shāng-dēh*).
28. Dites-moi le dernier prix, s'il vous plaît, monsieur; je n'aime pas à marchander.
29. Nous *n'*avons *qu'*un² prix, madame (*noū nā-vong keūng prēē mā-dām*).
30. Je n'ai qu'un prix (*je nay keūng prēē*), madame.
31. Je ne puis (*pu͡-ēē*) vous le donner à moins (*mo͡-aing*) je vous⌢assure (*jĕ voū zăs-sür*), madame.
32. Je peux vous le donner moins cher; mais cela ne sera pas la même (*maym*) qualité (*kă-lēē-tay*).
33. Ne pouvez-vous pas me le donner moins cher, monsieur?
34. Je peux me le procurer (*prō-cü-ray*) ailleurs (*ăh-yeūr*) à meilleur marché (*āh mĕ-yeūr mār-shay*).
35. Pardon (*pār-dŏng*), madame, vous vous trompez

vous trompez) ; you will surely (= at least [*du moins*]) get an inferior (*inférieure*) quality.

36. How can you ask me to let you have it (*que je vous le laisse*) at this price?

37. I cannot sell with loss (*à perte*). (*Pourtant* means yet, however, nevertheless, and cannot be rendered into English in this phrase.)

38. I assure you, I give it you at cost-price (*au prix coûtant*).

39. Tell me your lowest (*le juste*) price, please.

40. I assure you, sir, that is the very lowest (*c'est tout au juste*, idiomatic French expression).

41. Is that your lowest price?

42. I cannot give it you any cheaper (*à moins*). I never ask too much (= overcharge [*je ne surfais jamais*]). That is a fixed price.

43. Did you sell your horse?

44. For how much did you sell it?

45. This book sells (*se vend*) very well.

46. I should like to have a bonnet of white satin (*satin blanc*) trimmed (*garni*) with lace (*dentelles*).

47. Try (*essayez*) this one, if you please, madam; it is very becoming to you (*il vous va* or *fait très-bien*), I assure you.

48. Do you think so? Well, to speak frankly (*franchement*), I am of the same (= of your) opinion (*avis*).

49. This hat is exceedingly (*à merveille*) becoming to you.

50. This dress does not fit you.

(*trong-pay*); du moins vous‿aurez une qualité inférieure (*dü mŏ-āing· voū zō-rēh ŭn kā-lēē-tay aing-fay-
ryeŭr*).

36. Comment pouvez-vous demander que je vous le laisse
(*layss*) à ce prix ?

37. Je ne peux pourtant (*tāng*) pas vendre à perte (*vāng-
dr rā pĕrt*).

38. Je vous‿assure, je vous le donne au prix coûtant
(*jĕ voū zā-sür jĕ voū lĕ dŏn oh prēē coū-tāng*).

39. Dites-moi le juste prix (*lĕ jŭst prēē*), je vous prie.

40. Monsieur, je vous‿assure, que c'est tout‿au juste
(*kĕ say toūt tōh jŭst*).

41. Est-ce là votre dernier prix (*dĕr-nyēh prēē*) ?

42. Je ne puis vous le donner à moins. Je ne vous surfais (*sür-fay*) pas. C'est‿un prix fixe (*say teūng
prēē. fix*).

43. Avez-vous vendu (*vāng-dü*) votre cheval (*shĕ-vàhl*) ?

44. Combien (*or* à quel prix) l'avez-vous vendu ?

45. Ce livre se vend très-bien.

46. Je voudrais‿avoir un chapeau de satin blanc (*să-
taing blāng*) garni de dentelles (*garnēē dĕ dāng-tell*).

47. Essayez-le (*es-say-yēh lĕ*), s'il vous plaît, madame. Je
vous‿assure, qu'il vous va (*or* fait) très-bien.

48. Vous trouvez ? Eh bien ! Franchement (*frāng-shĕ-
māng*) je suis de votre‿avis (*vot-rāh-vēē*).

49. Ce chapeau vous va à *merveille* (*āh mer-vĕ-yĕ*).

50. Cette robe ne vous fait pas.

2.

FOUNDATION SENTENCE.

For instance, here is a ball-dress which I have

just bought for less than fifty francs.

Through

example ; pattern ; sample ; instance (*par exemple* means *for instance*).

here is ; there is ; there are ; behold [1]

a ball-dress [2]

which [3]

---

1) **Voici**, *here is*, and **voilà**, *there is*, are peculiarly constructed in connection with **pronouns.** The French always say for instance : *Here I am, me voilà*, or *me voici. There he is, le voilà. There they are, les voilà. Here we are, nous voilà. There we are arrived, nous voici arrivés.*

2) Why must this construction be used?

3) We have only **one relative** pronoun for **who, which** and ·that, viz., **qui.**—*Qui*, however, is always the *nominative case* and refers both to *persons* and *things* whether they are in the *singular* or the plural. For instance :

Le garçon *qui* l'a fait, est parti, the boy who has done it, is gone.

Les garçons *qui* l'ont fait, sont partis, the boys who have done it, are gone.

2.

FOUNDATION SENTENCE.

Par exemple, voici une robe de bal, que je
pār   ĕg-săngpl   voăh-sēĕ   ŭn   robe   dĕ   băhl   kĕ   jĕ

viens d'acheter pour moins de cinquante francs.
vyaing   dăsh-tay   poŭr   mŏ-aing   dĕ   saing-kăng   frăng.

Par (*pār*)

exemple (*ĕg-săng-pl*) [masc.]

voici[1] (*voăh-sēĕ*)

une robe de bal[2] (*ŭn robe de băhl*)

que[3] (*kĕ*)

Le livre *qui* est sur la table, est à mon frère, the book which is on
the table, belongs to my brother.
Les livres *qui* sont sur la table, sont à mon frère; the books which
are on the table, belong to my brother.
There is also only **one relative pronoun** for **whom, which** and
that when in *the accusative case*, viz., **que**; as:
*L'*homme *que* vous avez vu, l'a fait, the man whom you saw has
done it.
Le livre *que* vous avez lu, est à ma sœur, the book which you have
read, belongs to my sister.
Remark : The French *must* always express the relative, though
we frequently omit it in English.

I come ; I am coming[1]

from buying

I have just bought (The literal translation is : *I come from buy-ing*).

for

less

of

fifty

francs

for less than fifty francs (**Than** after a *comparative* is usually expressed by **que** ; but after **moins** and **plus** we have to use **de** when a *numeral* follows, as is the case here).

3.

1. Tell me the lowest price for (*de*) this bonnet.

2. Fifty francs, madam.

---

1) **Je viens**, *I come, I am coming,* is the *present tense* of the regulai verb *venir* of which the pupil may learn the following most impor-tant tenses :

Present.	*Imperfect.*
Je viens (*vyaing*),	Je venais (*vĕ-nay*),
tu viens (*vyaing*),	tu venais,
il vient (*vyaing*),	il venait,
nous venons (*vĕ-nong*),	nous venions (*vĕ-nyong*),
vous venez (*vĕ-nēh*),	vous veniez (*vĕ-nyĕk*),
ils viennent (*vyĕn*).	ils venaient (*vĕ-nay*).

je viens[1] (*vyaing*)

d'acheter (*dāsh-tay*)

je viens d'acheter (The English '*just, just now*' must be given by **venir de**, as : I have *just* seen, je *viens de* voir ; I have just received, *je viens de* recevoir).

pour (*poŭr*)

moins (*mo͡-aing*)

de (*dĕ*)

cinquante (*saing-kāng*)

francs (*frāng*)

pour moins de cinquante francs.

3.

1. Dites-moi le dernier prix de ce chapeau (*lĕ dĕr-nyĕh prēē dĕ sĕ shā-po*).
2. C'est cinquante francs, madame.

Future.	*Conditional.*
Je viendrai (*vyaing-drĕh*),	Je viendrais (*vyaing-dray*),
tu viendras (*vyaing-drāh*),	tu viendrais,
il viendra (*vyaing-drāh*),	il viendrait,
nous viendrons (*vyaing-drong*),	nous viendrions (*vyaing-drēē ong*),
vous viendrez (*vyaing-drĕh*),	vous viendriez (*vyaing-drēē-ĕh*),
ils viendront (*vyaing-drong*),	ils viendraient (*vyaing-dray*).

Perfect.   *Pluberfect.*

Je suis venu (*vĕ-nü*), &c.   J'étais venu (*vĕ-nü*), &c.

Imperative. **Viens** (*vyaing*), venons (*vĕ-nong*), venez (*vĕ-nĕh*).

3. You will surely let me have it for forty? (= You will pass [*vous passerez*] it me well at forty [*quarante*])?

4. No madam, that is the lowest (*c'est tout au juste*).

5. I cannot let you have it at a lower figure. I never make any overcharges (= I cannot give it you at less (*à moins*), I overcharge *never*, [*ne — jamais* [1]]).

6. I can get (*procurer*) it cheaper somewhere else (*ailleurs*).

7. You are mistaken (= you mistake yourself [*vous vous trompez*]), madam ; at least [*du moins*] you will get an inferior quality [*une qualité inférieure*]).

8. We sell at stated prices only (*ne — que*).

9. Very well (*eh bien*), let us split (= divide, *partageons*) the difference (*le différent*). I will give you forty-five (*quarante-cinq*) francs.

10. Quite impossible. We never ask too much. All our prices are marked (*sont marqués*) in plain figures (*en chiffres connus*).

11. The postman (*facteur*) has just brought a letter for you (= comes from bringing, &c.).

12. I just received this telegram and hope (*j'espère*) its contents (*contenu*) will prove satisfactory to you (= will satisfy you, *vous satisfera*).

13. My brother has just sold his furniture (*mobilier*).

---

1) **Never** is always expressed by ne - jamais ; **nothing** or **not anything** by ne - rien ; no one, not any one by ne - **personne** Ob.

3. Voụs me le passerẹz bien à quarante (*āh kāh-rāngt*)?

4. Non, madame, c'est tout au juste (*say toū toh jüst*).
5. Je ne puis vous le donner à moins. Je ne surfais jamais[1] (*jāh-may*).

6. Je peux me le procurer ailleurs à meilleur marché (*prŏ-kü-rēh āh-yeūr āh mĕ-yeūr mār-shay*).
7. Vous vous trompez (*trong-pēh*), madame; du moins vous ̂aurez une qualité inférieure (*ün kāh-lēē-tāy aing-fay-ryeūr*).
8. Nous ne vendons qu'à prix fixe (*nĕ vāng-dong kāh prēē fïx*).
9. •Eh bien, partageons le différent. Je vous donnerai quarante-cinq francs (*par-tāh-jong lĕ dif-fay-rāng. Jĕ voū dōn-nĕ-rēh kāh-rāng saing frāng*).
10. C'est ̂impossible (*taing-pōh-sēēbl*). Nous ne surfaisons jamais (*sür-fay-zong jă-may*). Tous nos prix (*prēē*) sont marqués (*mār-kay*) en chiffres connus (*āng shïfr cŏn-nü*).
11. Le facteur vient d'apporter une lettre pour vous.

12. Je viens de recevoir ce télégramme et j'espère que son contenu (*cong-tĕ-nü*) vous satisfera (*să-tïs-fĕ-răh*).

13. Mon frère vient de vendre son mobilier (*mō-bēē-yēh*).

---

serve that **ne** must be always placed before the verb (*without pas* accompanying it).

Did I tell you that he is going (*qu'il va*[1]) to live in
the country ?

14. It just struck nine. (= Nine hours come from sound-
ing).
15. Is Mrs. L. within ? No, madam, she has just gone
out.
16. Did you call on Mrs. T. ?
17. I went to her house, but did not find her. She had
just gone out (*trouvée* must be placed in the feminine, because the auxiliary is preceped by *la*).
18. I just met (*rencontrer*) Mr. A.

19. Does he get on well (*fait-il bien*) in business ?
20. Yes, his business goes very well.
21. I have my breakfast every day (= all the days, *tous
les jours*) for less than two francs.
22. If it is later than (*plus de*) five o'clock, do not go
to my physician's, for (*car*[2]) he is not at home.
23. I have bought for less than one franc some very
beautiful (*beau*) writing paper (*du papier à lettres*)
and five dozens (*douzaines*) of envelopes (*d'enveloppes*.

---

1) **Aller, to go,** is an *irregular* verb, the principal tenses of which
the student *must* know :

Present.	Imperfect.
Je vais (*vais*),·	J'allais (*jā-lay*),
tu vas (*vāh*),	tu allais,
il va (*vāh*),	il allait,
nous‿allons (*zā-long*),	nous‿allions (*zā-hong*),
vous‿allez (*zā-lēh*),	vous‿alliez (*zā-lvēh*),
ils vont (*vong*).	ils‿allaient (*zā-lay*).
Future.	Conditional.
J'irai (*jēē-rēh*).	J'irais (*jēē-rai*),
tu iras (*tū ēē-rāh*),	tu irais (*ēē-ray*),

Vous⁀ai-je dit qu'il *va*¹ demeurer à la campagne (*kāng-pān-yĕ*)?

14. Neuf⁀heures viennent (*vyĕn*) de sonner.

15. Madame L. est⁀elle chez⁀elle? Non Madame, elle vient de sortir (*sor-teer*).

16. Avez-vous⁀été voir Madame T. (*tay*)?

17. Je suis⁀allé chez⁀elle, mais je ne l'ai pas trouvée. Elle venait (*vĕ-nay*) de sortir.

18. Je viens de rencontrer (*rāng-cong-tray*)˙ monsieur A. (*āh*).

19. Fait⁀il bien ses⁀affaires?

20. Oui, son commerce va très-bien.

21. J'ai tous les jours (*toū lay joūr*) mon déjeuner pour moins de deux francs.

22. S'il est plus de cinq‿heures, *n'allez pas* chez mon médecin, *car*² il n'est pas chez lui.

23. J'ai acheté pour moins d'un franc (*deūng frang*) du papier à lettres très-beau et cinq douzaines d'enveloppes (*dü pāp-yĕh āh lett tray boh ay saing doū-zayn dāng-vĕ-lŏp*).

Future.	*Conditional.*
il ira (*ēēl ēē-rāh*),	il irait (*ēē-ray*),
nous‿irons (*zēē-rong*),	nous⁀irions (*zēē ryong*),
vous‿irez (*zēē-rēh*),	vous⁀iriez (*zēē-ryēh*),
ils‿iront (*zēē-rong*),	ils⁀iraient (*zēē-ray*).
Perfect.	*Pluperfect.*
Je suis⁀allé. &c.	J'étais⁀allé. &c.

Imperative. Va (*vāh*), go (thou), allons (*ā-long*) let us go, allez (*ā-lay*), go (you).

2) The student must distinguish between *for* as *preposition=pour*, and *for* as *conjunction* of *cause* or *reason=car*.

GRAMMATICAL REMARKS.

A.

Remarks on the Orthography of some verbs of the first conjugation.[1]

Some regular verbs ending in **er** are, for the sake of euphony, liable to the following modifications:

1. Some verbs ending in **ter** as: jeter, to throw; re-jeter, to throw back; and verbs ending in **eler,** as: appeler, to call; renouveler, to renew etc., double the **t** or **l**, when they are followed by an **e** *mute.* This is the case in some persons of the Present, Future and Imperative, viz:

Pres. Je je*tt*e, tu je*tt*es, il je*tt*e, nous jetons, vous jetez, ils je*tt*ent.

Imper. Je*tt*e, Pl. jetons, jetez.

Fut. Je je*tt*erai, tu je*tt*eras, &c.

Pres. J'appe*ll*e, tu appe*ll*es, il appe*ll*e, nous appelons, vous appelez, ils appe*ll*ent.

Imper. Appe*ll*e, Pl. appelons, appelez.

Fut. J'appe*ll*erai, tu appe*ll*eras, &c.

N.B. The verb **acheter,** *to buy,* is not conjugated in this manner; it never doubles the **t**, but takes the grave accent **è**:

Pres. J'achète, tu achètes, il achète, nous achetons, vous achetez, ils achètent (*ă-shayt*).

Fut. J'achèterai.

Imper. Achète, Pl. achetez.

---

1) These remarks on orthography may be studied later.

2. Verbs of two syllabes ending in **eler,** as : geler to freeze, and all others that have an **e** *mute* in the last syllable but one, such as :

> Semer, to sow ; mener, to lead ; lever, to lift up,

take the grave accent **è,** when followed by an **e** *mute.* Ex. :

> *Infinitive :* **Mener,** to lead.

Pres. Je mène, tu mènes, il mène, nous menons, vous menez, ils mènent.

Imperf. Je menais, tu menais, &c.

Fut. Je mènerai, tu mèneras, &c.

Imper. mène, menons, menez

The same change takes place with those verbs which have on the last syllable but one the *accent aigu*=**é.** They, however, retain the **é** in the Future and Conditional. Ex.:

> *Infinitive :* **Espérer,** to hope.

Pres. ''espère, tu espères, il espère, nous⌢espérons, vous⌢espérez, ils⌢espèrent.

Imperf. J'espérais.

Imper. Espère, espérons, espérez.

Fut. J'espérerai.

Such are: préférer, to prefer; posséder, to possess, &c.

3. In verbs ending in **ger,** as: juger (*jü-jêh*), to judge; partager (*pār-tāh-jêh*), to share or divide, the **e** is retained in those tenses where **g** is followed by the vowels **a** or **o,** in order to give the **g** the same soft sound as in all other tenses and persons. Ex. :

> *Infinitive :* **Manger** (*māng-jay*), to eat.

Pres. Je mange (*māng-sh*), — *Plur.* nous mangeons (*māng-jong*).

Part. pr. Mangeant (*māng-jāng*).

Imperf. Je mangeais (*māng-jay*), tu mangeais, il mangeait, nous mangions, vous mangiez, ils mangeaient.

Pret. Je mangeai (*māng jay*), tu mangeas, il mangea, nous mangeâmes, vous mangeâtes, ils mangèrent.

Imper. Mangeons.

Part. past. Mangé (*māng-jay*).

4. In verbs ending in **cer,** as : commencer, to begin, a cedille must be placed under the **c,** when this letter is followed by **a** or **o.** Ex.:

Infinitive : **Placer** (*plāh-sēh*), to place.

Pres. Je place (*plāhs*), tu places, &c. —*pl.* nous plaçons (*plāh-song*), &c.

Imperf. Je plaçais (*plāh-say*), tu plaçais, il plaçait, nous placions, vous placiez, ils plaçaient (*plāh-say*).

mper. Plaçons (*plāh-song*), &c.

Pret. Je plaçai, tu plaças, il plaça, nous plaçâmes (*plāh-sāhm*), &c.

Part. pr. Plaçant (*plāh-sāng*).

Part. passé, Placé.

5. Verbs ending in *ayer, oyer, uyer* change the *y* into *i,* whenever the letter *y* is immediately followed by an *e mute.* Such are :

Payer (*pay-yēh*), to pay; employer (*āng-ploāh-yēh*), to employ ;

effrayer (*ĕf-fray-yēh*), to frighten ; essuyer (*ĕs-s'wēē-yēh*), to wipe.

Pres. Je paie (*pay*), tu paies, il paie, *pl.* nous payons, vous payez, ils paient (*pay*).

Part. pres. Payant (*pay-yāng*).

Part. passé. Payé.

Pres. J'emploie (*jāng ploāh*), tu emploies, il emploie, *pl.* nous employons, vous employez (*vou zāng-ploāh-yēh*), ils emploient.

Part. pres. employant.

Pres. J'essuie (*jes-s'wee*), tu essuies, &c. — *pl.* ils essuient.

Imperf. Je payais, &c. — *pl.* nous payions, vous payiez, &c.

J'employais, &c. — *pl.* nous emploíons, &c.

J'essuyais, &c. — *pl.* nous essuyions, &c.

Fut. Je paierai, &c. ; j'emploierai, etc. ; j'essuierai, &c.

Imper. Paie — payez. Emploie — employez. Essuie — essuyez.

6. Verbs which in the Infinitive end in *ier*, as : prier (*prēē-ēh*), to pray ; crier (*krēē-ēh*), to cry, are in some cases spelt with double *ii.* This happens in the 1st and 2nd persons plural of the Imperfect of the Indicative, and of the Present of the Subjunctive. Ex. :

Infinitive : **Oublier** (*oū-blēē-ēh*), to forget.

Ind. Imperf. pl. Nous oubliions, vous oubliiez, ils oubliaient.

Subj. Pres. pl. Que nous priions, que vous priiez, &c.

B.

Formation of the Plural of Nouns.

The plural of nouns is generally formed, as in English, by adding **s** to the singular. *This **s** is not sounded.*

Singular.	Plural.		
Ex. : l'homme,	les hommes,	the man,	the men.
le livre,	les livres,	the book,	the books.
la personne,	les personnes,	the person,	the persons.
la banque,	les banques,	the bank,	the banks.

Exceptions :

1. Nouns ending in *s, x,* or *z* remain *unchanged* in the plural.

Singular.	Plural.		
Ex. : le fils,	les fils,	the son,	the sons.
le pas,	les pas,	the step,	the steps.
la noix (*n'woāh*)	les noix,	the nut,	the nuts.

2. Nouns ending in *au* or *eu* take *x* in the plural.

Singular.   *Plural.*

Ex.: le tableau (*tāh-blō*), les tableaux, the picture, the pictures.

le bateau (*bāh-tō*), les bateaux, the boat, the boats.

le feu (*feŭ*), les feux, the fire, the fires.

3. The greater part of the nouns ending in *al* or *ail* form their plural in **aux** (*ōh*).

Singular.   *Plural.*

Ex.: le cheval (*shĕ-vāhl*), les chevaux (*shĕ-vōh*), the horse, the horses.

'animal, (*lā-nĕĕ-māhl*), les animaux (*lay-zā-nĕĕ-mōh*), the animal, the animals.

le travail (*trā-vāy*), les travaux (*trā-vōh*), the work, the works.

4. Most nouns ending in *ou* take **s** in the plural, *except the following, which take* **x** :

Singular.   *Plural.*

Ex.: le bijou (*bĕĕ-joŭ*), les bijoux, the jewel, the jewels.

le genou (*jĕ-noŭ*), les genoux, the knee, the knees.

le chou (*shoŭ*), les choux, the cabbage, the cabbages.

5. The following *plurals* are **irregular:**

Singular.   *Plural.*

Ex.: le ciel (*syĕl*), les cieux (*syeŭ*), the heaven.[1]

l'oeil (*leŭyĕ*), les yeux (*lay zyeŭ*), the eye.

l'aïeul (*lā-yeŭl*), les aïeux (*lay zā-yeŭ*), the ancestor.

C.

The Partitive Article.

Such expressions as: 'Give me *some* wine.'— 'Have you *any* books?' — 'Bring me *some* eggs'— etc., are

---

1) *Ciel* forms also a regular plural with another signification, viz., *les ciels* = skies 'n a picture), or = the heads, or testers (of a bed).

rendered in French by the so-called *partitive article.* 'Donnez-moi *du* vin.'— 'Avez-vous *des* livres?'— Apportez-moi *des* oeufs.'

Now the *partitive article* is really the *genitive of the definite article,* as for instance: *du* vin, some wine; *de l'*eau, some water; *de la* bière, some beer; *des* magasins, some stores (*or* simply 'stores').[1]

Compare our *Sentence III.* and the remarks on the partitive article: 'Dites au garçon de m'apporter *des* tartines de beurre et *des* oeufs à la coque.'

In *questions,* the English use *any* instead of some, but in French this must always be rendered by the *partitive article,* as: "Have you *any* bread? Avez-vous *du* pain?"— "Has he bought *any* handkerchiefs? A-t-il acheté *des* mouchoirs?" — Has he made *any* purchases? A-t-il fait *des* emplettes?"

Important Remarks on the use of the partitive article.

1. Sometimes (but not often) the *adjective precedes the French noun. In such cases the partitive article is expressed simply by* **de**; as:

> Good bread (*or* some [any] good bread), de bon pain)[2].
> Bad coffee (*or* some [any] bad coffee), de mauvais café.
> Beautiful flowers (*or* some [any] fine flowers), de belles fleurs.

2. In the same manner **de** is used when a *negative* occurs in a French sentence.

---

1) *Some* is not always used in English, but in French we must employ the partitive article, whenever we imply that we mean *some part* or *parts* of a *totality.*

2) We have already seen that in French *the adjective* is usually placed *after the noun* so that the above rule holds good but in few cases.

Examples.

I do **not** drink (bois) wine,	Je ne bois (*b'woãh*) pas **de** vin.
I drink **no** water,	Je ne bois pas d'eau.
I have **no** change,	Je n'ai pas **de** monnaie.
I have **no** money,	Je n'ai pas d'argent (*dār-jāng*).

3. **De** is used after nouns expressing *measure*, *weight*, *quantity* or *number* where *of* is used in English.

Examples.

une bouteille **de** vin (*ün boū-tĕ-yĕ dĕ vaing*),	a bottle of wine.
une tasse de café,	a cup of coffee.
une paire de bas (*ün pair dĕ bāh*),	a pair of stockings.

4. **De** must be employed after the following *adverbs of quantity :*

Assez (*ā-say*), enough.

beaucoup (*bō-koū*), much, many, a great many, a great deal.

combien (*kong-byaing*), how much, how many.

peu (*peū*), little, few.

plus (*plü*), more.

moins (*mo-aing*), less.

rien, nothing.

quelque chose (*kel-kĕ shohs*) some-thing.

trop (*trōh*), too much, too many.

trop peu (*trōh peü*), too little, too few.

tant (*tāng*), so much, so many.

autant (*ōh-tāng*), as much, as many.

Examples.

Je n'ai pas assez d'argent sur moi (*pāh zās-say dār-jāng sür m'woãh*).

I have not *money enough* with me (= enough *of* money).

J'ai vu *beaucoup de* personnes,

I have seen *a great many* persons (= many *of* persons).

Combien d'échantillons avez-vous reçu (*kong-byaing day-shāng-tēĕ-yong a-vĕh voū rĕ-sü*) ?

How many patterns have you received (= how many *of* patterns)?

Il a lu *peu de* livres.

He has read *few* books (= few *of* books).

Vous avez fait *trop de* fautes (*foht*).	You have made *too many* mistakes (=too many *of* mistakes).
Apportéz-moi *plus d'*eau chaúde, garçon.	Waitér, bring me *more hot water* (= more *of* hot water).

5. **De** is used in' the place of our *English adjective describing a material*, as : .

Une bague *d'*or (*ün bā̆g dōr*), a gold ring.
Une cuillier *d'*argent (*ün k'wēē-yēh dār-jāng*), a silver spoon.
Une robe *de* soie, a silk dress.
Un chapeau *de* velours (*eūng shā-pŏh dĕ vĕ-loūr*), a velvet bonnet.
Une table *de* bois (*ün tāhbl dĕ b'woāh*), a wooden table.

N.B.—After numerals *no article at all* is used ; the same as in English :

Deux‿enfants (*deū sāng-fāng*), two children.
Dix‿écoliers (*dēĕ zay-kō-lyēh*), ten pupils.
Vingt francs (*vaing frāng*), twenty francs.

The most important Verbs of the first Conjugation :

parler (*pār-lēh*), to speak, to say.

causer (*kō-zēh*), to chat.

raconter (*rā-kóng-tēh*), to tell, to narrate.

affirmer (*af-fĭr-mēh*) to affirm.

nier (*nēē-ēh*), to deny.

demander (*dĕ-māng-dēh*), to ask.

répliquer, (*ray-plēē-kēh*), to reply, to answer.

prouver (*proū-vēh*),to prove.

approuver (*āp-proū-vēh*), to approve.

assurer (*ăs-sü-rēh*),to assure.

douter, (*doū-tēh*), to doubt.

1épéter (*ray-pay-tēh*), to repeat.

déclarer (*day-clā-rēh*), to declare.

penser (*pāng-sēh*), to think.

considérer (*cong-sēē-day-rēh*), to consider.

avouer (*ă-voŭ-ēh*), to avow, to acknowledge.

objecter (*ob-jĕk-tēh*), to object.

refuser (*rĕ-fü-zēh*), to refuse.

accorder (*ac-cor-dēh*), to accord.

expliquer (*ex-plēē-kēh*), to explain.

réciter (*ray-sēē-tēh*), to recite.

ignorer (*ĭn-yŏ-rēh*), to ignore, to be ignorant of.

oublier (*oŭ-blēē-ēh*), to forget.

deviner, (*dĕ-vēē-nēh*), to divine, to guess.

louer (*loŭ-ēh*), to praise, to let, to hire (dwellings).

admirer (*ād-mēē-rēh*), to admire.

blâmer (*blāh-mēh*), to blame.

imiter (*ēē-mēē-tēh*), to imitate.

enseigner (*āng-sĕn-yēh*), to teach, to instruct.

éviter (*ay-vēē-tēh*), to avoid.

reprocher (*rĕ-prŏ-shēh*), to reproach.

crier (*krēē-ēh*), to cry, to scream.

disputer (*dĭs-pü-tēh*), to dispute.

persuader (*pĕr-sü-ā-dēh*), to persuade.

aimer (*ay-mēh*), to love, to like.

caresser (*cā-rĕs-sēh*), to caress.

flatter (*flāt-tēh*), to flatter.

embrasser (*āng-brās-sēh*), to embrace.

mépriser (*may-prēē-zēh*), to despise.

dédaigner (*day-dĕn-yēh*), to disdain.

offenser (*of-fāng-sēh*), to offend.

insulter (*aing-sül-tēh*), to insult.

quereller (*kĕ-rĕl-lēh*), to quarrel.

braver (*brā-vēh*), to brave.

céler (*say-lĕh*), to conceal.

jurer (*jü-rēh*), to swear, to take an oath.

apaiser (*ā-pay-zēh*), to appease.

baiser (*bay-zĕh*), to kiss.

espérer (*ĕs-pay-rēh*), to hope.

donner (*don-nĕh*), to give.

honorer (*ŏ-nŏ-rēh*), to honor.

désirer (*day-zēē-rēh*), to desire.
souhaiter (*soū-ay-tēh*), to
wish.

remercier (*rĕ-mĕr-syēh*), to
thank.
estimer (*ĕs-tēē-mēh*), to esteem.

Translate the following

Exercise

into French, and then again, without assistance of the
book, into English:

What o'clock is it?—It is half-past seven.—Do you
know what o'clock it is?—I do not know (*je ne sais*) what
o'clock it is. I forgot to wind up (*remonter*) my watch;
it (*elle*) has stopped (*s'est arrêtée*).—Have you a time-table
(=the hours of departure, *les heures du départ*)? Please
see at what o'clock the first train leaves (*part*).—Did you
write to him?—Why did you not write to them?—Why
did you not write to him to send us another (*une autre*)
set (*collection*) of samples (*d'échantillons*, day-shāng-tēē-
yong)?—Why did you not write to them that we have
refused (*refusé*) the draft (*la traite*)?—Have the kindness
(*ayez la bonté*) to give us some information (*des renseignements*, rāng-sĕn-yĕ-māng) about (*sur*) Mr. B.—I take the
liberty (*je prends* [prāng] *la liberté*) to recommend (*recommander*, rĕ-com-māng-dēh) him to you.—Does Mr. N. live
here?—Yes sir, but master (*monsieur*) is not to be seen
now; he is very busy (*très-occupé*) at present (*à présent*, āh
pray-zāng). Will you please give him my card (*ma carte*)?

Translate the following

Exercise.

Buying some Cloth.

1) I should like to buy some cloth. — 2) I should like to buy some good cloth. — 3) Will you be kind enough (*donnez-vous la peine*=donnēh voū lā pain) to pass to the rear (*au fond*=oh fong) of the store, sir? — 4) Will you please show (*montrer*=mong-trēh) some cloth to the gentleman? — 5) What (*quelle*) sort of cloth do you wish, sir? — 6) Have you any samples (*or* patterns)? — 7) Yes, sir, here are (*voici*) samples of all the pieces of cloth (*de tous les draps*) which we have in stock. — 8) What is the price of this (*celui-ci*)? — 9) It costs twenty-five francs a metre (*le mètre*=maytr). — 10) That (*ça*=sāh) seems rather dear to me. — 11) I beg your pardon (*pardonnez-moi*), sir, that (*ce*) is not dear for this (*cette*) quality. Feel (*tâtez*), if you please, how fine it is (=how [*comme*] it is fine= *fin*, faing).—12) And that one (*celui-là*), what do you charge for that (=of what price is it)? — 13) The blue (*ce bleu-là* =sĕ bleū lāh)? I could not (*je ne pourrais*=jĕ nĕ poūr-ray) give it to you for (*à*) less than thirty (*trente*=trāngt) francs. — 14) That is very dear; it does not seem to me finer (*plus fin*=plü faing) than (*que*) the other. — 15) You are right, sir; it is similar (*semblable*=sāng-blā-bl) in (*pour*) quality (=*the* quality); but blue (=*the* blue) is always a little dearer (*plus cher*) than other colors (=*the* other colors, *couleurs*).

THE

𝕸𝖊𝖎𝖘𝖙𝖊𝖗𝖘𝖈𝖍𝖆𝖋𝖙 𝕾𝖞𝖘𝖙𝖊𝖒.

A SIMPLE AND PRACTICAL METHOD,

ENABLING

ANY ONE TO LEARN, WITH SLIGHT EFFORT, TO SPEAK
FLUENTLY AND CORRECTLY

𝕱𝖗𝖊𝖓𝖈𝖍, 𝕲𝖊𝖗𝖒𝖆𝖓, 𝕾𝖕𝖆𝖓𝖎𝖘𝖍, 𝖆𝖓𝖉 𝕴𝖙𝖆𝖑𝖎𝖆𝖓.

BY
DR. RICHARD S. ROSENTHAL,

*Late Director of the "Akademie für fremde Sprachen" in Berlin and Leipzig,
of the "Meisterschaft College" in London, and Principal of the
"Meisterschaft School of Practical Linguistry" in New York.*

FRENCH.

IN FIFTEEN-PARTS, EACH CONTAINING THREE LESSONS.

PART VI.

NEW YORK:
I. K. FUNK & CO., PUBLISHERS,
10 AND 12 DEY STREET.

TERMS.

WE have arranged with Dr. ROSENTHAL, the author of the "Meisterschaft System," for its introduction in America under his own supervision, and he has opened

The Meisterschaft School of Practical Linguistry

FOR NON-RESIDENTS.

The student does not need to leave his home. The lessons of each language are prepared by the Professor, and printed and sent in pamphlet shape to each member of the School wherever he may reside.

The course of study for each language—German, French, Italian, or Spanish—makes fifteen pamphlets of three lessons each.

All members of the School have

THE PRIVILEGE

of asking, by letter, questions concerning each lesson, or consulting on any difficulty which may have occurred to them. All exercises corrected and all questions answered by return post by Dr. ROSENTHAL or one of his assistants.

TERMS OF MEMBERSHIP.

Five Dollars is the price for membership in the school for each language. This amount ($5.) entitles the member to receive the fifteen books or pamphlets containing the lessons, also answers to his questions. Return postage for the answer must accompany the question.

State distinctly which language, or languages, you desire to study There are *no extra charges*. The price, **Five Dollars,** pays for one language ; **Ten Dollars** for two languages, etc. All exercise. and questions must be written on a separate sheet of paper, and must state full address of the pupil.

Remittances must be made in Post-Office Order or registered letter addressed to

I. K. FUNK & CO,
10 and 12 Dey Street, New York.

The Meisterschaft-System.

FRENCH.

PART VI.

VI.

(Continuation.)

24. For less than a franc I bought in a large (*grand*) Vienna store (*un magasin de Vienne*), where every thing is sold (*se vend*[1]) very cheap, a quire (= a hand, *une main*) of this English paper, some excellent steel-pens (*des plumes métalliques*) and six dozens of envelopes.

25. You wish (*or* want) a silk dress, madam? Will you please step up (*monter*) to the '*entre-sol*'?

26. Have you received any beautiful novelties (*nouveautés*)?

27. I can suit your taste (*or* serve you to your taste). We have just received a very large assortment (*assortiment*).

28. I do not like this shade (*nuance*) very much. I want something darker (*plus foncé*, i.e. with a deeper, richer color).

29. You have there (*là*) some brocaded silk (*de la soie moirée*). Please let me see it (*voyons-la*).

30. Here you are, madam. We have the same quality with a large satin stripe (*à large raie satinée*).

31. It is the most beautiful thing you can see.

---

1. The *passive voice* is often expressed by the *active with se*.

VI.

(Continuation.)

24. J'ai acheté pour moins d'un franc dans un grand magasin de Vienne où tout *se vend*[1] très-bon marché, une main (*ün maing*) de ce papier anglais, des plumes métalliques excellentes (*day plüm may-tā-lēēk zĕg-sĕl-lāngt*) et six (*sēē*) douzaines d'enveloppes (*doū-zayn dāng-vĕ-lŏp*).

25. C'est une robe de soie que vous désirez (*day-zee-ray*), madame? Veuillez monter à l'entre-sol (*lāng-tr-sŏl*)? [The *entre-sol* is an apartment between the ground-floor and the first story.]

26. Avez-vous reçu de belles nouveautés (*noū-voh-tay*)?

27. Je puis vous servir (*sĕr-vēēr*) à votre goût. Nous venons de recevoir un très-grand assortiment (*tās-sor-tēē-māng*).

28. Cette nuance (*nü-āngs*) ne me plaît pas trop. Je désire quelque chose de plus foncé (*fong-say*).

29. Vous avez là de la soie moirée (*m'woāh-ray*). Voyons-la (*voāh-yong lāh*), s'il vous plaît.

30. Voici, madame. Nous avons la même qualité à large raie satinée (*ray să-tēē-nay*).

31. C'est tout ce qu'on peut voir de plus beau. [Idiomatic phrase which is used very frequently.]

32. Is this Lyons-silk?

33. Certainly (*certainement*), madam. It would be impossible to find similar goods (*pareille marchandise*)
among (*dans*) English products (*les produits d'Angleterre*).

34. Will you please give me your address and I will
send the package (*le paquet*).

35. I should like to have some writing- (*or* note) paper
(*papier à lettres*), sir.

36. You wish small-sized paper (*petit format*), madam?

37. How do you sell the quire (*la main*) of this English
paper?

38. We sell a great deal (*beaucoup*) of this paper to a
number (*or* several, *plusieurs*) of offices.

39. Show me some good steel-pens (*plumes métalliques*).

40. How do you sell the gross (*la grosse*) by the box?

41. I should like to see (= to have) some linen (*de la
toile*) for shirts.

42. Do you want something nice (*or* beautiful)?

43. Of the best quality.

44. Here is some Dutch linen (*de la toile de Hollande*)
which is excellent.

45. How do you sell it?

46. Four francs a metre.

47. A dozen would cost me (*me reviendra*) therefore
(*ainsi*)?

48. You will (*surely*) make me a reduction (*une diminution*) on the price.

32. Est-ce là de la soie de Lyon (*lēē-ong*) ?

33. Certainement (*sēr-tain'-mǎng*) madame; il serait⌢impossible (*taing-pos-sēēbl*) de trouver pareille marchandise (*pā-rě-yě mār-shǎng-deeze*) dans les produits d'Angleterre (*prō-dwēēt dāng-lět-tayr*).

34. Veuillez me donner votre⌢adresse et je vous⌢enverrai le paquet (*je voū zāng-vĕr-rēh lē pǎ-kay*).

35. Je voudrais⌢avoir du papier (*pā-pyēh*) à lettres, monsieur.

36. Est-ce petit format (*formāh*) que vous désirez, madame?

37. Combien vendez-vous (*vāng-day-voū*) la main (*maing*) de ce papier anglais?

38. Nous vendons beaucoup de ce papier à plusieurs (*plü-z'yeūr*) bureaux (*bü-roh*).

39. Montrez-moi de bonnes plumes métalliques (*māytā-lēēk*).

40. Combien vendez-vous la grosse en boîte (*āng b'woāt*) ?

41. Je voudrais⌢avoir de la toile pour chemises (*twoǎhl poūr shě-mēēze*).

42. Voulez-vous quelque chose de beau (*bō*)?

43. De la meilleure qualité (*mě-yēur kā-lēē-tay*).

44. Voici de la toile de Hollande qui est⌢excellente (*tĕg-sěl-lǎngt*).

45. Combien la vendez-vous?

46. Quatre francs le mètre (*mayt'r*).

47. Ainsi la douzaine me reviendra (*aing-sēē lā doū-zayn mě rě-vyaing-drā*) ?

48. Vous me ferez bien une diminution (*dēē-mēē-nü-syong*) sur ce prix (*prēē*).

2.

Terms of politeness.[1]

A. Terms of asking.

1. May I ask (*or* beg) you to tell me....?

2. May I ask a favor of you ?

3. I have to make a request of you.
4. Be so kind (*or* Have the kindness) to tell me....
5. I have to ask you for a favor.
6. Would you be so kind as to do me a service ?

7. If I were not afraid of troubling you (*d'être indiscret*) I would beg you to....

8. Would you have the kindness to....?

9. Would you be so kind as to grant me (*de m'accor-der*) a moment's conversation (*or* interview) ?

10. If it were convenient to you to....
11. Do me this favor.
12. I beg (you) for it.
13. You would greatly oblige me if....

---

1) These phrases will be found very useful in every day conversation. I have often observed that foreigners are at a loss how to express themselves gracefully and naturally, not knowing how to make use of the words they really have mastered, and I beg that stu-

2.

Formules de politesse.[1]

A.· Formules de demande (for-mül dĕ dĕ-mängd).

1. Puis-je vous demander (*or* prier = *prēē-ēh*) de me dire (*dēēr*)....?
2. Pourrais-je vous demander une faveur (*dĕ-mäng-dēh ün fā-veūr*)?
3. J'ai une prière (*prēē-air*) à vous faire.
4. Ayez la bonté (*ay-yēh lā bong-tay*) de me dire....
5. J'ai une grâce à vous demander.
6. Voudriez-vous me rendre un service (*räng-dr eūng sĕr-vēēs*)?
7. Si je ne craignais pas (*crĕn-yay päh*) d'être indiscret (*aing-dis-cray*), je vous prierais de (*jē voū-prēē-ĕ-rĕh dĕ*)....
8. { Auriez-vous la bonté de....?
   { Auriez-vous l'obligeance de....?
9. Auriez-vous la bonté de m'accorder un moment d'entretien (*mo-mäng däng-tr'-tyaing*) (*or* un moment d'audience [*do-dyängs*])?
10. S'il vous convenait de....
11. Faites-moi ce plaisir.
12. Je vous en prie (*jĕ voū zäng prēē*).
13. Vous m'obligeriez (*mo-blēē-jĕ-ryēh*) beaucoup (*or* infiniment [*aing-fēē-nēē-mäng*]) si....

---

dents will study these phrases very thoroughly, as they are continually used in polite society, and serve to introduce various requests and statements. Similiar phrases will be given in the succeeding parts.

14. Count on (*sur*) my gratitude.

15. I should be very grateful (*reconnaissant*) to you if..
16. Would you please repeat what you were saying?
17. I beg your pardon, sir?
18. What was it you said, madam?
19. Please, listen to me (*écoutez-moi*).

FOUNDATION SENTENCE.

As I must leave for Germany to-night, I should

be very much obliged to you, if you were to ask

him to please send me the patterns at once, which

I selected three days ago.

1.

As I am obliged to leave for Germany to-night.

---

1) Liquid sound.
2) o-â is only one sound.

14. Comptez sur ma reconnaissance (*cong-tay sür mă rĕ-cŏ nais-săngs*).

15. Je vous serais très-reconnaissant (*rĕ-con-nai-săng*) si..

16. Veuillez répéter ce que vous‿avez dit (*dĕĕ*)?

17. Plaît-il (*play-tĕĕl*), monsieur ?

18. Vous disiez (*voŭ dĕĕ-zyĕh*), madame?

19. { Ecoutez-moi (*ay-kŏŏ-tĕh m'woāh*), s'il vous plait.
    { Daignez m'écouter (*dain-yĕh may-coŭ-tay*).

FOUNDATION SENTENCE.

Comme il faut que j'aille en Allemagne ce soir,

kŏm . ĕĕl ĭŏh · kĕ jā) ĕ [1] āng ā-lĕ-mān-yĕ . sĕ swoār[2]

je vous serais bien obligé si vous lui demandiez

jĕ voŭ sĕray byāing ob-lĕĕ-jay sĕĕ voŭ lŭ ĕĕ [3] dĕ māng-dyĕh

de m'envoyer sur-le-champ les‿échantillons que

dĕ māng-voāh-yĕh sür lĕ shāng lay zay-shāng-tĕĕ-yong kĕ

j'ai choisis il y a trois jours.

jay sh'woāh-zĕĕ ĕĕl ĕĕ ā tro-āh joŭr

1.

Comme il faut que j'aille en Allemagne ce soir.

kŏm ĕĕl fŏh kĕ jā yĕ āng ā-lĕ-mān-yĕ sĕ s'woār.

---

3) ŭ-ĕĕ is only one sound.

As

it is necessary *Présent :* il faut (*fŏh*). *Part. passé : fallu.*
Imp.: il fallait. *Futur :* il faudra (*fŏh-drāh*).
Défini : il fallu. *Prés. Subj.:* qu'il faille (*kĕĕl*
fā-yĕ).
English expressions as ' I must ; we are obliged,'
&c., must be rendered by ' il faut ' [1]).

that I may go

I go ; I am going ; (thou goest ; he goes, &c.)

I shall (*or* I will) go

that I may go (that thou mayst go, that he may go, that we may
go, that you may go, that they may go)

I must go, *or* I am obliged to leave

for (*aller* must be followed by *en* when one travels to *countries*, as :
Je vais en Angleterre)

Germany.

---

1. Mr. Daudet has gone (*or* left) ; and that is the reason why his brothers must go to France.

2. Did you not tell any one why I am obliged to go to
England ?

3. How much must I pay to the cab ?

---

1) RULE : ' il faut ' is used in the following way :
a) With the *simple infinitive :* il faut travailler (I, he, we, you,
or they) must work.
b) With *a personal conjunctive pronoun and the infinitive:* il me
faut vendre, I must sell ; il nous faut aller, we must go ; il vous faut
partir, you must leave.
c) With *que and the subjunctive mood :* Il faut que j'aille, I must
go. Il faut que le tailleur *fasse* mon habit, the tailor must make my
coat. Il faut que je *donne* ce livre à votre frère, I must give this
book to your brother.

Comme (*kŏm*)

il faut[1] (*ēĕl fōh*) (Is an irregular verb derived from the infinitive, *falloir*. It is used only in the third person singular)

que j'aille (*kĕ-jă-yĕ*) (Prés. Subjonc. of the irregular verb *aller*)

je vais (Present of aller), tu vas, il va, nous‿allons, vous‿allez, ils vont)

j'irai (*jēē-rę̄h*) (Future of aller)

que j'aille, que tu ailles, qu'il aille, que nous‿allions, que vous‿alliez, qu'ils‿aillent (*kēēl ză-yĕ*)

il faut que j'aille (*ēĕl fōh kĕ jā-yĕ*)

en (*āng*) (*aller* is followed by *à*, when one travels to *towns*, as: Je vais *à* Londres)

Allemagne (*ă-lĕ-mān-yĕ*)

---

1. Monsieur Daudet (*dō-day*) est parti; c'est pourquoi il faut que ses frères aillent en France (*ā-yĕ āng frāngs*).

2. N'avez-vous dit à personne pourquoi il faut que j'aille en Angleterre (*ăn-nāng-glĕ-tayr*)?

3. Combien faut-il que je donne[2] au cocher (*dŏn ōh cō-shay*)?

Any of these constructions may be used when the *subject* of the sentence happens to be a *pronoun* But the *third construction* only is admissible when the subject is a *noun*.

2) The pupil must now make himself familiar with the *subjunctive mood*. He ought now to learn, or rather to repeat *all* the tenses of *avoir*, *être* and *donner*. Then take *finir* (2d conjugation), and *vendre* (3d conjugation), which are given in the Grammatical Remarks of Part VI. A table giving the principal peculiarities of the French grammar accompanies the next lessons.

4. As I am obliged to go to Paris, please tell your brother to give me this address.
5. Where must I go this forenoon?
6. Tell him, if you please that he must make my coat to-day.
7. That *must* be so.
8. What must I get for dinner, madam?

9. The shoemaker must make my boots at once, as (*parce que*) I am going to leave.
10. What? You did not hear the thunder? (*Literally:* the clap [*le coup*] of thunder [*de tonnerre*])? You must sleep [*que vous dormiez* [2]] very heavily [*profondément*]).

11. Must I send the silk and velvet (*le velours*) to your house?
12. Am I obliged to pay beforehand (*d'avance*)?
13. What do you need? [*Il faut* signifies also *to need.*]
14. Waiter, give me another room. I need more air and light (*i. e.*, day-light = *jour*).
15. I need some money. .
16. How much do you need (*or* are you in need of)?
17. I need 33 (*trente-trois*) francs.
18. Did you breakfast?
19. I took (*j'ai pris*) a cup of coffee with milk.

---

1) Learn the *subjunctive mood* of the *present* of *faire* :
Que je fasse, that I may make. que nous fassions, that we may make. .
que tu fasses,   &c.   . que vous fassiez,   &c.
qu'il fasse,   &c.   qu'ils fassent,   &c.

4. Comme il faut que j'aille à Paris, dites à votre frère, je vous prie, de me donner cette adresse (*sĕt tā-drĕs*).

5. Où faut-il que j'aille ce matin ?

6. Dites-lui, s'il vous plaît, qu'il faut faire mon habit aujourd'hui (*mŏn nā-bēē ō-joūr-d'wēē*).

7. Il faut que cela soit (*s'woāh*).

8. Que faut-il *que je fasse*[1] pour le dîner (*dēē-nay*) madame ?

9. Il faut que le cordonnier *fasse*[1] mes bottes tout de suite, parce que je vais partir.

10. Comment ? Vous n'avez pas entendu (*zāng-tāng-dü* = heard) le coup de tonnerre (*coū dĕ ton-nayr* = thunder)? Il faut *que vous dormiez*[2] bien profondément (*pro-fong-day-māng* = deeply, profoundly).

11. Faut-il envoyer (*āng-voāh-yēh*) la soie et le velours (*vĕloūr*) chez vous ?

12. Faut-il payer d'avance (*dā-vāngs*) ?

13. Que vous faut-il (*kĕ voū fŏ-tēēl*) ?

14. Garçon, donnez-moi une autre chambre, il me faut plus d'air et plus de jour (*plü 'dair ay plü dĕ joūr*).

15. Il me faut de l'argent (*lārr-jāng*).

16. Combien vous faut-il ?

17. Il me faut trente-trois francs (*trāngt troāh frāng*).

18. Avez-vous déjà déjeuné ?

19. J'ai pris (*prēē*) une tasse de café au lait (*oh lay*).

---

2) The *subjunctive mood* of the *present* of *dormir*, to sleep :

Que je dorme, that I sleep.		que nous dormions, that we sleep.	
que tu dormes,	&c.	que vous dormiez,	&c.
qu'il dorme,	&c.	qu'ils dorment,	&c.

GRAMMATICAL REMARKS.

A.

Second Conjugation : Finir, to finish.[1]

INDICATIVE MOOD.

Present Tense.

SINGULAR.	PLURAL.
Je fin*is* (*fēē-nēē*), I finish.	nous fin*issons* (*fēē-nis-song*), we finish.
tu fin*is*, thou finishest.	
il fin*it*, he finishes.	vous fin*issez*, you finish.
elle fin*it*, she finishes.	ils fin*issent* (*fēē-niss*) ⎱ they elles fin*issent*. ⎰ finish.

Imperfect.

Je fin*issais* (*fēē-ni-say*), I finished.	nous fin*issions*, we finished.
tu fin*issais*, &c.	vous fin*issiez*, &c.
il fin*issait*, &c.	ils fin*issaient*(*fēē-ni-say*),&c.

Preterite.

Je fin*is* (*fēē-nēē*), I finished.	nous fin*îmes* (*fēē-nēēm*), we finished.
tu fin*is*, &c.	vous fin*îtes*, &c.
il fin*it*, &c.	ils fin*irent* (*fēē-nēēr*,) &c.

---

1) Be careful to always pronounce *finir* = *fēē-nēre* ; *je finissais* = *fēē nis-say* ; nous *finîmes* = *fēē-neme*, &c.

1st Future.

Je fin*irai* (*fēē-nēē-rēh*), I shall finish.

tu fin*iras*, &c.

il fin*ira*, &c.

nous fin*irons*, we shall finish.

vous fin*irez*, &c.

ils fin*iront*, &c.

1st Conditional.

Je fin*irais* (*fēē-nēē-ray*), I should finish.

tu fin*irais*, &c.

il fin*irait*, &c.

nous fin*irions*, we should finish.

vous fin*iriez*, &c.

ils fin*iraient*, &c.

INFINITIVE MOOD.

Fin*ir*, to finish.

de *or* à fin*ir*, to finish.

IMPERATIVE MOOD.

Fin*is*, finish.

fin*issons* (*fēē-nĭ-song*), let us finish.

fin*issez*, finish.

SUBJUNCTIVE MOOD.

Present.

Que je fin*isse* (*fēē-nĭss*), that I (may) finish.

que tu fin*isses*, &c.

qu'il fin*isse*, &c.

que nous fin*issions*, that we (may) finish.

que vous fin*issiez*, &c.

qu'ils fin*issent* (*fēē-nĭss*), &c.

Imperfect.

Que je fini*sse*, that I (might) finish.
que tu fini*sses*, &c.
qu'il fin*it*(*fēē-nēē*), &c.
que nous fin*issions*, that we (might) finish.
que vous fin*issiez*, &c.
qu'ils fin*issent* (*fēē-nĭss*), &c.

PARTICIPLES.

Present.	*Past.*
Fin*issant*, finishing.	Fini (*fēē-nēē*), *f.* finie,
en fin*issant*, by finishing, &c.	finished.

COMPOUND TENSES,

INFINITIVE MOOD.

Avoir fini (*fēē-nēē*), to have finished.

INDICATIVE MOOD.

Perfect.

J'ai fini (*fēē-nēē*), I have finished.
tu as fini, thou hast finished.
il a fini, he has finished.
nous avons fini, we have finished, &c.

Pluperfect.

J'avais fini, I had finished, &c.

Compound of the Preterite.

J'eus fini, I had finished, &c.

2d Future.

J'aurai fini, I shall have finished, &c.

2d Conditional.

J'aurais fini, }
J'eusse fini, } I should have finished, &c.

SUBJUNCTIVE MOOD.

Perfect.

Que j'aie fini, that I (may) have finished, &c.

Pluperfect.

Que j'eusse fini, that I (might) have finished, &c.

PARTICIPLES.

Ayant fini, having finished, &c.

Conjugate in the same manner: *bâtir*, to build ; *choisir*, to choose ; *remplir* (*rāng-pleer*), to fill, &c.

Remarks.

1) The verb *haïr*, to hate, loses in the *Present* and *Imperative singular* its *diæresis*. Otherwise it is quite regular and retains the two dots.
Pres. Je hais, tu hais, il hait, nous haïssons, vous haïssez, &c. *Imper.* Hais ; *Pl.* haïssons, haïssez. *Pret.* Je haïs I hated.

2) The verb *fleurir*, to flourish, has a second form for the *Imperfect tense*, Je florissais, and also a second for the *Part. present*, florissant, e, both of which are only used in a figurative sense, as : une ville florissante, a flourishing city, &c.

B.

Third Conjugation: Vendre, to sell.[1]

INDICATIVE MOOD.

Present Tense.

Je vends (*vāngd*), I sell.·   nous vendons, we sell.
tu vends, thou sellst.   vous vendez, you sell.
il vend, he sells.   ils vendent (*vāngd*), ⎱ they
elle (on)vend, she (one) sells.   elles vendent,   ⎰ sell.

Imperfect.

Je vendais (*vāng-day*), I sold.   nous vendions, we sold.
tu vendais, thou soldst.   vous vendiez, you sold.
il vendait, he sold.   ils vendaient, they sold.

Preterite.

Je vendis (*vāng-dēē*), I sold.   nous vendîmes, we sold.
tu vendis, &c.   vous vendîtes, &c.
il vendit, &c.   ils vendirent (*vāng-dēēr*), &c.

Future.

Je vendrai (*vāng-drēh*), I   nous vendrons, we
    shall sell.   shall sell.
tu vendras, &c.   vous vendrez, &c.
il vendra, &c.   ils vendront, &c.

---

1) Pronounce *vāng-dr; nous vendons = vāng-dong;* ils vendent = *vāng-d*, &c.

1st Conditional.

Je vend*rais*, (*vāng-dray*), I should sell.
tu vend*rais*, &c.
il vend*rait*, &c.

nous vend*rions*, we should sell.
vous vend*riez*, &c.
ils vend*raient*, &c.

IMPERATIVE MOOD.

Vend*s*, sell.

vend*ons*, let us sell.
vend*ez*, sell.

SUBJUNCTIVE MOOD.

Que je vend*e* (*vāngd*), that I (may) sell.
que tu vend*es*, - &c.
qu'il vend*e*, &c.
que nous vend*ions*, &c.
que vous vend*iez*, &c.
qu'ils vend*ent*, &c.

Imperfect.

Que je vend*isse* (*vāng-dĭss*), that I might sell.
que tu vend*isses*, &c.
qu'il vend*ît*, &c.
que nous vend*issions*, &c.
que vous vend*issiez*, &c.
qu'ils vend*issent*, &c.

PARTICIPLES.

Présent.
Vend*ant*, selling.
en vend*ant*, by selling.

Passé.
vend*u* (*vāng-dü*), *f.* vend*ue*,

COMPOUND TENSES.

INFINITIVE MOOD.

Avoir vendu, to have sold.

INDICATIVE MOOD.

Perfect.

J'ai vendu, I have sold.

tu as vendu, thou hast sold.

il a vendu, he has sold.

nous avons vendu, we have sold, &c.

Pluperfect.

J'avais vendu, I had sold, &c.

Preterite.

J'eus vendu, I had sold, &c.

2d Future.

J'aurai vendu, I shall have sold, &c.

2d Conditional.

J'aurais vendu,
J'eusse vendu, } I should have sold, &c.

SUBJUNCTIVE MOOD.

Perfect.

Que j'ai vendu, that I (may) have sold, &c.

Pluperfect.

Que j'eusse vendu, that I (might) have sold, &c.

PARTICIPLE.

Ayant vendu, having sold.

Conjugate after this model: perdre, to loose; attendre (*āt-tāng-dr*), to wait, to expect; répondre, to answer, &c.

The most Important Verbs of the First Conjugation.—Continued.

Traiter (*tray-tēh*), to treat.

maltraiter (*māhl-tray-tēh*), to illtreat, to abuse.

pleurer (*pleū-rēh*), to weep.

soupirer (*soū-pēē-rēh*), to moan.

consoler (*cong-sōh-lēh*), to console.

regretter (*rĕ-grĕt-tēh*), to regret.

pardonner (*pār-don-nēh*), to pardon.

excuser (*ex-cü-zēh*), to excuse.

venger (*vāng-jēh*), to revenge.

railler (*rā-yēh*), to joke, to make fun of.

toucher (*toū-shēh*), to touch.

goûter (*goū-tēh*), to taste:

regarder (*rĕ-gār-dēh*), to regard.

écouter (*ay-coū-tēh*), to listen to.

aller (*ā-lēh*), to go.

marcher (*mār-shēh*), to walk.

retourner (*rĕ-toūr-nēh*), to return.

rencontrer (*rāng-cong-trēh*), to meet, to encounter.

échapper (*ay-shāp-pēh*), to escape.

sauter (*sōh-tēh*), to jump.

tomber (*tong-bēh*), to fall.

danser (*dāng-sēh*), to dance.

jouer (*joū-ēh*), to play.

monter (*mong-tēh*), to mount, to bring up stairs; to get in.

songer (*song-jēh*), to dream.

rêver (*ray-vēh*), to dream.

manger (*māng-jēh*), to eat.

déjeuner (*day-jeū-nēh*), to breakfast.

dîner (*dēē-nēh*), to dine.

souper (*soū-pēh*), to sup.

mâcher (*māh-shēh*), to chew.

régaler (*ray-gā-leh*), to regale, to treat.

couper (*kōō-pēh*), to cut.

découper (*day-kōō pēh*), to carve, to cut up.

allumer (*ā-lü-mēh*), to light.

fumer (*fü-mēh*), to smoke.

bâiller (*bā-yēh*), to yawn.

siffler (*sïf-flēh*), to whistle.

tousser (*toūs-sēh*), to cough.

traîner (*tray-nēh*), to pull.

trembler (*trāng-blēh*), to tremble.

tirer (*tēē-rēh*), to draw, to drag.

montrer (*mong-trēh*), to show.

présenter (*pray-zāng-tēh*) to present.

accepter (*āc-cĕp-tēh*), to accept.

gâter (*gāh-tēh*), to spoil.

jeter (*jĕ-tēh*), to throw, to throw away.

ramasser (*ră-măs-sēh*), to pick up.

chercher (*shĕr-shēh*), to seek, to search.

trouver (*troū-vēh*), to find.

cacher (*că-shēh*), to hide.

nettoyer (*nĕt-t'w͡ə̄-ā-yēh*), to clean.

déchirer (*day-shēē-rēh*), to tear.

— briser (*brēē-zēh*), to pick to pieces.

porter (*por-tēh*), to carry.

apporter (*ăp-por-tēh*), to bring.

amener (*ă-mĕ-nēh*), to bring along.

mener (*mĕ-nēh*), to lead.

voyager (*vo͡ā-yā-jay*), to travel.

arriver (*ăr-rēē-vēh*), to arrive.

sonner (*sŏn-nēh*) to strike (of the clock), to ring (the bell).

entrer (*āng-trēh*), to enter.

fermer (*fĕr-mēh*), to lock.

marchander (*măr-shāng-dēh*) to bargain.

commander (*cōm-māng-dēh*), to order, to command.

envoyer (*āng-vo͡āh-yēh*), to send, to forward.

renvoyer (*rāng-vo͡āh-yēh*) to send back.

dédommager (*day-dom-māh-jay*), to idemnify.

acheter (*āsh-tēh*), to buy.

prêter (*pray-tēh*), to lend, to loan.

emprunter (*āng-preŭng-tēh*), to borrow.

rembourser (*rāng-boūr-sēh*), to reimburse, to repay.

débourser (*day-boūr-sēh*), to disburse, to pay out.

bonifier (*bō-nēē-fyēh*), to better.

payer (*pay-yēh*), to pay.

empaqueter (*āng-pā-kĕ-tēh*), to pack up.

dépaqueter (*day-pā-kĕ-tēh*), to unpack.

envelopper (*āng-vĕ-lop-pēh*), to envelop, to wrap up.

gagner (*gān-yēh*), to gain.

tromper (*trong-pēh*), to deceive.

voler (*vōh-lēh*), to steal.

étudier (*ay-tü-dyēh*), to study

compter (*kong-tēh*) to count, to reckon.

chiffrer (*shĭf-frēh*), to reckon.

additioner (*ad-dēē-syon-nēh*), to add.

multiplier (*mül-tēē-plēē-ēh*), to multiply.

diviser (*dēē-vēē-zēh*), to divide.

copier (*kō-pyēh*), to copy.

signer (*sĭn-yēh*), to sign.

dicter (*dĭc-tēh*), to dictate.

plier (*plēē-ēh*), to put together.

plisser (*plĭs-sēh*) to fold.

cacheter (*căsh-tēh*), to seal.

commencer (*com-māng-sēh*), to commence, to begin.

continuer (*cong-tēē-nü-ēh*), to continue.

cesser (*sĕs-sēh*), to cease.

achever (*ā-shĕ-vēh*), to perfect, to fulfil.

travailler (*trā-vā-yēh*), to work.

colorer (*co-lo-rēh*), to color.

dessiner (*dĕ-sēē-nēh*), to design.

laver (*lā-vēh*), to wash.

enregistrer (*āng-ray-jĭs-trēh*), to book, to check.

péser (*pē-zēh*), to weigh.

planter (*plāng-tēh*), to plant

Observation.

The student will see that most of these French verbs, which are originally derived from the Latin, are also found in the English tongue, though our pronunciation differs materially from the French. The pupil, with very little effort, can, therefore, put himself in possession *of 160 of the most necessary French verbs.*

Translate the following

Exercise

into English, and then render it into French without the help of the book :

1. On a Steamer.

1) Quand le bateau à vapeur (bā-tō āh vā-peūr=*steamer*), partira-t-il (par-tee-rā-teel=*going to leave ; start*) ?—Le bateau partira dans une heure. — 2) Quel est le prix du passage?—Les premières places (*plāhs*) sont de deux guinées et les secondes d'une guinée. — 3) Est-ce que tout est prêt (pray=*ready*)? — Oui, monsieur.—Eh bien, allons à bord!—4) Nous voici. Voyez (voah-yēh = *look; see*) quelle heure il est, pour savoir (sā-v'woār = *in order to know*) combien de temps nous aurons été à la traversée (trā-ver-say = *crossing*).—Il est deux heures précises. — 5) Combien de temps serons-nous en voyage?— Huit heures, je crois (kroāh = *I think*), si le temps (*weather*) est favorable (fā-vō-rābl = *favorable*). — 6) Avez-vous déjà été sur mer (*on sea*)? — 7) Oui, monsieur. Et vous?—J'ai été aussi (ŏ-sēē =*also*) plusieurs fois (plü-zyeūr-foāh = *several times*) sur mer; mais je ne suis pas sujet (sü-jay = *subject*) au mal de mer (*seasickness*).— 8) Vous changez (shāng-jay) de couleur. Qu'avez-vous? —La tête me tourne (*whirls; swims*); j'ai mal au coeur. —9) Vous paraissez (pā-rays-sēh = *seem*) vous trouver mal (*to feel bad*); ne vaudrait-il pas mieux (ne vō-dray-tēēl pāh myeū = *would it not be better*) de rentrer (rāng-tray) dans la cajute (kā-jüt = *cabin*) et de vous coucher (*lay down*)? — Je préfère (pray-fayr = *prefer*) rester sur le pont (pong = *deck*).

COMPANION TO THE
Revised Version of the New Testament.

Explaining the Reasons for the Changes Made on the Authorized Version. .

BY ALEXANDER ROBERTS, D.D.,
Member of the English Revision Committee.

WITH SUPPLEMENT BY A MEMBER OF THE AMERICAN COMMITTEE.

Containing a Brief History of the Revision of the Work and Co-operation of the New Testament Companies, of the Points of Agreement and Difference, and an Explanation of the Appendix to the Revised New Testament.

ALSO, A FULL TEXTUAL INDEX,

Being a Key to Passages in which Important Changes have been Made.

This book, having been carefully prepared by Members of both Revision Committees, carries official weight. It shows what changes have been made, and also the reasons which influenced the revisers in making them. It will be difficult to judge of the merits of the revision without the aid of this Companion volume. Our edition is printed by special arrangement with the English publishers. It is well known that, by an arrangement between the two Committees of Revision, the changes suggested by the American Committee, but which were not adopted by the English Revisers, are published as an Appendix to the Revised New Testament. The *Companion* volume is an explanation of *all* the changes adopted by both committees, and of those suggested by the American Committee, but not assented to by the English Committee, in their final revision. The book will be indispensable to a right understanding of the revision. This cheap edition of the combined books, although authorized and copyrighted, will be sold for 25 cents in paper, and 75 cents in cloth—sent postage free.

TESTIMONIALS.

T. W. CHAMBERS, D.D., a Member of the American Committee of Revision, says of this book: "Many persons have expressed a desire that, simultaneously with the issue of the Revised New Testament, there should appear an authentic explanation of the reasons for such changes as will be found in its pages. The work of Dr. Roberts is exactly fitted to meet this desire....Nowhere else in print can be found a statement so full and exact. It gives all needed information, and does it in an unexceptional way."

C. F. DEEMS, D.D., Pastor of the Church of the Strangers, New York, writes: "The Companion to the Revised Version seems to me almost indispensable. Even scholars who were not at the meeting of the Revisers would have a wearisome work in seeking to discover all the changes made, and to ordinary readers very much of the labor would be lost. ....All this is set forth by Dr. Roberts with admirable perspicuity. Those who have any intelligent interest in the Holy Scriptures, will find this little book absorbingly interesting. I shall urge every member of the church, of which I am pastor to give it a careful reading, and purpose to introduce it as a text-book in our Bible-classes."

"So valuable, interesting and useful is this publication, that we advise every one who wishes to know the why and wherefore of the revision, to obtain it immediately."—*New York Observer*.

Paper, 8vo size, 25 cents; Cloth, 16mo, 75 cents.

*** For Sale by Booksellers and Newsdealers, or sent postage-paid, on receipt of price, by

I. K. FUNK & CO., Publishers, 10 & 12 Dey St., N. Y.

THE TEACHER'S EDITION

OF THE

REVISED NEW TESTAMENT

**With New Concordance and Index, Harmony of the Gospels, Maps,
Historical and Chronological Tables, Parallel Passages printed
in full, Blank Pages Interleaved for manuscript notes, and
many other New and Indispensable Helps to the Study
of the Revised Version.**

After the excitement connected with the sale of the first copies of the new
revision, which lack the usual indexing headlines and marginal references
to parallel passages, and also the appendixes of tables, maps, etc.—all of
which helps preachers, teachers and Bible students have come to consider as
absolutely essential to a working copy of the Bible—there arises an imperative
demand for an edition of the Revised New Testament, containing all the
marginal and appendix helps of former TEACHERS' AND REFERENCE BIBLES,
adapted carefully and accurately to the Revised Version. We are, therefore, preparing, as rapidly as is consistent with accuracy, such an edition of
the Revised New Testament. The work is under the supervision of well-
known Bible scholars, with numerous helpers, and will be issued as early as
it can be done with thoroughness. In style and size the book will resemble
the Bagster Bible, "Fac-simile large edition," known as "the Moody Bible,"
being the same width and length and size of type. It will be supplied at
prices *within the reach of all.*

This "Teachers' Edition of the Revised New Testament" will be an exact,
certified reproduction of the entire Oxford and Cambridge Edition, including
the Preface and all the marginal readings and explanations. It will contain
the appendix notes of the American Revisers, printed in the margin of each
page by the side of the passages referred to. The parallel passages, to which
reference is m de in the "Bagster Bibles," with numerous others, so far as
appropriate, will be PRINTED IN FULL in the margin. The running headings,
usually printed at the tops of pages of the King James version, will be here
supplied. A small black mark will be inserted below the last letter of each
verse to facilitate reference, and aid in RESPONSIVE READING of the Revised
Version. The second half of the volume will consist of the most carefully
prepared HELPS TO THE STUDY OF THE REVISED NEW TESTAMENT, gleaned
from the best Teachers' Editions of the authorized version, and supplied
from various original sources—all being revised and adapted to harmonize
with the Revised Version. We shall introduce many other important features,
making this the most valuable edition of the New Testament ever issued.

Popular Cloth Edition—Ready in July—Price, Postage Free, $1.60.
Send for prospectus giving full description and prices of finer Bindings.
I. K. FUNK & CO., Publishers, 10 and 12 Dey St., New York.

THE

Meisterschaft System.

A SIMPLE AND PRACTICAL METHOD,

ENABLING

ANY ONE TO LEARN, WITH SLIGHT EFFORT, TO SPEAK
FLUENTLY AND CORRECTLY

French, German, Spanish, and Italian.

BY

DR. RICHARD S. ROSENTHAL,

*Late Director of the "Akademie für fremde Sprachen" in Berlin and Leipzig,
of the "Meisterschaft College" in London, and Principal of the
"Meisterschaft School of Practical Linguistry" in New York.*

FRENCH.

IN FIFTEEN PARTS, EACH CONTAINING THREE LESSONS.

PART VII.

NEW YORK:
I. K. FUNK & CO., PUBLISHERS,
10 AND 12 DEY STREET.

TERMS.

WE have arranged with Dr. ROSENTHAL, the author of the "Meisterschaft System," for its introduction in America under his own supervision, and he has opened

FOR NON-RESIDENTS.

The student does not need to leave his home. The lessons of each language are prepared by the Professor, and printed and sent in pamphlet shape to each member of the School wherever he may reside.

The course of study for each language—German, French, Italian, or Spanish—makes fifteen pamphlets of three lessons each.

All members of the School have

THE PRIVILEGE

of asking, by letter, questions concerning each lesson, or consulting on any difficulty which may have occurred to them. All exercises corrected and all questions answered by return post by Dr. ROSENTHAL or one of his assistants.

TERMS OF MEMBERSHIP.

Five Dollars is the price for membership in the school for each language. This amount (\$5.) entitles the member to receive the fifteen books or pamphlets containing the lessons, also answers to his questions. Return postage for the answer must accompany the question.

State distinctly which language, or languages, you desire to study There are *no extra charges*. The price, **Five Dollars,** pays for one language; **Ten Dollars** for two languages, etc. All exercise. and questions must be written on a separate sheet of paper, and must state full address of the pupil.

Remittances must be made in Post-Office Order or registered letter addressed to

I. K. FUNK & CO,

10 and 12 Dey Street, New York.

The Meisterschaft-System,

FRENCH.

PART VII.

VII.[1]

(*Continuation.*)

20. That is not sufficient (*assez*); you must eat something before dinner. (*Literally:* While [*en*[2]] awaiting [*attendant*] the dinner).

21. Have you any wine? Yes, sir; I have some.

22. If you need good sugar, we can furnish (*fournir*) you some at a very low price.

23. Show me some good steel pens. Here are some excellent ones.

24. Waiter, I have no napkin. Here is one, sir.

25. I do not like this room. Have you not (got) another one which you can give me? (*Literally:* to give to me.)

26. Yes, sir, we have several (*plusieurs*) unoccupied ones (= several free [*de libres*]).

---

1) To avoid breaking up the several tables in the Grammatical Remarks they have been consolidated into one part, thus shortening the Foundation Sentences for this Number.

2) *En* is a 'supplying pronoun,' and is used very frequently in French, though it cannot always be given in English. It is used

a) to express the words *some* and *any*, when they refer to some previously used substantive, as: Voici du jambon (ham): *en* voulez-vous? Donnez m'en, s'il vous plaît. Here is some ham; do you want some? Give me *some*, please.

b) *En* is used instead of *it* or *them*, when the *French verb* requires *de* (*i.e.*, governs the genitive). This rule refers almost only to *things, rarely* to persons. (It is immaterial what preposition is used in English.) *Ex.:* Vous parlez de son malheur (*mä-leur*)?

VII.

(Continuation.)

20. Ce n'est pas͡assez ; il vous faut manger (*māng-jay*) quelque chose, en attendant (*ān-nāt-tāng-dāng*) le dîner.

21. Avez-vous du vin (*vaing*)? Oui monsieur, j'en [1] ai (*jān-nai*).

22. S'il vous faut de bon sucre, nous pouvons vous͡en fournir (*foūr-nēēr*) à bien bon-marché.

23. Montrez-moi de bonnes plumes métalliques. En voici d'excellentes (*dĕg-sĕl-lāngt*).

24. Garçon, je n'ai pas de serviette. En voici une, monsieur. ('*En*' *can frequently not be expressed in English, but must be given in French.*)

25. Cette chambre ne me plaît pas. N'en avez-vous pas͡une autre à me donner (*nān-nà-vēh voŭ pāh zŭn nōtr āh mĕ don-nēh*)?

26. Oui, monsieur, nous͡en͡avons plusieurs de libres (*plü-zyeūr dĕ lēēbr*).

Non monsieur, je n'*en* parle pas. You are speaking of his misfortune? No, sir ; I am not speaking *of it*. — J'ai fait une faute (*fôht*), et *j'en* suis puni (*pŭ-nēē*). I have committed a fault and I am punished *for it*. — Vous m'avez rendu service (*rāng dŭ sĕr-vēēse*); je vous *en* remercie (*rĕ-mĕr-sēē*). You have rendered me a service ; I thank you *for* it. *En* is always placed *before* the verb (like the personal conjunctive pronouns). But when *en* meets with another personal pronoun it is placed *last*, as : Je *m'en* souviens (*soŭ-vyaing*), I remember. It is placed, however, *after* the *affirmative imperative*, as : Donnez-lui-en, give him some. (*Moi* and *toi* with the affirmative imperative are changed into *m'* and *t'* before *en*, as : Donnez-m'en, give me some.

27. Do you need a large room, or will you be satisfied (*vous contenterez-vous*) with a (*d'une*) room (*pièce*) with (*à*) one window?

28. I have received a letter from Paris and must answer it at once.

29. Will you please do your correspondence (*faire votre courrier*) in the coffee-room? You will find writing materials there. (*Literally :* You find there [*y*] everything which you need for writing.)

30. It is of the utmost importance (= *il faut absolument*) that this letter leaves to-day.

31. Waiter, a decanter of ice-water (*une carafe frappée*), if you please.

32. We have not got any, sir, but I'll bring you (*or* get you) some ice (*de la glace*) on a plate, if you like it.

33. This roast duck is excellent. May I help you to some? (*Vous en servirai-je?*) [*May I,* in such and similiar phrases, must be rendered through the future tense.]

34. This roast-beef looks very nice. Will you please cut me a slice of it (*m'en couper une tranche*)?

35. This meat (*cette viande*) is very tender; may I offer you another small piece (*un petit morceau*)?

36. Give me a very small piece only (*seulement*).

37. You are giving me too much (*trop*); give me only (*ne-que*) half of it (*la moitié*).

38. Do you want a fork? Thanks, I have one.

39. I must go to London for some weeks (*semaines*) on family-business (*pour affaires de famille*).

27. Vous faut⁀il une grande chambre, ou vous contenterez-vous (*cong-tāng-tĕ-rēh-voŭ*) d'une pièce à une
fenêtre (*dün pēē-ays āh ün fĕ-naytr*) ?

28. J'ai reçu une lettre de Paris et il faut que je réponde
tout de suite (*r̃ay-pongd toūt s'wēēt*).

29. Veuillez faire votre courrier dans la salle des voyageurs; vous⁀y (*voŭ-zēē*) trouverez tout ce qu'il faut
pour écrire (*ay-krēēr*).

30. Il faut⁀absolument (*tāb-so-lü-māng*) que cette lettre
parte aujourd'hui.

31. Garçon, une carafe frappée, s'il vous plaît.

32. Nous n'en⁀avons pas, monsieur, mais si vous voulez
je vous⁀apporterai de la glace sur une assiette.

33. Ce caneton (*kā-nĕ-tong*) est⁀excellent ; vous⁀en servirai-je encore (*ay-tĕg-sĕl-lāng ; voŭ zāng· sĕr-vēē-rēh-jĕ
āng-kor*).

34. Ce filet a très-bonne mine ; veuillez m'en couper une
tranche (*trāngsh*) ?

35. Cette viande (*vēē-āngd*) est très-tendre (*tāng-dr*),
vous⁀en offrirai-je encore un petit morceau (*voŭ zāng
nŏf-frēē-rēh-jĕ āng-kor eŭng p'tēe mor-soh*) ?

36. Donnez-m'en seulement (*seŭl-māng*) un tout petit
morceau.

37. Vous m'en donnez trop ; ne m'en donnez que la moitié (*m'woāh-tyēh*).

38. Voulez-vous⁀une fourchette ? Merci, j'en‿ai une.

39. Il faut que j'aille à Londres pour quelques semaines
(*sĕ-mayn*) pour affaires de famille (*fā-mēē-yĕ*).

GRAMMATICAL REMARKS.

A.

The Adjective.

The adjective agrees in gender and number with the · substantive or pronoun it relates to. Le *bon‿*enfant (*bon nāng-fāng*), the good child. *La bonne* femme (*făm*), the good woman. *Elle* est‿*heureuse* (*ĕl lay teū-reūse*), she is happy.

FORMATION OF THE FEMININE FORM.

The feminine of adjectives and participles is generally formed by the addition of the letter *e.*

Masc.	*Fem.*	
vrai,	vraie,	true.
joli,	jolie,	pretty.
connu,	connue,	known.
général (*jay-nay-rāhl*),	générale,	general.
charmant (*shār-māng*)	charmante,	charming.

Exceptions.

Adjectives ending in *e* mute remain unchanged in the feminine, as :

Masc.	*Fem.*	
sage,	sage,	wise.
aimable (*ay-māhbl*),	aimable,	amiable.

Adjectives ending in *f*, change *f* into *ve* in the feminine.

Masc.	*Fem.*	
actif (*āc-tĕĕf*),	active,	active.
bref,	brève,	short.
neuf,	neuve,	new.
vif (*vĕĕf*).	vive,	quick.

Adjectives ending in *l* double it in the feminine:

Masc.	Fem.	
cruel (*krü-ĕl*),	cruelle,	cruel.
pareil (*pă-rĕ-yĕ*)	pareille,	similar.
nul (*nühl*),	nulle,	no *or* null.
éternel, (*ay-ter-nĕl*),	éternelle,	eternal.
gentil (*jăng-tĕĕl*),	gentille (*jăng-tĕĕ-yĕ*),	pretty.
tel,	telle,	such.
vermeil (*ver-mĕ-yĕ*),	vermeille,	vermilion.

In the same manner monosyllables in *s, n* and *t* are formed; viz., doubling *s, n* and *t* in the feminine:

Masc.	Fem.	
bon (*bong*),	bonne, (*bŏnn*),	good.
gros (*grŏ*),	grosse (*grŏss*),	big.
sòt (*sŏ*),	sotte (*sŏtt*),	stupid.

To these belong also the following:

épais (*ay-pay*), *fem.* épaisse, thick.

exprès (*ex-pray*), *fem.* expresse, express.

muet (*mü-ay*), *fem.* muette, dumb.

sujet (*sü-jay*) *fem.* sujette, subject.

Adjectives ending in *x* change the same into *se:*

Masc.	Fem.	
heureux (*eŭ-reŭ*),	heureuse (*eŭ-reŭse*),	happy.
jaloux (*jă-loŭ*),	jalouse (*jă-loŭse*),	jealous.
paresseux (*pă-rĕs-seŭ*),	paresseuse (*pa-rĕ-seŭse*),	lazy.

But *faux* (*fŏ*), false, makes its feminine *fausse* (*fŏss*).

Adjectives ending in *er* and *et* take in the feminine the *grave accent:*

Masc.	Fem.	
léger (*lay-jay*),	légère (*lay-jayr*),	light.
complet (*cong-plĕh*),	complète (*cong-playt*),	complete.

Of the adjectives ending in *c* the following three change this *c* into *che :*

Masc.	Fem.	
˙blanc (*blāngk*),	blanche (*blāngsh*),	white.
franc (*frāngk*),	franche (*frāngsh*),	frank.
sec (*sĕck*)	sèche (*saysh*),	dry.

The others ending in *c* take *que :*

Masc.	Fem.	
public (*pü-blēĕk*),	publique,	public.
turc (*türk*),	turque,	Turkish.
caduc (*kā-dük*),	caduʻque,	decrepit.
grec (*grĕk*),	grecque,	Greek.

The following adjectives do not follow any of the above rules :

Masc.	Fem.	
long,	longue,	long.
aigu (*ai-gü*),	aiguë,	acute.
frais (*fray*),	fraîche (*fraysh*),	fresh.
doux (*dōō*),	douce (*doōs*),	sweet, soft.
malin (*mă-laing*),	maligne (*mā-lĕĕn-yĕ*),	wicked.
bénin (*bai-naing*),	bénigne (*bai-nĕĕn-yĕ*),	benign.

The following are more irregular in the formation of their feminine, as :

Masc.	Fem.	
Beau [bel] (*bōh*),	belle,	beautiful.
nouveau [nouvel] (*noū-vōh*),	nouvelle (*noū-vĕl*),	new.
mou [mol] (*moū*),	molle (*mŏll*),	soft.
fou [fol] (*foū*),	folle (*fŏll*),	foolish.
vieux [vieil] (*vyeū*),	vieille (*vyĕ-yĕ*),	old.

N.B. The above words in parentheses, *bel, nouvel*, etc., are used before *masculine nouns* beginning with *a vowel or h mute*, as: *un bel⌣arbre*, a fine tree; *un nouvel⌣ordre*, a new order; *un fol⌣espoir*, a foolish hope, etc.

B.

Of the Plural of Adjectives.

The rules given for the plural of substantives apply
also to adjectives. *Ex.:*

	Plural.
Grand, *f.* grande ; grand.	grands, *f.* grandes.
gras, *f.* grasse ; fat.	gras, *f.* grasses.
royal (*roãh-yãhl*), *f.* royale; royal.	royaux (*roãh-yoh*), *f.* royales.
beau (*bõh*), *f.* belle ; beautiful.	beaux (*bõh*), *f.* belles.
vieux (*vyeũ*), *f.* vieille (*vyĕ-yĕ*); old.	vieux, *f.* vieilles.

Fou, mou and *bleu-* (blue) make in *the plural* fous,
mous and bléus.

POSITION OF ADJECTIVES IN A SENTENCE.

Adjectives are generally placed *after* the nouns which
they qualify ; as, for instance:

le tailleur français,	the French tailor.
l'homme heureux (*eũ-reũ*),	the happy man.
de l'eau fraîche,	some fresh water.

But the following, in their common acceptation, are
generally placed *before* their nouns :

autre, other.	demi (*dĕ-mēē*), half.
beau, fine.	grand, great.
bon, good.	gros, large.
brave (*bɩãhv*), brave.	jeune, young.
cher, dear.	joli, pretty.
méchant (*may-shãng*), wicked.	petit (*p'-tĕē*), small.
mauvais (*mõ-vēh*), bad.	saint (*saing*), holy.
meilleur (*mĕ-yeũr*), better.	tout (*toũ*), all.
moindre (*mõ-aing-dr*), less.	vieux (*vyeũ*), old.
nouveau (*noũ võh*), new.	vrai (*vray*), true.

Many of these, however, may be constantly found in French books placed *after*, and many of the others may be found *before* their nouns. The safe rule is to place the adjective *after* its noun.

The **following adjectives** have a **different meaning,** according as they stand *before* or *after* their noun:

Mon *cher* ami, my dear friend (denoting affection).	Un livre *cher*, a dear book (denoting the price).
un *brave* homme, an honest man.	un homme *brave*, a brave (= courageous) man.
un *onnête homme*, an honest man.	un homme *honnête*, a civil *or* polite man.
une *fausse* clef, a false key, skeleton-key, a picklock.	une clef *fausse*, a wrong key.
une *sage*-femme, a midwife.	une femme *sage*, a wise woman.
la *dernière* année, the last year (of certain space of time).[1]	l'année *dernière*, last year (the past year).

C.

Degrees of Comparison.

The *Comparative* is formed by placing the adverb *plus*, more, before the adjective, while *le plus* or *la plus* (fem.) is prefixed to denote the *Superlative*.

Positive.	*Comparative.*
haut (*ōh*), (*m.*) haute (*ōht*) (*f.*) } high.	plus haut plus haute } higher.
beau (*bōh*), (*m.*) belle (*bĕl*), (*f.*) } beautiful.	plus beau plus belle } more beautiful.

-----

1) For instance: He spent the last year of his life at Paris, il passa la *dernière année de sa vie* à Paris.

Superlative.

le plus haut \
la plus haute } the highest.

le plus beau \
la plus belle } the most beautiful.

There is in French also a *lower* and *lowest degree* which is formed by the words *moins*, less, for the Comparative, and *le* (*la*) *moins*, the least, for the Superlative.

Positive.	*Comparative.*
cher (*m.*) } dear.	moins cher } less dear, *i.e.*,
chère (*f.*) }	moins chère } cheaper.

Superlative.

le moins cher \
la moins chère } the least dear, *i.e.*, the cheapest.

The following three adjectives have an

IRREGULAR COMPARISON ·

Bon, *f.* bonne, good ; *comp.* meilleur, e, better ; *super.* le meilleur, la meilleure, the best.

Mauvais, e, (*mŏh-vay*), in the meaning wicked ; *comp.* pire (*pēĕr*), · worse ; *sup.* le pire, *f.* la pire, the worst.

Petit, e ; *comp.* moindre (*mo-āing-dr*), less ; *sup.* le moindre, *f.* la moindre, the least.

Remarks :

As before an adjective is rendered by *aussi* ; *as* after · it, and *than* are both translated by *que*. Ex. :

Il est *aussi* bon *que* moi, he is *as* good *as* I am.

Elle est plus belle *que* sa cousine, she is handsomer *than* her cousin.

TABLE.

Nouns and Adjectives.

Nouns.

ARTICLE.

Masc.	*Fem.*	*Apostr.*	*Plural.*
N. le	la	l'	les
G. du	de la	de l'	des
D. au	à la	à l'	aux
A. le	la	l'	les

PLURAL OF NOUNS.

maison,	maisons.
fils,	fils.
tableau,	tableaux.
cheval,	chevaux.

IRREGULAR PLURAL.

ciel,	cieux.
l'oeil,	yeux.
aïeul,	aïeux.

Adjectives.

grand, grande ;	grands, grandes.
bon, bonne ;	bons, bonnes.
neuf, neuve ;	neufs, neuves.
heureux, heureuse ;	heureux, heureuses.
blanc, blanche ;	blancs, blanches.
public, publique ;	publics, publiques.
vieux, vieille ;	vieux, vieilles.
doux, douce ;	doux, douces.
long, longue ;	longs, longues.

IRREGULAR COMPARISON.

bon ; meilleur ; le meilleur.

mauvais ; pire ; le pire.

petit ; moindre ; le moindre.

Pronouns.

Conjunctive Personal.	Disjunctive Personal.

Conjunctive Personal.
je, me
tu, te.
il, lui, le.
elle, lui, la.
nous, nous.
vous, vous.
ils, leur, les.
elles, leur, les.

Disjunctive Personal.

moi, toi, lui, elle.
nous, vous, eux, elles.

Possessive Pron.: (Adject.)

mon, ma, mes.   notre, nos.
ton, ta, tes.   votre, vos.
son, sa, ses.   leur, leurs.

Possessive Pronouns (Substant.)

le mien, la mienne ;   les miens, les miennes.
le tien, la tienne ;   les tiens, les tiennes.
le sien, la sienne ;   les siens, les siennes.
le nôtre, la nôtre ;   les nôtres.
le vôtre, la vôtre ;   les vôtres. } both genders.
le leur, la leur ;   les leurs.

Demonstrative Pronouns.

ce, cet, cette ;   ces.
celui, celle ;   ceux, celles.
celui-ci, celle-ci ;   ceux-ci, celles-ci.
celui-là, celle-là ;   ceux-là, celles-là.

Relative Pronouns.

qui ; que.
lequel, laquelle ; lesquels, lesquelles.
dont ; en ; y.

Conjugaison du verbe ÊTRE.

Premier mode.

INDICATIF.

PRÉSENT.

Je suis,
tu es,
il est,
nous sommes,
vous êtes,
ils sont.

IMPARFAIT.

J'étais,
tu étais,
il était,
nous étions,
vous étiez,
ils étaient.

PASSÉ DÉFINI.

Je fus,
tu fus,
il fut,
nous fûmes,
vous fûtes,
ils furent.

PASSÉ INDÉFINI.

J'ai été,
tu as été,
il a été,
nous avons été,
vous avez été,
ils ont été.

PASSÉ ANTÉRIEUR.

J'eus été,
tu eus été,
il eut été,
nous eûmes été,
vous eûtes été,
ils eurent été.

PLUS-QUE-PARFAIT.

J'avais été,
tu avais été,
il avait été,
nous avions été,
vous aviez été,
ils avaient été.

FUTUR.

Je serai,
tu seras,
il sera,
nous serons,
vous serez,
ils seront.

FUTUR ANTÉRIEUR.

J'aurai été,
tu auras été,
il aura été,
nous aurons été,
vous aurez été,
ils auront été.

Deuxième mode.

CONDITIONNEL.

PRÉSENT.

Je serais,
tu serais,
il serait,
nous serions,
vous seriez,
ils seraient.

PASSÉ (1re forme).

J'aurais été,
tu aurais été,
il aurait été,
nous aurions été,
vous auriez été,
ils auraient été.

PASSÉ (2me forme).

J'eusse été,
tu eusses été,
il eût été,
nous eussions été,
vous eussiez été,
ils eussent été.

Troisième mode.

IMPERATIF.

PRÉSENT ou FUTUR.

Sois,
soyons,
soyez.

Quatrième mode.

SUBJONCTIF.

PRÉSENT ou FUTUR.

Que je sois,
que tu sois,
qu'il soit,
que nous soyons,
que vous soyez,
qu'ils soient.

IMPARFAIT.

Que je fusse,
que tu fusses,
qu'il fût,
que nous fussions,
que vous fussiez,
qu'ils fussent.

PASSÉ.

Que j'aie été,
que tu aies été,
qu'il ait été,
que nous ayons été,
que vous ayez été,
qu'ils aient été.

PLUS-QUE-PARFAIT.

Que j'eusse été,
que tu eusses été,
qu'il eût été,
que nous eussions été,
que vous eussiez été,
qu'ils eussent été.

Cinquième mode.

INFINITIF.

PRÉSENT.

Être.

PASSÉ.

Avoir été.

PARTICIPE PRÉSENT.

Étant.

PARTICIPE PASSÉ.

Été.

Conjugaison du verbe AVOIR.

Premier mode.

INDICATIF.

PRÉSENT.

J'ai,
tu as,
il a,
nous avons,
vous avez,
ils ont.

IMPARFAIT.

J'avais,
tu avais,
il avait,
nous avions,
vous aviez,
ils avaient.

PASSÉ DÉFINI.

J'eus,
tu eus,
il eut,
nous eûmes,
vous eûtes,
ils eurent.

PASSÉ INDÉFINI.

J'ai eu,
tu as eu,
il a eu,
nous avons eu,
vous avez eu,
ils ont eu.

PASSÉ ANTÉRIEUR.

J'eus eu,
tu eus eu,
il eut eu,
nous eûmes eu,
vous eûtes eu,
ils eurent eu.

PLUS-QUE-PARFAIT.

J'avais eu,
tu avais eu,
il avait eu,
nous avions eu,
vous aviez eu,
ils avaient eu.

FUTUR.

J'aurai,
tu auras,
il aura,
nous aurons,
vous aurez,
ils auront.

FUTUR ANTÉRIEUR.

J'aurai eu,
tu auras eu,
il aura eu,
nous aurons eu,
vous aurez eu,
ils auront eu.

Deuxième mode.

CONDITIONNEL.

PRÉSENT.

J'aurais,
tu aurais,
il aurait,
nous aurions,
vous auriez,
ils auraient.

PASSÉ (1re forme).

J'aurais eu,
tu aurais eu,
il aurait eu,
nous aurions eu,
vous auriez eu,
ils auraient eu.

PASSÉ (2me forme).

J'eusse eu,
tu eusses eu,
il eût eu,
nous eussions eu,
vous eussiez eu,
ils eussent eu.

Troisième mode.

IMPERATIF.

PRÉSENT ou FUTUR.

Aye,
Ayons,
Ayez.

Quatrième mode.

SUBJONCTIF.

PRÉSENT ou FUTUR.

Que j'aie,
que tu aies,
qu'il ait,
que nous ayons,
que vous ayez,
qu'ils aient.

IMPARFAIT.

Que j'eusse,
que tu eusses,
qu'il eût,
que nous eussions,
que vous eussiez,
qu'ils eussent.

PASSÉ.

Que j'aie eu,
que tu aies eu,
qu'il ait eu,
que nous ayons eu,
que vous ayez eu,
qu'ils aient eu.

PLUS-QUE-PARFAIT.

que j'eusse eu,
que tu eusses eu,
qu'il eût eu,
que nous eussions eu,
que vous eussiez eu,
qu'ils eussent eu.

Cinquième mode.

INFINITIF.

PRÉSENT.

Avoir.

PASSÉ.

Avoir eu.

PARTICIPE PRÉSENT.

Ayant.

PARTICIPE PASSÉ.

Eu, ayant eu.

Première Conjugaison, en ER.

INDICATIF.

PRÉSENT.

Je chante,
tu chantes,
il chante,
nous chantons,
vous chantez,
ils chantent.

IMPARFAIT.

Je chantais,
tu chantais,
il chantait,
nous chantions,
vous chantiez,
ils chantaient.

PASSÉ DÉFINI.

Je chantai
tu chantas,
il chanta,
nous chantâmes,
vous chantâtes,
ils chantèrent.

PASSÉ INDÉFINI.

J'ai chanté,
tu as chanté,
il a chanté,
nous avons chanté,
vous avez chanté
ils ont chanté.

PASSÉ ANTÉRIEUR.

J'eus chanté,
tu eus chanté,
il eut chanté,
nous eûmes chanté,
vous eûtes chanté,
ils eurent chanté.

PLUS-QUE-PARFAIT.

J'avais chanté,
tu avais chanté,
il avait chanté,
nous avions chanté,
vous aviez chanté,
ils avaient chanté.

FUTUR.

Je chanterai,
tu chanteras,
il chantera,
nous chanterons,
vous chanterez,
ils chanteront.

FUTUR ANTÉRIEUR.

J'aurai chanté,
tu auras chanté,
il aura chanté,
nous aurons chanté,
vous aurez chanté,
ils auront chanté.

CONDITIONNEL.

PRÉSENT.

Je chanterais,
tu chanterais,
il chanterait,
nous chanterions,
vous chanteriez,
ils chanteraient.

PASSÉ (1re forme).

J'aurais chanté,
tu aurais chanté,
il aurait chanté,
nous aurions chanté,
vous auriez chanté,
ils auraient chanté.

PASSÉ (2me forme).

J'eusse chanté,
tu eusses chanté,
il eût chanté,
nous eussions chanté
vous eussiez chanté
ils eussent chanté.

IMPERATIF.

Chante,
chantons,
chantez.

SUBJONCTIF.

PRÉSENT ou FUTUR.

Que je chante,
que tu chantes,
qu'il chante,
que nous chantions,
que vous chantiez.
qu'ils chantent.

IMPARFAIT.

Que je chantasse,
que tu chantasses,
qu'il chantât,
que nous chantassions,
que vous chantassiez,
qu'ils chantassent.

PASSÉ.

Que j'aie chanté,
que tu aies chanté,
qu'il ait chanté,
que nous ayons chanté,
que vous ayez chanté,
qu'ils aient chanté.

PLUS-QUE-PARFAIT.

Que j'eusse chanté,
que tu eusses chanté,
qu'il eût chanté,
que nous eussions chanté,
que vous eussiez chanté,
qu'ils eussent chanté.

INFINITIF.

PRÉSENT.

Chanter.

PASSÉ.

Avoir chanté.

PARTICIPE PRÉSENT.

Chantant.

PARTICIPE PASSÉ.

Chanté, chantée, ayant chanté.

Deuxième Conjugaison, en IR.

INDICATIF.

PRÉSENT.

Je finis,
tu finis,
il finit,
nous finissons,
vous finissez,
ils finissent.

IMPARFAIT.

Je finissais,
tu finissais,
il finissait,
nous finissions,
vous finissiez,
ils finissaient.

PASSÉ DÉFINI.

Je finis,
tu finis,
il finit,
nous finîmes,
vous finîtes,
ils finirent.

PASSÉ INDÉFINI.

J'ai fini,
tu as fini,
il a fini,
nous avons fini,
vous avez fini,
ils ont fini.

PASSÉ ANTÉRIEUR.

J'eus fini,
tu eus fini,
il eût fini
nous eûmes fini,
vous eûtes fini,
ils eurent fini.

PLUS-QUE-PARFAIT.

J'avais fini,
tu avais fini,
il avait fini,
nous avions fini,
vous aviez fini,
ils avaient fini.

FUTUR.

Je finirai,
tu finiras,
il finira,
nous finirons,
vous finirez,
ils finiront.

FUTUR ANTÉRIEUR.

J'aurai fini,
tu auras fini,
il aura fini,
nous aurons fini,
vous aurez fini,
ils auront fini.

CONDITIONNEL.

PRÉSENT.

Je finirais,
tu finirais,
il finirait,
nous finirions,
vous finiriez,
ils finiraient.

PASSÉ, (1re forme).

J'aurais fini,
tu aurais fini,
il aurait fini,
nous aurions fini,
vous auriez fini,
ils auraient fini.

PASSÉ (2me forme).

J'eusse fini,
tu eusses fini,
il eût fini,
nous eussions fini,
vous eussiez fini,
ils eussent fini.

IMPERATIF.

Finis,
finissons,
finissez.

SUBJONCTIF.

PRÉSENT ou FUTUR.

Que je finisse,
que tu finisses,
qu'il finisse,
que nous finissions,
que vous finissiez,
qu'ils finissent.

IMPARFAIT.

Que je finisse,
que tu finisses,
qu'il finît,
que nous finissions,
que vous finissiez,
qu'ils finissent.

PASSÉ.

Que j'aie fini,
que tu aies fini,
qu'il ait fini,
que nous ayons fini,
que vous ayez fini,
qu'ils aient fini.

PLUS-QUE-PARFAIT.

Que j'eusse fini,
que tu eusses fini,
qu'il eût fini,
que nous eussions fini
que vous eussiez fini,
qu'ils eussent fini.

INFINITIF.

PRÉSENT.

Finir.

PASSÉ.

Avoir fini,

PARTICIPE PRÉSENT.

Finissant.

PARTICIPE PASSÉ.

Fini, finie, ayant fini.

Troisième Conjugaison, en RE.

INDICATIF.

PRÉSENT.

Je rends,
tu rends,
il rend,
nous rendons,
vous rendez,
ils rendent.

IMPARFAIT.

Je rendais,
tu rendais,
il rendait,
nous rendions,
vous rendiez,
ils rendaient.

PASSÉ DÉFINI.

Je rendis,
tu rendis,
il rendit,
nous rendîmes,
vous rendîtes,
ils rendirent.

PASSÉ INDÉFINI.

J'ai rendu,
tu as rendu,
il a rendu,
nous avons rendu,
vous avez rendu,
ils ont rendu.

PASSÉ ANTÉRIEUR.

J'eus rendu,
tu eus rendu,
il eut rendu,
nous eûmes rendu,
vous eûtes rendu,
ils eurent rendu.

PLUS-QUE-PARFAIT.

J'avais rendu,
tu avais rendu,
il avait rendu,
nous avions rendu,
vous aviez rendu,
ils avaient rendu.

FUTUR.

Je rendrai,
tu rendras,
il rendra,
nous rendrons,
vous rendrez,
ils rendront.

FUTUR ANTÉRIEUR.

J'aurai rendu,
tu auras rendu,
il aura rendu,
nous aurons rendu,
vous aurez rendu,
ils auront rendu.

CONDITIONNEL.

PRÉSENT.

Je rendrais,
tu rendrais,
il rendrait,
nous rendrions,
vous rendriez,
ils rendraient.

PASSÉ (1re forme).

J'aurais rendu,
tu aurais rendu,
il aurait rendu,
nous aurions rendu,
vous auriez rendu,
ils auraient rendu,

PASSÉ (2me forme).

J'eusse rendu,
tu eusses rendu,
il eût rendu,
nous eussions rendu,
vous eussiez rendu,
ils eussent rendu.

IMPERATIF.

Rends.
Rendons,
Rendez.

SUBJONCTIF.

PRÉSENT ou FUTUR.

Que je rende
que tu rendes,
qu'il rende,
que nous rendions,
que vous rendiez
qu'ils rendent.

IMPARFAIT.

Que je rendisse,
que tu rendisses,
qu'il rendît,
que nous rendissions,
que vous rendissiez,
qu'ils rendissent.

PASSÉ.

Que j'aie rendu,
que tu aies rendu,
qu'il ait rendu,
que nous ayons rendu
que vous ayez rendu,
qu'ils aient rendu.

PLUS-QUE-PARFAIT.

Que j'eusse rendu,
que tu eusses rendu,
qu'il eût rendu,
que nous eussions rendu,
que vous eussiez rendu,
qu'ils eussent rendu.

INFINITIF.

PRÉSENT.

Rendre.

PASSÉ.

Avoir rendu.

PARTICIPE.

PRÉSENT.

Rendant.

PASSÉ.

Rendu, rendue, ayant
rendu.

The following table contains all the *endings* of the three conjugations, viz. :

the 1st *Conjugation* ending in **er** (= donn-*er*)

" 2d " " " **ir** (= fin-*ir*)

" 3d " " " **re** (= rend-*re*).

This table ought to be continually used by the student, who had better paste it on a stiff paper-board.

INDICATIF. PRÉSENT.

1st conj.	2d conj.	3d conj.
e	is	s
es	is	s
e	it	–
ons	issons	ons
ez	issez	ez
ent	issent	ent

IMPARFAIT.

ais	issais	ais
ais	issais	ais
ait	issait	ait
ions	issions	ions
iez	issiez	iez
aient	issaient	aient

PASSÉ DÉFINI.

ai	is	is
as	is	is
a	it	it
âmes	îmes	îmes
âtes	îtes	îtes
èrent	irent	irent

FUTUR.

erai	irai	rai
eras	iras	ras
era	ira	ra
erons	irons	rons
erez	irez	rez
eront	iront	ront

CONDITIONNEL. PRÉSENT.

erais	irais	rais
erais	irais	rais
erait	irait	rait
erions	irions	rions
eriez	iriez	riez
eraient	iraient	raient

IMPERATIF.

e	is	s
ons	issons	ons
ez	issez	ez

SUBJONCTIF. PRÉSENT.

e	isse	e
es	isses	es
e	isse	e
ions	issions	ions
iez	issiez	iez
ent	issent	ent

IMPARFAIT.

asse	isse	isse
asses	isses	isses
ât	ît	ît
assions	issions	issions
assiez	issiez	issiez
assent	issent	issent

INFINITIF. PRÉSENT.

er	ir	re

PARTICIPE. PRÉSENT.

ant	issant	ant

PASSÉ.

é, ée.	i, ie.	u, ue.

Translate the following

Exercises

into English, and then again, without assistance of the book, into French:

1. At Dinner.

Auriez-vous la bonté de faire la salade pendant que je vais (jĕ vay = *I am going*) découper (*carve*) le rôti (*roast*). Prendrez-vous (prāng-dṛēh vōu = *will you take*) du rôti ? Aimez-vous le gras (grāh = *fat*) ? Donnez-moi du maigre (maygr = *lean*), s'il vous plaît. J'espère que vous trouvez ce morceau (mŏr-sōh = *piece*) à votre goût (goū). Vous n'avez pas de sauce. Comment trouvez-vous le rôti ? Permettez-moi de vous servir (sĕr-vēēr = *to serve*) un morceau de ....? Vous n'avez pas mangé de .... Desservez (day-sĕr-vēh = *clear the things off*) et apportez-nous du café.

2. A Business Letter.

PARIS, le treize (trayse = 13th) janvier (jāng-vyēh = *January*).

Monsieur Charles Toussaint à Lyon (toū-saing āh Lēē-ong).

Monsieur,

Occupés (oc-cü-pay = *busy, occupied*) du règlement (ray-glĕ-māng = *regulation*) de nos écritures (ay-krēē-tür = *books*), nous vous envoyons ci-inclus votre compte pour l'année passée (*last year*), en vous priant (āng voū prēē-āng = *requesting, begging*) de vouloir bien le faire examiner, et si vous êtes d'accord (*in accord, accordance*), avec nous, de nous créditer sur le nouveau (noū-vōh = *new*) compte du solde (*balance*) en notre faveur (*favor*) de dix mille francs.

Agréez l'assurance (ā-gray-ēh lā-sü-rāngs = *accept the assurance*) de la parfaite considération (pār-faite cong-sēē-dĕ-rāh-syong = *highest esteem*) de

Vos très-humbles (eūng-bl = *humble*) serviteurs (sĕr-vēē-teūr = *servants*),

GAILLARD & CIE. (gā-yār ay cong-pān-yēē).

3.

—— 1) Monsieur, je représente (re-pray-zăṅgt) la maison de B. et Compagnie (B. & Cie.) à Lyon (lēē-ong), et je viens vous faire mes offres de service.—2) Ah, je m'en souviens (soū-vyaing = *remember*), nous avons déjà fait des affaires ensemble (zāng-sāṅg-bl = *together*). Mais je ne puis vous donner d'ordre aujourd'hui.—3) J'en suis bien fâché (*sorry*). Je ne puis cependant (sĕ-pāng-dāng = *however*) vous quitter sans vous montrer quelques échantillons entièrement (āng-tyairĕmāng=*entirely*) nouveaux (noū-vōh). — 4) Ne vous en donnez pas la peine (pain = *trouble*); je ne commanderai (*order*) rien (*nothing*) pour le moment. Ce n'est pas une peine du tout ; je m'en ferai un plaisir.—5) Si vous voulez bien prendre la peine d'examiner (deg-zāh-mēē-nay) mes échantillons, je suis convaincu (cong-vaing-kü = *convinced*) que vous me donnerez un ordre au moins pour essai (*trial*).—6) Voyez, voici une nouvelle espèce (*species*) de mousseline de laine (moū-zĕ-lēēn de laine) qui se porte (*is worn*) beaucoup en France. — 7) On la porte beaucoup pour robes d'été (*summer-dresses*); nous en avons vendu l'impossible (laing-po-sēēbl).

4.

Comment trouvez-vous la nouvelle pièce de monsieur N.? A parler franchement (frāng-shĕ-māng=*frankly*), la pièce est ennuyeuse (ăng-n'wee-yeūse=*tedious*). La pièce manque (mānk=*is wanting in*) d'action (dăc-zyong = *in action*). Le dénoûment est forcé (lĕ day-noū-māng ay for-say = *the catastrophe is forced*). L'intrigue (laing-treeg = *the plot*) n'a pas le sens commun (lĕ sāng commeūng = *common sense*). Comment avez-vous trouvé les couplets du vaudeville (*the couplets, songs*)? Assez jolis (*rather pretty*); mais je ne suis pas enchanté (āng-shāng-tay = *enchanted, charmed*), ni (nee = *neither*) de vos chanteurs (shāng-teūr = *singers*), ni de vos cantatrices,(cāng-tāh-trees = *lady-singers*). Ils chantent (shāngt = *sing*) presque tous faux (presk toū fōh = *almost all false*). Un théâtre de vaudeville ne peut pas être bien monté en chanteurs.

Translate the following

Exercises.

1.

1) May I ask you to tell me if Mr. Grévy is at home? 2) I am very sorry (*je regrette bien*), sir; Mr. Grévy is not at home; he has just gone out (*sortir* = sor-tēēr).— 3) May I ask you to tell me where you have bought this beautiful dress and how much you have paid for it? — 4) Be so kind to pass me the salt (*le sel*). — 5) Have the kindness to read this letter; I do not understand (*je ne comprends pas* = jĕ nĕ cong-prāng pāh) English. — 6) Have the kindness to give my card to Mr. Bronsard (brong-sār) and tell him, if you please, that I have just arrived by (*par*) this train. —7) If I were not afraid of troubling you I would beg you to accompany me this morning. I have some shopping to do. — 8) Would you have the kindness to send me some patterns of the best Lyons silk you have in stock? — 9) Would you have the kindness to get me a physician? My sister is very ill (*malade* = mā-lāhd). — 10) If it were convenient to you to give me some information (*des renseignements* = day rāng-sĕn-yĕ-māng) about (*sur*) Mr. Beauregard, I should feel (= be) very much (*bien*) obliged (*obligé* =

ob-lēē-jay) to you. — 11) You would greatly oblige me
if you would give (=if you gave [Imperfect]) this letter
to Mrs. Tourville. — 12) I did not understand you.
Will you please repeat what you have said? — 13) Would
you be so kind as to grant me a moment's interview? I
have just received a letter from my uncle in Paris and
hope that its contents will be quite satisfactory to you.—
14) You have greatly obliged me, sir, and you may count
on my gratitude. — 15) Do me this favor. I beg *for it*
(*en*). — 16) Be so kind as to write to Mr. B. that I want
two front-rooms.

2.

1) Tell the boy (*garçon*) that he must go to the station at half past five at the latest, as the train arrives at
4.40. — 2) The dressmaker (*la couturière* = koū-tü-ryair)
must finish my dress to-day as I am going to leave for
Saratoga to-night. — 3) At what o'clock must you be at
your physician's? — 4) How much money do you need?
— 5) If the tailor should come [*Imperfect*], tell him that
I have no time to try (*essayer*) the coat on this morning.
He must call again (*revenir*) to-morrow at a quarter to
twelve. — 6) Waiter, I have no knife.—Here is one, sir.
7) If you want good gloves, go to the French glovemaker's in Church street. He keeps (= *has*) excellent
ones. — 8) Mr. Littré must go to Rouen for some weeks.
He wants to visit (*visiter*) his aunt, who is very ill. —
·9) Since when are you in Paris? — Since last night. —
10) Well, I hope you will do me the favor to dine with
me to-day, as I am obliged to go to England to-morrow
morning at half past four. — 11) If you want to leave by
this boat, you must hurry (*vous dépêcher*). — 12) If I were
not afraid of troubling you I would beg you to hand (*donner*) this little package to my sister. But you must go
there (*y*) at once, as she will stay (*rester*) only one day in
Paris.

COMPANION TO THE
Revised Version of the New Testament.

Explaining the Reasons for the Changes Made on the Authorized Version.

BY ALEXANDER ROBERTS, D.D.,
Member of the English Revision Committee.

WITH SUPPLEMENT BY A MEMBER OF THE AMERICAN COMMITTEE.

Containing a Brief History of the Revision of the Work and Co-operation of the New Testament Companies, of the Points of Agreement and Difference, and an Explanation of the Appendix to the Revised New Testament.

ALSO, A FULL TEXTUAL INDEX,

Being a Key to Passages in which Important Changes have been Made.

This book, having been carefully prepared by Members of both Revision Committees, carries official weight. It shows what changes have been made, and also the reasons which influenced the revisers in making them. It will be difficult to judge of the merits of the revision without the aid of this Companion volume. Our edition is printed by special arrangement with the English publishers. It is well known that, by an arrangement between the two Committees of Revision, the changes suggested by the American Committee, but which were not adopted by the English Revisers, are published as an Appendix to the Revised New Testament. The *Companion* volume is an explanation of *all* the changes adopted by both committees, and of those suggested by the American Committee, but not assented to by the English Committee, in their final revision. The book will be indispensable to a right understanding of the revision. This cheap edition of the combined books, although authorized and copyrighted, will be sold for 25 cents in paper, and 75 cents in cloth—sent postage free.

TESTIMONIALS.

T. W. CHAMBERS, D.D., a Member of the American Committee of Revision, says of this book: "Many persons have expressed a desire that, simultaneously with the issue of the Revised New Testament, there should appear an authentic explanation of the reasons for such changes as will be found in its pages. The work of Dr. Roberts is exactly fitted to meet this desire....Nowhere else in print can be found a statement so full and exact. It gives all needed information, and does it in an unexceptional way."

C. F. DEEMS, D.D., Pastor of the Church of the Strangers, New York, writes: "The Companion to the Revised Version seems to me almost indispensable. Even scholars who were not at the meeting of the Revisers would have a wearisome work in seeking to discover all the changes made, and to ordinary readers very much of the labor would be lost. ....All this is set forth by Dr. Roberts with admirable perspicuity. Those who have any intelligent interest in the Holy Scriptures, will find this little book absorbingly interesting. I shall urge every member of the church of which I am pastor to give it a careful reading, and purpose to introduce it as a text-book in our Bible-classes."

"So valuable, interesting and useful is this publication, that we advise every one who wishes to know the why and wherefore of the revision, to obtain it immediately."—*New York Observer.*

Paper, 8vo size, 25 cents; Cloth, 16mo, 75 cents.

*** For Sale by Booksellers and Newsdealers, or sent postage-paid, on receipt of price, by

I. K. FUNK & CO., Publishers, 10 & 12 Dey St., N.Y.

THE TEACHER'S EDITION
OF THE
REVISED NEW TESTAMENT

With New Concordance and Index, Harmony of the Gospels, Maps,
Historical and Chronological Tables, Parallel Passages printed
in full, Blank Pages Interleaved for manuscript notes, and
many other New and Indispensable Helps to the Study
of the Revised Version.

After the excitement connected with the sale of the first copies of the new
revision, which lack the usual indexing headlines and marginal references
to parallel passages, and also the appendixes of tables, maps, etc.—all of
which helps preachers, teachers and Bible students have come to consider as
absolutely essential to a working copy of the Bible—there arises an imperative
demand for an edition of the Revised New Testament, containing all the
marginal and appendix helps of former TEACHERS' AND REFERENCE BIBLES,
adapted carefully and accurately to the Revised Version. We are, therefore, preparing, as rapidly as is consistent with accuracy, such an edition of
the Revised New Testament. The work is under the supervision of well-
known Bible scholars, with numerous helpers, and will be issued as early as
it can be done with thoroughness. In style and size the book will resemble
the Bagster Bible, "Fac-simile large edition," known as "the Moody Bible,"
being the same width and length and size of type. It will be supplied at
prices *within the reach of all.*

Thi; "Teachers' Edition of the Revised New Testament" will be an exact,
certified reproduction of the entire Oxford and Cambridge Edition, including
the Preface and all the marginal readings and explanations. It will contain
the appendix notes of the American Revisers, printed in the margin of each
page by the side of the passages referred to. The parallel passages, to which
reference is m de in the "Bagster Bibles," with numerous others, so far as
appropriate, will be PRINTED IN FULL in the margin. . The running headings,
usually printed at the tops of pages of the King James version, will be here
supplied. A small black mark will be inserted below the last letter of each
verse to facilitate reference, and aid in RESPONSIVE READING of the Revised
Version. The second half of the volume will consist of the most carefully
prepared HELPS TO THE STUDY OF THE REVISED NEW TESTAMENT, gleaned
from the best Teachers' Editions of the authorized version, and supplied
from various original sources—all being revised and adapted to harmonize
with the Revised Version. We shall introduce many other important features,
making this the most valuable edition of the New Testament ever issued.

Popular Cloth Edition—Ready in July—Price, Postage Free, $1.60.
Send for prospectus giving full description and prices of finer Bindings.

I. K. FUNK & CO., Publishers, 10 and 12 Dey St., New York.

THE

Meisterschaft System,

A SIMPLE AND PRACTICAL METHOD,

ENABLING

ANY ONE TO LEARN, WITH SLIGHT EFFORT, TO SPEAK
FLUENTLY AND CORRECTLY

French, German, Spanish, and Italian,

BY

DR. RICHARD S. ROSENTHAL,

Late Director of the "Akademie für fremde Sprachen" in Berlin and Leipzig,
of the "Meisterschaft College" in London, and Principal of the
"Meisterschaft School of Practical Linguistry" in New York.

FRENCH.

IN FIFTEEN PARTS, EACH CONTAINING THREE LESSONS.

PART VIII.

NEW YORK:
I. K. FUNK & CO., Publishers,
10 AND 12 Dey Street.

TERMS.

WE have arranged with Dr. ROSENTHAL, the author of the "Meisterschaft System," for its introduction in America under his own supervision, and he has opened

FOR NON-RESIDENTS.

The student does not need to leave his home. The lessons of each language are prepared by the Professor, and printed and sent in pamphlet shape to each member of the School wherever he may reside.

The course of study for each language—German, French, Italian, or Spanish—makes fifteen pamphlets of three lessons each.

All members of the School have

THE PRIVILEGE

of asking, by letter, questions concerning each lesson, or consulting on any difficulty which may have occurred to them. All exercises corrected and all questions answered by return post by Dr. ROSENTHAL or one of his assistants.

TERMS OF MEMBERSHIP.

Five Dollars is the price for membership in the school for each language. This amount ($5.) entitles the member to receive the fifteen books or pamphlets containing the lessons, also answers to his questions. Return postage for the answer must accompany the question.

State distinctly which language, or languages, you desire to study There are *no extra charges.* The price, **Five Dollars,** pays for one language ; **Ten Dollars** for two languages, etc. All exercise. and questions must be written on a separate sheet of paper, and must state full address of the pupil.

Remittances must be made in Post-Office Order or registered letter addressed to

I. K. FUNK & CO,

10 and 12 Dey Street, New York.

The Meisterschaft-System,

FRENCH.

PART VIII.

VIII.

FOUNDATION SENTENCE.

(*Continuation.*) .

I should be much obliged to you.

1.

1. I am very much (*infiniment*) obliged to you.

2. I am sorry, but I cannot do it.

3. With the best will (*la volonté*) in the world (*du monde*), I could not (*je ne pourrais*) do so (= it).

4. I should be much obliged to you, if you were to tell me how I could find the new (*nouvelle*) address of this gentleman.

---

1) **Je pourrai,** *I shall be able,* is the irregular future of *pouvoir,* which is conjugated thus :

Present.	*Imperfect.*
Je peux (*peü*), } I can,	Je pouvais (*poü-vay*), I could, &c.
Je puis, } &c.	tu pouvais,
tu peus (*peü*),	il pouvait,
il peut (*peü*),	nous pouvions (*poü-vyong*),
nous pouvons (*poü-vong*),	vous pouviez (*poü-vyèh*), -
vous pouvez,	ils pouvaient (*poü-vay*).
ils peuvent (*peüv'*).	

VIII.

FOUNDATION SENTENCE.

(Continuation.)

Je vous serais bien obligé.

jĕ   voŭ ˙ sĕ ray   byaing   ŏb-lēē-jay.

˙1.

1. Je vous suis⌢infiniment⌢obligé (*jĕ voŭ s'wēē zaing-fēē-nēē-māng tŏb-lēē-jay*).

2. J'en suis fâché (*jāng s'wēē fāh-shay*), mais je ne puis le faire.

3. Avec la meilleure volonté du monde, je ne pourrais le faire (*ā-vēk lā mĕ-yeūr vō-long-tay dŭ mongd jĕ nĕ pour-rēh lĕ fair*).

4. Je vous serais bien⌢obligé si vous me disiez, comment *je pourrai*[1] trouver la nouvelle adresse de ce monsieur (*lā noŭ-vĕl ā-drĕs dĕ sĕ mŏ-syeŭ*).

Preterite.

Je pus (*pŭ*), I could, &c.
tu pus,
il put,
nous pûmes (*pŭm*),
vous pûtes (*pŭt*),
ils purent (*pŭr*).

Conditional.

Je pourrais (*poŭr-ray*),
tu pourrais,
il pourrait,
nous pourrions (*poŭr-ryong*),
vous pourriez,
ils pourraient.

Future.

Je pourrai (*poŭr-rēh*), I shall be able, &c.
tu pourras,
il pourra,
nous pourrons (*poŭr-rong*),
vous pourrez,
ils pourront.

Subj. Present.

Que je puisse (*pŭ-is*),
que tu puisses,
qu'il puisse,
que nous puissions,
que vous puissiez,
qu'ils puissent.

Of the health.

5. How do you do?

6. How are you? (*Literally:* How do you go?)

7. How do you do?

8. How is (= goes) your health?

9. Is your health good?

10. Thanks (*merci*), pretty good. (*Literally :.* It goes pretty well.)

11. How is your father? [The French say more politely *Mr. your father; Madam your mother.*]

12. Is every one (*tout le monde*) well at your house?

13. They are all (*tous*) in good health.

14. Thank you (*Je vous remercie*), my whole family (*toute ma famille*) is very well.

15. How have you been since (*depuis que*) I saw you?

16. How is your friend?

17. { Is your mother well?
     { Is your mother in good health?

18. She is not well; she is a little (i.e. *rather = un peu*) indisposed.

19. { What is the matter with her?
     { What ails her?

---

1) *Bien portant = well, healthy,* is the opposite to *malade, ill,* or *indisposé, indisposed.* But of a healthy *clime* or *food* the French

Dè la santé (*sāng-tay*).

5. Comment vous portez-vous ?

6. Comment‿allez-vous (*cŏ-māng, tā-lēh-voū*) ?

7. { Comment cela va-t-il ?
{ Comment ça va-t-il (*kŏ-māng sā vā-tēēl*) ?

8. Comment va la santé ?

9. Votre santé est‿elle bonne (*vōt' sāng-tay ay-tĕll bŏr*) ?

10. { Merci, ça va assez bien.
{ Merci, cela va assez bien (*mĕr-cēē s'lāh vā ă-say*
{ *byaing*).

11. { Comment se porte monsieur votre père ?
{ Comment va monsieur votre père ?

12. Tout le monde (*toū-lĕ-mong*) se porte-t-il bien chez vous ?

13. Ils sont tous‿en bonne santé (*toūs zāng bŏn sāng-tay*).

14. Je vous remercie (*rē-mĕr-sēē*), toute ma famille est bien portante [1] (*toūt māh fā-mēē-yĕ ay byaing por-tāngt*).

15. Comment vous‿êtes-vous porté depuis que je vous‿ai vu (*dĕ-pü-ēē kĕ jĕ voū zay vü*) ?

16. Comment se porte votre‿ami ?

17. { Votre mère est-elle bien ?
{ Votre mère est-elle en bonne santé (*ay-tĕll āng bŏn*
{ *sāng-tay*) ?

18. Elle ne se porte pas bien ; elle est‿un peu indisposée (*ĕll lay teūng peū aing-dĭs-po-zay*).

19. { Quelle maladie (*mă-lā-dēē*) a-t-elle ?
{ Qu'a-t-elle (*kāh-tĕll*) ?

---

use the word *sain* (*saing*), *healthy*, and *malsain* (*māhl-saing*), un-healthy.

20. She has a headache (*mal à la tête*) and is obliged to keep the room.

21. Your wife[1] has been rather indisposed (*souffrante*)?

22. Yes, sir. Mrs. B. (*or* my wife) had taken cold, but she has quite recovered (= she *is* quite recovered [*entière-ment retablie*]).

23. I have a cold.

24. Mrs. B. has a cold (in the head).

25. Returning from the ball (*or* On my way home from the ball) I took cold.

26. I should like to go to bed; I do not feel well (*je suis mal à mon aise* = ease, comfort).

27. I do not know what ails me.

28. I have a headache.

29. He is suffering with the toothache.

30. I have a sore throat (*la gorge*).

31. I have the stomach-ache.

32. He is sick (*mal au coeur* = ill at the heart).

33. Am I not pale? Yes, sir, you are looking badly.

34. Get me a physician (*médecin*).

35. Do you know (*connaissez-vous*) an English physician?

36. We must hope (*or* Let us hope) that this will not amount to much (= will be nothing).

37. There is not anything the matter with me (= I have nothing).

---

1) In speaking about one's own wife, or of the wife of another party, the French say simply *Madame*.

20. Elle a mal à la tête et est⌒obligé de garder .a chambre (*shāng-br*).

21. Madame[1] a été un peu souffrante (*soū-frāngt*)?

22. Oui monsieur. Madame B. avait pris froid (*or* s'était refroidie); mais⌒elle est⌒entièrement rétablie (*a-vay prēē froāh* [*say-tay rĕ-froāh-dēē*], *may zĕll lay tāng-tyai-rĕ-māng rĕ-tāh-blēē*).

23. ⎰ Je suis⌒enrhumé[2] (*zāng-rü-may*).
    ⎱ J'ai le rhume (*rüm*).

24. Madame B. est⌒enrhumée (du cerveau) (*ay-tāng-rü-may dü sĕr-vōh*).

25. En revenant du bal j'ai pris froid (*or* je me suis refroidi [*rĕ-froāh-dēē*]).

26. Je voudrais bien aller au lit; je suis mal à mon aise (*ā-lēh ōh lēē, jĕ s'wēē māhl lāh mon nayze*).

27. Je ne sais ce que j'ai (*jĕ nĕ say sĕ kĕ jay*).

28. J'ai mal à la tête.

29. Il a mal aux dents (*dāng*).

30. J'ai mal à la gorge.

31. J'ai mal au ventre (*vāng-tr*).

32. Il a mal au coeur (*keūr*). (Refers only to nausea.)

33. Ne suis-je pas pâle (*pāhl*)? Oui monsieur, vous⌒avez mauvaise mine (*mēēn*).

34. Envoyez chercher (*āng-vōāh-yēh shĕr-shēh*) un médecin.

35. Connaissez-vous (*cŏ-nay-sēh-voŭ*) un médecin anglais?

36. Il faut espérer que cela ne sera rien (*rēē-aing*).

37. Je n'ai rien.

---

2) *Je suis⌒enrhumé*, ı have a cold; *le rhume* and *la toux* are *not* synonymous. *Le rhume* is *the cold* (in one's head), but *la toux* is *the cough.*

234

38. I am delighted (*charmé*) to see you in such good health.
39. I have been coughing (= I am coughing [*je tousse*]) for [*depuis*] two days.
40. How hoarse (*enroué*) you are!
41. I am afraid (*Je crains* or *j'ai peur*) I will take (*or catch*) cold.
42. You ought to take care of yourself (*vous ménager*).
43. You will get ill (= You will make an illness of it [*en*]).
44. What is it hurts him?
45. Has he consulted a physician?

46. Did he feel (*a-t-il tâté*) his pulse?
47. I am very glad (*ravi*) to see you looking so well.

48. He will not outlast the winter (*l'hiver*).
49. He is out of danger (*hors de danger*) now.

50. I suffer frequently (*souvent*) with the headache (toothache.)

_____

2.

B. Terms of thanking.

1. I thank you very much, sir.
2. Thanks!
3. My best thanks!
4. Thank you *very* much.

38. Je suis charmé de vous vòir en bonne santé. .

39. J'ai la toux (*toŭ*) (*or* je tousse) depuis deux jours.

40. Comme vous‿êtes‿enroué (*zāng-roŭ-ay*)!

41. Je crains (*or* j'ai peur) de m'enrhumer (*jĕ craĭng de māng-rü-may*).

42. Il faut vous ménager (*may-nā-jay*).

43. Vous‿en ferez une maladie.

44. Qu'est-ce que lui fait mal (*kāys kĕ lü-ēē fay māhl*)?

45. A-t-il consulté un médecin (*kong-sül-tay eūng mayď-saing*).

46. Lui a-t-il tâté le pouls?

47. Je suis ravi (*rā-vēē*) (*or* enchanté [*āng-shāng-tay*]) de vous voir si bonne mine (*mēēn*).

48. Il ne passera pas l'hiver (*lēē vayr*).

49. Il est hors de danger maintenant (*or dĕ dāng-jay maing-tĕ-nāng*).

50. J'ai souvent des maux de tête (des maux de dents [*day mōh dĕ dāng*]).

2.

B. Formules de remercîments (rĕ-mĕr-sēē-māng).

1. Je vous remercie (*rĕ-mĕr-sēē*) beaucoup, monsieur.

2. Mille remercîments (*mēēl rĕ-mĕr-sēē-māng*).

3. { Tous mes remercîments (*toŭ may rĕ-mĕr-sēē-māng*).
   { Grand merci (*grāng mĕr-sēē*).

4. Je vous fais tous mes remercîments.

5. I am very much obliged to you.

6. You are very kind.

7. That would be an abuse of your kindness.

·8· I am very grateful (*sensible*) for your kindness.

9. On the contrary, *I* ought to thank *you*.

10. I do not know how to thank you sufficiently.

C. Terms of excuse.

1. I beg your pardon, sir.

2.. Don't mention it, pray.

3. I beg you will excuse me.

4. I may be mistaken ; I *surely am* mistaken, but I believe that....

5. I beg your pardon, sir, but the affair is quite different.

6. Do not take it amiss, please.

7. Do not be angry, pray.

8. Please, do not feel annoyed on that account (*pour cela*).

---

1) *Dois* is the irregular present of *devoir*.
2) *Saurais* is the irregular conditional of *savoir*, to *know*, and is

5. Je vous suis bien (*or* infiniment) obligé (*ŏb lēē-jay*).

6. { Vous‿êtes bien bon.
   { Vous‿avez trop de bonté (*trŏ dĕ bong-tay*).

7. Ce serait‿abuser de votre complaisance (*tă-bü-zay dĕ vot' cong-play-zăngs*).

8. Je suis très-sensible (*săng-sēēbl*) à votre bonté.

9. C'est moi, au contraire, qui dois[1] vous‿en remercier (*d'woăh voū-zăng rĕ-mĕr-zyēh*).

10. Je ne saurais[2]‿assez vous‿en remercier (*jĕ nĕ so-ray zăs-say voū zăng rĕ-mĕr-syēh*).

C. Formules d'excuse (*dĕx-küs*).

1. { Je vous demande pardon (*dĕ-măngd părdong*), mon-
   {   sieur.
   { Pardon (*păr-dong*), monsieur.

2. { Il n'y a pas de mal (*ēēl nēē ăh păh dĕ măhl*), mon-
   {   sieur.
   { Pas de mal, monsieur.

3. { Mille pardons (*mēēl păr-dong*).
   { Pardon mille fois (*foăh*).

4. Je puis me tromper (*trong-pay*), je me trompe sans doute (*săng doūt*) mais je crois que (*jĕ croăh kĕ*).....

5. Je vous demande pardon, mais l'affaire est tout‿autre.

6. { Ne le trouvez-vous pas mauvais (*mō-vày*).
   { Ne le prenez pas‿en mauvaise part (*zăng mō-vayze păr*).

7. { Ne m'en voulez pas.
   { Ne m'en veuillèz pas (*veū-yēh păh*).

8. { Ne m'en voulez pas pour cela.
   { Ne m'en veuillez pas pour cela.

quite synonymous with the *Je ne puis;* it is used when mental actions are spoken of.

If you were to ask him to send me immediately the patterns which I selected three days ago.

If (We say in English *if you would ask him*, but in French we must always use the *imperfect* or the *present* after *si*)

you were to ask *him ;* you would ask *him*

to ask; to demand; to inquire for

to ask for some one; to inquire for a person

to ask a person for something (Observe the different construction in French)

Do you want to see the master or mistress?

to send me

on

the field

at once; immediately

which I have chosen (*choisis* has to be spelled with an *s*. Compare page 86, Note 1)

there; in it; on them; on it (See rules on *en*, page 204)

there is; there are

three days ago.

Si vous lui demandiez de m'envoyer sur-le-
sēē   voū lŭ-ēē dĕmăng-dyĕh   dĕ măng-voăh-yĕh   sur lĕ

champ les échantillons que j'ai choisis il y a trois
shăng   lay zay-shăng-tēē-yong kĕ   jay sh'woăh-zēē il yăh troăh

jours.
joūr.

Si (*sēē*) (is constructed either with the Present or Imperfect, but
never with the Conditional)

vous lui demandiez (*voū lŭ-ēē dē-măng-dyēh*)

demander (*dĕ-măng-dēh*)

demander quelqu'un (*kēl-keūng*) (Observe the construction)

demander quelque chose à quelqu'un (Observe the construction)

demandez-vous Monsieur ou Madame ?

de m'envoyer (*dĕ măng-voăh-yēh*)

sur (*sür*)

le champ (*lĕ shăng*)

sur-le-champ (*sür-lĕ-shăng*)

que j'ai choisis (*kĕ jay sh'woăh-zēē*) (See rules on the past participle of verbs conjugated
with *avoir*, page 86, Note I)

y (*ēē*) (is used like *en*)

il y a (*ēēl yăh*)

il y a trois jours (*ēēl yăh troăh joūr*).

GRAMMATICAL REMARKS.

3.

Numerals.

We have two kinds of Numerals, the Cardinal and the Ordinal. The **Cardinal Numerals** (or numbers) are:

1 un (*eŭng*)		21	vingt *et* un
2 deux (*deŭ*)		22	vingt-deux
3 trois (*troā*)		23	vingt-trois
4 quatre (*kăt*)		24	vingt-quatre
5 cinq (*saing*)		25	vingt-cinq
6 six (*sĕĕ*)		26	vingt-six
7 sept (*sĕt*)		27	vingt-sept
8 huit (*h'wēĕt*)		28	vingt-huit
9 neuf (*neŭv*)		29	vingt-neuf
10 dix (*dēēz*)		30	trente (*trāngt*)
11 onze (*ŏngs*)		31	trente *et* un
12 douze (*doŭze*)		32	trente-deux
13 treize (*trayze*)		33	trente-trois
14 quatorze (*kā-torz*)		34	trente-quatre
15 quinze (*kaingz*)		35	trente-cinq
16 seize (*sayz*)		36	trente-six
17 dix-sept (*dēē-sĕt*)		37	trente-sept
18 dix-huit (*dēē-z'wēĕt*)		38	trente-huit
19 dix-neuf		39	trente-neuf
20 vingt (*vaing*)		40	quarante (*kā-rāngt*)

41 quarante *et* un

42 quarante-deux

43 quarante-trois

44 quarante-quatre

45 quarante-cinq

46 quarante-six

47 quarante-sept

48 quarante-huit

49 quarante-neuf

50 cinquante (*saing-kāngt*)

51 cinquante *et* un

52 cinquante-deux

53 cinquante-trois

54 cinquante-quatre

55 cinquante-cinq

56 cinquante-six

57 cinquante-sept

58 cinquante-huit

59 cinquante-neuf

60 soixante (*s'woā-sāngt*)

61 soixante *et* un

62 soixante-deux

63 soixante-trois

64 soixante-quatre

65 soixante-cinq

66 soixante-six

67 soixante-sept

68 soixante-huit

69 soixante-neuf

70 soixante-dix

71 soixante *et* onze

72 soixante-douze

73 soixante-treize

74 soixante-quatorze

75 soixante-quinze

76 soixante-seize

77 soixante-dix-sept

78 soixante-dix-huit

79 soixante-dix-neuf

80 quatre-vingts (*kāt'r-vaing*)

81 quatre-vingt-*un*

82 quatre-vingt-deux

83 quatre-vingt-trois

84 quatre-vingt-quatre

85 quatre-vingt-cinq

86 quatre-vingt-six

87 quatre-vingt-sept

88 quatre-vingt-huit

89 quatre-vingt-neuf

90 quatre-vingt-dix

91 quatre-vingt-onze

92 quatre-vingt-douze

93 quatre-vingt-treize

94 quatre-vingt-quatorze

95 quatre-vingt-quinze

96 quatre-vingt-seize

97 quatre-vingt-dix-sept

98 quatre-vingt-dix-huit

99 quatre-vingt-dix-neuf

100 cent (*sāng*)

101 cent-*un*

102 cent deux, &c.

200 deux cents

201 deux cent un

202 deux cent deux, &c.

1,000 mille (*mēēl*)

2,000 deux mille

1,000,000 un million (*mēēl-yong*).

Remarks.

1) The numbers 21, 31, 41, 51, 61, and 71 are written vingt *et* un, trente *et* un, &c., but 8: and 101 are written quatre-vingt-un, cent-un, without the copula *et*.

2) Quatre-vingts, 80, has a final *s* which is omitted in all subsequent numbers.

3) Deux cents, 200, trois cents, 300, &c., are written with a final *s;* but when these numbers are followed by any other number they drop the *s;* as : deux cent un, 201, trois cent quatre, 304, &c.

4) Mille *never* takes the *s*.

5) There being no modern French number to express 70 or 90 (the old forms septante and nonnante being almost obsolete, and only used in Switzerland) one counts from 60 to 80, and from 80 to 99, continuously, as though one were to say in English, eighty-eight, eighty-nine, eighty-ten, eighty-eleven, &c.

6) The expression, *I am* 20, 30, 40, &c., years old, cannot be rendered literally, but must be expressed thus: *J'ai* vingt ans, — *j'ai* trente ans, &c.—How old are you? is translated: Quel âge avez-vous? *Ex.:*

Quel âge a votre ami ? how old is your friend ?
Il a dix-huit ans, he is eighteen years old.

Ordinal Numbers.

Except le premier (*lĕ prĕ-myēh*) and le second (*lĕ sĕ-gong*), the ordinal numbers are formed from the cardinal by changing *e* mute into *ième;* and by adding this syllable to those which end in another consonant. Among these, however, cinq takes *u* before *ième* (*cinquième*), and neuf changes the *f* into *v* (*neuvième*). The *ordinal numbers* are as follows:

Le premier (*prĕ-myēh*) ⎱ the
la première (*prĕ-myair*) ⎰ first.

le second (*sĕ-gong*)   ⎫
la seconde (*sĕ-gongd*)   ⎬ the
le, la deuxième (*deū-*   ⎭ second.
 zyaim)

le troisième (*troā-zyēhm*) the third.

le quatrième, the fourth.

le cinquième (*saing-kyēhm*), the fifth.

le sixième (*sĕē-zyēhm*), the sixth.

le septième, the seventh.

le huitième, the eight.

le neuvième, the ninth.

le dixième, the 10th.

le onzième, the 11th.

le douzième, the 12th.

le treizième, the 13th.

le quatorzième, the 14th.

le quinzième, the 15th.

le seizième, the 16th.

le dix-septième, the 17th.

le dix-huitième, the 18th.

le dix-neuvième, the 19th.

le vingtième, the 20th.

le vingt-unième, the 21st.

le vingt-deuxième, the 22d, &c.

le trentième, the 30th.

le quarantième, the 40th.

le cinquantième, the 50th.

le soixantième, the 60th.

le soixante-dixième, the 70th.

le soixante-onzième, the 71st.

le soixante-douzième, the 72d, &c.

le quatre-vingtième, the 80th.

le quatre-vingt-unième, the 81st.

le quatre-vingt-dixième, the 90th.

le centième, the 100th.

le cent et unième, the 101st.

le cent deuxième, the 102d, &c.

le cent vingtième, the 120th.

le deux-centième, the 200th.

le six cent soixante-quinzième, the 675th.

le millième, the 1000th.

le dernier, the last.

Remarks.

1) *Unième* is used only after *vingt, trente, quarante,* &c., as: Charles est le trente-unième de sa classe, Charles is the 31st of his class.

2) Days of tne month (except *le premier* and *le dernier*) are expressed by cardinal numbers, as :

The first of April, le premier avril ; but :

The fifth of January, le cinq janvier (*jăng-vyĕh*).

The 2d, 3d, 4th, &c. of May, le deux, trois, quatre, &c., mai (*or* de mai).

The eleventh of March, le onze (without apostrophe) mars.

The twentieth of June, le vingt juin (*j'wŏaing*).

The question, ' What day of the month is to-day ? ' is translated :

    Quel jour du mois avons-nous aujourd'hui? *or :*

    Quel quantième (*kĕll kăngt-yĕhm*) sommes-nous? (*or* avons nous])?

Answer : C'est aujourd'hui le dix, *or :*

    Nous sommes le dix, *or* nous⁀avons le dix.

The English ' on the sixth,' &c., is rendered in French le six. *Ex.:* On the sixth of May, le six mai (*may*).

3) Proper names of princes, too, take in French the cardinal numbers without the article, except *the first* and sometimes *the second*, as :

Henri premier, Henri the first.

Charles second *or* deux, Charles the second ; but Henry *quatre*, Henry the fourth.

4) The *distinctive* numbers (adverbs of number) are formed from the ordinal by adding *-ment* or *-ement* to the final letter :

    Premièrement (*prĕ-myĕh-rĕ-măng*), first ; in the first place.

    Deuxièmement (*dĕŭ-zyĕh-mĕ-măng*), secondly.

    Troisièmement (*troă-zyĕh-mĕ-măng*), thirdly, &c.

5) *Fractional* numbers are expressed by ordinal numbers, as in English, but only from five upwards, as :

Un cinquième, a fifth.	Un huitième, an eighth.
Un sixième, a sixth.	Un dixième, a tenth.

The others are as follows:

A half = un demi (*dĕ-mēē*), f. une demie. The half = la moitié (*mō-ă-tyēh*).

A third = un tiers. A quarter *or* fourth = un quart (*kār*).

One pound and a half = une livre et demie (*dĕ mēē*).

Names of the months.

janvier (*jăng-vyēh*), January.

février (*fay-vrēē-ĕh*), February.

mars (*mārs*), March.

avril (*ă-vrēē-yĕ*), April.

mai (*maў*), May.

juin (*j'ūāing*), June.

juillet (*j'wēē-yĕh*), July.

août, (*a-oū*), August.

septembre (*set-tăng-br*), September.

octobre (*oct-to-br*), October.

novembre (*no-văng-br*), November.

décembre (*day-săng-br*), December.

en janvier, in January.

Names of the days.

dimanche (*dēē-măngsh*), Sunday.

lundi (*leūng-dēē*), Monday.

mardi (*mār-dēē*), Tuesday.

mercredi (*mĕr-kr-dēē*), Wednesday.

jeudi (*jeū-dēē*), Thursday.

vendredi (*văng-dr-dēē*), Friday.

samedi (*săm-dēē*), Saturday.

on Tuesday, (le) mardi.

Words.

Les Meubles (meū-bl), (m.). The Furniture.

une armoire (*ār-m'woār*), a wardrobe.

la commode, the bureau.

le tiroir (*tēē-ro-ār*), the drawer.

la table, the table.

la chaise (*shayze*), the chair.

le fauteuil (*fōh-teū-yĕ*), the armchair.

la couverture (*coū-vĕr-tür*), the blanket.

une étagère (*ay-tāh-jayr*), a whatnot.

le tapis (*tāh-pēē*), the carpet.

le tapis de table, the table-cover.

le lit (*lēē*), the bed.

le lit de fer, the iron bedstead.

le dos (*dŏh*), the back.

le sofa, the sofa.

la glace (*glāhs*), the (large) mirror.

le miroir (*mēē-ro-ār*), the (small) mirror.

le tableau (*tā-blŏ*), the picture.

le cadre (*cāh-dr*), the frame.

la cheminée (*shĕ-mēē-nay*), the chimney.

le chambranle (*shāng-brāngl*), the chimney-piece.

une pelle (*pell*), a shovel.

des pincettes (*paing-sĕt*), tongs.

une pendule (*pāng-dül*), a clock.

le traversin (*trā-vĕr-saing*), the bolster.

le matelas (*mă-t'-lāh*), the mattress.

un sommier élastique (*som-yĕh ay-lā-stēĕk*), a spring-mattress.

l'oreiller (*lŏh-rĕ-yĕh*), the pillow.

le drap (*drāh*), the sheet.

faire le lit, to make the bed.

mettre des draps blancs, to put on fresh sheets.

une lampe (*lāngp*), a lamp.

des allumettes (*day ză-lü-mĕt*), matches.

une bougie (*boū-jēē*), a waxlight.

Translate the following

Exercise

into English and then render it again into French :

Appartements à louer (*āp-pār-tĕ-māng āh loū ēh*).

Avez-vous des appartements (dāy zāp-pār-t'māng) à louer?—J'en ai plusieurs et de différents prix (dif-fay-rāng prēē). — Voulez-vous un appartement meublé ou non meublé ?—J'ai besoin de chambres meublées. Il me faudrait un salon et deux chambres à coucher. — Je puis vous satisfaire (*satisfy*), madame.—Donnez-vous la peine d'entrer (dāng-tray). Je vais vous faire voir (*let you see ; show you*) les chambres. — L'escalier (les-kā-lyeh = *the stair-case*) est un peu rapide (rā-pēēd = *steep*). — Il en a l'air, mais il est très-doux (doū = *easy*) à monter.—Est-il éclairé (*lighted up*) le soir? — Cela va sans dire (*Why, certainly ; of course*).—Vous voyez que le salon est sur le devant (dĕ-vāng = *to the front*) et que les chambres à coucher sont sur le derrière.—Quel est le prix du loyer (*rent*)? — Il est de cent francs.—C'est très-cher.— Veuillez remarquer, madame, que c'est ici le plus beau quartier (kār-tyĕh = *part ; quarter*) de la ville et que la maison est très-bien habitée (ā-bēē-tay = *inhabited by very respectable people*).

In order to get a thorough mastery over the French verbs the student may now place the following verbs in proper form.

Exercise.

Give the

Indicative Present

of the following verbs :

Je *mener.*—Nous *avancer.*—Il *acheter.*—Vous *appeler.*—Trop de plaisir *ennuyer.*—Ces élèves *répéter* comme des perroquets (per-ro-kĕh = *parrots*).—L'intempérance (laing-tāng-pay-rāngs = *intemperance*) *abréger* (*shorten*) la vie (vēē = *life*).—La nature (nā-tür) est un miroir fidèle (fēē-dayl=*true*) qui *réfléter* (*repeat*) à nos yeux la grandeur de Dieu (*grāng-deūr dĕ dyeū* = *the greatness of God*).

Imperfect.

Je *commencer.*—Nous *régner* (*to reign*).—Il *jeter.*—L'armée *avancer*, les ennemis (lay zĕ-nĕ-mēē) *engager* le feu ; la victoire (vĭc-t'woāre = *victory*) *balancer.*—Nous *établir.*—Vous *rougir* (*to blush*).—Ils *bâtir* (*to build*).—Le jeune garçon *unir* la douceur à la modestie.—Il *défendre.*—Nous *correspondre.*

Future.

Nous *avouer.*—Est-ce toi qui *distribuer ?*—Je l'*aimer.*—Dieu nous *protéger.*—Vous *regretter* le temps perdu (*lost*).—Vous *saisir* (*to seize*). —Le travail (trā-vā-ȳĕ=*labor*) vous *enrichir* (ăng-rēē-shēēr=*to enrich*). — Nous *répondre.*—Vous *perdre.*

Conditional.

Nous *perdre.*—Tu *entendre* (ăng-tāng-dr = *to hear*).—Sans la vertu (*virtue*) vous *prétendre* vainement (vain'-māng = *in vain*) au bonheur (bon-neūr = *happiness*).—Vous *prier.*—Nous *diner.*

Subjunctive Present.

Il faut que vous *certifier* (cĕr-tēē-fȳĕh.—Il faut que chacun (shāh-keūng = *every one*) *payer* son tribut à la nature (nā-tür).—Il faut qu'il *abréger.*—Il faut qu'il *envoyer* les échantillons.

Put the following singulars into the corresponding persons of the plural :

Je *prétends.*—Tu as *défendu.* — J'avais *rompu.* —Je *perdrais* si je *jouais,* mais je ne *joue* pas.—Ton maître ne *veut* pas que tu l'*interrompes.*—Je *hais.*—Que je *vienne.*—Je *vais.*—Il *ira.*—Je *faiblissais.*— Il *plaisante.*—Il *assure.*—Tu as *donné.*—Je suis *venu.*—Elle était *parti.* —Il *peut.*—Je *pourrai.*—Je suis *allé.*

Translate the following

Exercises

into English, and then again, without assistance of the book, into French :

At a theatre.

Où voulez-vous que nous⌢allions⌢aujourd'hui ?—Allons‿aux Français.[1]—Je le veux bien. — Qu'est-ce qu'on donne ce soir? Voyons l'affiche (lā-feesh = *hand-bill, poster*). *Les Fourchambault* (*the Fourchambault* [foūr-shăng-bol] *family*), comédie (cŏ-may-dēē) en cinq actes par (*by*) Emile Augier. Le nom de l'auteur (lō-teūr = *the author*) suffit (*is sufficient*) pour me décider (day-see-day = *to decide*). J'entends dire (jāng-tāng dēēr = *I hear it said, I am told*) que c'est‿une très-belle pièce (*very good* [*fine*] *piece*). Quelle place prendrons-nous (prāng-drong noū = *shall we take*)? Quelles sont les meilleures (*the best*) places? Pour les⌢hommes (*gentlemen*) les⌐fauteuils d'orchestre (fō-teū-yĕ dor-shĕs-tr=*orchestra-stalls*) ; mais les dames ne vont qu'aux premières ou aux secondes loges (*go only to the boxes on the first or secod tier*). " *L'entr'-acte* (lāng-tr-āct) messieurs, le programme détaillé (day-tā-yay = *detailed*) du spectacle! Les noms (nōng = *names*) de tous les⌢acteurs (*actors*) qui jouent (jew = *play*) dans les pièces de ce soir (s'wōar=*evening*) ! " — Qu'est-ce qu'ils crient (krēē = *scream*) donc ces⌢individues (say-zaing-dēē-vēē-dü = *these individuals*) ?—Ils⌢offrent (eel-zŏffr = *they are offering*) les petits journaux de théâtre (lay-p'tee joūr-nō = *the small journals*). — A Paris, ces journaux remplacent (rāng-plās = *take the place of*) le programme qui est distribué (dĭs-tree-bü-ay = *distributed*) en Amérique par l'administration (lād-mēē-nĭs-trā-zyong = *administration*) du théâtre (tay-āh-tr). — Combien ce journal? Vingt centimes (sāng-tēēm).

---

1) The best French theatre in Paris, or rather in France.

Words.

La Ville (vēēl).	*The Town.*
Une rue pavée (*pāh-vay*), a paved street.	la deuxième à droite (*deŭ-zyēhm*), second turning to the right. —
traverser, to cross.	un passage (*pāh sāge*), a thorough-fare. —
passer de l'autre côté, to cross over ; to go to the other side.	
le trottoir (*trot-t'woār*), the foot-path.	une place (*plāhs*), un square (pronounced in the English way), } a square.
le coin (*ko-aing*) de rue, the street corner,	l'édifice (*lay-dēē-fēēs*), the building. —
au bout de la rue (*oh boŭ dĕ lā rü*), at the end of the street.	un monument (*moh-nü-māng*), a monument.
tout droit (*toŭ droāh*), straight ahead !	une église (*ay-glēēze*), a church. .
l'ambassade (*lāng-bās-sāhd*), the embassy.	un palais (*pāh-lay*), a palace. .
la police (*pŏ-lēēs*), the police.	l'hôtel de ville, the Town-hall ; City-hall.
un sergent de ville (*ser-jāng dĕ vēĕl*), a police-officer.	le cocher (*kŏh-shay*), the cabman. .
le gaz, the gas.	une course, a tour ; drive. .
un réverbère, a street-lamp.	à l'heure, by the hour. . —
une voiture (*voāh-tür*), a carriage.	à la course, by the mile. —
une voiture de remise, un remise, (*rĕ-mēēze*) } livery-coach ; fly ; hackney-coach.	le pourboire (*poŭr-b'woār*), a tip.
	une station de fiacres (*ün stā-syong de fēē-ākr*), a cab-stand. —
le pont (*pong*), the bridge.	un omnibus (*büs*), an omnibus.
	l'intérieur est complet (*laing-tayr-yeŭr ay cong-play*), full inside.

COMPANION TO THE
Revised Version of the New Testament.

Explaining the Reasons for the Changes Made on the Authorized Version.

BY ALEXANDER ROBERTS, D.D.,
Member of the English Revision Committee.

WITH SUPPLEMENT BY A MEMBER OF THE AMERICAN COMMITTEE.

Containing a Brief History of the Revision of the Work and Co-operation of the New Testament Companies, of the Points of Agreement and Difference, and an Explanation of the Appendix to the Revised New Testament.

ALSO, A FULL TEXTUAL INDEX,
Being a Key to Passages in which Important Changes have been Made.

This book, having been carefully prepared by Members of both Revision Committees, carries official weight. It shows what changes have been made, and also the reasons which influenced the revisers in making them. It will be difficult to judge of the merits of the revision without the aid of this Companion volume. Our edition is printed by special arrangement with the English publishers. It is well known that, by an arrangement between the two Committees of Revision, the changes suggested by the American Committee, but which were not adopted by the English Revisers, are published as an Appendix to the Revised New Testament. The *Companion* volume is an explanation of *all* the changes adopted by both committees, and of those suggested by the American Committee, but not assented to by the English Committee, in their final revision. The book will be indispensable to a right understanding of the revision. This cheap edition of the combined books, although authorized and copyrighted, will be sold for 25 cents in paper, and 75 cents in cloth—sent postage free.

TESTIMONIALS.

T. W. CHAMBERS, D.D., a Member of the American Committee of Revision, says of this book: "Many persons have expressed a desire that, simultaneously with the issue of the Revised New-Testament, there should appear an authentic explanation of the reasons for such changes as will be found in its pages. The work of Dr. Roberts is exactly fitted to meet this desire....Nowhere else in print can be found a statement so full and exact. It gives all needed information, and does it in an unexceptional way."

C. F. DEEMS, D.D., Pastor of the Church of the Strangers, New York, writes: "The Companion to the Revised Version seems to me almost indispensable. Even scholars who were not at the meeting of the Revisers would have a wearisome work in seeking to discover all the changes made, and to ordinary readers very much of the labor would be lost. ....All this is set forth by Dr. Roberts with admirable perspicuity. Those who have any intelligent interest in the Holy Scriptures, will find this little book absorbingly interesting. I shall urge every member of the church of which I am pastor to give it a careful reading, and purpose to introduce it as a text-book in our Bible-classes."

"So valuable, interesting and useful is this publication, that we advise every one who wishes to know the why and wherefore of the revision, to obtain it immediately."—*New York Observer.*

Paper, 8vo size, 25 cents; Cloth, 16mo, 75 cents.

*** For Sale by Booksellers and Newsdealers, or sent postage-paid, on receipt of price, by

I. K. FUNK & CO., Publishers, 10 & 12 Dey St., N. Y.

THE TEACHER'S EDITION

OF THE

REVISED NEW TESTAMENT

With New Concordance and Index, Harmony of the Gospels, Maps,
Historical and Chronological Tables, Parallel Passages printed
in full, Blank Pages Interleaved for manuscript notes, and
many other New and Indispensable Helps to the Study
of the Revised Version.

After the excitement connected with the sale of the first copies of the new revision, which lack the usual indexing headlines and marginal references to parallel passages, and also the appendixes of tables, maps, etc.—all of which helps preachers, teachers and Bible students have come to consider as absolutely essential to a working copy of the Bible—there arises an imperative demand for an edition of the Revised New Testament, containing all the marginal and appendix helps of former TEACHERS' AND REFERENCE BIBLES, adapted carefully and accurately to the Revised Version. We are, therefore, preparing, as rapidly as is consistent with accuracy, such an edition of the Revised New Testament. The work is under the supervision of well-known Bible scholars, with numerous helpers, and will be issued as early as it can be done with thoroughness. In style and size the book will resemble the Bagster Bible, "Fac-simile large edition," known as "the Moody Bible," being the same width and length and size of type. It will be supplied at prices *within the reach of all.*

This "Teachers' Edition of the Revised New Testament" will be an exact, *certified reproduction* of the entire Oxford and Cambridge Edition, including the Preface and all the marginal readings and explanations. It will contain the appendix notes of the American Revisers, printed in the margin of each page by the side of the passages referred to. The parallel passages, to which reference is made in the "Bagster Bibles," with numerous others, so far as appropriate, will be PRINTED IN FULL in the margin. The running headings, usually printed at the tops of pages of the King James version, will be here supplied. A small black mark will be inserted below the last letter of each verse to facilitate reference, and aid in RESPONSIVE READING of the Revised Version. The second half of the volume will consist of the most carefully prepared HELPS TO THE STUDY OF THE REVISED NEW TESTAMENT, gleaned from the best Teachers' Editions of the authorized version, and supplied from various original sources—all being revised and adapted to harmonize with the Revised Version. We shall introduce many other important features, making this the most valuable edition of the New Testament ever issued.

Popular Cloth Edition—Ready in July—Price, Postage Free, $1.60.

Send for prospectus giving full description and prices of finer Bindings.

I. K. FUNK & CO., Publishers, 10 and 12 Dey St., New York.

39. Ah, tous ces objets sont usagés (*toū say zob-jay song tü-zā-jay*).

40. Conducteur (*kong-düc-teūr*), deux placès pour Lyon (*plāhs poūr lēē-ong*), s'il vous plaît,

41. Il n'y en a plus dans ces waggons (*ēēl nēē͡ān͡nāh plü dāng cĕ vă-gong*), messieurs ; descendez le train (*m'syeūh ; dĕ-sāng-dēh lĕ traing*).

42. Y a-t-il encore une place (*āng-cŏr rün plāhs*), messieurs?

43. Non monsieur, nous sommes au complet (*oh cong-play*).

44. Je vous demande pardon (*pār-dong*), il y en a encore une (*ēēl yāh nāh āng-cor rün*).

45. Y a-t-il quelque chose (*ēē-āh-tēēl kĕl-kĕ shōhs*) poūr moi, garçon.

46. Je suis souffrant (*soū-frāng*) (*or* indisposé [*aing-dis-po-zay*]). Est-ce qu'il y a une pharmacie anglaise près de l'hôtel (*ays kēēl yāh ün fār-māh-sēē āng-layze pray dĕ lō-tĕll*).

47. Oui monsieur, il y a un pharmacien (*phār-mā-syaing*) anglais aū bout (*oh boū*) de la rue.

48. Y a-t-il des lettres au nom de monsieur B. (*day lĕttr' oh nong dĕ mŏ-syeūh bay*) ?

49. Mon nom s'écrit (*mong nong say-krēē*).....

50. Y a-t-il encore loin d'ici aux Champs-Elysées (*āng-kor lo͡-aing dēē-sēē ōh shāng-zay-lēē-zēh*) ?

51. Cette rue n'y conduit point dù tout (*nēē cong-d'wēē po͡-aing dü toū*).

52. { Vous êtes à l'opposé.
{ Vous y tournez le dos (*vou zēē toūr-nēh lĕ dōh* = *you turn your back to it*).

53. What can I do for you? (*Literally :* What is there for your service) ?

54. Take care, sir (*prenez garde, monsieur*) ; there are two steps down there (*là-bas*).

55. There were a great many people (*beaucoup de monde*) at the concert.

56. There are already (*déjà*) some people there.

57. We have company (*du monde*) to dinner to-day.

58. There was an enormous crowd (*un monde fou*) there.

59. It's always crowded here (= There is always crowd [*foule*] here).

60. Is there salt enough on it ?

61. What is the news in the papers (= What is there *of* news in the papers) ?

62. I have not yet read (*lu*) to-day's paper.

63. How do you like (*trouvez-vous*) Mr. B.'s new piece ?

64. There are some very nice verses (*vers*) in it, but — to speak frankly — the development (*dénoûment*) is forced (*forcé*).

65. Could you not call your employer (*votre patron*) ?

66. He is not in, sir ; he is gone out on (*pour*) business.

67. Look at this hat (*or* bonnet), please. It is the latest thing out (*c'est tout ce qu'il y a de plus nouveau*).

68. I cannot give it you at a cheaper price (*à moins*). I do not gain (*or* make = *gagne*) a centime by it.

53. Qu'y a-t-il pour·votre service (*kēē-āh-tēēl poūr vot' sĕr-
vēēs*) ?

54. Prenez garde, monsieur ; il y a encore deux marches.
là-bas (*ēēl yāh āng-kor deū mārsh lā-bāh*).

55. Il y avait beaucòup de monde au concert (*ēēl yā-vay
boh-koū dĕ mongd'ōh cong-sair*).

56. Il y a déjà du monde (*day-jāh dü mongd*).

57. Nous⌢avons⌢aujourd'hui du monde à dîner (*āh dēē-
nēh*).

58. Il y avait un monde fou [*fou* means literally *foolish*].

59. Il y a toujours foule ici (*toū-joūr fōōl ēē-sēē*).

60. Y a-t-il assez de sel (*ā-say dĕ sĕl*) ?

61. Qu'y a-t-il de nouveau dans les journaux (*kēē-āh-tēēl
dĕ noū-vōh dāng lay joūr-noh*) ?

62. Je n'ai pas encore lu le journal d'aujourd'hui [*lu* is
the past participle of *lire*, to read].·

63. Comment trouvez-vous la nouvelle pièce de monsieur B. (*com-māng troū-vēh voū lāh noū-vĕll pee-āys dĕ
mŏ-syeūh bay*) ?

64. Il y a de très-beaux vers, mais — à parler franchement — le dénoûment (*dĕ tray bōh vayr, may āh pār-
lēh frāng-sh' māng lĕ day-noū-māng*) est forcé.

65. Ne pourriez-vous pas⌢appeller votre patron (*vŏt pā-
trong*) ?

66. Il n'y est pas, monsieur ; il est sorti pour affaires.

67. Regardez ce chapeau, s'il vous plaît. C'est tout ce qu'il
y a de plus nouveau (*say toū s'keēl yāh dĕ plü noū-vōh*).

68. Je ne puis vous le donner à moins. Je n'y gagne
un centime (*gān-yĕ eūng sāng-tēēm*).

69. Do you not need any gloves, sir?

70. Yes, I need two pairs.

71. { This pair is too large for me.
    { This pair is too narrow for me.

72. { They are too short in the fingers (*les doigts*).
    { They are too long in the fingers.

73. Please pass them to me; I'll put a little powder (*poudre*) in them.

74. Were there many people at the theatre yesterday?

75. The parquette (*le parterre*) was full (*plein*), but there was hardly any one in the boxes (*les loges*).

76. Had you a good seat? (*Literally:* Were you well seated?)

77. Yes, I was near the orchestra.

78. The orchestra-stalls (*les fauteuils d'orchestre*) are the best seats for gentlemen.

79. Ladies of fashion (*les dames comme il faut*) go to the boxes of the first and second tier only (*literally:* go only to the first and second boxes).

80. Did you go to the soirée of Mrs. L. on Monday?

81. Yes, why didn't you come there?

82. I was at the theatre.

83. What did they play (= give)?

84. They performed (= gave) Iphigenia, with a comedy (*un vaudeville*) afterwards (= at the end, *à la fin*); but I went to see the tragedy only.

69. Ne vous faut-il pas de gants, monsieur ?

70. Oui, il m'en faut deux paires (*ēēl māng fōh deū pair*).

71. { Cette paire m'est trop large (*may trōh lārje*).
     { Cette paire m'est trop étroite (*trōh ay-troāht*).

72. { Les doigts (*d'wo-āh*) sont trop courts (*trōh coūr*).
     { Les doigts (*d'wo-āh*) sont trop longs.

73. Passez-les-moi, s'il vous plaît ; j'y mettrai un peu de poudre (*jēē mě-tray eūng peū dě poū-dr*).

74. Y avait-il beaucoup de monde hier au spectacle (*ēē-ayr oh spec-tākl*).

75. Le parterre était plein (*plaing*), mais il n'y avait presque (*prěsk*) personne dans les loges (*loje*).

76. Etiez-vous bien placé (*byaing plāh-say*) ?

77. Oui, j'étais près de l'orchestre (*pray dě lör-shěs-tr*).

78. Pour les hommes, les fauteuils d'orchestre sont les meilleures places (*poūr lay zŏm lay fō-teū-yě dor-shěs-tr song lay mē-yeūr plāhs*).

79. Les dames comme il faut ne vont qu'aux (*ně vong kōh*) premières ou aux secondes loges.

80. Est-ce que vous êtes allé (*ays-kě voū zayt zāh-lay*) à la soirée de madame L., lundi (*leūng-dēē*) ?

81. Oui, pourquoi n'y êtes-vous donc pas venu (*nēē ayt voū dong pāh vě-nü*) ?

82. J'ai été au spectacle.

83. Qu'est-ce qu'on donnait (*kays kong don-nay*) ?

84. On a donné Iphigénie (*ēē-fēē-jay-nēē*), avec un vaude-ville à la fin (*eūng vohd'-vee-yě āh lā faing*), mais je n'y suis allé que pour voir la tragédie (*may jě nēē s'wēē zāh-lay kě poūr voār lā trǎ-jay-dēē*).

3.

GRAMMATICAL REMARKS.

A.

Possessive Adjectives.

The following adjectives are mostly placed under the head of pronouns; as, however, they may be more properly termed *adjectives*, I have thought it better to insert them in this place.

SINGULAR.		PLURAL.
Masc.	*Fem.*	*Both genders.*
1. mon (*mong*),	ma (*māh*),	mes (*may*), my.
2. ton (*tong*)	ta (*tāh*),	tes (*tay*), thy.
3. son (*song*)	sa (*sāh*),	ses (*say*), his, her, *or* its.

SINGULAR.	PLURAL.
Masc. and Fem.	*Both genders.*
1. notre (*nŏt'*),	nos (*nŏ*), our.
2. votre (*vŏt'*),	vos (*vŏ*), your.
3. leur (*leūr*),	leurs (*leūr*), their.

These pronominal adjectives agree in gender and number with the nouns which they qualify; as:

mon tableau (*tā-blŏ*), my picture.
ma clef (*klay*), my key.
mes enfants (*may zāng-fāng*), my children.
son portrait (*por-tray*), his (*or* her) portrait.
ses maisons (*may-zong*) his (*or* her) houses.

notre lavabo (*lā-vā-bŏ*), our washstand.

nos serviettes (*sĕr-vyĕt*), our towels.

leur banquier (*bānk-yēh*), their banker.

leurs acquits (*zā-kĕĕ*), their receipts.

Observations.

1. The masculine forms *mon*, *ton*, *son*, and **not** *ma*, *ta*, *sa*, are used before nouns of the feminine gender beginning with a vowel or unaspirated *h*, for the sake of euphony, and to avoid the meeting of two vowels; as:

mon opinion (*mon-no-pĕĕ-nyong*), (f.) my opinion.

ton humeur (*ton nü-meŭr*), (f.) thy temper.

son histoire (*son nĭs-twoār*), (f.) his (*or* her) history.

2. The pronominal adjectives *notre*, our, and *votre*, your, have no circumflex accent (to distinguish them from the possessive pronouns *le nôtre*, *le vôtre*, see next Part), and are pronounced *short*, almost as if written *not'*, *vot'*.

Demonstrative Adjectives.

The Demonstrative Adjective, sometimes called a demonstrative pronoun, is thus declined:

Singular.		*Plural.*	
Masc. ce	} this *or* that.	*Masc.*	} ces, these *or* those.
Fem. cette		*Fem.*	

The demonstrative adjective agrees with its noun in gender and number; as:

ce cheval (*cĕ shĕ-vāhl*),   this horse.

cette maison (*cĕt may-zong*),   this house.

ces enfants (*say sāng-fāng*),   these children.

The form *cet* is employed for the masculine instead of *ce*, when preceding a noun beginning with a vowel *or* mute *h ;* as:

cet‿homme (*cĕ tòm*),	this man.
cet‿arbre (*cĕ tãrbr*),	this tree.
cet‿agent (*cĕ tãh-jãng*),	this agent.

Relative, Interrogative, and Admirative Adjectives.

The Relative, Interrogative, and Admirative Adjective **quel** is thus declined:

Singular.		*Plural.*	
Masc. quel (*kĕl*),	} which *or* what.	*Masc.* quels	{ which *or* what.
Fem. quelle (*kĕl*),		*Fem.* quelles	

It agrees in gender and number with the noun which it qualifies; as:

quel‿homme? (!) (*kĕl lòm*) which man? *or* what a man !
quelle femme? (!) (*kĕl fãmm*), which woman? *or* what a woman !
quels chevaux (*shĕ-vòh*)? (!) which horses? *or* what horses !
quelles fleurs (*fleŭr*)? (!) which flowers? *or* what flowers !

B.

Of Passive Verbs.

Passive verbs are formed, in French as in English, by joining the Participle past of an active verb to the auxiliary verb to be, *être;* for instance: of the verb *donner,* the passive voice is **être donné,** to be given; of *finir,* **être fini,** to be finished; of *vendre,* **être vendu,** to be

THE

𝕸𝖊𝖎𝖘𝖙𝖊𝖗𝖘𝖈𝖍𝖆𝖋𝖙 𝕾𝖞𝖘𝖙𝖊𝖒,

A SIMPLE AND PRACTICAL METHOD,

ENABLING

ANY ONE TO LEARN, WITH SLIGHT EFFORT, TO SPEAK FLUENTLY AND CORRECTLY

𝕱𝖗𝖊𝖓𝖈𝖍, 𝕲𝖊𝖗𝖒𝖆𝖓, 𝕾𝖕𝖆𝖓𝖎𝖘𝖍, 𝖆𝖓𝖉 𝕴𝖙𝖆𝖑𝖎𝖆𝖓,

BY

DR. RICHARD S. ROSENTHAL,

Late Director of the "Akademie für fremde Sprachen" in Berlin and Leipzig,
of the "Meisterschaft College" in London, and Principal of the
"Meisterschaft School of Practical Linguistry" in New York.

FRENCH.

IN FIFTEEN PARTS, EACH CONTAINING THREE LESSONS.

PART IX.

NEW YORK:
I. K. FUNK & CO., PUBLISHERS,
10 AND 12 DEY STREET.

TERMS.

WE have arranged with Dr. ROSENTHAL, the author of the "Meis-terschaft System," for its introduction in America under his own supervision, and he has opened

The Meisterschaft School of Practical Linguistry

FOR NON-RESIDENTS.

The student does not need to leave his home. The lessons of each language are prepared by the Professor, and printed and sent in pamphlet shape to each member of the School wherever he may reside.

The course of study for each language—German, French, Italian, or Spanish—makes fifteen pamphlets of three lessons each.

All members of the School have

THE PRIVILEGE

of asking, by letter, questions concerning each lesson, or consulting on any difficulty which may have occurred to them. All exercises corrected and all questions answered by return post by Dr. ROSEN-THAL or one of his assistants.

TERMS OF MEMBERSHIP.

Five Dollars is the price for membership in the school for each language. This amount ($5.) entitles the member to receive the fifteen books or pamphlets containing the lessons, also answers to his questions. Return postage for the answer must accompany the question.

State distinctly which language, or languages, you desire to study There are *no extra charges*. The price, **Five Dollars,** pays for one language ; **Ten Dollars** for two languages, etc. All exercise, and questions must be written on a separate sheet of paper, and must state full address of the pupil.

Remittances must be made in Post-Office Order or registered letter addressed to

I. K. FUNK & CO.,

10 and 19 Dey Street, New York.

The Meisterschaft-System.

FRENCH.

PART IX.

IX.

1.

1. At whose place did you find the new address of Mr. B. who lived in Bank Street two months ago?

2. Ask the bookseller on your way (*en passant*), when he will send me the Italian book which I bought a fortnight ago. (*Literally : fifteen days ago* [*il y a quinze jours*].)

3. Are you going to the bank? No, sir, I am not going there (*y*).

4. Do you think of it (*y*)? Yes, I am thinking thereof (*y*).

5. Go there!

6. Think of (*or* reflect about) it (*y*).

7. Drive me (*or* lead me) there.

8. There are not more than (*or* not above) two *or* three persons there.

9. There is no longer (*ne-plus*) any one there.

10. I could not tell you whether (*si*) it is more than three months since (*que*) Mrs. D. has left here (*or* has gone from here).

11. Is it longer than (*plus de*) two days since you did not see him?

IX.

(Continuation.)

1.

1. Chez qui avez-vous trouvé la nouvelle adresse de monsieur B. qui demeurait rue de la Banque, il y a deux mois (*mŏ-syeūh bay kēē dĕ-meū-ray rü d'lā bānk ēil yāh deū m'woāh*).

2. Demandez en passant (*āng pā-sāng*) au libraire, quand est-ce qu'il m'enverra[1] (*kāng ays kēēl māng-vēr-rā*) le livre italien (*ēē-tā-lyaing*) que j'ai acheté il y a quinze jours.

3. Allez-vous à la banque ? Non monsieur, je n'v vais pas (*jĕ nēē vay pāh*).

4. Y pensez-vous ? Oui, j'y pense (*jēē pặngs*).

5. Allez-y ! [For rules on *y*, see page 204 rules on *en*.]

6. Réfléchissez-y (*ray-flay-shĭs-say-zēē*) !

7. Conduisez-y-moi (*kong-dwēē-zay-zēē-m'woāh*) !

8. Il n'y a pas plus de deux ou trois personnes (*ēēl n'yāh pāh plü dĕ deū zoū troāh pĕr-sŏn*).

9. Il n'y a plus personne.

10. Je ne pourrais vous dire s'il y a plus de trois mois que madame D. est partie d'ici (*kĕ mā-dām day ay pār-tēē dēē-sēē*).

11. Y a-t-il plus de deux jours que vous ne l'avez vu ? [After *il y a* the second negation *pas* is left out when the *perfect tense* follows.]

12. Is it a long time (*longtemps*) since you received news from your brother?

13. Yes, it is quite a long time (*un peu de temps*) since he wrote us. [The French say : Since he has *not* written to us.]

14. There is no one there.

15. There are a great many people (*beaucoup de monde*) there.

16. There is a pretty large number of people there.

17. Is there any room (*de la place*)? No, sir, this compartment is full.

18. What is the matter?

19. It's an age since we saw you. (*Literally :* since one did not see you.)

20. We left a week ago. (*Literally :* eight days ago.)

2.

21. The matter presents two sides; *or*, There are two sides to this affair. (*Literally :* There is something in favor [*pour*], and something against it [*contre*]).

22. Many thanks. (*Literally :* I thank you very much.)

23. Don't mention it, pray. (*Or ;* You are very welcome.)

24. I beg your pardon, sir,

12. Y a-t-il longtemps que vous⌢avez reçu des nouvelles de monsieur votre frère (*yāh-tēēl long-tāng kĕ voū zā-vĕh rĕ-sü day noū-vĕll dĕ mŏ-syeŭh vŏt frair*)?

13. Oui, il y a un peu de temps qu'il ne nous⌢a écrit (*ēēl yāh eūng peū dĕ tāng kēēl nĕ noū zăh ay-krēē*).

14. Il n'y a personne.

15. Il y a beaucoup de monde (*bō-koū dĕ mongd*). [*Monde* means literally *world.*]

16. Il y a passablement de monde (*pā-sāh-blĕ-māng dĕ mongd*).

17. Y a-t-il de la place (*plāhs*)? Non monsieur, ce‿ compartiment est (au) complet (*kong-play*).

18. Qu'y a-t-il donc (*kēē-ā-tēēl dong*)?

19. Il y a un siècle (*syāy-kl'*) qu'on (*kong*) ne vous⌢a vu. [*Siècle* means literally *a century.*]

20. { Il y a huit jours que nous sommes partis (*pār-tēē*).
    { Nous sommes partis il y a huit jours (*ēēl yāh h'wēēt joŭr*).

2.

21. Il y a du pour et du contre (*ēēl yāh dü poūr ay dü cong-tr*).

22. Je vous remercie beaucoup. [*Très* is *never* used with verbs, but only with *adjectives and adverbs.*]

23. { Il n'y a pas de quoi (*ēēl neē-āh pāh dĕ k'woāh*).
    { Pas de quoi (*pāh de k'woāh*). [Standing phrases.]

24. { Je vous demande pardon (*pār-dong*), monsieur.
    { Pardon (*or* mille pardons [*mēēl pār-dong*]), monsieur.

25. Please don't apologize; *or*, It's of no consequence; don't mention it.

26. One ticket, second-class, Paris!

27. There is no second-class; this is an express-train. (*Literally :* There is not of it [*en*]; this is an express.)

28. There are only first-class tickets sold.

29. What is the fare first-class? (*Literally :* How much the first-class ?)

30. { Is there any connection (*correspondance*)?
    { Do these trains connect (*correspondent*)?

31. Please go into the waiting-room. I'll join (*rejoindrai*) you there in (*dans*) two minutes.

32. Do not enter (*or* don't let us go) into this compartment; there are two small children in it.

33. You are right; they are not very delightful company on a journey. (*Literally :* That is not a very agreeable company in [*en*] journey.)

34. Have you anything to declare (*i.e.* at the custom-house) ?

35. You must open your trunk.

36. Here is the key.

37. What have you (*literally :* What is there) in this portmanteau ?

38. Undo (*défaites*) these straps (*courroies*), if you please.

25. { Il n'y a pas de mal, monsieur (*ēēl nēē-āh pāh dĕ māhl mŏ-syeūh*).
Pas de mal, monsieur.

26. Une seconde, Paris (*ŭn sĕ-congd, pā-rēē*).

27. Il n'y en a pas; c'est un express (*ēēl nēē ān nāh pāh; say teūng nĕx-pray*). [If *y* and *en* happen to be used in one sentence, *y precedes en.*]

28. Il n'y a que des premières (*ēēl nēē āh kĕ day prĕ-myair*).

29. Combien les premières (*kong-byaing lay prĕ-myair*)?

30. { Y a-t-il correspondance (*cor-rĕs-pong-dāngs*)?
Est-ce que ces trains correspondent (*ays kĕ say traing cor-rĕs-pongd*)?

31. Veuillez passer à la salle d'attente. Je vous y rejoindrai (*jĕ voū zēē rĕ-joaing-dray*) dans deux minutes (*mēē-nüt*).

32. N'entrez pas dans ce compartiment; il y a deux petits enfants (*nāng-trēh pāh dāng cĕ cong-pār-tēē-māng; ēēl yāh deū p'tēē zāng-fāng*).

33. Vous avez raison ; ce n'est pas une compagnie bien agréable en voyage (*voū zāh-vēh ray-zong ; cĕ nay pāh zün cong-pān-yēē byaing ā-gray-āhbl ăng voāh-yāsh.*)

34. N'avez-vous rien (*rēē-aing*) à déclarer ?

35. Il faut ouvrir votre malle (*ēēl fōh toū-vrēēr vŏt māhll*).

36. Voici la clef (*klay*).

37. Qu'est-ce qu'il y a dans ce sac de voyage (*kays kēēl yāh dāng cĕ săc dĕ voāh-yāsh*) ?

38. Défaites ces courroies (*day-fate say koūr-roāh*), s'il vous plaît.

39. Ah, all these objects have been in use (*or* worn [*sont usagés*]).

40. Conductor, two places for Lyons, if you please!

41. There are none (= no more) in these carriages; further down. (*Literally:* Descend the train.)

42. Any room, gentlemen? (*Literally:* Is there a seat here?)

43. No, sir, every seat is occupied (= we are full [*au complet*]).

44. I beg your pardon, there is one.

45. Has there anything come for me, waiter? (*Literally:* Is there anything? &c.)

46. I am not well (*souffrant* or *indisposé*). Is there an English druggist (= drugshop [*pharmacie*]) near (*près de*) the hotel?

47. Yes, sir, there is an English druggist (*pharmacien*) at the bottom (*au bout*) of the street.

48. Are there (*y a-t-il*) any letters addressed to (*au nom de*) Mr. B.?

49. My name is spelled (*s'écrit*)....

50. Is it far from here (*loin d'ici*) to the Champs-Elysées?

51. This street does not lead (*conduit*) to it at all (*point du tout*).

52. You are going in the opposite direction (*à l'opposé*).

sold, &c. It is to be observed that in French the *Participle past varies according to the gender and number of the noun or pronoun* it relates to and which stands as the *subject* of the sentence.

INFINITIVE MOOD.

Être loué, to be praised.

INDICATIVE MOOD.

Present.

Je suis loué (*or* louée, *fem.*), I am praised,
tu es loué (*or* louée, *fem.*), thou art praised,
il est loué, he is praised,
elle est louée, she is praised,
nous sommes loués (*or* louées, *fem.*), we are praised,
vous êtes loués (*or* louées, *fem.*), you are praised,
ils sont loués,
elles sont louées, } they are praised.

Imperfect.

J'étais loué (*or* louée, *fem.*), I was praised,
tu étais loué (*or* louée, *fem.*),   &c.
il était loué,   &c.
elle était louée,   &c.

Preterite.

Je fus loué *or* louée, I was praised, &c.

1st Future.

Je serai loué *or* louée, I shall be praised, &c.

1st Conditional.

Je serais loué *or* louée, I should be praised, &c.

IMPERATIVE MOOD.

Sois loué *or* louée, be praised,
soyons loués *or* louées, let us be praised,
soyez loués *or* louées, be praised.

SUBJUNCTIVE MOOD.

Present.

Que je sois loué *or* louée, that I (may) be praised, &c.

Imperfect.

Que je fusse loué *or* louée, that I (might) be praised, &c.

PARTICIPLE.

Étant loué *or* louée, being praised.

COMPOUND TENSES.

INFINITIVE MOOD.

Avoir été loué, louée, to have been praised.

INDICATIVE MOOD.

Perfect.

J'ai été loué, louée, I have been praised,
tu as été loué, louée, thou hast been praised, &c.

Pluperfect.

J'avais été loué, louée, I had been praised, &c.

Compound of the Preterite.

J'eus été loué, louée, I had been praised, &c.

2d Future.

J'auräi été loué, louée, I shall have been praised, &c.

2d Conditional.

J'aurais été loué, louée, ⎱ I should *or* I would have been
J'eusse été louée, louée, ⎰   praised, &c.

SUBJUNCTIVE MOOD.

Perfect.

Que j'aie été loué, louée, that I (may) have been praised,
    &c.

Pluperfect.

Que j'eusse été loué, louée, that I (might) have been
    praised.

PARTICIPLE.

Past. Ayant été loué, louée, having been praised.

Remarks :

The English preposition *by*, after the passive voice,
must be rendered by *de*, when the verb denotes a *sentiment or an inward act of soul,* and by *par*, when it expresses
an *outward action,* which by the by is mostly the case.
Ex. :

> He is esteemed by everybody.
> Il est estimé *de* tout le monde.
> This book is written by him.
> Ce livre est écrit par lui.

C.

Neuter or Intransitive Verbs.

The *neuter verbs* admit no *direct object*, as *aller*, to go, *arriver*, to arrive, &c.

Among the neuter verbs there are some which take *être* in the compound tenses instead of *avoir*. Ex. : *être arrivé*, to have arrived. These are conjugated as follows:

Pres.	J'arrive.	*Fut.*	J'arriverai.
Imperf.	J'arrivais.	*Cond.*	J'arriverais.
Pret.	J'arrivai.		

Perfect.

Je *suis* arrivé *or* arrivée, I have (am) arrived.
tu es arrivé *or* arrivée, &c.

Pluperfect.

J'étais arrivé *or* arrivée, I had arrived, &c.

2d Future.

Je serai arrivé *or* arrivée, I shall have (be) arrived, &c.

2d Conditional.

Je serais arrivé *or* arrivée, I should have arrived, &c.

The most important verbs of this class which are conjugated with *être* are:

être allé, to have gone.
être sorti, to have gone out.
être tombé, to have fallen.
être venu, to have come.
être resté, to have remained.

Translate the fóllowing

Exercises

into English and then again into French:

1. *To ask for a street.*

Monsieur, pourriez-vous me faire le plaisir de m'indiquer (maing-dēē-kĕh = *to direct me*) la rue de Richelieu (rēē-shĕ-lyeū)?—Oui monsieur; prenez la première à droite (*to the right*), et ensuite (āng-s'wēēt = *then*) la seconde à gauche (gōsh = *to the left*). — Je vous remercie bien, monsieur. — Quel est, s'il vous plaît, le chemin (shĕ-maing = *way*) pour aller aux boulevards?—Suivez (s'wēē-vēh = *follow*) cette rue, elle va vous y (*thereto*) conduire (kong-d'wēēr = *lead; bring*).—Merci bien.—Eh bien, vous ne vous êtes pas perdu (*lost*)?—Non, mais j'ai été obligé de demander mon chemin trois fois (foāh = *three times*).

2. *Terms used during a call.*

Tenez (*ah! why!*), comment ça va-t-il donc? Je ne m'attendais pas (*I did not expect*) à avoir le plaisir de vous voir ce matin. Je vous croyais encore à la campagne. Depuis quand êtes-vous donc revenu? — Voilà que j'arrive (jā-rēēv); je n'ai pas encore été à la maison.—Avez-vous déjeuné (day-jeū-nay)? — Non, pas encore. — Eh bien, venez donc avec moi, nous déjeunerons ensemble (day-jeū-nĕ-rong zāng-sāng-bl) au Palais Royal (roā-yāhl).

3.

1) **G**ood morning, my dear friend. How are you?
I am very glad to see you. — 2) When did you arrive in
Paris and where do you stay? — 3) How is your father?
Is he any better (*mieux*)? — 4) How have you been since
I had the pleasure to see you?—Thank you, I have been
very well indeed; but my wife has been quite ill. — 5) I
am very sorry to hear you say so. Why, what is the matter with her? — 6) She was very ill last winter, but she is
now out of danger. — 7) The egoist (*l'égoiste*) is loved by
no one. — 8) The Arabians (*les Arabes*) invented (*inven-
ter*) the numbers (*les chiffres*). — 9) The numbers have been
invented by the Arabians. — 10) The emperor (*l'empereur*)
was assassinated in the midst (*au milieu*) of his people (*ses
gens*). — 11) The birth (*la naissance*) of Christ (*Christ*) was
announced by a star (*une étoile*). — 12) The earth (*la terre*)
was refreshed (*rafraîchie*) by the rain (*la pluie*). — 13)
Happy the people which is governed by wise (*sages*) laws
(*lois*). — 14) We were astonished (*étonnés*) by his wisdom
(*la sagesse*).

4.

Bruxelles, October 10th, 1881.

Messrs. Toussaint, La Rue & Cⁱᴱ., Rouen.

Gentlemen:

Would you have the kindness to give us some information about (*sur*) the firm in B. the name of which you
will find at the foot of this letter (= of which [*dont*] you

will find the name at the foot [*au-dessous*]). This house possesses a great reputation for (*de*) integrity (*moralité*), and as I am going to do a pretty heavy (*assez importante*) business with it, I am desirous (*je désire*) to know if this is true (*méritée*).

I thank you in advance (*d'avance*=dā-vāngs) for (*de*) the trouble you are going to have (= you will take, *vous prendrez*), and beg you will count (*compter*) on my gratitude (*ma reconnaissance*) and discretion.

Very respectfully yours.

Translate the following

Exercise

into French :

1) Are you going to Paris? — Do you go as far as (*jusqu'à* = jüs-kāh) Paris? — Then I shall have the pleasure of your society (*société* = so-syēh-tay), for I am going there too (*aussi*=ō-sēē). — 2) I am very glad of it (*en*). — It is very disagreeable (*désagréable* = day-zāh-gray-ābl) to travel (*voyager*) quite alone (*seul* = seūl). — But when (*quand*) one is in society (*en compagnie*) one talks, chats (*cause*) and the time passes (*se passe*). — 3) When (*quand*) do you think we shall arrive in Paris? — I hope we shall arrive this afternoon (*cet après-midi*).— 4) Here we are at the first station. — How long (*combien de temps*) are we going to stop (*rester*) here? — We shall stop here (*y*) but (*ne-que*) three minutes. — There we are

off (*partis*) again (*de nouveau*). — What is that (*qu'est-ce-que*) I see in front of us (= before us, *devant nous*)? — That's a tunnel (*un souterrain* = soū-tĕr-raing). — We are in darkness (*l'obscurité* = lob-scü-rēē-tay). — Here is another station. Are we going to stop (*s'arrêter*) there? — Yes, we are going to stop there five minutes. — Where are we now? — We are passing over (*sur*) a viaduct (*un viaduc* = vēē-āh-düc). — We shall be soon at the end (*au terme*) of our journey. — This is the last station. — Here we are at the depot. — Let us look for (= let us go to seek, *allons chercher*) our luggage. — Let us make haste; there is a great crowd of people here.

Words.

Poste ; Télégraphie. — *Post ; Telegraph.*

la grande poste (*lăh grāng pòst*), The General Post-Office.

le porte, the postage.

le bureau de poste (*bü-ro dĕ pòst*), the post-office.

un timbre-poste (*taing-br'-pòst*), a postage-stamp.

le facteur (*fāc-teūr*), the postman.

le papier à lettres (*păp-yĕh āh lĕt*), note-paper.

la boîte (*b'woāt*) (aux lettres), the letter-box.

une feuille (*feū-yĕ*), a sheet.

mettre une lettre à la poste, to post a letter.

une enveloppe (*āng-vĕ-lop*), an envelope.

une lettre affranchie (*ă-frāng-shĕĕ*), a prepaid letter.

le bureau télégraphique (*tay-lay-grā-fĕĕk*), the telegraph-office.

une lettre chargée (*shār-jay*), a registered letter.

le télégramme, the telegram.

une dépêche (*day-paysh*), a dispatch.

une lettre recommandée (*rĕ-cŏ-māng-day*), a registered letter.

télégraphier (*tay-lay-grā-fyĕh*), to dispatch.

le câble, the cable.

COMPANION TO THE
Revised Version of the New Testament.

Explaining the Reasons for the Changes Made on the Authorized Version.

BY ALEXANDER ROBERTS, D.D.,
Member of the English Revision Committee.

WITH SUPPLEMENT BY A MEMBER OF THE AMERICAN COMMITTEE.

Containing a Brief History of the Revision of the Work and Co-operation of the New Testament Companies, of the Points of Agreement and Difference, and an Explanation of the Appendix to the Revised New Testament.

ALSO, A FULL TEXTUAL INDEX,
Being a Key to Passages in which Important Changes have been Made.

This book, having been carefully prepared by Members of both Revision Committees, carries official weight. It shows what changes have been made, and also the reasons which influenced the revisers in making them. It will be difficult to judge of the merits of the revision without the aid of this Companion volume. Our edition is printed by special arrangement with the English publishers. It is well known that, by an arrangement between the two Committees of Revision, the changes suggested by the American Committee, but which were not adopted by the English Revisers, are published as an Appendix to the Revised New Testament. The *Companion* volume is an explanation of *all* the changes adopted by both committees, and of those suggested by the American Committee, but not assented to by the English Committee, in their final revision. The book will be indispensable to a right understanding of the revision. This cheap edition of the combined books, although authorized and copyrighted, will be sold for 25 cents in paper, and 75 cents in cloth—sent postage free.

TESTIMONIALS.

T. W. CHAMBERS, D.D., a Member of the American Committee of Revision, says of this book: "Many persons have expressed a desire that, simultaneously with the issue of the Revised New Testament, there should appear an authentic explanation of the reasons for such changes as will be found in its pages. The work of Dr. Roberts is exactly fitted to meet this desire.... Nowhere else in print can be found a statement so full and exact. It gives all needed information, and does it in an unexceptional way."

C. F. DEEMS, D.D., Pastor of the Church of the Strangers. New York, writes: "The Companion to the Revised Version seems to me almost indispensable. Even scholars who were not at the meeting of the Revisers would have a wearisome work in seeking to discover all the changes made. and to ordinary readers very much of the labor would be lost. ....All this is set forth by Dr. Roberts with admirable perspicuity. Those who have any intelligent interest in the Holy Scriptures, will find this little book absorbingly interesting. I shall urge every member of the church of which I am pastor to give it a careful reading, and purpose to introduce it as a text-book in our Bible-classes."

. "So valuable, interesting and useful is this publication, that we advise every one who wishes to know the why and wherefore of the revision, to obtain it immediately."—*New York Observer.*

Paper, 8vo size, 25 cents; Cloth, 16mo, 75 cents.

*** For Sale by Booksellers and Newsdealers, or sent postage-paid, on receipt of price, by

I. K. FUNK & CO., Publishers, 10 & 12 Dey St., N. Y.

THE TEACHER'S EDITION

OF THE

REVISED NEW TESTAMENT

With New Concordance and Index, Harmony of the Gospels, Maps,
Historical and Chronological Tables, Parallel Passages printed
in full, Blank Pages Interleaved for manuscript notes, and
many other New and Indispensable Helps to the Study
of the Revised Version.

After the excitement connected with the sale of the first copies of the new revision, which lack the usual indexing headlines and marginal references to parallel passages, and also the appendixes of tables, maps, etc.—all of which helps preachers, teachers and Bible students have come to consider as absolutely essential to a working copy of the Bible—there arises an imperative demand for an edition of the Revised New Testament, containing all the marginal and appendix helps of former TEACHERS' AND REFERENCE BIBLES, adapted carefully and accurately to the Revised Version. We are, therefore, preparing, as rapidly as is consistent with accuracy, such an edition of the Revised New Testament. The work is under the supervision of well-known Bible scholars, with numerous helpers, and will be issued as early as it can be done with thoroughness. In style and size the book will resemble the Bagster Bible, "Fac-simile large edition," known as "the Moody Bible," being the same width and length and size of type. It will be supplied at prices *within the reach of all.*

This "Teachers' Edition of the Revised New Testament" will be an exact, *certified reproduction* of the entire Oxford and Cambridge Edition, including the Preface and all the marginal readings and explanations. It will contain the appendix notes of the American Revisers, printed in the margin of each page by the side of the passages referred to. The parallel passages, to which reference is m de in the "Bagster Bibles," with numerous others, so far as appropriate, will be PRINTED IN FULL in the margin. The running headings, usually printed at the tops of pages of the King James version, will be here supplied. A small black mark will be inserted below the last letter of each v:.se to facilitate reference, and aid in RESPONSIVE READING of the Revised Version. The second half of the volume will consist of the most carefully)ared HELPS TO THE STUDY OF THE REVISED NEW TESTAMENT, gleaned ..om the best Teachers' Editions of the authorized version, and supplied ˮ om various original sources—all being revised and adapted to harmonize ith the Revised Version. We shall introduce many other important features, making this the most valuable edition of the New Testament ever issued.

Popular Cloth Edition—Ready in July—Price, Postage Free, $1.60.

Send for prospectus giving full description and prices of finer Bindings.

I. K. FUNK & CO., Publishers, 10 and 12 Dey St., New York.

THE

Meisterschaft System.

A SIMPLE AND PRACTICAL METHOD,

ENABLING

ANY ONE TO LEARN, WITH SLIGHT EFFORT, TO SPEAK
FLUENTLY AND CORRECTLY

French, German, Spanish, and Italian.

BY
DR. RICHARD S. ROSENTHAL,

Late Director of the "Akademie für fremde Sprachen" in Berlin and Leipzig,
of the "Meisterschaft College" in London, and Principal of the
"Meisterschaft School of Practical Linguistry" in New York.

FRENCH.

IN FIFTEEN PARTS, EACH CONTAINING THREE LESSONS.

PART X.

NEW YORK:
I. K. FUNK & CO., Publishers,
10 AND 12 Dey Street.

TERMS.

We have arranged with Dr. ROSENTHAL, the author of the "Meisterschaft System," for its introduction in America under his own supervision, and he has opened

The Meisterschaft School of Practical Linguistry

FOR NON-RESIDENTS.

The student does not need to leave his home. The lessons of each language are prepared by the Professor, and printed and sent in pamphlet shape to each member of the School wherever he may reside.

The course of study for each language—German, French, Italian, or Spanish—makes fifteen pamphlets of three lessons each.

All members of the School have

THE PRIVILEGE

of asking, by letter, questions concerning each lesson, or consulting on any difficulty which may have occurred to them. All exercises corrected and all questions answered by return post by Dr. ROSENTHAL or one of his assistants.

TERMS OF MEMBERSHIP.

Five Dollars is the price for membership in the school for each language. This amount ($5.) entitles the member to receive the fifteen books or pamphlets containing the lessons, also answers to his questions. Return postage for the answer must accompany the question.

State distinctly which language, or languages, you desire to study There are *no extra charges.* The price, **Five Dollars,** pays for one language ; **Ten Dollars** for two languages, etc. All exercise and questions must be written on a separate sheet of paper, and must state full address of the pupil.

Remittances must be made in Post-Office Order or registered letter addressed to

I. K. FUNK & CO.,

10 and 12 Dey Street, New York.

The Meisterschaft-System.

FRENCH.

PART X.

X.

(*Continuation.*)

FOUNDATION SENTENCE.

(*No. VI.*)

1.

Of Dress and Dressing.

1. Hasten to dress yourself (*de vous habiller*).

2. I shall not be long in dressing (*m'habiller*).

3. What! you are not yet dressed? It is a quarter to ten.

4. I was very tired (*fatigué*) this morning.

5. I got up (*or* I rose = *je me suis levé*) late; I shall soon (*bientôt*) be ready.

6. Give me my shirt, stockings, garters, shoes, and trousers.

7. Wash (*lavez-vous*) your (= the) hands and face (*le visage*).

8. My hands are very dirty (*sales*).

9. Why did you not wash your hands?

10. Wipe (*essuyez*) your hands with this towel (*cette serviette*).

X.

(*Continuation.*)

FOUNDATION SENTENCE.

(*No. VI.*)

1.

De l'habillement (*de lā-bēē-yĕ-māng*).

1. Dépêchez-vous de vous‿habiller (*day-pay-shay vŏū dĕ voū-zā-bēē-yēh*).
2. Je ne serai pas lōngtemps à m'habiller (*āh mā-bēē-yēh*).
3. Comment! vous n'êtes pas‿encore habillé? Il est dix heures moins‿un quart (*dēē-zeūr mō-aing zeūng kār*).
4. J'étais bien fatigué (*fā-tēē-gay*) ce matin.
5. Je me suis levé tard (*tār*) ; je vais‿être bientôt prêt (*jĕ vay zay-tr byaing-tōh pray*).
6. Donnez-moi ma chemise, mes bas, mes jarretières,·mes souliers et mon pantalon (*may bāh, may jā-rē-tyair, may soū-lyēh ay mong pāng-tā-long*).
7. Lavez-vous les mains et le visage (*lay maing ay lĕ vēē-zāje*).
8. Mes mains sont très-sales (*may maing song tray sāhl*).
9. Pourquoi ne vous‿êtes-vous pas lavé les mains (*ne voū zayt voū pāh lā-vay lay maing*) ?
10. Essuyez vos mains avec cette serviette (*ĕs-s'wēē-yēh voh maing ā-vĕk sĕt sĕr-vyĕt*).

11. Clean (*décrottez*) my boots and brush my clothes, please.

12. Did you black (*ciré*) my shoes?

13. Have this coat mended (*raccommoder*).

14. Send me a tailor who understands (*se charge de*) repairing (*réparations*); there are some buttons off (= it wants some buttons, *il manque quelques boutons à*) this waistcoat.

15. This waistcoat is torn (*déchiré*).

16. There! I have torn my dress!

17. Oh, that's only a slight tear (*un petit accroc*); I am going to put a stitch (*faire un point*) into it.

18. That will not be seen.

19. Put on (*mettez*) this dress.

20. Wait (*attendez*) a moment; I have only to put on my necktie.

21. Put on your hat (*or* bonnet).

22. I am putting (*je mets*) my stockings on.

23. She dresses herself (*elle se met*) with a great deal of taste.

24. Take off (*ôtez*) your hat (*or* bonnet).

25. Button up (*boutonnez*) your dress.

26. A buttonhole (*une boutonnière*) of this waistcoat is torn out (*défaite*).

27. This dress (*or* coat) is very becoming to you.

11. Décrottez mes bottes et brossez mes habits, s'il vous plaît (*may zā-bēē*).

12. Avez-vous ciré mes souliers (*sēē-ray may soū-lyēh*) ?

13. Faites raccommoder cet habit (*sĕ tā-bēē*).

14. Envoyez-moi donc un tailleur qui se charge de réparations; il manque quelques boutons à ce gilet (*āng-voāh-yĕh m'woāh dong eūng tā-yeūr kēē sĕ shārje dĕ ray-pā-rā-syong; ēēl mānk kĕl kĕ boū-tong āh sĕ jēē-lay*).

15. Ce gilet est déchiré (*day-shēē-ray*).

16. Voilà que je déchire ma robe (*kĕ jĕ day-shēēr mā robe*).

17. Ce n'est qu'un petit accroc; je vais vous y faire un point (*sĕ nay keūng p'tēē tā-kroc, jĕ vay voū zēē fāir eūng po-aing*).

18. Ça ne se verra pas (*sā nĕ sĕ ver-rā pāh* [*verra* is the irregular future of *voir*, to see].

19. Mettez cet habit (*sē tā-bēē*).

20. Attendez un moment (*āt-tāng-day zeūng mō-māng*); je n'ai plus que ma cravate à mettre.

21. Mettez votre chapeau (*vŏt shā-pōh*).

22. Je mets mes bas (*jĕ may may bāh*). [*Je mets* is the irregular present of *mettre*].

23. Elle se met avec beaucoup de goût (*ĕll sĕ may tā-vĕk bōh-koū dĕ goū*).

24. Otez votre chapeau.

25. Boutonnez votre habit (*vŏt rā-bēē*).

26. Une boutonnière de ce gilet est défaite (*boūtŏn-nyair dĕ sĕ jēē-lay ay day-fait*).

27. Cet habit vous va fort bien (*voū vāh fŏr byaing*).

28. Which shoemaker works for you (*vous chausse* or *botte*) at present (*à présent*)?

29. These boots are too tight for me (= press me, *me gênent* or *serrent*).

30. Will you try these boots?

31. I cannot put (*or* get) them on.

32. Stretch your leg out (*allongez votre jambe*), please.

33. All right; now put your foot on the ground (*par terre*).

34. They are too tight on the instep (*du coude-pied*).

35. You know (*vous savez*) the first time one tries on (*on met*) a pair of boots, the foot feels always a little tight (*on a toujours le pied un peu gêné*).

36. Yes, but they squeeze me (*elles me serrent*) too hard; I cannot walk with them (*marcher avec*).

37. I prefer (*j'aime mieux*) you to make me another pair. [After *aimer mieux* the Subjunctive has to follow.]

38. Undress yourself.

39. Take off your dress (*or* coat).

40. I must take off my dress.

41. Undress (*déshabillez*) this child.

42. You are not yet half (*à moitié*) undressed.

43. Hasten to undress yourself.

44. He is taking his boots off.

45. I shall not be long undressing.

28. { Quel cordonnier vous chausse à présent (*kĕl cŏr-don-nyēh voŭ shŏss āh pray-zāng*) ?

Quel bottier vous botte maintenant (*maing-tĕ-nāng*) ?

29. Ces bottes me gênent. (*jane* or *serrent* [*sĕr*]) beaucoup.

30. Voulez-vous essayer ces bottines (*zĕ-say-yēh say bŏt-tēēn*) ?

31. Je ne peux pas les mettre.

32. Allongez votre jambe (*ā-long-jay vŏt jāng*), s'il vous plaît.

33. Bien, mettez le pied (*pyēh*) par terre à présent.

34. Elles me gênent (*jane*) du coude-pied (*coŭd-pyēh*).

35. La première fois qu'on met des bottes, comme vous savez, on a toujours le pied un peu gêné (*lĕ pyēh eŭng peŭ jay-nay*).

36. Oui, mais elles me serrent trop (*sĕr trōh*), je ne peux pas marcher avec (*mār-shay ā-vek*).

37. J'aime mieux (*m'yeŭ*) que vous m'en fassiez (*māng fās-yēh*) une autre paire.

38. Déshabillez-vous (*day-ză-bēē-yēh voŭ*).

39. Otez votre habit.

40. Il faut que j'ôte mon habit (*ēēl fō kĕ jōht mon nā-bēē*).

41. Déshabillez cet enfant (*day-zā-bēē-yēh sĕ tāng-fāng*).

42. Vous n'êtes pas encore à moitié déshabillé (*āh m'woā-tyēh day-zā-bēē-yēh*).

43. Dépêchez-vous (or *Hâtez-vous*) de vous déshabiller.

44. { Il tire (*or* Il ôte) ses bottes (*ēēl tēēr* [*ōht*] *say bŏt*).

Il se débotte.

45. Je ne serai pas longtemps à me déshabiller.

2.

46. Have you (got) a pin (*une épingle*)?

47. This bonnet (*or* hat) is very becoming (*vous coiffe*) to you. [*Of hats, bonnets, &c., the expression* **coiffer** *is used in the sense of* **to be becoming**; *but of dresses one says* **faire** *or* **aller.**] Compare phrase 27.

48. I dress my hair (*je me coiffe*) to suit my own taste.

49. This is a very fine hat, and it is quite fashionable (*or* quite the style [*à la mode*]).

50. The shape (*la forme*) is rather large (*un peu large*).

51. Are you done with your toilette? Is your toilette completed?

52. This dress is very becoming to you (*or* fits you very well).

53. This dress fits you beautifully (*vous serre bien*) in the waist (*la taille*).

54. It is very well finished (*or* made).

55. She is not very (*tout-à-fait*) fashionably dressed (*habillée à la mode*). .

56. I must go to this barber's (*or* hairdresser's = *coiffeur*).

57. To have your hair cut (*faire couper les cheveux*) *or* dressed (*faire coiffer*)?

58. I must have my hair cut.

59. He is shaving (*il se fait la barbe*).

60. Shave me, please.

2.

46. Avez-vous⁀une épingle (*āh-vēh-voŭ zün nay-pain-gl'*)?

47. Ce chapeau vous coiffe bien (*sĕ shā-pōh voŭ k'woāf byaing*).

48. Je me coiffe à ma façon (*or* à mon goût) (*jĕ mĕ k'woāf āh ma fᾱsong*).

49. C'est⁀un chapeau qui est très-fin et à la mode (*say teŭng shā-pōh kēē ay tray faing ay āh lāh mōde*).

50. La forme est un peu large.

51. { Votre toilette est-elle finie (*vŏt t'woā-lĕt ay-tĕll fēē-nēē*)? { Avez-vous⁀achevé votre toilette (*zā-sh'vay vŏt t'woā-lĕt*)?

52. Cet⁀habit vous va fort bien. (Compare phrase 47.)

53. Cet⁀habit vous serre (*or* vous prend) bien la taille (*sē tā-bēē voŭ sĕrr [prāng] byaing lāh tā-yĕ*).

54. Il est très-bien fait.

55. Elle n'est pas‿habillée tout-à-fait à la mode (*ĕll nay pāh zā-bēē-yēh toŭ-tā-fay āh lāh mode*).

56. Il faut que j'entre chez ce coiffeur (*kĕ jāng-tr' shay sĕ k'woā-feŭr*).

57. Pour vous faire couper les cheveux, ou pour vous faire coiffer?

58. Il faut que je me fasse couper les cheveux (*coŭ-pĕh lay shĕ-veŭ.*)

59. Il se fait la barbe.

60. Faites-moi la barbe.   La barbe, s'il vous plaît.

61. Take a seat (*asseyez-vous*[1]), please.
62. Please raise (*levez*) your head a little.

63. A little to this side, pray.

64. Does the razor (*le rasoir*) hurt you (*vous fait-il mal*), sir?

65. A little powder, sir?
66. Please (*faites*).
67. Curl the hair, sir?
68. No, please. Comb it a little.

69. Part my hair, please.
70. Here you are, sir. Please pay at the office.

---

1) **Asseyez-vous**, *be seated*, is the imperative of the irregular verb *s'asseoir* (*sās-swoār*), to sit down. It is conjugated in the following manner:

Present.

Je m'assieds (*mās-syēh*).
tu t'assieds (*tăs-syēh*).
il s'assied (*săs-syēh*).
nous nous asseyons (*zās-say-yong*).
vous vous asseyez (*zās-say-yēh*).
ils s'asseient (*sās-say*).

Imperfect.

Je m'asseyais (*mās-say-yay*).
tu t'asseyais (*tăs-say-yay*).
il s'asseyait (*săs-say-yay*).
nous nous asseyions (*zās-say-yiong*).
vous vous asseyiez (*zās-say-yiēh*).
ils s'asseyaient (*sās-say-yay*).

Preterite.

Je m'assis (*mās-sēē*).
tu t'assis (*tăs-sēē*).
il s'assit (*săs-sēē*).
nous nous assîmes (*zās-sēēm*).
vous vous assîtes (*zās-sēēt*).
ils s'assirent (*sās-sēēr*).

Perfect.

Je me suis assis (*zās-sēē*).
tu t'es assis (*zās-sēē*).
il s'est assis (*tăs-sēē*).
nous nous sommes assis (*zās-sēē*).
vous vous êtes assis (*zās-sēē*).
ils se sont assis (*tās-sēē*).

Future.

Je m'assiérai *or* Je m'asseierai (*mās-sēē-ĕ-rēh* or *mās-sĕ-yĕ-rēh*).
tu t'assiéras *or* tu t'asseieras.
il s'assiéra *or* il s'asseiera.

61. Asseyez-vous[1] (*ās-sey-yēh*), s'il vous plaît.

62. Levez‿un peu la tête, s'il vous plaît (*lě-vēh zeŭng peŭ lāh tayt*).

63. Un peu de ce côté-ci, je vous prie (*eŭng peŭ dě sě co-tay-see, jě voŭ prēē*).

64. Le rasoir (*lě rāh-z'woār*) vous fait-il mal, monsieur?

65. Un peu de poudre de riz (*pōō-dr' d'rēē*), monsieur?

66. Faites (*or* Oui, s'il vous plaît).

67. Un coup[2] de fer, monsieur (*eŭng coŭ d'fěr m'syeŭh*)?

68. Oh non, je vous‿en prie. Un coup de brosse, s'il vous plaît (*jě voŭ zāng prēē; eŭng coŭ dě bross, sēē voŭ play*).

69. Faites-moi la raie, s'il vous plaît.

70. Voilà, monsieur. Au comptoir[3] s'il vous plaît (*ōh cong-t'woār sēē voŭ play*).

---

nous nous assiérons *or* nous nous asseierons.
vous vous assiérez *or* vous vous asseierez.
ils s'assiéront *or* ils s'asseieront.

Pres. Subj.	*Imperative.*
Que je m'asseie (*mās-sey*).	Assieds-toi (*ās-syēh twoāh*).
que tu t'asseies.	asseyons-nous (*ăs-sĕ-yong noŭ*).
qu'il s'asseie.	asseyez-vous (*ăs-sĕ yēh voŭ*).
que nous nous asseyions.	*Participles.*
que vous vous asseyiez.	s'asseyant (*să-sĕ-yāng*).
qu'ils asseient.	assis (*ăs-sēē*).

2) **Le coup** (*koŭ*) means literally the *blow, stroke, knock,* and is used almost as frequently as the verb *to fix* by Americans. Thus we say in French: *Un coup de peigne* (*eŭng koŭ dě-pĕn-yě*), s'il vous plaît, please comb my hair (*literally :* a stroke of the comb, *peigne*). *Un coup de brosse,* s'il vous plaît, please brush my hair (= a stroke of the brush, *brosse*).—Donnez *un coup de balai* à cette chambre (*don-nēh zeŭng koŭ d'bā-lay āh sět shāng-br*), sweep this room, please (=give a stroke of the broom [*balai*] to this room), &c., &c.

3) All the money is received in French shaving-saloons and in most other mercantile establishments·by the *dame du comptoir* (*dāhm dü cong-t'woār*), lady-cashier. One pays for shaving by saying : *Une barbe ;* for hair-cutting by saying : *Une taille* or *Une coupe.*

3.

Terms of Regret.

1. I am sorry that....

2. I am very sorry for it.

3. I regret it exceedingly.

4. I am very sorry to....

5. With the best will (*la volonté*) in the world I could not do so.

6. I could not do so, even if (*quand même*) I should like to.

7. I am exceedingly sorry that I cannot render you this service.

---

1) It will be observed that hardly any of these terms have been translated literally. The French are more polite—at least in expressions—than we are, and the French idioms must therefore be committed to memory.

2) The *irregular verb* **vouloir** (*voŭ-p̄woãr*), *to be willing*, is thus conjugated:

Present.	*Imperfect.*
Je veux (*veŭ*).	Je voulais, I was willing; I de-
tu veux (*veŭ*).	sired; I wanted.
il veut (*veŭ*).	tu voulais.
nous voulons (*voŭ-long*).	il voulait.
vous voulez (*voŭ-lĕh*).	nous voulions.
ils veulent (*veŭl*).	vous vouliez.
	ils voulaient.

3.

Formules de regrets.[1]

1. Je suis fâché que (*with the subjunctive mood following*).

2. { J'en suis fâché.
   { Cela me fait de la peine (*pain*).

3. { J'en suis désolé (*jăng swēē day-zō-lay*).
   { J'en suis au désespoir (*ōh day-sĕs-p'woār*). (*Literally :*
   {   in despair).

4. Je regrette beaucoup (*or* bien; fort; infiniment) que (with the subjunctive mood).

5. Avec la meilleure volonté du monde je ne ne pourrais le faire (*ā-vĕk lāh mĕ-yeūr vō-long-tay dü mongd*).

6. Je ne saurais le faire quand même je le voudrais[2] (*jĕ nĕ sō-ray lĕ fair kăng maim jĕ lĕ voū-dray*).

7. Je suis au désespoir de ne pouvoir vous rendre ce service (*jĕ s'wēē ōh day-zĕs-p'woār dĕ nĕ poū-v'woār voū răng-dr sĕ sĕr-vēēse*).

Future.	*Conditional.*
Je voudrai.	Je voudrais, I should like to ; I
tu voudras.	want to.
il voudra.	tu voudrais.
nous voudrons.	il voudrait.
vous voudrez.	nous voudrions.
ils voudront.	vous voudriez.
Subj. Pres.	ils voudraient.
Que je veuille (*veū-yĕ*).	
que tu veuilles (*veū-yĕ*).	*Imperative.*
qu'il veuille (*veū-yĕ*).	Veuillez (*veū-yēh*), be so kind as;
que nous voulions (*voū-lyong*).	will you please ?
que vous vouliez (*voū-lyēh*).	
qu'ils veuillent (*veū-yĕ*).	

GRAMMATICAL REMARKS.

A.

Reflective Verbs.

Verbs are called *reflective* or *reflected* because their subject and object are the same person or thing. The subject acts therefore upon itself, and is at the same time the agent and the object of the action. Reflected verbs have therefore, besides the subject, always another personal pronoun, viz., *me, te, se* (myself, thyself, himself, herself, itself), for the singular; *nous, vous, se* (ourselves, yourselves, themselves), for the plural. It frequently happens that, in English, this second pronoun is omitted, whereas it must be expressed in French. *Ex.:* to repent, *se repentir ; Pres.* I repent, *je* me *repens,* &c.

Observe that all reflected verbs, without exception, are conjugated with the auxiliary **être,** as: I have hurt myself, *je me* suis *blessé,* and *not* je m'ai blessé.

The conjugation of the following verb may serve as a model for all the reflected verbs.

Se réjouir (*sĕ ray-joū-ēēr*), to rejoice.

INDICATIVE MOOD.

Present Tense.

Je *me* réjouis (*jĕ mĕ ray-joū-ēē*), I rejoice.

tu te réjouis, thou rejoicest.

il (elle) se réjouit, he (she) rejoices.

nous nous réjouissons (*ray-joŭ-ĭs-song*), we rejoice.
vous vous réjouissez, you rejoice.
ils (elles) se réjouissent (*ray-joŭ-ĭs*), they rejoice.

Imperfect.

Je me réjouissais (*ray-joŭ-ĭs-say*), I rejoiced, &c.

Preterite.

Je me réjouis (*ray-joŭ-ēĕ*), I rejoiced, &c.

1*st Future.*

Je me réjouirai (*ray-joŭ-ēĕ-rēh*), I shall rejoice, &c.

1*st Conditional.*

Je me réjouirais (*ray-joŭ-ēĕ-ray*), I should rejoice, &c.

IMPERATIVE MOOD.

Réjouis-toi, rejoice.
réjouissons-nous, let us rejoice.
réjouissez-vous, rejoice.

SUBJUNCTIVE MOOD.

Present.

Que je me réjouisse (*ray-joŭ-ĭs*), that I (may) rejoice, &c.

Imperfect.

Que je me réjouisse (*ray-joŭ-ĭs*), that I (might) rejoice, &c.

PARTICIPLE.

Se (me, te, &c.) réjouissant (*ray-joŭ-ĭs-sāng*), rejoicing.

COMPOUND TENSES.

INFINITIVE MOOD.

S'être réjoui, réjouie (*ray-joŭ-ēē*), to have rejoiced.

INDICATIVE MOOD.

Perfect.

Je me *suis* réjoui, -e (*ray-joŭ-ēē*), I have rejoiced.
tu t'*es* réjoui, -e (*tŭ tay ray-joŭ-ēē*), thou hast rejoiced.
il s'*est* réjoui, he has rejoiced.
elle s'*est* réjouie, she has rejoiced.
nous nous *sommes* réjouis, -ies, we have rejoiced.
vous vous *êtes* réjoui(s), -ie(s), you have rejoiced.

ils se *sont* réjouis, ⎫
elles se *sont* réjouies, ⎭ they have rejoiced.

Pluperfect.

Je m'*étais* réjoui, -e, I had rejoiced.
tu t'*étais* réjoui, -e, thou hadst rejoiced, &c.

Compound of the Preterite.

Je me *fus* réjoui, -e, I had rejoiced.
tu te *fus* réjoui, -e, &c.

2d Future

Je me *serai* réjoui, -e, I shall have rejoiced.
tu te *seras* réjoui, -e, &c.

2d Conditional

Je mè *serais* réjoui, -e, I should have rejoiced.
tu te *serais* réjoui, -e, &c.

Second Compound of the Preterite.

Si je me *fusse* réjoui, -e, if I had rejoiced, &c.

SUBJUNCTIVE MOOD.

Perfect.

Que je me *sois* réjoui, -e, that I (may) have rejoiced.
que tu te *sois* réjoui, -e, &c.
qu'il se *soit* réjoui (qu'elle se *soit* réjouie), &c.

Pluperfect.

Que je me *fusse*, réjoui, -e, that I (might) have rejoiced. ·
que tu te *fusses* réjoui, -e, &c.

PARTICIPLE.

S'*étant* (m'*étant*, &c.) réjoui, -e, having rejoiced.

In questions

se réjouir is thus conjugated :

Present.

Me réjouis-je (*better :* est-ce que je me réjouis [*ays kě jě mě ray-jou-ēē*]), do I rejoice?
te réjouis-tu (*or* est-ce que tu te réjouis), dost thou rejoice ?
se réjouit-il (*or* est-ce qu'il se réjouit) ? &c.
nous réjouissons-nous ? &c.
vous réjouissez-vous ? &c.
se réjouissent-ils (-elles) ? &c.

Perfect.

Me suis-je réjoui, -e, have I rejoiced?
t'es-tu réjoui, -e, hast thou rejoiced ?
s'est-il réjoui, has he rejoiced ?

nous sommes-nous réjouis, -ies, have we rejoiced?
vous êtes-vous réjoui(s), -ie(s), have you rejoiced?
se sont-ils réjouis,
se sont-elles réjouies, } have they rejoiced?

With the negation.

Present.

Je ne me réjouis pas, I do not rejoice.
tu ne te réjouis pas,   do.
il (elle) ne se réjouit pas,   do.
nous ne nous réjouissons pas, · do.
vous ne vous réjouissez pas,   do.
ils (elles) ne se réjouissent pas. .

Imperative.

Ne *te* réjouis pas, do not rejoice.   .
ne *nous* réjouissons pas, let us not rejoice.
ne *vous* réjouissez pas, ·do not rejoice.

Perfect.

Je ne me suis pas réjoui, -e, I have not rejoiced.
tu ne t'es pas réjoui, -e, &c.
il (elle) ne s'est pas réjoui, -e, &c.
nous ne nous sommes pas réjouis, -ies, we have not rejoiced.
vous ne vous êtes pas réjouis(s), ie(s), &c.
ils (elles) ne se sont pas réjouis, -ies, &c.

Infinitive.

Ne pas se réjouir, not to rejoice,
ne pas s'être réjoui, -e, not to have rejoiced.

With negation and interrogation.

Present.

Ne me réjouis-je pas? *or* } do I not rejoice?
Est-ce que je ne me réjouis pas? }

ne te réjouis-tu pas?　dost thou not rejoice?

ne se réjouit-il pas?　does he not rejoice? &c.

Perfect.

Ne me suis-je pas réjoui, -e?　have I not rejoiced?

ne t'es-tu pas réjoui? -e, &c.

ne s'est-il (-elle) pas réjoui, -e? &c.

ne nous sommes-nous pas réjouis, -ies? &c.

ne vous êtes-vous pas réjoui(s), -ie(s)? &c.

ne se sont-ils (elles) pas réjouis, -ies? &c.

Remarks.

1) A great many verbs having no reflective pronouns in English are reflected in French. The following are most commonly used:

Regular reflective verbs of the 1st Conj.

S'affliger (*să-flēē-jĕh*), to be sorry.

s'approcher (*să-pro-shĕh*), to come near.

s'arrêter (*săr-ray-tēh*), to stop.

se baisser (*bais-sēh*), to stoop.

se coucher (*coū-shĕh*), to go to bed.

se fier (*fēē-ĕh*), to trust.

se figurer (*fēĭ-gü-rēh*), } to fancy,
s'imaginer (*sēē-mă-jēē-nĕh*), } to imagine.

se hâter, to make haste.

se lever, to rise, to get up.

se marier, (*măr-yĕh*), to marry.

se dépêcher (*day pay-shĕh*), to make haste.

s'écrier (*say-krēē-ĕh*), to exclaim, to cry out.

s'enrhumer (*sāng-rü-mĕh*), to take cold.

s'étonner (*say-tŏ-nĕh*), to wonder.

s'éveiller (*say-vĕ-yĕh*), to awake.

se moquer (*mŏ kĕh*); to mock, scoff.

se promener, to take a walk

se reposer, to rest.

se soucier (*soŭ-syĕh*), to care.

se tromper (*trong-pĕh*), to be mis-taken.

se vanter (*vāng-tĕh*), to boast.

Examples.

I rise, I get up, je *me* lève.—*Get up*, levez-vous!

I have risen *or* got up, je *me* suis levé.

We have stopped, nous *nous* sommes_arrêtés, &c.

2. Óbserve also these expressions:

How are you? comment vous portez-vous?

I am well, je me porte bien.

I am mistaken, je me trompe (*trongp*).

I have been mistaken, je me suis trompé.

He is silent, il *se* tait (*tay*). Be still! taisez-vous!

B.

Impersonal Verbs.

1. In every language there are some verbs which are only used in the third person singular. They are called impersonal verbs. Their compound tenses in French are formed by means of the auxiliary *avoir*. Such are:

Neiger (*nay-jay*), to snow ;

pleuvoir (*pleŭ-v'woār*), to rain ;

grêler, to hail ;

tonner, to thunder ;

geler (*jĕ-lĕh*), to freeze ;

dégeler (*day-jĕ-lĕh*), to thaw ;

importer (*aing-por-tĕh*), to matter ;

Pres. il neige, it snows.

il pleut, it rains.

il grêle, it hails.

il tonne, it thunders.

il gèle (*jail*), it freezes.

il dégèle (*day-jail*), · it thaws.

il importe (*aing-port*), it matters.

Some other verbs become impersonal, when employed in the same manner, viz., in the third person singular.

Examples.

il suffit (*süf-fēē*), it suffices.
il semble (*säng-bl'*), it seems.
il vaut mieux (*vōh m'yeŭ*), it is better.
il me tarde, I long.
il manque (*mängk*), it wants.
il s'agit (*sā-jēē*), it is the question.

il convient, (*cong-vyaing*), it is convenient.
il arrive (*ar-rēēv*), it happens.
il reste, there remains.
il ne tient pas à moi (*ēēl nĕ tyaing pāh zāh m'woāh*), it does not depend on me.

Important Remark.

The *Subjunctive Mood with* **que** must always be used after the following *impersonal* verbs and expressions :

il convient (*kŏng-vyaing*), it is proper.
il faut, it is necessary.
il importe (*aing-pòrt*), it is important, it matters, it concerns.
il suffit (*süf-fēē*), it is sufficient.
il vaut mieux (*voh-m'yeŭ*), it is better.

And also after :

il est fâcheux (*fāh sheŭ*), it is sad.

il est temps (*täng*), it is time.
il est juste (*jüst*), it is just, right.
il est difficile (*dif-fēē-sēēl*), it is difficult.
il est possible (*pos-sēē-bl*), it is a matter of course, it is possible.
il se peut, it may be.
c'est dommage (*dom-māhsh*), it is a pity.
c'est un malheur (*say teŭng māhl-eŭr*), it is a misfortune.

Examples.

Il faut **que vous le fassiez** tout de suite (*făs-syĕh toŭt s'wēēt*). You must do it at once.

Il importe beaucoup **que vous y soyez** (*ēēl aing-pŏrt bŏh-kōō kĕ voŭ zēē s'woāh-yĕh*). It is of great consequence that you should be there.

Il faudrait, pour vous donner des conseils (*day congk-sĕ-yĕ*), **que je connaisse** vos affaires (*kĕ jĕ con-naiss vŏh zāf-fair*). In order to give you some advice (*des conseils*), it would be necessary to know your affairs.

Il suffit **que vous le disiez** (*dēē-zyĕh*). It is sufficient that you say so.

Il est possible (*pos-sēē-bl'*) **qu'il revienne** à sept heures (*rĕ-vyĕn āh sĕt teŭr*). He may possibly come back at 7 o'clock.

Translate the following

Exercises

into English and, then again, without assistance of the book, into French :

Au bureau.

1.

Veuillez faire le compte-courant (lĕ congt coū-rāngt = *the account*) de N. et Cie. — Il est déjà fait, monsieur. Après déduction (day-düc-syong) faite de leurs factures (făc-tür = *accounts*) et de leur à-compte. (*on account payment*), il nous revient (rĕ-vyaing = *there comes to us*) en-

core mille francs. Ils proposent (prō-pōz) de nous remettre un billet à trois mois (*a three months' note*). — Mais
ce sont dés déboursés (*cash expenses*). Ils auraient du
(*past part. of dévoir*) les compter (cong-tēh = *pay*) depuis
longtemps. Ils ont beaucoup perdu (*lost*) dans la fail-
lite (fā-yēēt=*failure*) de D. et Cie., mais la maison jouit
(*enjoys*) d'une très-bonne réputation (ray-pü-tā-syong) et
a toujours payé bien ponctuellement (pong-tü-ĕl-lĕ-māng
= *punctually*). — Eh bien! en leur envoyant l'extrait
(*statement*) de leur compte (*account*), écrivez-leur (*write to
them*) que nous ne pouvons leur accorder trois mois, mais
que nous disposerons sur eux (*we will draw on them*) à
soixante jours.

2.

Voulez-vous me dire à combien se monte (mongt =
amounts) mon compte? Je vais vous le solder (*pay*). —
Le voici; il se monte à cinq mille trois cent trente-huit
francs. — Voulez-vous le quittancer (kĕt-tāng-say = *to
receipt*)? Voici cinq mille francs en or; vous pouvez vé-
rifier (vay-rēē-fyĕh = *verify*) les rouleaux (roū-lōh=*rolls*).
Pour ce qui reste (*for the rest; remainder*), vous m'obligeriez si vous vouliez me prendre ce billet à-ordre (*note*).
— Quand est-il payable (pay-yā-bl')? — Dans un mois.
— Tenez, voyez! ' *Au quinze juillet prochain* (prō-shaing
= *next*) *je paierai à monsieur La Rue, ou à son ordre, la
somme de trois cent quarante francs, valeur* (vā-leūr = *value*)
reçue comptant. Paris, le treize Avril 1881.' — Quel est
ce nom-là. — Je ne connais pas le souscripteur (soū-

scrĭp-teūr = *maker*), mais les endosseurs (lay-zāng-dō.
seūr = *the indorsers*) sont bons. — Je n'aimerais pas être
obligé de le faire protester.

Exercise.

The pupil must put all the verbs in *italics* in their tense
and person :

Future.

Je (*se frapper*). — Nous (*se rendre*). — Vous (*se tromper*). — Ils (*se
réjouir*). —Il (*s'arrêter*). — Vous (*se dépêcher*). — Nous (*s'étonner*). —
Vous (*s'enrhumer*).

Plusqueparfait.

Elle (*se douter*). — Vous (*se tromper*). — Ils (*se nourrir*). — Elle (*se
nommer*). — Elles (*se réjouir*). — Nous (*se flatter*). — Vous (*s'imaginer*).
—Elle (*se promener*).— Je (*se vanter*). — Elle (*se hâter*). — Vous (*se marier*). — Nous (*se lever*).

Negative—Interrogative. Perfect.

Tu (*s'égarer*)? — Il (*s'avancer*)? — Elle (*s'enrichir*)? — Nous (*s'ar
rêter*)? — Vous (*se tromper*)? — Ils (*se fâcher*)? — Elles (*se moquer*)?
Nous (*se fier*)? — Je (*se figurer*)? — Elles (*se reposer*)?

Negative. Present.

Je (*se nommer*). — Il (*se tromper*). — Tu (*s'adresser*). — Elle (*se rendre*).
—Nous (*se flatter*).— Vous (*se blâmer*).— Ils (*se baisser*).—Elles (*se ré-
jouir*). — Tu (*s'enrhumer*). — Nous (*se coucher*). — Vous (*s'étonner*). —
Ils (*s'éveiller*). — Elles (*s'écrier*). — Tu (*se dépêcher*).

COMPANION TO THE
Revised Version of the New Testament.

Explaining the Reasons for the Changes Made on the Authorized Version.

BY ALEXANDER ROBERTS, D.D.,
Member of the English Revision Committee.

WITH SUPPLEMENT BY A MEMBER OF THE AMERICAN COMMITTEE.

Containing a Brief History of the Revision of the Work and Co-operation of the New Testament Companies, of the Points of Agreement and Difference, and an Explanation of the Appendix to the Revised New Testament.

ALSO, A FULL TEXTUAL INDEX,

Being a Key to Passages in which Important Changes have been Made.

This book, having been carefully prepared by Members of both Revision Committees, carries official weight. It shows what changes have been made, and also the reasons which influenced the revisers in making them. It will be difficult to judge of the merits of the revision without the aid of this Companion volume. Our edition is printed by special arrangement with the English publishers. It is well known that, by an arrangement between the two Committees of Revision, the changes suggested by the American Committee, but which were not adopted by the English Revisers, are published as an Appendix to the Revised New Testament. The *Companion* volume is an explanation of *all* the changes adopted by both committees, and of those suggested by the American Committee, but not assented to by the English Committee, in their final revision. The book will be indispensable to a right understanding of the revision. This cheap edition of the combined books, although authorized and copyrighted, will be sold for 25 cents in paper, and 75 cents in cloth—sent postage free.

TESTIMONIALS.

T. W. CHAMBERS, D.D., a Member of the American Committee of Revision, says of this book: "Many persons have expressed a desire that, simultaneously with the issue of the Revised New Testament, there should appear an authentic explanation of the reasons for such changes as will be found in its pages. The work of Dr. Roberts is exactly fitted to meet this desire....Nowhere else in print can be found a statement so full and exact. It gives all needed information, and does it in an unexceptional way."

C. F. DEEMS, D.D., Pastor of the Church of the Strangers, New York, writes: "The Companion to the Revised Version seems to me almost indispensable. Even scholars who were not at the meeting of the Revisers would have a wearisome work in seeking to discover all the changes made, and to ordinary readers very much of the labor would be lost. ....All this is set forth by Dr. Roberts with admirable perspicuity. Those who have any intelligent interest in the Holy Scriptures, will find this little book absorbingly interesting. I shall urge every member of the church of which I am pastor to give it a careful reading, and purpose to introduce it as a text-book in our Bible-classes."

"So valuable, interesting and useful is this publication, that we advise every one who wishes to know the why and wherefore of the revision, to obtain it immediately."—*New York Observer.*

Paper, 8vo size, 25 cents; Cloth, 16mo, 75 cents.

*** For Sale by Booksellers and Newsdealers; or sent postage-paid, on receipt of price, by

I. K. FUNK & CO., Publishers, 10 & 12 Dey St., N. Y.

THE TEACHER'S EDITION

OF THE

REVISED NEW TESTAMENT

With New Concordance and Index, Harmony of the Gospels, Maps,
Historical and Chronological Tables, Parallel Passages printed
in full, Blank Pages Interleaved for manuscript notes, and
many other New and Indispensable Helps to the Study
of the Revised Version.

After the excitement connected with the sale of the first copies of the new
revision, which lack the usual indexing headlines and marginal references
to parallel passages, and also the appendixes of tables, maps, etc.—all of
which helps preachers, teachers and Bible students have come to consider as
absolutely essential to a working copy of the Bible—there arises an imperative
demand for an edition of the Revised New Testament, containing all the
marginal and appendix helps of former TEACHERS' AND REFERENCE BIBLES,
adapted carefully and accurately to the Revised Version. We are, therefore, preparing, as rapidly as is consistent with accuracy, such an edition of
the Revised New Testament.   The work is under the supervision of well-
known Bible scholars, with numerous helpers, and will be issued as early as
it can be done with thoroughness.   In style and size the book will resemble
the Bagster Bible, "Fac-simile large edition," known as "the Moody Bible,"
being the same width and length and size of type. It will be supplied at
prices *within the reach of all.*

This "Teachers' Edition of the Revised New Testament" will be an exact,
certified reproduction of the entire Oxford and Cambridge Edition, including
the Preface and all the marginal readings and explanations.   It will contain
the appendix notes of the American Revisers, printed in the margin of each
page by the side of the passages referred to.   The parallel passages, to which
reference is m. de in the "Bagster Bibles," with numerous others, so far as
appropriate, will be PRINTED IN FULL in the margin.   The running headings,
usually printed at the tops of pages of the King James version, will be here
supplied.   A small black mark will be inserted below the last letter of each
verse to facilitate reference, and aid in RESPONSIVE READING of the Revised
Version.   The second half of the volume will consist of the most carefully
prepared HELPS TO THE STUDY OF THE REVISED NEW TESTAMENT, gleaned
from the best Teachers' Editions of the authorized version, and supplied
from various original sources—all being revised and adapted to harmonize
with the Revised Version. We shall introduce many other important features,
making this the most valuable edition of the New Testament ever issued.

Popular Cloth Edition—Ready in July—Price, Postage Free, $1.00.

Send for prospectus giving full description and prices of finer Bindings.

I. K. FUNK & CO., Publishers, 10 and 12 Dey St., New York.

THE

Meisterschaft System.

A SIMPLE AND PRACTICAL METHOD,

ENABLING

ANY ONE TO LEARN, WITH SLIGHT EFFORT, TO SPEAK
FLUENTLY AND CORRECTLY

French, German, Spanish, and Italian.

BY

DR. RICHARD S. ROSENTHAL,

Late Director of the "Akademie für fremde Sprachen" in Berlin and Leipzig,
of the "Meisterschaft College" in London, and Principal of the
"Meisterschaft School of Practical Linguistry" in New York.

FRENCH.
IN FIFTEEN PARTS, EACH CONTAINING THREE LESSONS.

PART XI.

NEW YORK:
I. K. FUNK & CO., Publishers,
10 AND 12 DEY STREET.

TERMS.

WE have arranged with Dr. ROSENTHAL, the author of the "Meisterschaft System," for its introduction in America under his own supervision, and he has opened

The Meisterschaft School of Practical Linguistry

FOR NON-RESIDENTS.

The student does not need to leave his home. The lessons of each language are prepared by the Professor, and printed and sent in pamphlet shape to each member of the School wherever he may reside.

The course of study for each language—German, French, Italian, or Spanish—makes fifteen pamphlets of three lessons each.

All members of the School have

THE PRIVILEGE

of asking, by letter, questions concerning each lesson, or consulting on any difficulty which may have occurred to them. All exercises corrected and all questions answered by return post by Dr. ROSENTHAL or one of his assistants.

TERMS OF MEMBERSHIP.

Five Dollars is the price for membership in the school for each language. This amount ($5.) entitles the member to receive the fifteen books or pamphlets containing the lessons, also answers to his questions. Return postage for the answer must accompany the question.

State distinctly which language, or languages, you desire to study There are *no extra charges*. The price, **Five Dollars,** pays for one language ; **Ten Dollars** for two languages, etc. All exercise and questions must be written on a separate sheet of paper, and must state full address of the pupil.

Remittances must be made in Post-Office Order or registered letter addressed to

I. K. FUNK & CO.,

10 and 12 Dey Street, New York.

The Meisterschaft-System.

FRENCH.

PART XI.

XI.

1.

To Ask and Answer.

1. Who is there?
2. Who are you?
3. To whom have I the honor to speak?

4. What is your name? My name is Garnier. (*Literally:* I call myself Garnier.)
5. What is it you want? (What do you want?)
6. What do you desire?
7. I want to speak to you.
8. I have something to say to you. (I must tell you something.)
9. Do you know me?—I have not the honor of knowing you.

10. Listen to me. — I am listening to you.

11. Do you understand me? — I do not understand you. — I did not understand you.
12. Why do you not answer?

13. I did not quite understand. (I did not hear well.)
14. I beg your pardon, sir?

XI.

1.

Pour Questionner et Répondre (kĕst-yon-nēh ay ray-pong-dr').

1. Qui est là (*kēē ay lāh*)?
2. Qui êtes-vous?
3. A qui ai-je l'honneur de parler (*āh kēē ai-jĕ lon-neŭr dĕ pār-lĕh*)?
4. Comment vous appelez-vous (*kom-māng voŭ zāp-pĕ-lēh voŭ*)? Je m'appelle Garnier.
5. Que voulez-vous?
6. Que désirez-vous (*kĕ day-zēē-rēh voŭ*)?
7. J'ai besoin (*bĕ-zo-aing*) de vous parler.
8. J'ai quelque chose à vous dire (*jay kĕl-kĕ shōhs āh voŭ dēēr*).
9. Me connaissez-vous? Je n'ai pas l'honneur de vous connaître (*mĕ cŏ-nais-sēh-voŭ? jĕ nay pāh lon-neŭr dĕ voŭ con-nay-tr*).
10. Ecoutez-moi. — Je vous écoute (*ay-coŭ-tēh m'wōāh; jĕ voŭ zay-coŭt*).
11. Me comprenez-vous? — Je ne vous comprends (*cong-prāng*) pas. Je ne vous ai pas compris (*cong-prēē*).
12. Pourquoi ne répondez-vous pas (*ray-pong-dēh-voŭ pāh*)?
13. J'avais mal entendu (*māh lāng-tāng-dü*).
14. Plaît-il (*play-tēēl*)?

15. What do you mean?
16. Come nearer (= approach, *approchez*); I have something to say to you.
17. I have to tell you some little thing (= word, *mot*).
18. What can I do for you?

19. Can I do anything for you?
20. Do you understand?
21. Do you understand me?
22. Do you understand me now (*maintenant*)?
23. I understand you very well (*fort bien*).

24. Do you understand what I am telling you?
25. What do you say (*or* What are you saying)?
26. What in the world do you mean (*or* What is that you are saying)?
27. What did you say?
28. I did not say anything.
29. Do you understand what I say?

30. Will you please repeat it?
31. Will you have the kindness to repeat it?

32. Did you not tell me that.... (*or* Have you not told me that....)?
33. Who told you that (*cela*)?
34. Who in the world has told you that?

35. I have been told so (= One has told it me).
36. Somebody told me so.
37. I have heard it said.

15. Que voulez-vous dire (*dēēr*) ?

16. Approchez (*ăp-pro-shēh*) ; j'ai quelque chose à vous dire (*kĕl-kĕ shōhs äh voū dēēr*).

17. J'ai un petit mot (*p'tēē mōh*) à vous dire (*dēēr*).

18. Qu'y a-t-il pour votre service (*kēē äh tēēl poūr vŏt sĕr-vēēs*) ?

19. Qu'est-ce qu'il y a (*kays kēēl ēē-äh*) pour votre service ?

20. Entendez-vous (*āng-tāng-dēh-voū*) ?

21. M'entendez-vous (*māng-tāng-dēh-voū*) ?

22. M'entendez-vous maintenant (*maing-tĕ-nāng*) ?

23. Je vous̑entends fort bien (*jĕ voū zāng-tāng fōhr by-aing*).

24. Entendez-vous ce que je dis (*sĕ.kĕ jĕ dēē*) ?

25. Que dites-vous (*kĕ dēēt-voū*) ?

26. Qu'est-ce que vous dites (*kays-kĕ voū dēēt*) ?

27. Qu'avez-vous dit (*kāh-vēh voū dēē*) ?

28. Je n'ai rien dit (*jĕ nay rēē-aing dēē*).

29. Comprenez-vous ce que je dis (*cong-prĕ-nēh-voū sĕ kĕ jĕ dēē*) ?

30. Voulez-vous bien répéter (*byaing ray-pay-tēh*) ?

31. Voulez-vous̑avoir la bonté de répéter (*zā-v'woār lāh bong-tay dĕ ray-pay-tēh*) ?

32. Ne m'avez-vous pas dit que...̇..?

33. Qui vous̑a dit cela (*kēē voū zāh dēē sĕ-lāh*) ?

34. Qui est-ce qui vous‿a dit cela (*kēē ays kēē voū zāh dēē sĕ-lāh*) ?

35. On me l'a dit (*ong mĕ lāh dēē*). •

36. Quelqu'un (*kĕl-keūng*) me l'a dit.

37. Je l'ai entendu dire (*jĕ lay āng-tāng-dü dēēr*).

38. How do you call this?

39. How is this called?

40. That is called....

41. That is called....

42. May I ask you? (*or* May I inquire of you? *or* May I beg you)?

43. What is it?
44. What is the use of that?

45. What is this?

46. What does that mean (= What will this say)?

2.

To Affirm or Deny.

1. I say yes.
2. I say no.
3. I tell you that....
4. I assure you that....
5. I tell you it is true.
6. It is certain.
7. It is a fact.
8. I warrant it (*or* I guarantee it).
9. I guarantee you the fact.

---

1) *il sert* is the third person singular of the irregular present of

38. Comment‿appelez-vous cela (*kŏm-mäng täp-pĕ-lēh voū s'lāh*) ?

39. Comment cela s'appelle-t-il (*kŏm-mäng s'lāh säp-pĕl-tēēl*) ?

40. {
   On appelle cela....
   Cela s'appelle....
}

41. C'est ce qu'on nomme (*says-kong nŏm*).

42. {
   Puis-je vous demander ?
   Oserais-je vous demander ?
   Oserais-je vous prier (*prēē-ēh*) ?
   Peut-on vous demander ?
}

43. Qu'est-ce que c'est (*kays-kĕ say*) ?

44. A quoi cela sert-il ?[1]

45. {
   Qu'est-ce que cela (*kays-kĕ s'lāh*) ?
   Qu'est-ce que ç'est que cela (*kays-kĕ say kĕ s'lāh*) ?
}

46. Qu'est-ce que cela veut dire ?

2.

Pour Affirmer ou Nier.

1. Je dis **que** oui (*jĕ dēē kĕ oū-ēē*).

2. Je dis **que** non.

3. Je vous dis que....

4. Je vous‿assure que (*jĕ voū zäs-sür kĕ*)....

5. Je vous dis que c'est vrai (*kĕ say vray*).

6. Cela est certain (*cĕr-taing*).

7. C'est‿un fait (*say teūng fay*).

8. Je vous le garantis (*gä-räng-tēē*).

9. Je vous garantis le fait.

---

servir, to serve, to help. *Pres.:* Je sers, tu sers, il sert nous servons, vous servez, ils servent (*sĕrv*).

10. I suppose so.

11. I do not suppose so.

12. I fancy so.

13. You can easily conceive (*or* understand) that....

14. Do you think so ?

15. I do not think so.

16. I don't know what you mean.

17. Is it true that....?

18. Yes, it is certain.

19. I answer for it.

20. I am certain of it.

21. I am sure of it.

22. You may be convinced of it.

23. You may believe me as to that (*en*).

24. I can assure you of it.

25. It cannot be true.

---

1) The pupil must learn the *irregular* verb **savoir** (*sā-vwoār*), to know.

Present.	*Preterite.*
Je sais (*say*).	Je sus (*sü*).
tu sais (*say*).	tu sus.
il sait (*say*).	il sut.
nous savons (*sāh-vong*).	nous sûmes (*süm*).
vous savez (*sāh-vĕh*).	vous sûtes (*süt*).
ils savent (*sāhv*).	ils surent (*sür*).

Imperfect.	*Future.*
Je savais.	Je saurai (*sŏh-rĕh*).
tu savais.	tu sauras (*sŏh-rā*).
il savait.	il saura (*sŏh-rā*).
nous savions.	nous saurons (*sŏh-rong*).
vous saviez.	vous saurez (*sŏh-rĕh*).
ils savaient.	ils sauront (*sŏh-rong*).

10. Je suppose **que** oui (*jĕ süp-poz kĕ ou-ēē*).

11. Je suppose **que** non (*jĕ süp-poz kĕ nong*).

12. J'imagine (*jēē-mā-jĕēn*) **que** oui.

13. Vous comprenez facilement que (*fā-sēē-lē-māng*) ....

14. Le pensez-vous (*lĕ pāng-sēh voŭ*) ?

15. Je ne le pense pas.

16. Je ne sais [1] ce que vous voulez dire (*jĕ nĕ say s'kĕ voŭ voŭ-lēh dēēr*).

17. Est-il vrai que (*ay-tēēl vray kĕ*).....

18. Oui, cela est certain (*cĕr-taing*).

19. Je vous en réponds (*jĕ voŭ zāng ray-pong*).

20. J'en suis certain (*jāng s'wēē cĕr-taing*).

21. J'en suis sûr (*jāng s'wēē sür*).

22. Soyez en bien persuadé (*s'woāh-yēh zāng byaing-pĕr-sü-āh-day*).

23. Vous pouvez [2] m'en croire (*māng kroār*).

24. Je puis [2] vous l'assurer (*lās-sü-rēh*).

25. Cela ne peut [2] être vrai (*s'lāh nĕ peŭ taytr' vray*).

Conditional.	*Subj. Pres.*
Je saurais.	Que je sache (*sāsh*).
tu saurais.	que tu saches (*sāsh*).
il saurait.	qu'il sache (*sāsh*).
nous saurions.	que nous sachions (*sā-shyong*).
vous sauriez.	que vous sachiez (*sā-shyēh*).
ils sauraient.	qu'ils sachent (*sāsh*).

Participles.

Sachant (*sāh-shāng*).
sû (*sü*).

2) *Pouvoir*, to be able. *Part. Pres.*: pouvant.—*Part. past.*: pu.—*Present:* Je peux (*or* je puis), (*puis* is only used in the first person sing. *I cannot* is mostly expressed by *je ne puis* (without pas) or by *je ne peux pas*), tu peux, il peut, nous pouvons, vous pouvez, ils peuvent.—*Imperfect.*: Je pouvais, tu pouvais, &c.—*Pret.*: Je pus, tu pus, il put, nous pûmes, vous pûtes, ils purent (*pür*).—*Fut.*: Je pourrai, tu pourras, il pourra, nous pourrons, vous pourrez, ils pourront.—*Condit.*: Je pourrais, tu pourrais, il pourrait, &c.—*Subjunct.*: Que je puisse, que tu puisses, qu'il puisse, que nous puissions, que vous puissiez, qu'ils puissent (*pü-is*).

26. That is true (= That's the truth).
27. I assure you it is so.

28. It cannot be. (It is impossible.)
29. I assure you it is not so.
30. You are right.
31. You are wrong.
32. There is no doubt of it.
33. Every one will tell you so.
34. Upon my word of honor!

35. That is a matter of course.

36. I can hardly believe you.
37. I do not know anything about it.
38. There is nothing in it.
39. Are you in earnest?
40. Are you talking seriously?
41. Are you not mistaken?

42. I see I am mistaken.
43. Is not this an error (*or* mistake)?
44. I doubt it.
45. You are jesting (*or* joking).
46. That is incredible.
47. You are altogether wrong.

48. Some one has imposed upon you.

---

1) *Dire*, to say; to tell. — *Part. pres.:* disant (*dēē-zäng*). — *Part. past.:* dit.—*Pres.:* Je dis, tu dis, il dit, nous disons, vous *dites*, ils disent (*dēēz*).—*Imperf.:* Je disais, tu disais, &c.—*Pret.:* Je dis (*dēē*),

26. C'est la vérité.

27. Je vous‿assure qu'il en‿est‿ainsi (*jĕ voū zās-sür kĕēl āng nay-taing-sēē*).

28. Cela ne se peut pas!

29. Je·vous‿assure **que** non (*jĕ voū zās-sür kē nong*).

30. Vous‿avez raison (*ray-zong*).

31. Vous‿avez tort (*tor*).

32. Il n'y a pas de doute (*dōōt*).

33. Tout le monde vous le dira[1] (*dēē-rāh*).

34. D'honneur (*or* Sur mon‿honneur, *or* Ma parolᴊ d'honneur)!

35. Cela s'entend (*s'la sāng-tāng*) (*or* C'est bien‿entendu (*byaing nāng-tāng-dü*).

36. J'ai de la peine à·vous croire.

37. Je n'en sais rien (*rēē-aing*).

38. Il n'en‿est rien (*ēēl nāng-nay rēē·aing*).

39. Est-ce tout de bon?

40. Parlez-vous sérieusement (*say-rēē-eū-zĕ-māng*).

41. Ne vous trompez-vous pas (*nĕ voū trong-pēh voū pāh*)?

42. Je vois (*jĕ v'woāh*) que je me suis trompé.

43. N'est-ce pas‿une‿erreur (*naysĕ pāh zün nĕr-reūr*)?

44. J'en doute (*jāng dōōt*).

45. Vous plaisantez (*play-zāng-tēh*).

46. C'est‿incroyable (*say taing-kroāh-yābl*).

47. Vous‿êtes dans la plus profonde‿erreur (*pro-fŏng-dĕr-reūr*).

48. On vous‿en‿a imposé (*ong voū zāng-nāh-aing-po-zay*).

---

tu dis, il dit, nous dîmes (*dēēm*), vous dîtes, ils dirent (*dēēr*).—*Fut.:* Je dirai (*dēē-rēh*), tu diras, &c.—*Subjunct.:* Que je dise (*dēēz*), &c.— *Subj. Imp.:* Que je disse (*dĭs*), &c.—*Imperative:* Dis, disons, dites.

FOUNDATION SENTENCE.

This Irish waiter looked as if he had had a

drop too much, when he came to take my letters

to the post-office.

1.

This Irish waiter looked as if he had had a
drop too much.

This [1]

waiter (boy; bachelor)

Irish

had

the look (the air; the melody)

of having [2]

---

1) Before a masculine noun which begins with *a vowel* or *h* mute, *cet* is used instead of *ce*. Ex.: cet‿enfant (*sĕ tăng-fāng*), this child ; cet‿homme (*sĕ tŏm*). this man ; cet‿arbre (*sĕ tărbr*), this tree. In the plural there is no difference. Ex.: ces‿enfants (*say zăng-fāng*), these children ; ces‿hommes (*say zŏm*), these men.

FOUNDATION SENTENCE.

Ce garçon irlandais avait l'air d'avoir trop
sĕ gär-song ïr-läng-day ä-vay layr dä-v'woär trŏh

bu, lorsqu'il est venu chercher mes lettres, pour
bü lors-kĕĕl ay ve-nü shĕr-shay may lĕttr' poŭr

les mettre à la poste.
lay mĕtt-räh läh -pŏst.

1.

Ce garçon irlandais avait l'air d'avoir trop bu.
sĕ gär-song ïr-läng-day ä-vay layr dä-v'woär trŏh bü.

Ce[1] (*sĕ*) (*fem.* cette ; *plur.* ces, these)

garçon (*gär-song*)

irlandais (*ïr-läng-day*)

avait (*ä-vay*)

l'air (*layr*) (*m.*)

d'avoir[2] (*dä-v'woär*)

---

2) Expressions such as : the desire *of seeing* you, the honor *of knowing* her, &c., must be rendered by the *Infinitive with. de*, i.e. le désir *de* vous *voir*, l'honneur *de* la *connaître*. Il est *temps de partir*, it is time to start ; Il avait l'air *d'avoir* trop bu ; J'ai l'honneur *de* vous *saluer* (*sä-lü-ēh*), &c.

too much

drunk[1]

---

1. Why do you look so angry? (*Literally :* Why have you the look of such bad humor (*de si mauvaise humeur*)?
2. Mrs. N. looked very angry when (*lorsque*) I told her that he would not come (*qu'il ne viendrait*[2] *pas*).

---

1) **Boire** (*b'woãr*), *to drink,* is an *irregular* verb.

Present.	*Preterite*
Je bois (*b'woãh*).	Je bus.
tu bois.	tu bus.
il boit.	il but.
nous *buvons* (*bü-vong*).	nous bûmes (*büm*).
vous *buvez*.	vous bûtes (*büt*).
ils boivent (*b'woãv*).	ils burent (*bür*).

Imperfect.	*Subj. Present.*
Je buvais.	Que je boive.
tu buvais.	que tu boives.
il buvait.	qu'il boive.
nous buvions.	que nous *buvions*.
vous buviez.	que vous *buviez*.
ils buvaient.	qu'ils boivent.

Future.	*Imperative.*
Je boirai.	bois.
tu boiras.	*buvons*.
il boira.	*buvez*.
nous boirons.	*Participles.*
vous boirez.	buvant.
ils boiront.	bu.

2) The *irregular verb* **venir** (*vĕ-nēēr*), *to come,* is thus conjugated :

Present.	*Preterite.*
Je viens (*vyaing*).	Je vins (*vaing*).
tu viens.	tu vins (*vaing*).
il vient.	il vint (*vaing*).
nous venons (*vĕ-nong*).	nous vînmes (*vaingm*).
vous venez.	vous vîntes (*vaingt*).
ils viennent (*vyĕn*).	ils vinrent (*vaingr*).

trop (*trōh*)

bu[1] (*bü*) (*Partic. past* of the irregular verb *boire* (*b'woār*) to drink).

---

1. Pourquoi avez-vous l'air de si mauvaise humeur (*dĕ sēē mō-vayze ü-meūr*) ?

2. Madame N. avait l'air de très mauvaise humeur, lorsque jē lui ai dit, qu'il ne viendrait[2] pas (*k̄ēēl nĕ vyaing-dray pāh*).

Imperfect.
Je venais.
tu venais.
il venait.
nous venions.
vous veniez.
ils venaient. –

Perfect.
Je **suis** venu, I have come.
tu es venu, &c.
il est venu, &c.

Future.
Je viendrai.
tu viendras.
il viendra.
nous viendrons.
vous viendrez.
ils viendront.

Imperative.
viens (*vyaing*).
venons.
venez.

Conditional.
Je viendrais (*vyaing-dray*).
tu viendrais.
il viendrait.
nous viendrions.
vous viendriez.
ils viendraient.

Subj. Pres.
Que je vienne (*vyĕn*).
que tu viennes.
qu'il vienne.
que nous *venions*.
que vous *veniez*.
qu'ils viennent (*vyĕn*).

Sub. Imperf.
Que je vinsse (*vaings*).
que tu vinsses.
qu'il **vînt**.
que nous vinssions.
que vous vinssiez.
qu'ils vinssent.

Participles.
venant (*vĕ-nāng*).   venu (*vĕ-nü*).

In the same manner are conjugated : *convenir* (*kōng-vĕ-nēĕr*), to agree, to suit ; *devenir*, to become ; *parvenir*, to attain, to reach ; *prévenir*, to be beforehand with, to inform ; *se souvenir*, to remember (je me souviens [*soŭ-vyaing*], I remember) ; *revenir*, to come back, to return (cela me revient à l'esprit [*s'lāh mĕ rĕ-vyaing-āh lĕs-prēē*], there occurs to me).

GRAMMATICAL REMARKS.

Exercises and Words used in Common Conversation.

Conjugation of S'en aller, to go away.

I give the conjugation of the irregular reflective verb *S'en aller*, to go away, on account of its difficulty to English students. Observe that **en** is *never separated* from the reflective personal pronouns *m'*, *t'*, *s'*, *nous, vous, s'.* This is especially noticeable in the compound tenses, viz.: Je *m'en* suis allé, &c.

Present.

Je m'en vais (*jĕ māng vay*).

tu t'en vas (*tü tāng vāh*).

il s'en va (*ēēl sāng vāh*).

nous nous en allons (*noŭ-noŭ-zāng-nāh-long*).

vous vous en allez (*voŭ-voŭ-zāng-nāh-lēh*).

ils s'en vont (*ēēl sāng vong*).

Je ne m'en vais pas (*je nĕ māng vay pāh*).

tu ne t'en vas pas.

il ne s'en va pas.

nous ne nous en allons pas.

vous ne vous en allez pas.

ils ne s'en vont pas.

Imperfect.

Je m'en allais (*je māng-nāh-lay*).

Je ne m'en allais pas.

Preterite.

Je m'en allai (*jĕ măng-năh-*   Je ne m'en allai pas.
lēh).

Perfect.

Je m'en suis allé (*jĕ măng*   Je ne m'en suis pas allé.
s'wēē zāh-lay).

tu t'en es allé.   tu ne t'en es pas allé.

il s'en est allé.   il ne s'en est pas allé.

nous nous en sommes allés   nous ne nous en sommes
(*noū-noū-zāng sŏm zāh-lay*).   pas allés.

vous vous en êtes allés.   vous ne vous en êtes pas
                              allés.

ils s'en sont allés.   ils ne s'en sont pas allés.

Pluperfect.

Je m'en étais allé.   Je ne m'en étais pas allé.

2d Pluperfect.

Je m'en fus allé.   Je ne m'en fus pas allé.

Future.

Je m'en irai.   je ne m'en irai pas.

2d Future.

Je m'en serai allé.   Je ne m'en serai pas allé.

Imperative.

Va-t'en.   Ne t'en va pas.

(qu'il s'en aille.)   (qu'il ne s'en aille pas.)

allons-nous-en.   ne nous en allons pas.

allez-vous-en.   ne vous en allez pas.

(qu'ils s'en aillent.)   (qu'ils ne s'en aillent pas.)

Interrogatively. · Negative-Interrogative.

Present.

M'en vais-je ?	Ne m'en vais-je pas ?
t'en vas-tu ?	ne t'en vas-tu pas ?
s'en va-t-il ?	ne s'en va-t-il pas ?
nous en allons-nous ?	ne nous en allons-nous pas ?
vous en allez-vous ?	ne vous en allez-vous pas ?
s'en vont-ils ?	ne s'en vont-ils pas ?

Imperfect.

M'en allais-je ?	Ne m'en allais-je pas ?

Preterite.

M'en allai-je ?	Ne m'en allai-je pas ?

Perfect.

M'en suis-je allé ?	Ne m'en suis-je pas allé ?
t'en es-tu allé ?	ne t'en es-tu pas allé ?
s'en est-il allé ?	ne s'en est-il pas allé ?
nous en sommes-nous al-lés ?	ne nous en sommes-nous pas allés ?
vous en êtes-vous allés ?	ne vous en êtes-vous pas allés.
s'en sont-ils allés ?	ne s'en sont-ils pas allés ?

Pluperfect.

M'en étais-je allé ?	Ne m'en étais-je pas allé ?

2d Pluperfect.

M'en fus-je allé ?	Ne m'en fus-je pas allé ?

Future.

M'en irai-je ?   Ne m'en irai-je pas ?

2d *Future.*

M'en serai-je allé ?   Ne m'en serai-je pas allé ?

Words.

Carte du Restaurant.   *Bill of Fare.*

1. Potages.   Soups.

Un consommé, beef soup.   un potage au riz (*rēē*), rice-soup.
une julienne (*jül-yĕn*), Julienne.   un potage au vermicelle, Ver-
                                              micelli soup.

2. Poissons (*p'woä-song*) (m. pl.).   Fish.

Le saumon (*sōh-mong*), salmon.   un turbot (*tür-bō*), turbot.
la sole, sole.   le maquereau (*măkĕ-rōh*), mack-
une truite (*trü-ēēt*), trout.   erel.
un hareng (*āh-raing*), herring.   un homard en salade, lobster-
une anguille (*āng-ghēē-yĕ*), eel.   salad.
un homard (*ō-mär*), lobster.   le brochet (*brō-shĕh*), pike.
                                              des huîtres (*day z'wēē-t'r*), oysters.

3. Boeuf (*beüf*) (m.).   Beef.

le biftek,   }   saignant (*sĕn-yāng*), rare.
le beefsteak,   } beefsteak.   le filet (*fēē-lĕh*), fillet.
un beefsteak à l'anglaise, beef-   un filet aux truffes (*ōh trüff*),
steak.   fillet with truffles.
bien cuit (*byaing-k'wēē*), well-   un rosbif aux pommes (*ōh pŏm*),
done.   roast-beef and potatoes.

4. Mouton (*mōō-tong*) (m.).   Mutton.

une côtelette, cutlet ; chop.   un filet de mouton (*mōō-tong*),
un gigot (*jēē-gōh*), leg of mutton.   roast-mutton.

5. Veau (*vōh*) (f.).   Veal.

une côtelette, cutlet.   un ris de veau (*vōh*), sweet-bread.
des rognons (*rŏn-yong*), kidneys.

6. Volaille (*vō-lǎ⁚yĕ*) (m.).   Poultry.

un chapon (*shǎ-pong*), capon.   un poulet en salade (*sā-lǎhd*),
un poulet (*poŭ-lay*), chicken.   chicken-salad.
un poulet en mayonnaise, Ma-   un caneton (*kǎhnĕ-tong*), duck.
yonnaise of chicken.   une oie (*o-āh*), goose.
un pigeon (*pēĕ-jong*), pigeon.   un dindon (*daing-dong*), turkey.

7. Gibier (*jēĕ-byĕh*) (m.).   Game.

une perdrix (*pĕr-drēĕ*), partridge.   un filet de chevreuil (*shĕ-vreŭ-yĕ*),
une caille (*kǎ-yĕ*), quail.   venison.

8. Pâtisseries (*pāh-tĭs-sĕ-rēĕ*) (f. pl.).   Pastry.

un pâté chaud de légumes (*lay-gŭm*), hot vegetable pie.

un pâté de foies gras, ⎰ Pâté de foies gras.
⎱ goose-liver pastry.

9. Salades (*sā-lǎhd*) (f. pl.).   Salads.

une salade de céleri, celery sal-   une salade de concombres (*cong-
ad.   congŏ'r*), cucumber-salad.

une laitue (*lay-tü*), lettuce-salad.   du cresson (*crĕ-song*), cresses.

10. Légumes (*lay-gŭm*) (m. pl.).   Vegetables.

des‿asperges (*day zǎs-pĕrjĕ*) (f.),   des pommes de terre, potatoes.
asparagus.   des pommes frites (*frēĕt*), fried
des petits pois (*p'woāh*), (au   potatoes.
beurre), green peas.   des‿épinards (*day-zay-pĕĕ-nār*)
des‿artichauts frits (*day zār-tēĕ   (m.), spinach.
shō frēĕ*), artichokes (fried).   des carottes (f.), carrots.
des‿haricots verts (*day-zār-rĕĕ-coh   des‿oignons (*day z'woān-yong*)
vayr*), French beans.   (m.), onions.
des choux-fleurs (*shoo-fleūr*) (m.),   du macaroni, macaroni.
cauliflowers.

11. Entremets au sucre.
(*āng-tr'-may ōh sü-cr'*).

une omelette, omelet.
une omelette au rhum, omelet
with rum.

12. Dessert (*dĕ-sayr*) (m.).

du fruit (*frü-ēē*), fruit.
des pruneaux (*prü-no*) (m. pl.),
stewed prunes.
une compote de pommes (*cong-pŏ dĕ pŏm*), stewed apples.
des confitures de groseilles (*kong-fēē-tür dĕ-gro-zĕ-yĕ*), red currant
jam.
de la gelée de groseilles, red currant jelly.
une marmelade d'abricots (*dā-brēē-kŏh*), marmalade of apricots.
une meringue à la crême (*kraym*),
meringue with jelly.
des macarons (*mā-kā-rong*) (m.
pl.), macaroons.

Sweet dishes.

des beignets (*bĕn-yēh*), de pommes, apple fritters.

Desserts.

des biscuits (m. pl.), biscuits.
une compote de pêches (*paysh*),
stewed peaches.
des (quatre-) mendiants (*māng-dyāng*) (m. pl.), raisins, figs,
nuts, and almonds.
du fromage à la crême, cream
cheese.
du fromage de Gruyère, Gruyère
cheese.
du fromage de Brie (*brēē*), Brie
cheese.
du fromage de Roquefort, Roquefort cheese.
des prunes à l'eau-de-vie (*lōh-dĕ-vēē*), prunes in brandy.

Translate the following

Exercise

into English and then render it again into French:

On sonne (*Somebody is ringing*). Serait-ce monsieur
B.? — Madame, veut-elle recevoir monsieur B.? — Faites-
le entrer dans le petit salon. — Madame, j'ai l'honneur

de vous souhaiter (*to wish*) le bonjour. — Bonjour monsieur ; donnez-vous donc la peine de vous asseoir. Comment vous portez-vous ? — Très-bien, madame, je vous
remercie ; et vous-même ? — J'ai été un peu enrhumée,
mais je vais très-bien aujourd'hui. — Je suis charmé de
vous voir rétablie. — Vous êtes bien aimable d'avoir
pensé à moi. — Je me suis présenté (pray-zăng-tay) plusieurs fois chez vous, mais je n'ai pas eu l'avantage (lă-
văng-tăhjc=*the happiness*) de vous rencontrer (*meet*). On
doit (*they must*) vous avoir remis (*given*) ma carte. — En
effet (*yes, indeed*), et je regrette bien de ne pas m'être
trouvée chez moi pour vous recevoir. — Comment va
monsieur votre père ? — Il est indisposé depuis quelques
jours, il est obligé de garder la chambre. — J'en suis bien
fâché. J'espère que cela ne sera rien. — C'est peu de
chose (*it is a mere trifle*) ; mais à son âge il lui faut des
soins (*he must be careful*).

With a Physician.

1) I have taken (*pris* = prēē) the liberty to send (*envoyer chercher*) for you, doctor. — Why, what is the matter with you ? How do you feel (*comment vous trouvez-
vous*) ? — I am not at all (*du tout*) well. I feel (*je me
sens* = săng) very ill. — 2) Since when are you ill ? —
How did this (*cela*) begin ? — It (*cela*) took me yesterday
in consequence of (*par*) a chill (*un frisson*=frĭs-song) ; and
then (*ensuite* = ăng-s'wēēt) I perspired (*transpirer*=trăng-
spēē-rēh) very much. — 3) Did you feel sick (= Have
you felt [*senti*=săng-tēē] sick [*des maux de coeur*]) ? — Yes,

I feel sick.and am inclined to vomit (= and have inclination [*des envies* = day zăng-vēē] to vomit). — Show me (*voyons*) your tongue (*langue*). — You will have (*il vous faudra*) to take a little medicine (*une petite médecine*).— 4) Give me your arm (*bras* = brāh). Your pulse (*pouls*) is rather high (*un peu élevé*). There is some fever (*de la fièvre* = fēē-ay-vr'). — You have a little fever. — 5) Do you think my illness dangerous (*dangereuse* = dăng-jĕ-reūse)? — No, but we must take care (*prendre garde*) so that it may not become (*devienne*) so. — 6) What have I to do? — Have I anything else (*autre chose*) to do? — No, only take care (*ayez soin* = s'woaing) to keep yourself warm (*chaudement*). — Be careful not to take cold. — 7) What kind of a night did you pass (= How have you passed the night)? — I feel.much better, thank you. — I have slept (*dormi* = dor-mēē) a little, and the fever is quite gone down (*diminuée* = dēē-mēē-nü-ay). — 8) Very well, I can assure you that this will be nothing serious (*rien de sérieux* = rēē-aing dĕ say-ryeū). — In two or three days you will be well (*guéri* = cured).

Exercise.

Which is the way to the Northern railway station (*la gare du Nord*), please? — Go straight ahead, sir. — Which is the nearest (*le plus court* = lĕ plü coūr) way to go to St. Honoré Street? — Go straight ahead; you cannot miss your way (= you cannot mistake [*vous tromper*] of [*de*] the way). — Can you tell me if this road (*cette route*) leads (*conduit* = kong-d'wēē) to Amiens? —

You are on (*dans*) the right (*vrai*) road, sir. — You are not on the right road, sir. — To (*de*) which side must I go? — Follow (*suivez*=s'wēē-vēh) this street, it will lead (*conduira*) you to the great road. — How far may it be from here (=How much can it there have [*y avoir*] from here)? — It may be about a mile (= It can there have a mile [*un mille* = mēēl]). — It is not (*il n'y a pas*) more than a mile. — It is (*il y a*) scarcely (*à peine*) a mile. It is (*il y a*) â good mile. — It is a little more than a mile.

Exercise.

Lettre d'introduction et de crédit.

LYONS, 3 janvier 1881.

Messieurs MICHELET ET CIE., à Paris.

Messieurs:

Nous prenons (*we take*) la liberté d'introduire (*introduce*) chez vous par ces lignes (*lines*) et de vous recommander à un accueil obligeant (*kind reception*, i.e. *to your kindness*) Mr. Chas. Fruston de cette place.

Nous l'accréditons chez vous pour la somme de dix mille francs. Veuillez bien lui payer jusqu'à cette concurrence (*up to this amount*) l'argent dont (*whereof*) il aura besoin et nous en débiter.

Agréez (*accept*) l'assurance de notre parfait dévouement   D. ET CIE.

COMPANION TO THE
Revised Version of the New Testament.

Explaining the Reasons for the Changes Made on the Authorized Version.

BY ALEXANDER ROBERTS, D.D.,

Member of the English Revision Committee.

WITH SUPPLEMENT BY A MEMBER OF THE AMERICAN COMMITTEE.

Containing a Brief History of the Revision of the Work and Co-operation of the New Testament Companies, of the Points of Agreement and Difference, and an Explanation of the Appendix to the Revised New Testament.

ALSO, A FULL TEXTUAL INDEX,

Being a Key to Passages in which Important Changes have been Made.

This book, having been carefully prepared by Members of both Revision Committees, carries official weight. It shows what changes have been made, and also the reasons which influenced the revisers in making them. It will be difficult to judge of the merits of the revision without the aid of this Companion volume. Our edition is printed by special arrangement with the English publishers. It is well known that, by an arrangement between the two Committees of Revision, the changes suggested by the American Committee, but which were not adopted by the English Revisers, are published as an Appendix to the Revised New Testament. The *Companion* volume is an explanation of *all* the changes adopted by both committees, and of those suggested by the American Committee, but not assented to by the English Committee, in their final revision. The book will be indispensable to a right understanding of the revision. This cheap edition of the combined books, although authorized and copyrighted, will be sold for 25 cents in paper, and 75 cents in cloth—sent postage free.

TESTIMONIALS.

T. W. CHAMBERS, D.D., a Member of the American Committee of Revision, says of this book: " Many persons have expressed a desire that, simultaneously with the issue of the Revised New Testament, there should appear an authentic explanation of the reasons for such changes as will be found in its pages. The work of Dr. Roberts is exactly fitted to meet this desire.....Nowhere else in print can be found a statement so full and exact. It gives all needed information, and does it in an unexceptional way."

C. F. DEEMS, D.D., Pastor of the Church of the Strangers, New York, writes: "The Companion to the Revised Version seems to me almost indispensable. Even scholars who were not at the meeting of the Revisers would have a wearisome work in seeking to discover all the changes made, and to ordinary readers very much of the labor would be lost. ....All this is set forth by Dr. Roberts with admirable perspicuity. Those who have any intelligent interest in the Holy Scriptures, will find this little book absorbingly interesting. I shall urge every member of the church of which I am pastor to give it a careful reading, and purpose to introduce it as a text-book in our Bible-classes."

"So valuable, interesting and useful is this publication, that we advise every one who wishes to know the why and wherefore of the revision, to obtain it immediately."—*New York Observer.*

Paper, 8vo size, 25 cents ; Cloth, 16mo, 75 cents.

*** For Sale by Booksellers and Newsdealers, or sent postage-paid, on receipt of price, by

I. K. FUNK & CO., Publishers, 10 & 12 Dey St., N.Y.

THE TEACHER'S EDITION

OF THE

REVISED NEW TESTAMENT

With New Concordance and Index, Harmony of the Gospels, Maps,
Historical and Chronological Tables, Parallel Passages printed
in full, Blank Pages Interleaved for manuscript notes, and
many other New and Indispensable Helps to the Study
of the Revised Version.

After the excitement connected with the sale of the first copies of the new revision, which lack the usual indexing headlines and marginal references to parallel passages, and also the appendixes of tables, maps, etc.—all of which helps preachers, teachers and Bible students have come to consider as absolutely essential to a working copy of the Bible—there arises an imperative demand for an edition of the Revised New Testament, containing. all the marginal and appendix helps of former TEACHERS' AND REFERENCE BIBLES, adapted carefully and accurately to the Revised Version. We are, therefore, preparing, as rapidly as is consistent with accuracy, such an edition of the Revised New Testament. The work is under the supervision of well-known Bible scholars, with numerous helpers, and will be issued as early as it can be done with thoroughness. In style and size the book will resemble the Bagster Bible, "Fac-simile large edition," known as "the Moody Bible," being the same width and length and size of type. It will be supplied at prices *within the reach of all.*

This "Teachers' Edition of the Revised New Testament" will be an exact, *certified reproduction* of the entire Oxford and Cambridge Edition, including the Preface and all the marginal readings and explanations. It will contain the appendix notes of the American Revisers, printed in the margin of each page by the side of the passages referred to. The parallel passages, to which reference is made in the "Bagster Bibles," with numerous others, so far as appropriate, will be PRINTED IN FULL in the margin. The running headings, usually printed at the tops of pages of the King James version, will be here supplied. A small black mark will be inserted below the last letter of each verse to facilitate reference, and aid in RESPONSIVE READING of the Revised Version. The second half of the volume will consist of the most carefully prepared HELPS TO THE STUDY OF THE REVISED NEW TESTAMENT, gleaned from the best Teachers' Editions of the authorized version, and supplied from various original sources—all being revised and adapted to harmonize with the Revised Version. We shall introduce many other important features, making this the most valuable edition of the New Testament ever issued.

Popular Cloth Edition—Ready in July—Price, Postage Free, $1.60.

Send for prospectus giving full description and prices of finer Bindings.

I. K. FUNK & CO., Publishers, 10 and 12 Dey St., New York.

THE

𝕸𝖊𝖎𝖘𝖙𝖊𝖗𝖘𝖈𝖍𝖆𝖋𝖙 𝕾𝖞𝖘𝖙𝖊𝖒,

A SIMPLE AND PRACTICAL METHOD,

ENABLING

ANY ONE TO LEARN, WITH SLIGHT EFFORT, TO SPEAK
FLUENTLY AND CORRECTLY

𝕱𝖗𝖊𝖓𝖈𝖍, 𝕲𝖊𝖗𝖒𝖆𝖓, 𝕾𝖕𝖆𝖓𝖎𝖘𝖍, 𝖆𝖓𝖉 𝕴𝖙𝖆𝖑𝖎𝖆𝖓,

BY

DR. RICHARD S. ROSENTHAL,

*Late Director of the "Akademie für fremde Sprachen" in Berlin and Leipzig,
of the "Meisterschaft College" in London, and Principal of the
"Meisterschaft School of Practical Linguistry" in New York.*

FRENCH.

IN FIFTEEN PARTS, EACH CONTAINING THREE LESSONS.

PART XII.

NEW YORK:

I. K. FUNK & CO., Publishers,

10 AND 12 Dey Street.

TERMS.

WE have arranged with Dr. ROSENTHAL, the author of the "Meisterschaft System," for its introduction in America under his own supervision, and he has opened

The Meisterschaft School of Practical Linguistry

FOR NON-RESIDENTS.

The student does not need to leave his home. The lessons of each language are prepared by the Professor, and printed and sent in pamphlet shape to each member of the School wherever he may reside.

The course of study for each language—German, French, Italian, or Spanish—makes fifteen pamphlets of three lessons each.

All members of the School have

THE PRIVILEGE

of asking, by letter, questions concerning each lesson, or consulting on any difficulty which may have occurred to them. All exercises corrected and all questions answered by return post by Dr. ROSENTHAL or one of his assistants.

TERMS OF MEMBERSHIP.

Five Dollars is the price for membership in the school for each language. This amount ($5.) entitles the member to receive the fifteen books or pamphlets containing the lessons, also answers to his questions. Return postage for the answer must accompany the question.

State distinctly which language, or languages, you desire to study There are *no extra charges*. The price, **Five Dollars,** pays for one language ; **Ten Dollars** for two languages, etc. All exercises and questions must be written on a separate sheet of paper, and must state full address of the pupil.

Remittances must be made in Post-Office Order or registered letter addressed to

I. K. FUNK & CO,

10 and 12 Dey Street, New York.

The Meisterschaft-System.

FRENCH.

PART XII.

XII.

(*Continuation.*)

3. The old lady with whom you were at church is not
beautiful, but she has a very distinguished appearance
(*l'air très distingué*).
4. Why did that English waiter look so angry?

5. My clerk is a[1] Frenchman, but he looks like an
Englishman (*il a l'air anglais*).
6. Your Irish servant looks like a Frenchman.

7. The old tailor whom my brother had in Berlin, did
not look like a German.
8. He looks good-natured (*il a l'air bon*).
9. I met Miss B.; she was looking very sad (*elle avait
l'air très triste*).
10. He is very angry. (*Literally :* He is *of* very bad
humor.)

---

1. A.) The *indefinite article* is *omitted* before *national and professional
names* when the *subject* of the sentence is either a *noun* or a *personal
pronoun. Ex.:* Ce médecin est *allemand* (*tāh-lě-māng*), This physician
is *a* German. — Je suis *anglais* (*süĕĕ zāug-lay*), I am *an* Englishman.
— Mon père était *avocat* (*tā-vo-kāh*), My father was *a* lawyer. — Il est
américain (*tā-may-rĕĕ kaing*), He is *an* American.

B.) But after *c'est, voici* and *voilà* and when *the noun is qualified by*
an adjective, un must be used. *Ex.:* C'est un français, He (*or* it) is a
Frenchman.—Voici un médecin, Here is a physician.—Robert était

XII.

(Continuation.)

3. La vieille dame avec laquelle (*lă vyĕ-yĕ dāhm avek lă̠-kĕll*) vous‿avez‿été à l'église, n'est pas belle, mais‿elle a l'air très distingué (*dĭs-taing-gay*).
4. Pourquoi le garçon anglais avait-il l'air de si mauvaise humeur (*dĕ sēē mō-vayze ümeūr*)?
5. Mon‿employé (*mōng-nāng-plŏāh-yēh*) est français[1] mais‿il‿a l'air anglais (*zēēl lāh lair rāng-lay*).
6. Votre domestique (*dō-mĕs-tēēk*) irlandais a l'air français.
7. Le vieux tailleur que mon frère avait à Berlin (*bĕr-laing*), n'avait pas l'air allemand (*lair āh-lĕ-māng*).
8. Il a l'air bon.
9. J'ai rencontré (*rāng-cong-tray*) Mademoiselle B.; elle avait l'air très triste.
10. Il est de très mauvaise humeur.

---

un officier (*of-fēē-syĕh*) distingué, Robert was a distinguished officer.

C.) When one substantive is used to qualify another—in the so-called *apposition*—the *indefinite article* must be omitted in French. *Ex :* Berlin, *ville* d'Allemagne, Berlin, a city of Germany.—Jeanette, *fille* de monsieur Hachette, Jane, a daughter of Mr. Hachette.

The *indefinitive article* must also be omitted after the word *what*, when used to express *surprise. Ex : What* a noise you make! *Quel bruit* vous faites !—*What* a man ! *Quel* homme !

11. I am very angry.

12. Don't you think that this gentleman looks like a pedant ?

13. You look very ill indeed. (*Literally :* You have really [*bien*] the look of being ill).

14. He looks severe (*dur*).

15. This German minister looks like a man of the world.

16. I do not like this Irish coachman ; he looks suspicious (*mauvais*).

17. I saw your brother-in-law in the waiting-room of the Northern Station ; he looks very well (*bien portant*).

18. Your sister looks ill ; is anything the matter with her ?

19. How well you are looking ! (*Literally :* What air you have !)

20. He looks healthy. (*Literally :* He has the air of having health [*de la santé*])

21. Why are you so angry ? (*Literally :* Why are you *of* such [*si*] bad humor?)

22. Your employer (*patron*) is in (*de*) a very bad humor; he is very angry (*fâché*) with (*de*) you.

23. For the past three days (*il y a trois jours que*) our coachman has been very angry (=*is of bad* humor).

24. This young man looks like a good-for-nothing (*a l'air d'un vaurien*).

25. He is not so stupid as (*or*, He is not such a fool as) he looks.

26. How does he look ?

11. Je suis de très mauvaise humeur.

12. Ne pensez-vous pas, que ce monsieur a l'air d'un pédant (*pay-dāng*)?

13. Vous⁀avez bien la mine (*mēēn, or* bien l'air) d'être malade.

14. Il a l'air dur.

15. Ce ministre⁀allemand a l'air d'un⁀homme du monde (*deūn-nŏm dü mōngd*).

16. Je n'aime pas ce cocher irlandais; il a l'air mauvais.

17. J'ai vu monsieur votre beau-frère à la salle d'attente de la gare du Nord; il a l'air bien portant (*pŏr-tāng*).

18. Mademoiselle votre soeur a l'air malade; a-t-elle quelque chose (*kēlkĕ shohs*)?

19. Quel⁀air vous⁀avez (*kĕl lair voū zā-vēh*)!

20. Il a l'air d'avoir de la santé (*sāng-tay*).

21. Pourquoi êtes-vous de si mauvaise humeur?

22. Votre patron (*pā-trong*) est de très mauvaise humeur; il est très fâché (*fā-shay*) *de* vous.

23. Il y a trois jours que notre cocher est de très mauvaise humeur.

24. Ce jeune⁀homme a l'air d'un vaurien (*sĕ jeū-nŏm āh lair deūng voh-rēē-aing*).

25. Il n'est pas si stupide (*stü-pēēd*) qu'il en⁀a l'air (*kēēl ăng-nāh lair*).

26. Quelle mine a-t-il (*kell mēēn nā-tēēl*)?

27. {
He looks happy (*or* amused [*enjoué*]).

He looks sad (*triste*).

He looks contented (*content*).
}

28. The affairs look well.   (The affairs look bad.)

29. How does the matter look (*or* stand) ?

30. You are looking well.

31. She looks angry.

32. This young Englishman looks like a physician.

33. Ah ! you take an air of unconsciousness (*or* you make believe not to know it = Ah ! [*allons !*] you give yourself the air of not knowing it).

34. He gives himself the airs of a scholar (*de savant*).

35. Whenever I call on this man, instead of receiving me

---

1)   The *irregular verb* **aller**, *to go*, is thus conjugated :

Present.
Je vais (*vay*).
tu vas (*vāh*).
il va (*vāh*).
nous allons (*zāh-long*).
vous allez (*zāh-lēh*).
ils vont (*vong*).

Imperfect.
J'allais.
tu allais.
il allait.
nous allions.
vous alliez.
ils allaient.

Preterite.
J'allai.
tu allas.
il alla.
nous allâmes (*zāh-lāhm*).
vous allâtes (*zāh-lāht*).
ils allèrent (*zāh-layr*).

Future.
J'irai (*jēē rēh*).
tu iras (*ēē-rāh*).
il ira (*ēē-rāh*).
nous irons (*zēē-rong*).
vous irez (*zēē-rēh*).
ils iront (*zēē-rong*).

Conditional.
J'irais (*jēē-ray*).
tu irais (*ēē-ray*).
il irait (*ēē-ray*).
nous irions (*zēē-ryong*).
vous iriez (*zēē-ryēh*).
ils iraient (*zēē-ray*).

Perfect.
Je **suis** allé, I have gone.
tu es allé, &c.

Pluperfect.
J'étais allé, I had gone.
tu étais allé, &c.

Subj. Pres.
Que j'aille (*kē-jā-yē*).
que tu ailles (*ā-yē*).
qu'il aille (*ā-yē*)
que nous *allions* (*zāhl-yong*).
que vous *alliez* (*zāhl-yēh*).
qu'ils aillent (*zā-yē*).

Subj. Imperf.
Que j'allasse (*iāh-lās*).
que tu allasses (*āh-lās*),
qu'il *allât* (*āh-lāh*).
que nous a'lassions (*zāh-lās-yong*)
que vous allassiez (*zāh-lās-yēh*).
qu'ils allassent (*zāh-lās*).

27. { Il a l'air enjoué (*āng-joū-ay*).
Il a l'air triste.
Il a l'air content (*cong-tāng*).

28. Les affaires *sont* bien. (Les affaires *sont* mal.)

29. Où en est la chose (*où āng-nay lāh shōhs*) ?

30. Vous avez l'air de vous bien porter.

31. Elle a l'air fâché (*fāh-shay*).

32. Ce jeune anglais a l'air d'un médecin.

33. Allons![1] vous vous donnez l'air de ne pas le savoir (*sā-v'woār*).

34. Il se donne des airs de savant (*sā-vāng*).

35. Quand je vais voir[2] cet homme, au lieu de (*ō lyeū dĕ*)

Imperative.	*Participles.*
Va (*vāh*).	Allant.
allons.	allé.
allez.	

2) The irregular verb **voir** (*v'woār*), *to see*, is conjugated in the following manner :

Present.	*Imperfect.*
Je vois (*v'woāh*).	Je voyais (*v'woā-yay*).
tu vois.	tu voyais.
il voit.	il voyait.
nous voyons (*v'woāh-yong*).	nous voyions.
vous voyez (*v'woā-yĕh*).	vous voyiez.
ils voient (*v'woāh*).	ils voyaient.

Preterite.	*Future.*
Je vis (*vēĕ*).	Je verrai (*vĕr rēh*).
tu vis.	tu verras (*vĕr-rāh*).
il vit.	il verra.
nous vîmes (*vēĕm*).	nous verrons.
vous vîtes (*vēĕt*).	vous verrez.
ils virent (*vēĕr*).	ils verront (*vĕr-rong*).

Imperative.	*Participles.*
Vois (*v'woāh*).	Voyant (*v'woā-yāng*).
voyons (*v'woā-yong*).	vu (*vü*).
voyez (*v'woā-yĕh*).	

Observe that **to call upon a person** is rendered either by **aller voir** *quelqu'un* or **venir voir** *quelqu'un*.

pleasantly, he frowns (= When I go to see this man instead of [au lieu de] *making me good face* [*bonne mine*], *he makes me a bad face* [*mauvaise mine*]).

36. I drink but little wine.
37. Do you want ale? No, thanks, I prefer water.

38. I must first (*d'abord*) drink something.
39. I am dying with thirst.
40. Hand me (*servez-moi*) a glass of wine.
41. I should like to take another glass (*encore un verre*).

---

1) The *irregular verb* **faire**, *to do, to make*, is conjugated in the following manner:

Present.		Future.
Je fais (*fay*).		Je ferai (*fĕ-rĕh*).
tu fais.		tu feras (*fĕ-rāh*).
il fait.		il fera (*fĕ-rāh*).
nous *faisons* (*fay-zong*).		nous ferons (*fĕ-rong*).
vous *faites* (*fait*).		vous ferez (*fĕ-rĕh*).
ils *font* (*fong*).		ils feront (*fĕ-rong*).

Imperfect. — *Subj. Pres.*

Je faisais. — Que je fasse (*făss*).
tu faisais. — que tu fasses.
il faisait. — qu'il fasse.
nous faisions. — que nous fassions (*făss-yong*).
vous faisiez. — que vous fassiez (*făss-yĕh*).
ils faisaient. — qu'ils fassent (*făss*).

Preterite. — *Subj. Imperf.*

Je fis (*fĕĕ*). — Que je fisse (*fiss*).
tu fis (*fĕĕ*). — que tu fisses.
il fit (*fĕĕ*). — qu'il fît.
nous fîmes (*fĕĕm*). — que nous fissions (*fis-yong*).
vous fîtes (*fĕĕt*). — que vous fissiez (*fis-yĕh*).
ils firent (*fĕĕr*). — qu'ils fissent (*fiss*).

Imperative. — *Participles.*

Fais. — Faisant.
faisons. — fait.
faites.

2) The *irregular verb* **mourir**, *to die*, is conjugated:

Present.

Je meurs (*meŭr*). — nous *mourons* (*moŭ-rong*).
tu meurs. — vous *mourez* (*moŭ-rĕh*).
il meurt. — ils meurent (*meŭr*).

me faire[1] bonne mine, il me fait mauvaise mine (*mō-vayze mēēn*).

36. Je bois peu de vin.
37. Voulez-vous de la bière? Non, merci, je préfère de l'eau.
38. Il faut d'abord que je boive.
39. Je meurs[2] de soif (*meūr dě s'woāf*).
40. Servez[3]-moi un verre de vin (*vaing*).
41. Je boirais bien encore un verre.

Preterite.	*Subj. Pres.*
Je mourus (*moŭ-rŭ*).	Que je meure (*meūr*).
tu mourus.	que tu meures.
il mourut.	qu'il meure.
nous mourûmes (*moŭ-rŭm*).	que nous *mourions* (*moŭ-ryong*).
vous mourûtes (*moŭ-rŭt*).	que vous *mouriez* (*moŭ-ryèh*).
ils moururent (*moŭ-rŭr*).	qu'ils meurent (*meūr*).
Future.	*Imperative.*
Je mourrai (*moŭr-rēh*).	Meurs.
tu mourras.	mourons.
il mourra.	mourez.
nous mourrons.	*Participles.*
vous mourrez.	Mourant.
ils mourront.	mort (*more*).

Se mourir means *to be near dying, to be fainting*, as: *elle se meurt, she is fainting.*

3) **Servir**, *to serve, to help to*, is thus conjugated:

Present.	*Preterite.*
Je sers (*sayr*).	Je servis (*sěr-vēē*).
tu sers.	tu servis.
il sert (*sayr*).	il servit.
nous servons (*sěr vong*).	nous servîmes (*sěr-vēēm*).
vous servez (*sěr-věh*).	vous servîtes (*sěr-věēt*).
ils servent (*sěrv*).	ils servirent (*sěr-věēr*).

Future.

Je servirai (*sěr-vēē-reh*).	nous servirons (*sěr-vēē-rong*).
tu serviras.	vous servirez.
il servira.	ils serviront.

Participles.

servant (*sěr-vāng*).	servi (*sěr-vēē*).

Se **servir**, *to make use of*, and **desservir**, *to clear the table*, are conjugated in the same manner.

42. I have the honor of drinking your health and that of your family.

43. That is the best wine which one can drink.

44. He is drinking out of (*dans*) a large glass.

45. He is pouring out something.

46. Pour me out some water.

47. What will you drink with your dinner?

48. Do you drink beer or porter?

49. From preference I take water.

50. Please give me a glass of water; I am dying with thirst.

51. To what can I help you (*or*, What may I offer you)?

52. Do you take soup?

53. Thanks. I will trouble you for a little beef. It looks so nice.

54. Do you like it well done (*bien cuit*) or rare (*peu cuit* = little cooked)?

55. Not too much done, pray.

2.

Phrases used during a Ceremonial Call.

1. Does Mr. N. live here?

2. Is this Mr. N.'s (*or* Does Mr. N. live here)?

3. Is Mr. N. in (*or* within? *or* Is Mr. N. at home)?

---

1) After the *Superlative* followed by a relative sentence, the *Subjunctive mood* is used when the relative clause expresses the *views* and *opinions* of the *subject*: *C'est le plus grand* des maux que je *connaisse*, That is the greatest evil I know. If, however, I wish to represent the thing as *certain* or as a *matter of fact*, the *Indicative* must

42. J'ai l'honneur de boire à votre santé et à celle de toute votre famille (*fah-mēē-yĕ*).

43. C'est le meilleur vin que l'on puisse[1] boire.

44. Il boit *dans*[2] un grand verre.

45. Il verse à boire.

46. Versez-moi de l'eau.

47. Que voulez-vous boire à votre diner (*dēē-nay*).

48. Buvez-vous de la bière ou du porter?

49. Je prendrai par préférence (*pray-fay-rāngs*) de l'eau.

50. Donnez-moi, s'il vous plait, un verre d'eau ; je meurs de soif.

51. Que vous servirai-je?

52. Prendrez-vous de la soupe, monsieur?

53. Je vous remercie. Je vous demanderai un peu de boeuf. Il a si bonne mine (*mēēn*).

54. Le voulez-vous bien cuit ou peu cuit (*k͡üēē*)?

55. Pas trop cuit, s'il vous plait.

2.

Visite de cérémonie.

1. Monsieur N. demeure-t-il ici (*dĕ-meŭr-tēēl-lēē-sēē*)?

2. { C'est ici (*say tēē-sēē*) chez monsieur N.?
{ Est-ce ici (*ays sēē-sēē*) chez monsieur N.?

3. Monsieur N. est-il chez lui?

---

be employed. Ex.: Ce ne sont pas les hommes *les plus riches* qui *sont* les plus heureux, The richest people are not the happiest.

2) The French say : *boire* **dans** un (not d'un) verre, to drink *out of* a glass ; *fumer* **dans** une pipe (*pēĕp*), to smoke out of a pipe.

4. Is Mr. N. at home? (*i.e.* for callers).

5. He is not in (*or* He is not at home).

6. Is Mrs. N. also not[1] at home?

7. Yes, Mrs. N. is at home.

8. Will you please tell me your name?

9. Whom shall I announce?

10. Whom have I the honor of announcing?

11. Will you take my card?

12. Please walk in. (Walk in, if you please.)

13. Will you please walk in (*or* Step this way, if you please).

14. Whom have I the honor of addressing (*or* With whom have I the honor)?

15. My name is B.

16. May I *inquire* whom I have the honor of addressing?
    [The French say more correctly: May I *know* Puis-je *savoir?*]

17. My name is B.

18. Have I not the honor of addressing Mr. N.?

19. That's my name, sir.

20.
    { I beg of you, be seated.
    { Sit down, pray.
    { Will you please take a seat?

---

1) Must be translated thus. Ex.: Are you going to the concert? —No, I am not going there.—*Neither am I.*—Allez-vous au concert? —Non, je n'y vais pas.—*Ni moi non plus.*

2) S'asseoir (*sâs-swoâre*), to sit down.—*Part. pres.* s'asseyant (*sâs-say-yàng*).—*Part pr.:* assis (*ás-séë*).—*Pres.:* Je m'assieds (*jĕ mâs-syèh*), tu t'assieds, il s'assied, nous nous asseyons (*nôô nôô zâs-sèh-yong*), vous vous asseyez, ils s'asseient.—*Imp. :* Je m'asseyais (*jĕ mâs-sèh-*

4. Monsieur N. est-il visible (*ay-tēēl vēē-zēē-bl'*)?

5. Il n'y est pas.

6. Madame n'y est pas non plus?[1]

7. Oui monsieur, madame N. est chez elle.

8. Voudriez-vous me dire votre nom (*nong*) (*or* Votre nom, s'il vous plait)?

9. Qui annoncerai-je (*kēē ăn-nong-sĕ-ray-jĕ*)?

10. Qui aurai-je l'honneur d'annoncer (*dăn-nong-sēh*)?

11. Veuillez remettre ma carte (*or* Voici ma carte, *or* Remettez ma carte).

12. Veuillez entrer (*zăng-trēh*) (*or* Entrez, s'il vous plait).

13. Donnez-vous la peine d'entrer (*dāng-trēh*). [The most usual and polite form.]

14. A qui ai-je l'honneur de parler?

15. Monsieur B. [Must be answered thus.]

16. Puis-je *savoir* à qui j'ai l'honneur de parler?

17. Monsieur B. [Any other answer would be wrong.]

18. { Est-ce à monsieur N. que j'ai l'honneur de parler?
{ C'est à monsieur N. que j'ai l'honneur de parler?

19. Moi-même, monsieur (*or* C'est moi-même). [This is the only way of answering such questions.]

20. { Donnez-vous la peine de vous asseoir[2] (*vōō-zās-s'woāre*).
{ Veuillez-vous asseoir.
{ Asseyez-vous, s'il vous plaît.

---

yĕh), tu t'asseyais, il s'asseyait, &c.—*Pret.:* Je m'assis (*jĕ mā-sēē*), tu t'assis, il s'assit, nous nous assîmes (*nōō nōō zās-sēēm*), vous vous assîtes, ils s'assirent (*ēēl sās-sēēr*).—*Fut.:* Je m'asseierai, tu t'asseieras, il s'asseiera, &c., *or* Je m'assiérai, tu t'assiéras, il s'assiéra, &c.—*Pres. Subj.:* Que je m'asseie, que tu t'asseies, qu'il s'asseie. — *Imperat.:* Assieds-toi (qu'il s'asseie), asseyons-nous, asseyez-vous.

336

21. *Take a seat* on the sofa. (*Take a seat* on this chair.) [*Prendre place* cannot be used without designating some particular article of furniture on which to be seated.]

3.

22. What can I do for you?

23. How can I be of use to you?

24. I shall be (*je suis*) at your service in a moment.

25. What procures me (*or* To what do I owe) the honor of your visit? [*Of your visit* need not be translated.]
26. Will you grant me a few moments' conversation?

27. I have something to communicate privately (*en particulier*).

28. Can I have the honor of paying my compliments to Mrs. N.?

29. Good morning (*or* Good evening, &c.) [These phrases are used in taking leave.]

---

1) *Prendre* (*prăng-dr'*), to take.—*Part. pres.:* prenant (*prĕ-năng*).—*Part. p.:* pris (*prĕĕ*).—*Pres.:* Je prends (*prăng*), tu prends, il prend, nous prenons (*prĕ-nŏng*), vous prenez, ils prennent (*prĕn*).—*Imperf.:* Je prenais, tu prenais, il prenait, &c.—*Pret.:* Je pris (*prĕĕ*), tu pris, il prit, nous prîmes (*prĕĕm*), vous prîtes, ils prirent (*prĕĕr*). — *Fut.:* Je prendrai (*prăng-drĕh*), tu prendras, &c. — *Pres. Subj.:* Que je

21. Prenez [1] place sur le sofa. (Prenez place sur cette chaise.)

3.

22. Qu'y a-t-il pour votre service (*kēē āh-tēēl poūr vŏt' sĕr-vēēs'*)?

23. En quoi puis-je vous_être agréable (*āh gray-ābl'*)? [This phrase is more polite than the preceding one.]

24. Je suis à vos_ordres dans_un_instant (*dāng-zeūng-naing-stāng*).

25. Qu'est-ce qui me procure l'avantage (*kays kēē mĕ prŏ-kür lā-vāng-tāhje*)?

26. Voudriez-vous m'accorder un moment d'entretien (*mō-māng-dāng-tr'-tyaing*)?

27. { J'ai quelque chose à vous dire en particulier (*dēēr āng pār-tēē-cü-lyēh*).
{ J'aurais à vous parler en particulier.

28. { Pourrais-je présenter mes_hommages (*pray-zāng-tēh may zŏm-māhje*) à madame N.?
{ Pourrais-je rendre mes devoirs à Mme. N.?

29. { Je vous salue (*sāh-lü*), monsieur.
{ J'ai l'honneur de vous saluer.
{ J'ai l'honneur.

---

prenne (*prĕn*), que tu prennes, qu'il prenne, que nous prenions, que vous preniez, qu'ils prennent (*kĕĕl prĕn*).—*Imperat.:* Prends (*prāng*), prenons, prenez. — *N.B.* Conjugate in the same manner the compounds of *prendre:* apprendre, to learn ; *rapprendre*, to learn over (*or* again) ; *comprendre*, to understand ; *entreprendre* (*āng tr'-prāng-dr'*), to undertake ; *surprendre*, to surprise.

GRAMMATICAL REMARKS.

Demonstrative Pronouns.

These are:

Masc.	*Fem.*
Celui (*s'lü-ēē*),	celle (*cĕll*), that.
Pl. ceux (*seū*),	celles (*cĕll*), those.
celui-ci (*sēē*),	celle-ci, this *or* the latter.
Pl. ceux-ci (*seū-sēē*),	celles-ci, these.
celui-là (*s'lü͡ēē-lāh*),	celle-là, that (one) *or* the former.
Pl. ceux-là (*seū-lāh*).	celles-là, those.

Neuter.

ce and cela (abridged ça), that; ceci (*sĕ-sēē*) this.

Observations.

1. *Ce* has only *one* form for both genders and numbers. *Ex.:* *Ce* fut *mon ami; ce* fut *mon amie ; ce* furent *mes amis ; ce* furent *mes amies.*

2. *Ce* is frequently used before the third person singular or plural of the auxiliary verb être, and means either *this* or *that. C'est* quelque chose que je ne connais pas. That is something (which) I do not know.—*Est-ce* là votre malle? Oui, *c'est* ma malle. Is that your trunk? Yes, that is my trunk. — *Sont-ce* là vos bas? Oui, *ce sont* mes bas. Are these your stockings? Yes, these are my stockings.

3. *Celui-ci celle-ci, ceux-ci, celles-ci,* are translated *this, these,* or *this one,* etc. These pronouns are used in speaking either of persons or things, when it is necessary to *indicate clearly which person or thing is spoken of :* This is my hat, celui-ci est mon chapeau.

Celui-là, celle-là, ceux-là, celles-là, are used in the same manner, and must be translated by *that, those, that one,* &c.

4. *Celui-ci, celle-ci, ceci,* point out objects *nearest* to the speaker, while *celui-là, celle-là, cela,* signify those farthest from him, as : Voici deux livres; prenez *celui-ci,* Charles gardera *celui-là,* here are two books; you take *this one* and Charles will keep *that one.*

5. Celui, celle, &c., must be used instead of celui-ci, celle-ci, celui-là, celle-là, ceux-là, &c., before a relative pronoun or preposition. They are then translated very frequently by *the one who,* or *he who, she who, they who.*

It is my father's (that of my father),	c'est celui de mon père.
This horse is the one of which I spoke to you,	ce cheval est celui dont je vous ai parlé.

Translate the following

Examples.

Heureux *celui qui* trouve un vrai ami.—C'est *celui-là qui* m'a frappé. — Voyez-vous ces deux maisons? *Celle-ci qui* a coûté cinquante mille francs, ne vaut pas (*is not worth as much*), *celle-là que* j'ai eue pour la moitié de cette somme. — Voulez-vous *ceci* ou *cela ?* — La rose et la tulipe (*tü-lëëp, tulip*) sont deux fleurs charmantes (*charming flowers*); mais *celle-ci* est sans odeur (*odor*) et *celle-là*

exhale un parfum (*păr-feŭng*, *perfume*) délicieux. C'est
surtout (*especially*) à l'état .de domesticité (*in a domestic
state*) que le chien (*shēē-aing*, *dog*) et le chat (*shāh*, *cat*)
montrent la différence de leur charàctère; *celui-ci* s'attache à son maitre '(*master*), *celui-là* ne s'attache qu'à la
maison.

Of Possessive Pronouns.

1. The possessive pronouns are formed from the possessive adjectives *mon, ton, son*, etc. They are:

Le mien (*myaing*),	*la mienne* (*myĕn*), mine (my own).
le tien (*tyaing*),	*la tienne*, thine.
le sien (*syaing*),	*la siénne*, his, hers, its own.
le nôtre (*nōtr'*),	*la nôtre*, ours.
le vôtre (*vōtr'*),	*la vôtre*, yours.
le leur (*leŭr*),	*la leur*, theirs.

Pl. *les miens*, f. *les miennes* ;—*les nôtres*, *les vôtres*, etc.

2. They agree in gender and number with the object possessed: Avez-vous votre billet? Oui, j'ai le *mien*. Have
you your ticket? Yes, I have mine. Votre soeur est plus
âgée que la mienne, Your sister is older than mine. Mon
intention (*aing-tāng-syong*) est aussi bonne que la vôtre,
My intention is as good as yours.

Translate the following

Exercise

into French:

1) Have you (any) rooms to let (*à louer*)? Yes, sir, we
have several. What kind of (*quelles*) rooms do you want?
Do you want a furnished apartment (*un appartement*

meublé) or *an unfurnished one* (= *or* not furnished)? I need (*j'ai besoin de*) furnished rooms.—I would need (*il me faudrait*) four bedrooms, a drawing-room and a kitchen. — 2) Will you be kind enough to walk in (*entrer*). I will (= I am going to) show you the rooms. Here is the parlor. — It is not very large, but it will do (= it can do my business).—You see there is everything you can want, sir (= everything that is necessary, *il faut*). There are four arm-chairs, six chairs, a new carpet, a very nice looking-glass, and some very elegant curtains. Besides (*de plus*) there are some wardrobes. — 3) Let me see the sleeping-rooms, if you please.—Here (*par ici*) sir, please. Let mè see (*voyons*) if the bed is good, for that is *the main thing* (*le principal* = lĕ praing-sēē-pāhl). *As long as* (= when, *quand*) I have a good bed, I don't care (*je ne mie soucie guère*) for the (*du*) rest. — 4) You cannot wish for a better one, sir. Does this room lie (*donne*) towards the street?—No, sir, towards the garden (*le jardin* = jār-daing).—So much the better (*tant mieux* = tāng m'yeū).—I think the bed is quite good. Now how much do you ask for the five rooms and the kitchen? — 5) I have always let (*loué*) the parlor with one bedroom for twenty francs. You can have the five rooms for forty francs per week. — I think that is a great deal of money (= much money). — But you must consider (*considérer*), sir, that this is one of the most beautiful parts (*quartiers*) of the city, where all the houses rent at a very high figure (= where the houses are of an exorbitant price).—Very well, I will pay you your price, but I need a part of your cellar (*la cave* = kāhv) to put some wood (*du bois*) and coal (*du charbon*). — 6) Of course (*cela va sans dire*). You shall have a place which can be locked (=locked with a key [*fermée à clef*]). When do you think you will take (= to take) possession (*possession* = pŏs-sĕs-syong) of your lodgings?—I think to sleep here to-night. — You can come as soon as you like (=: as soon as it will please you [*aussitôt qu'il vous plaira*]).

Interrogative Pronouns.

1. **Lequel** (*lĕ-kĕll*)? **Laquelle** (*lă-kĕll*)?

SINGULAR.   PLURAL.

	Masc.	*Fem.*	*Masc.*	*Fem.*
N. & *Ac.*	lequel?	laquelle?	lesquels?	lesquelles?
Gen.	duquel?	de laquelle?	desquels?	desquelles?
Dat.	auquel?	à laquelle?	auxquels?	auxquelles?

This pronoun is used either *without* a noun, or is sep-arated from it by *de ;* but it agrees with the noun it re-fers to in gender and number. When the pronoun *which* (*of*) is used *interrogatively*, it is always expressed by *lequel, laquelle*, &c., as:

Lequel de ses fils est malade? Which of his sons is ill? Laquelle de vos soeurs est mariée? Which of your sis-ters is married?

Voici plusieurs appartements. Lequel choisirez-vous (*lĕ kĕll sh'woă-zēē-rēh-voŭ*)? Here are several apart-ments. Which will you choose?

Auquel de ces messieurs avez-vous donné ma lettre? To which of these gentlemen have you given my letter?

2. Qui (*kēē*)? **Quoi** (*k'wōāh*)? **Que** (*kĕ*)?

	Masc. and Fem.	*Neuter.*
Nom.	*Qui,* who?	*Que, quoi,* what?
Gen.	*de qui,* whose, of whom? from whom?	*de quoi,* { of what? from what?
Dat.	*à qui,* to whom, whom?	*à quoi,* to what, at what?
Acc.	*qui,* whom?	*que, quoi,* what?

Remarks.

1. The interrogative pronoun *qui?* is only used-of *persons.* Ex.:

Qui est arrivé? Who has arrived?

Qui est là? Who is there?

De qui parlez-vous? Of whom are you speaking?

A qui est cette malle? To whom does this trunk belong?

Qui cherchez-vous? Whom are you looking for?

2. *Whose,* when used interrogatively, must be rendered in French by *à qui.* Ex.:

Whose book is this? *à qui est ce livre?*

Whose trunk is this? à qui est cette malle?

3. *Quoi, what,* is disjunctive, and is used either by itself, or after a preposition, as:

De quoi parlez-vous? Of what are you speaking?

Quoi! vous êtes marié! What! you are married!

Quoi! il ne veut pas le faire? What! he will not do it?

4. *Que?* what? is *conjunctive*, and is only used before verbs, as :

Que voulez-vous? What do you want?

Que demandez-vous? What do you desire?

Qu'avez-vous vu? What have you seen?

Qu'avez-vous? What is the matter with you?

Que as an interrogative means *what*, **never whom.**

5. Instead of the simple form *qui?* the form *qui est-ce qui, who?* is very frequently used for the Nominative, and *qui est-ce que*, whom? for the Accusative (*i.e.*, Objective case).

Qui est-ce *qui* rit (*rēē*)? Who is laughing?

Qui est-ce *que* vous cherchez? Whom are you looking for?

Qui est-ce *qui* l'a fait? Who has done it?

Qui est-ce que vous avez-vu? Whom have you seen?

6. Instead of the simple form *que, what?* the form *qu'est-ce que?* or even *qu'est-ce que c'est que?* is frequently used, *but only for the Accusative* (Objective case).

Qu'est-ce que vous voulez? What do you want?

Qu'est-ce que vous faites là? What are you doing there?

7. *What—when Nominative—*may be given by *qu'est-ce* **qui?** It must, however, be always the subject of the sentence and the pupil must be careful not to confound **qui** est-ce *qui? who?* with **qu**'est-ce *qui, what?*

Qu'est-ce qui vous afflige (*āf-flēēje*)? What afflicts you?

Qu'est-ce qui vous étonne? What astonishes you?

Qu'est-ce qui vous manque? What are you missing?

8. Observe the following idiomatic phrases:

Qu'est-ce que cela (kays-kĕ sĕlāh) ?
Qu'est-ce que c'est que cela (kays kĕ say kĕ sĕ-lāh)? } what is that?

Qu'est-ce que la vie (vēē) ?
Qu'est-ce que c'est que la vie ? } what is life?

Qu'y a-t-il de nouveau ?
Qu'est-ce qu'il y a de nouveau ? } what is the news?

Note.—The interrogative adjective *what*, joined to a noun, is always expressed by *quel*, fem. *quelle.*—Ex. : *Quelle* est la difficulté
qui vous arrête, what is the difficulty that detains you ?

Exercise.

Qu'est-ce que [1] vous désirez ? — *Qui est-ce qui* veut venir
ce soir ? — *Qui est-ce que* je vois ? — *À qui* avez-vous parlé
de cette affaire ?—*À qui est-ce que* vous avez parlé de cette affaire ? — *De qui est-ce que* vous parlez ?—*Est-ce que*
vous êtes fatigué, mon cher ami ?—*Qu'est-ce qu'*il vous a
dit ? — Il m'a dit, que vous alliez vous marier (mār-yēh
= to get married). — *De qui est-ce que* vous parliez quand
je suis entré ? — *Qui* avez-vous entendu (zāng-tāng-dü,
heard) prêcher (pray-shēh, preach) dimanche dernier ?—
Monsieur B.; il a fait un sermon (sĕr-mong) très élo-
quent (tray-zay-lō-kāng). — *Qu'*allez-vous faire demain
matin ? Je vais écrire au négociant (nay-go-zyāng=
merchant) *de qui* je viens de recevoir une lettre. —
C'est une maladie *dont* on ne connaît pas la cause.

---

1) Give the rules why these relative pronouns have been used.

Words.

Couleurs (*cōō-leŭr*) f. pl.	*Colors.*
Une couleur claire,	A light color.
Une couleur foncée (*fong-say*),	A dark color.
L'incarnat (*laing-cār-nāh*)*m.*	The carnation.
L'azur (*lā-zür*) *m.*,	The azure.
blanc, blanche (*blāng, blāngsh*),	white.
bleu (*bleŭ*),	blue.
bleu clair,	light blue.
bleu foncé,	dark blue.
brun (*breŭng*),	brown.
châtain (*shā-laing*),	chestnut.
cramoisi (*crā-m'woā-zēē*),	crimson.
écarlate (*ay-cār-lāht*),	scarlet.
gris (*grēē*),	grey.
jaune (*jone*),	yellow.
noire (*n'woār*),	black.
olive,	olive.
orangé (*o-rāng-jay*),	orange.
pourpre,	purple.
rouge (*rōōje*),	red.
roux (*rōō*),	russet.
vert (*vayr*),	green.
Le vermillon (*vĕr-mēē-yong*),	The vermilion.
violet (*vēē-o-lĕh*),	violet.

COMPANION TO THE
Revised Version of the New Testament.

Explaining the Reasons for the Changes Made on the Authorized Version.

BY ALEXANDER ROBERTS, D.D.,
Member of, the English Revision Committee.

WITH SUPPLEMENT BY A MEMBER OF THE AMERICAN COMMITTEE.

Containing a Brief History of the Revision of the Work and Co-operation of the New Testament Companies, of the Points of Agreement and Difference, and an Explanation of the Appendix to the Revised New Testament.

ALSO, A FULL TEXTUAL INDEX,
Being a Key to Passages in which Important Changes have been Made.

This book, having been carefully prepared by Members of both Revision Committees, carries official weight. It shows what changes have been made, and also the reasons which influenced the revisers in making them. It will be difficult to judge of the merits of the revision without the aid of this Companion volume. Our edition is printed by special arrangement with the English publishers. It is well known that, by an arrangement between the two Committees of Revision, the changes suggested by the American Committee, but which were not adopted by the English Revisers, are published as an Appendix to the Revised New Testament. . The *Companion* volume is an explanation of *all* the changes adopted by both committees, and of those suggested by the American Committee, but not assented to by the English Committee, in their final revision. The book will be indispensable to a right understanding of the revision. This cheap edition of the combined books, although authorized and copyrighted, will be sold for 25 cents in paper, and 75 cents in cloth—sent postage free.

TESTIMONIALS.

T. W. CHAMBERS, D.D., a Member of the American Committee of Revision, says of this book: " Many persons have expressed a desire that, simultaneously with the issue of the Revised New Testament, there should appear an authentic explanation of the reasons for such changes as will be found in its pages. The work of Dr. Roberts is exactly fitted to meet this desire....Nowhere else in print can be found a statement so full and exact. It gives all needed information, and does it in an unexceptional way."

C. F. DEEMS, D.D., Pastor of the Church of the Strangers. New York, writes: "The Companion to the Revised Version seems to me almost indispensable. Even scholars who were not at the meeting of the Revisers would have a wearisome work in seeking to discover all the changes made, and to ordinary readers very much of the labor would be lost. ....All this is set forth by Dr. Roberts with admirable perspicuity. Those who have any intelligent interest in the Holy Scriptures, will find this little book absorbingly interesting. I shall urge every member of the church of which I am pastor to give it a careful reading, and purpose to introduce it as a text-book in our Bible-classes."

"So valuable, interesting and useful is this publication, that we advise every one who wishes to know the why and wherefore of the revision, to obtain it immediately."—*New York Observer.*

Paper, 8vo size, 25 cents ; Cloth, 16mo, 75 cents.

*** For Sale by Booksellers and Newsdealers, or sent postage-paid, on receipt of price, by

I. K. FUNK & CO., Publishers, 10 & 12 Dey St., N. Y.

THE TEACHER'S EDITION

OF THE

REVISED NEW TESTAMENT

With New Concordance and Index, Harmony of the Gospels, Maps,
Historical and Chronological Tables, Parallel Passages printed
in full, Blank Pages Interleaved for manuscript notes, and
many other New and Indispensable Helps to the Study
of the Revised Version.

After the excitement connected with the sale of the first copies of the new revision, which lack the usual indexing headlines and marginal references to parallel passages, and also the appendixes of tables, maps, etc.—all of which helps preachers, teachers and Bible students have come to consider as absolutely essential to a working copy of the Bible—there arises an imperative demand for an edition of the Revised New Testament, containing all the marginal and appendix helps of former TEACHERS' AND REFERENCE BIBLES, adapted carefully and accurately to the Revised Version. We are, therefore, preparing, as rapidly as is consistent with accuracy, such an edition of the Revised New Testament. The work is under the supervision of well-known Bible scholars, with numerous helpers, and will be issued as early as it can be done with thoroughness. In style and size the book will resemble the Bagster Bible, "Fac-similè large edition," known as "the Moody Bible," being the same width and length and size of type. It will be supplied at prices *within the reach of all.*

This "Teachers' Edition of the Revised New Testament" will be an exact, *certified reproduction* of the entire Oxford and Cambridge Edition, including the Preface and all the marginal readings and explanations. It will contain the appendix notes of the American Revisers, printed in the margin of each page by the side of the passages referred to. The parallel passages, to which reference is made in the "Bagster Bibles," with numerous others, so far as appropriate, will be PRINTED IN FULL in the margin. The running headings, usually printed at the tops of pages of the King James version, will be here supplied. A small black mark will be inserted below the last letter of each verse to facilitate reference, and aid in RESPONSIVE READING of the Revised Version. The second half of the volume will consist of the most carefully prepared HELPS TO THE STUDY OF THE REVISED NEW TESTAMENT, gleaned from the best Teachers' Editions of the authorized version, and supplied from various original sources—all being revised and adapted to harmonize with the Revised Version. We shall introduce many other important features, making this the most valuable edition of the New Testament ever issued.

Popular Cloth Edition—Ready in July—Price, Postage Free, $1.00.

Send for prospectus giving full description and prices of finer Bindings.

I. K. FUNK & CO., Publishers, 10 and 12 Dey St., New York.

THE

𝕸𝖊𝖎𝖘𝖙𝖊𝖗𝖘𝖈𝖍𝖆𝖋𝖙 𝕾𝖞𝖘𝖙𝖊𝖒,

A SIMPLE AND PRACTICAL METHOD,

ENABLING

ANY ONE TO LEARN, WITH SLIGHT EFFORT, TO SPEAK
FLUENTLY AND CORRECTLY

𝕱𝖗𝖊𝖓𝖈𝖍, 𝕲𝖊𝖗𝖒𝖆𝖓, 𝕾𝖕𝖆𝖓𝖎𝖘𝖍, 𝖆𝖓𝖉 𝕴𝖙𝖆𝖑𝖎𝖆𝖓,

BY

DR. RICHARD S. ROSENTHAL,

*Late Director of the "Akademie für fremde Sprachen" in Berlin and Leipzig,
of the "Meisterschaft College" in London, and Principal of the
"Meisterschaft School of Practical Linguistry" in New York.*

FRENCH.

IN FIFTEEN PARTS, EACH CONTAINING THREE LESSONS.

PART XIII.

NEW YORK:
I. K. FUNK & CO., Publishers,
10 AND 12 Dey Street.

TERMS.

WE have arranged with Dr. ROSENTHAL, the author of the "Meisterschaft System," for its introduction in América under his own supervision, and he has opened

The Meisterschaft School of Practical Linguistry

FOR NON-RESIDENTS.

The student does not need to leave his home. The lessons of each language are prepared by the Professor, and printed and sent in pamphlet shape to each member of the School wherever he may reside.

The course of study for each language—German, French, Italian, or Spanish—makes fifteen pamphlets of three lessons each.

All members of the School have

THE PRIVILEGE

of asking, by letter, questions concerning each lesson, or consulting on any difficulty which may have occurred to them. All exercises corrected and all questions answered by return post by Dr. ROSENTHAL or one of his assistants.

TERMS OF MEMBERSHIP.

Five Dollars is the price for membership in the school for each language. This amount ($5.) entitles the member to receive the fifteen books or pamphlets containing the lessons, also answers to his questions. Return postage for the answer must accompany the question.

State distinctly which language, or languages, you desire to study There are *no extra charges*. The price, **Five Dollars,** pays for one language ; **Ten Dollars** for two languages, etc. All exercises and questions must be written on a separate sheet of paper, and must state full address of the pupil.

Remittances must be made in Post-Office Order or registered letter addressed to

I. K. FUNK & CO.,

10 and 12 Dey Street, New York.

The Meisterschaft-System.

FRENCH.

PART XIII.

30. I beg your pardon (*or* Pardon me) for having disturbed you (*de vous avoir dérangé*).

31. I hope you will pay me another visit shortly. (*Literally :* Do me the honor of renewing [*de renouveler*] your visit shortly [*bientôt*]).

32. The honor is mine (*pour moi*).

33
{
I am exceedingly honored.

I am exceedingly flattered. [These phrases, which no English-speaking person would use, are commonly employed by the French.]
}

Phrases during a Friendly Call.

1. May I be permitted to enter ?

2.
{
Do I intrude ?

I hope I don't intrude ?
}

3. Pray do not let me interrupt you.

XIII

(Continuation.)

1.

30. Je vous demande pardon (*pār-dŏng*), de vous_avoir dérangé (*day-rāng-jĕh*).
31. Faites-moi l'honneur de renouveler bientôt votre visite (*dĕ rĕ-noo-vĕlĕh byaing-tōh votr' vēē-zēēt*).

32. L'honneur est *pour moi.*

33. { *Je me trouve* bien_honoré.
     { *Je suis* bien flatté.   [Standing phrases.]

Visite familière.

1. Est-il permis d'entrer (*ay-tēēl pĕr-mēē dāng-trēh*)? [Per-
mis *past partic.* of the irregular verb *permettre.* Comp.
mettre page 352].
2. { Est-ce que je vous dérange (*day-rāng-j'*)?
    { Je vous dérange peut-être (*peŭ-taytr'*).
    { Je ne vous dérange pas?
3. { Je vous prie (*prēē*) de ne pas vous déranger (*day-
    {   rāng-jĕh*).
    { Ne vous dérangez pas, je vous_en prie (*jĕ voŭ-zāng-
    {   prēē*).

4. If I disturb you, I will leave (*je me sauve*) at once.

5. {
   Not at all.
   Not by any means.
   Not the least in the world.
}

6. On thé contrary, I am very happy to see you.

7. I am very glad (*or* happy) to see you.

8. You are a stranger (*or* We are glad to see you again at last [*enfin*]).

9. What has become of you?

10. It is an eternity (*un siècle*) since I saw you.

11. It is long since we have heard from you. (*Literally :* that we have not had any news from you [**de**[2] *vos nouvelles*].)

12. It is long since I have heard from your brother (**de** *nouvelles de monsieur votre frère*).

13. Have you had any news from him (**de** *ses nouvelles*)?

14. I shall wait till I hear from you before writing (Observe : **de** *vos nouvelles*).

---

1) The *Infinitive preceded by de* must be used after the adjective *digne* (*dēēn-yé*), worthy of ; *capable* (*cā-pā-bl'*), capable of ; *incàpable* (*aing-cā-pā-bl'*), incapable of ; *enchanté, charmé,* glad, happy,—in fact, after *most* adjectives. (*Adjectives* which take *the Infinitive with à* will be given later.)

2) These phrases with *nouvelles* (news) cannot be translated literally and must be commited to memory. The **de** is idiomatic.

3) *Ecrire* (*ay-krēēr*), to write.—*Part. pr.:* écrivant (*ay-krēē-vāng*).— *Part. p.:* écrit (*ay-krēē*).—*Pres.:* J'écris (*jay-krēē*), tu écris, il écrit,

4. Si je vous dérange, *je me sauve* tout de suite (*jĕ mĕ sŏv' tōōt-sŭēēt*).

5. {
  Pas du tout (*pāh dü tōō*).
  Point du tout (*po͡-aing dü-tōō*).
  Pas le moins du monde.
}

6. Au contraire (*cŏng-trayr*), je suis͡ enchanté (*zāng-shāng-tĕh*) de[1] vous voir.

7. Je suis bien͡aise (*or* Je suis charmé, *or* Je suis ravi [*rā-vēē*]) de vous voir.

8. {
  Enfin (*āng-faing*) on vous revoit.
  Vous voilà enfin.
}

9. Que devenez-vous donc? [Comp. *venir*, page 163, No. 1.]

10. Il y a un siècle que je ne vous ai vu. (Comp. page 253, No. 11.)

11. Il y a bien longtemps͡ que *nous n'avons͡ eu* de *vos nouvelles*[2] (*kĕ noŭ nā-vong zü dĕ vōh noŭ-vĕll*).

12. Il y a longtemps que je n'ai eu de nouvelles de monsieur votre frère.

13. Avez-vous eu de ses nouvelles?

14. {
  J'attendrai de vos nouvelles pour écrire.[3]
  Je n'écrirai pas avant d'avoir de vos nouvelles.
}

---

nous écrivons (*nōō-zay-krēē-vong*), vous écrivez, ils écrivent (*ĕĕl-zay-krēēv*). — *Imperf.:* J'écrivais, tu écrivais, &c. — *Pret.:* J'écrivis (*jay-krēē-vēē*), tu écrivis, il écrivit, &c. — *Fut.:* J'écrirai (*jay-krēē-rēh*), tu écriras, il écrira, nous écrirons, &c.—*Pres. Subj.:* Que j'écrive (*kĕ jay-krēēv*),que tu écrives, qu'il écrive, &c.—*Imperat.:* Ecris, écrivons, écrivez. — *N.B.* Thus are conjugated: *Décrire*, to describe ; *circonscrire* (*cīr-kong-skrēēr*), to circumscribe ; *inscrire* (*aing-skrēēr*), to inscribe ; *prescrire*, to prescribe, to order ; *récrire*, to write again, to reply ; *souscrire* (*sōō-skrēēr*), to subscribe ; *transcrire* (*trāngs-krēēr*), to transcribe.

15. { You are quite a stranger.
{ You have become quite a stranger.

16. And how are you? [It is impossible to put these overpolite French phrases into common-sense English.]

17. I am glad to see you. (*Literally :* Be welcome.)

18. It is very kind **of** *you* (**de** votre part *or.* à vous) to call upon me.

19. I am *so* glad (**que** *je suis content*) to see you at last (*enfin*).

20. My father will be particularly glad [1]) to see you.

21. My mother will be very glad.

22. And my cousin too.

23. But pray be seated.

24. Don't you prefer (*or* Would you not rather sit ' on) the sofa?

25. Thanks, I have but little time; I cannot sit down.

26. Thanks, I am [3]) very well here.

27. I must go now.

28. Why are you in such haste?

---

1) If a noun is specially emphasized, *c'est qui* must be used with the *subject* of a *sentence.—Ex.: C'est* votre soeur *qui* m'a vu, *Your sister* saw me.—*C'est* votre patron *qui* l'a envoyé, *Your employer* sent it.—Before other members of sentences *c'est que* must be employed. *Ex.: C'est* à votre mère *que* j'ai donné ce billet, I gave this ticket *to your mother. C'est* hier que je le lui ai donné, I gave it to him *yesterday.*

2) *Mettre,* to put, to place. *Part. pres. :* mettant. — *Part. p. :* mis (*mèè*). — *Pres.:* Je mets (*may*), tu mets, il met, nous mettons, vous mettez, ils mettent (*mèt*).—*Imperf. :* Je mettais, tu mettais, &c.— *Pret.:* Je mis (*mèè*), tu mis, il mit, nous mîmes (*mèèm*), vous mîtes, ils mirent (*mèèr*).—*Fut.:* Je mettrai, tu mettras, &c.—*Pres. Subj :* Que je mette, que tu mettes, qu'il mette, &c. — *Imperf. Subj. :* Que je misse (*miss*), que tu misses, qu'il mît (*mèè*), &c.—Thus: *Admettre,* to

15. { Vous devenez rare (*rāhr*).
    On ne vous voit plus.
    On vous voit rarement (*rāh-rĕ-māng*).

16. Permettez-moi de vous demander (*dĕ-māng-dēh*) des nouvelles de votre santé (*sāng-tay*).

17. { Soyez *le* bienvenu (*byaing vĕ-nü*) [to a gentleman].
    Soyez *la* bienvenue [to a lady].

18. C'est bien aimable *de votre part* (*or* C'est bien aimable *à vous*) de venir me voir.

19. **Que** je suis content (*cong-tāng*) de vous revoir enfin (*āng-faing*).

20. C'est mon père[1] qui sera content de vous revoir.

21. Que ma mère sera contente (*cōng-tāngt*).

22. Et mon cousin donc (*kōō-zaing dong*).

23. Mais asseyez-vous donc, je vous prie.

24. N'aimez-vous pas mieux vous *mettre*[2] sur le sofa ?

25. Merci, j'ai peu de temps, je ne m'assiérai pas.

26. Merci, *je suis*[3] très-bien ici.

27. Il faut que je m'en aille[4] maintenant.

28. Etes-vous donc si pressé ?

---

admit ; *commettre*, to commit ; *démettre*, to turn out ; *omettre*, to omit ; *permettre*, to permit, to allow ; *promettre*, to promise ; *compromettre* (*cong-pro-metr'*), to compromise, to expose ; *remettre*, to replace, to hand over ; *soumettre* (*sōō-mĕtr'*), to submit ; *transmettre* (*trāngs-mĕtr'*), to transmit.

N.B.—*Se mettre à* signifies *to begin*, as Il se mit à pleurer, he began to cry.

N.B.—*Mettre* signifies frequently *to sit down, to be seated* when the place where one sits down is either given or self-understood.

3) *Etre* signifies often *to sit down* or *to stand*, especially when the place is understood. *Ex.:* Was he *sitting down* or did he stand ? Etait-il assis ou debout (*dĕ-bōō*)?—He stood, Il était debout.—Where, où donc ?—*He was standing* at the window, il était à la fenêtre.

4) Compare page 314.

29. I do not like leaving you, but I really must be off. (*Literally :* I leave you [*je vous quitte*] with [*à*] regret, but it really [*absolument*] must be.)

30. Call soon again.

31. Don't be such a stranger.

32. Call again (= another time [*une autre fois*]).

33. You will do me a great favor (*or* You will confer a great favor upon me) by calling soon.

34. My regards to all at home, if you please (*or* Remember me to all at home, please).

2.

When he came to get your letters.

When

he came [1]

to seek ; to search ; to look for [2]

your (pl.)

letters.

---

1) The following *intransitive verbs* must always be conjugated with *être :*

Aller, to go.
venir, to come.
devenir, to become.
intervenir (*aing-tĕr-vĕ-nēer*), to intervene.
parvenir, to attain, to reach.
revenir, } to come back, to re-
retourner, } turn.
tomber (*tong-bĕh*) to fall.

Arriver (*ār-rēē-vēh*), to arrive.
partir pour, to start for, to leave for.
entrer (*āng-trēh*), to enter.
sortir, to go out.
mourir (*moū-rēēr*), }
décéder, } to die.
naître, to be born.

As : Je suis allé ; je suis tombé ; il est parti ; nous sommes arrivés, &c.

2) The *Infinitive without preposition* is used :
a) after *verbs of motion*, as *aller, venir, courir*, and *envoyer*.

29. Je vous quitte à regret, mais il le faut absolument
(*jĕ vōō kĭt tāh rĕ-grăy may zēēl lĕ foh tāb-so-lü-māng*).

30. Revenez-nous bientôt.

31. Ne soyez pas si rare (*rāhr*). [Must be translated thus.]

32. Venez-nous voir une autre fois (*fo-āh*).

33. Vous nous ferez grand plaisir si vous veniez nous voir une autre fois.

34. Mes compliments (*cong-plēē-māng*) chez vous, s'il vous plait.

2.

Lorsqu'il est venu chercher vos lettres.

lors-kēēl   ay   vĕ-nü   shĕr-shēh   vō   lĕttr'.

Lorsque (*lorsk*)

il est venu [1] (*ēēl lay vĕnü*)

chercher [2] (*shĕr-shēh*)

vos (*vō*) (pl.)

lettres (*lettr'*) (pl.)

(Observe that *aller chercher* means to fetch, to get ; *aller trouver*, to look for ; *aller voir*, to pay a call ; *venir chercher* or *prendre*, to call for ; *envoyer chercher*, to send for.)

b) after verbs that denote a *perception of the senses* as entendre (*āng-tāng-dr*), voir (*vō-ār*), sentir (*sāng-teēr*). Ex.: Je l'entends venir, I hear him coming.

c) The *simple Infinitive* is governed further by the verbs : aimer, when used in the Conditional, *i.e.* j'aimerais, *I should like ;* préférer, to prefer ; il vaut mieux, it is better. Ex.:

J'aimerais le *voir*, I should like to see him.
Il vaut mieux *céder*, It is better to yield.
Je préfère *rester* à la maison, I prefer staying at home.

Note. When, however, in the second member of a comparison, a second *Infinitive* follows que, this latter must take de before it. Ex.:

l'aime mieux mourir que de *trahir* mon secret (*sĕ-cray*), I will rather die than betray my secret.

1. I am very thirsty; will you please give me something to drink?

2. There is no more wine in the bottle; I must go into the cellar (*la cave*).

3. That is not worth while; give me some water (*only*).

4. That in the pitcher (*de la carafe*) is not fresh; I am going to get some more (*d'autre*).

5. Some one has rung, Pauline; go and open² the door.

6. Will you please go and tell Mr. B. that the gentleman is waiting for him (*l'attend*)?

7. Where are you going to pass your vacation this year?

8. I don't know yet; perhaps I shall go to³ France.

9. Well, how do you do this morning?

10. I am much better, thank you.

11. You ought⁴ to get up; we would like to (*nous irions*) take a walk (*faire un tour*).

12. I have a good mind (*J'ai encore envie*) to sleep⁵ a little longer (=yet).

13. In that case (*or* Then) I am going to take a walk by myself (*tout seul*).

---

1) Some of the following sentences are taken from *Le Page*, '*L'Echo de Paris*' (London, 48th edition), edited in Germany by *Dr. Fliess-bach*, and reproduced in America from the London edition, but without acknowledgment.

2) *Ouvrir*, to open.—*Part. pr.*: ouvrant.—*Part. p.*: ouvert.—*Pres.* J'ouvre, tu ouvres, il ouvre, nous ouvrons, vous ouvrez, ils ouvrent. — *Pret.*: J'ouvris, &c.—*Fut.*: J'ouvrirai, &c.—*Imperat.*: Ouvre, ouvrons, ouvrez.

3) *Aller* is followed by *à* when one travels to *towns*, but by *en* when reference is made to *countries*, as: Je vais *à* Paris; *but* je vais *en* France; Je vais *en* Angleterre.

4) *Devoir*, to owe (ought to).—*Part. pr.*: devant.—*Part. p.*: dû.—

1. J'ai bien soif ; voulez-vous, s'il vous plait, me donner à boire [1] (*bŏ-āre*) ?

2. Il n'y a plus de vin dans la bouteille (*boū-tāy-yĕ*), il faut que j'aille à la cave (*kāhv*).

3. Ce n'est pas la peine (*pain*) ; donnez-moi de l'eau seulement (*seūl-mäng*).

4. Celle de la carafe (*kā-rāf*) n'est pas fraiche : je vais⁀en⁀aller chercher d'autre.

5. On⁀a sonné Pauline ; allez donc ouvrir [2] la porte.

6. Voulez-vous⁀aller dire à monsieur B., que monsieur l'attend (*lā-tāng*) ?

7. Où irez-vous passer vos vacances cette‿année ?

8. Je ne sais pas⁀encore ; j'irai peut-être‿en [3] France (*āng frāngs*).

9. Eh bien, comment ça va-t-il ce matin ?

10. Ça va mieux, je vous remercie.

11. Vous devriez [4] vous lever ; nous⁀irions faire‿un tour (*tōōr*).

12. J'ai encore‿envie (*rāng-véé*) de dormir. [5]

13. En ce cas-là, j'irai me promener tout seul.

Pres. : Je dois (*dwoāh*), tu dois, il doit, nous devons, vous devez, ils doivent (*dwoāhv*).—*Imperf.* : Je devais, &c.—*Pret.* : Je dus (*dü*), tu dus, il dut, nous dûmes, vous dûtes, ils durent (*dür*).—*Fut.*: Je devrai, tu devras, il devra, &c.—*Condit.*: Je devrais, tu devrais, il devrait, nous devrions, &c.—*Subj. Pres.*: Que je doive, que tu doives, qu'il doive, &c.—*Subj. Imp.*: Que je dusse.—*Je dois*, followed by a verb, corresponds to our *I am to*, *I must*, while the Conditional, *Je devrais*, signifies *I ought to*, *I should*.

5) *Dormir*, to sleep.—*Part. pr.*: dormant.—*Part. p.*: dormi (*dor-méé*).—*Pres.*: Je dors, tu dors, il dort, nous dormons, vous dormez, ils dorment (*dorm*).—*Pret.*. Je dormis (*dor-méé*), &c.—*Subj.* : Que je dorme.

14. Do you know[1] Mr. B. ? [*To know=to be personally acquainted with,* must always be given by *connaître,* **never** by *savoir.*]

15. Yes, very well; we have been school-fellows.

16. They say (*or* People say) he is going to get married.

17. If any one should come[2] to inquire for me, porter, you'll please say that I have gone to the exposition (*au palais de l'exposition*).

18. If any one should call [*i.e.* to inquire for me], please say that I shall be back about 9 o'clock.

19. Please tell all callers that they must come before 10 o'clock in the morning. (*Literally:* Will you please tell to all persons, who should come [*qui viendront*] to inquire for me that, &c. ?)

20. If Mr. B. should come, tell him, that I could not wait for him any longer (*plus longtemps*).

21. If the tailor should come with my coat (= to bring my coat), tell him that he must call again (*repasser*) to-morrow morning.

22. Did any one call during my absence?

23. I must reproach you (= I have some reproaches to make to you).

24. Why so? — Because you have not yet called upon us since we moved (*depuis que nous sommes délogés*).

---

1) *Connaître,* to know.—*Part. pr.:* connaissant.—*Part. p.:* connu. —*Pres.:* Je connais, tu connais, il connaît, nous connaissons, vous connaissez, &c.—*Imperf.:* Je connaissais, &c. — *Pret.:* Je connus, &c.—*Fut.:* Je connaîtrai, &c.—Thus: *Méconnaître,* to mistake, not to acknowledge; *reconnaître,* to recognize, to know again.

14. Connaissez-vous [1] monsieur B. ?

15. Oui, très bien ; nous⁀avons⁀été camarades d'école.
16. On dit qu'il va se marier (*măr-yĕh*).

17. Concierge (*kong-syĕrje*), si [2] l'on vient me demander, vous direz que je suis⁀allé au palais (*pă-lay*) de l'exposition (*lĕx-pŏ-zēē-syong*).
18. Si quelqu'un vient (*or* venait) me demander, dites, s'il vous plait, que je rentrerai vers neuf⁀heures.
19. Veuillez dire à toutes les personnes qui viendront me demander (*kēē vyaing-drong' mĕ dĕ-măng-dēh*) qu'il faut venir avant dix⁀heures du matin.

20. Si monsieur B. venait, dites-lui que je n'ai pu l'attendre plus longtemps (*lăt-tăng-dr' plü long-tăng*).
21. Si le tailleur venait m'apporter mon⁀habit, dites-lui qu'il faut repasser demain matin.

22. Est-on venu me demander pendant mon⁀absence (*păng-dăng mŏn-năb-sāngs*) ?
23. J'ai des reproches (*rĕ-prōsh*) à vous faire.

24. Pourquoi donc ?—Parce que vous n'êtes pas⁀encore venu nous voir depuis que nous sommes délogés.

---

2) After *si, if,* the *Present, Imperfect* or *Pluperfect must* always follow (but never the *Future* or *Conditional*), while in the main sentence the *Conditional* must be employed, as : *Si vous veniez* me voir, *vous seriez* bien reçu. You would be received well, if you were to come to see me.

25. If you wish to behave amiably, you would come to dine with us on Friday next.

26. Would you do me the favor to accompany me after breakfast to make some purchases (*or* to do some shopping)?

27. Please send[1] the laundress to me one of these days.

28. I am going (*j'irai*) to see her to-night and I can tell her to call upon you to-morrow morning.

29. Will you come and take a walk (*vous promener*)?

30. I come to bid you good-bye.

31. What! are you going to leave us (*nous quitter*)?

32. Yes, I am going to London to seek a place.

33. Please don't go yet; breakfast will be served at once.

34. I have come (=I am coming) to take you with me.

35. To go where?

36. To come with me to the Museum, to look at the new pictures.

37. What is the news?

38. Didn't you read[2] the paper this morning? It is said (*or* reported) we are going to war with England (*nous allons avoir la guerre avec l'Angleterre*).

---

1) *Envoyer*, to send. — *Part. pr.*: envoyant.- *Part. p.*: envoyé.— *Pres.*: J'envoie (*jäng võ-äh*), tu envoies, il envoie. nous envoyons, vous envoyez, ils envoient.—*Imperf.*: J'envoyais.—*Pret.*: J'envoyai. *Fut.* · J'enverrai (*jäng-vĕr-rêh*), tu enverras, il enverra, nous enverrons, vous enverrez, ils enverront.—*Condit.* . J'enverrais.

25. Si vous‿étiez bien‿aimable, vous viendriez dîner avec nous vendredi prochain (*vǎng-drĕ-dēē prō-shaing*).

26. Voudriez-vous me faire le plaisir de venir avec moi après le déjeûner, faire des‿emplettes ?

27. Envoyez-moi[1] donc la blanchisseuse ces jours-ci.

28. J'irai la voir ce soir, et je peux lui dire de venir vous parler demain matin.

29. Voulez-vous venir vous promener ?

30. Je viens vous faire mes‿adieux (*may zā-dyeŭ*).

31. Comment? est-ce que vous‿allez nous quitter (*kit-tēh*) ?

32. Oui, je vais à Londres chercher une place (*plāhs*).

33. Ne vous‿en‿allez donc pas ;, on va servir la collation (*cǒ-lā-syong*) tout de suite.

34. Je viens vous chercher.

35. Pour aller où donc ?

36. Pour venir avec moi au Musée (*mü-zay*) voir les nouveaux tableaux (*nǫō-vō tā-blō*).

37. Qu'est-ce qu'il y a de nouveau ?

38. Vous n'avez pas lu[2] le journal ce matin ? On dit que nous‿allons‿avoir la guerre avec l'Angleterre (*lāng-glĕ-tĕr*).

---

2) *Lire* (*lēēr*), to read —*Part. pr.* · lisant (*lēē zāng*).—*Part. p.* · lu — *Pres.:* Je lis (*lēē*), tu lis, il lit, nous lisons (*lēē-zong*), vous lisez, ils lisent (*lēēz*).—*Pret. :* Je lus, tu lus, il lut, nous lûmes, vous lûtes, &c. — *Fut. :* Je lirai (*lēē-rēh*), tu liras, il lira (*lēē rāh*), &c. — *Imperf. Subj.:* Que je lusse.

GRAMMATICAL REMARKS.

Exercises and Words used in Common Conversation.

_____

Exercise.

Does Mr. N. live in this house?—No, sir, I do not know this gentleman. — But isn't this No. 68 (= Is not this then here [*ce n'est donc pas ici*] No. 68)?—Certainly, sir. — Then he must have moved (= It is necessary then that he *have* moved [*déménagé*]).—A person of this name has never lived in this house since I have been here (=Never [*jamais*] a person of this name has not [*n'a*] lived in the house since [*depuis que*] I here [*y*] am). — Is Mr. N. at home? — I am not sure of it (*en*). He usually (*d'habitude*) does not go out till noon (= he only [*ne—que*] goes out [*sort*] at noon). — Mr. N. is not at home any more (not any more = [*ne-plus*]). — He has just gone out (= He comes from going out).—Can't you tell me when *he will come home* (*il rentrera*)? — I really cannot tell you. — Will you please give him this card? — Yes, sir, with pleasure. — But do not forget it; *I am very anxious that* (*je tiens à ce que*) Mr. N. *should know* (*sache*) that I have called on him (=That I have [*suis*] come *in order to* [*pour*] see him). — He shall have it as soon as he comes in (= He shall have it on [*en*] re-entering [*rentrant*]). — Is this Mr. N.'s? — Yes, sir, but master cannot be seen. — Tell him that a stranger is here who is going to leave in a few days (= Tell him that it is [*c'est*] a stranger who leaves [*part*] in several days). — I'll see, but I do not believe that Mr. N. can (*puisse*) receive (*recevoir*) you. — Whom have I the honor of announcing? — Mr. B. — *My master* (*monsieur*) is very sorry (=regrets very much, *infiniment*), but he is not well and cannot receive any one. — Then (*en ce cas*) give him (= you will give him) this letter which I was charged to put (*remettre*) *in his own hands* (*en main propre*).

Exercise.

Will you please give me my key (*ma clef*)? It is Number 22.—Here, sir (*la voici, monsieur*); don't forget your candle (*votre bougie*=boū-jēē).—Will you please give me some matches (*quelques allumettes*)? — You are going to leave to morrow, sir? — Yes; *I have just come home* (*je rentre*) to pack my trunk (*faire ma malle*). — You are wrong, sir; you ought to stay a fortnight longer (=*encore*).—At what o'clock do you leave? — The train leaves at 7 A.M. (*du matin*). You must order a cab for 6 o'clock. — Have you had the kindness to make up my bill for (*de*) last week (*la semaine dernière*)? — Yes, sir, I am just about (*je suis en train*) finishing it. Here it is. — Thanks, will you please see (*regarder*) if this is all right (*si c'est bien* or *si cela fait bien votre compte*)? — That's all right (*c'est cela même*), sir, thank you. Allow me to receipt (*acquitter*) your bill and to put (*mettre*) a stamp (*un timbre*) on it (*y*). — May I (*puis-je*) hope that you will recommend my hotel to your countrymen?—With the greatest pleasure.—I shall be greatly obliged to you, sir.

Relative Pronouns.

The interrogative pronouns *qui, quoi,* and *lequel* serve also as *relative pronouns.* The declension of quoi and lequel has been given. That of *qui,* when relative, differs from the interrogative qui.

Sing. and *Plur.* *Masc.* and *Fem.*

Nom. *Qui,* who, which, that.
Gen. **de qui** and **dont,** whose, of (from) whom, of which.
Dat. *à qui,* to whom.
Acc. *que,* whom, which, that.

1. *Who, which,* and *that* are rendered by **qui,** when they are in the *Nominative* case, whether they refer to persons or things, both for the singular and plural.

L'employé **qui** a écrit cette lettre, n'est pas ici.
The clerk who wrote this letter is not here.
Passez-moi le plat **qui** est sur la table.
Hand me the dish which is on the table.
Les hommes **qui** l'ont dit, sont partis hier soir.
The men who said it left last night.

2. The same pronouns—when in the *Accusative—whom, which, that,* are rendered by **que.**

Est-ce là le chapeau neuf **que** vous avez acheté ?
Is that the new hat which you have bought ?
La leçon **que** vous m'avez donnée, est très difficile.
The task which you have given me is very difficult.

Observe that *the French must always express the relative pronoun,* though we frequently omit it.

3. **Dont,** *whose, of which,* is used for persons and things of both genders and numbers.

Voíci la dame **dont** je vous ai parlé.

Here is the lady of whom I spoke to you.

C'est le monsieur **dont** il a acheté le cheval.

That is the gentleman whose horse he bought.

C'est une maladie **dont** on ne seconnait point la cause.

That is an illness the cause of which is unknown.

Est-ce là le jardin **dont** vous m'avez parlé?

Is that the garden of which you spoke to me?

4. *The Genitive de qui* (both singular and plural) and the *Dative à qui, to whom,* are used only when referring to *persons.*[1]

Le négociant **de qui** j'ai reçu ces échantillons, vient de faire banqueroute.

The merchant from whom I received these patterns has just become bankrupt.

Voilà le monsieur **à qui** j'ai donné votre lettre.

There is the gentleman to whom I gave your letter.

When, however, *animals* or *inanimate objects* are spoken of, *auquel, à laquelle, auxquels,* or *auxquelles,* must be used.

Tel est le bonheur *auquel* j'aspire (*jãs-pēēr*).

Such is the fortune to which I aspire.

C'est le chien *auquel* j'ai donné à manger.

That is the dog which I fed (=to which I gave to eat).

C'est une occasion *à laquelle* je ne pensais pas.

That is an occasion I did not think of.

---

1) *Qui* is mostly used after prepositions when persons are referred to ; but after *entre,* between, and parmi (*pār-mēē*), among, we must always write *lesquels* or *lesquelles, whether persons* or things are spoken of.

Les sciences (*sēē-āngs*) *auxquelles* je m'intéresse.

The sciences in which I am interested.

5. *Difference between* **dont, de qui,** and the genitives of **lequel.**

Dont is used when it is governed by a noun which stands either in the *Nominative* or *Accusative case*, as :

Voici le monsieur **dont** je vous ai parlé.

There is the gentleman of whom I spoke to you.

Voilà une fleur **dont** la forme est très curieuse.

There is a flower whose form is very strange.

La dame **dont** vous voyez le portrait, est à présent à Berlin.

The lady whose portrait you see is at present in Berlin.

Le monsieur **dont** j'instruis les enfants, est très riche.

The gentleman whose children I instruct is very rich.

But **de qui** or **duquel, de laquelle,** &c., must be employed when the *noun* which follows *whose* is in *any other case than the Nominative or Accusative* or is *governed by a preposition*. (*De qui refers only to persons,* while duquel, de laquelle, &c., may be used both for persons and for things), as :

Les amis **sur qui** vous comptez, vous abandonneront.

The friends on whom you count will forsake you.

C'est un homme *à la discrétion* **de qui** vous pouvez vous fier.

He is a man to whose discretion you may trust.

J'honore cet homme aux bontés **duquel** (or **de qui**) je dois ma fortune.

I honor this man, to whose kindness I owe my fortune.

C'est un régiment (*ray-jēē-māng*) à la valeur **duquel** ᵥl'ennemi n'a pu résister.

That's a regiment whose valor the enemy has been unable to resist.

C'est un jeune homme sur la parole **de qui** (or **duquel**) on ne peut pas compter.

That is a young man upon whose word one cannot rely.

6. *Lequel, laquelle*, &c., are used after prepositions when
reference is made to things, while *qui* must be employed
when persons are referred to. *Ex. :*

Voilà le banc *sur lequel* je me suis assis.

Here is the bench on which I sat.

C'est une condition (*kong dēē-zyong*) **sans laquelle** il ne
veut rien faire.

That is a condition without which he will do nothing.
But :

Le marchand *avec qui*[1] j'ai voyagé, est mort.

The merchant with whom I travelled died.

7. *Lequel, laquelle*, &c., must be used instead of *qui* or
que, when by the use of the two latter pronouns an am-
biguity might arise. As :

La tante de mon ami *laquelle* demeure à Londres.

My friend's aunt who lives in London.

(*qui* demeure à Londres, would mean : The aunt of my
friend who is living in London, and would signify that
the friend lives in London.)

J'ai vu le cocher de votre cousine, **lequel** viendra vous
voir.

I have seen your cousin's coachman, who will call on
you.

---

1) *Qui* remains always unchanged, even before a vowel or *h voyelle*,
as : L'homme *qui* arrive ;—à *qui* il parle ;—à *qui* elle pense ;—de *qui*
on se plaint.

8. Such expressions as *he who, she who, they who, those who* must be rendered by *celui qui, celle qui* (fem.); *ceux qui* (pl. m.); *celles qui* (pl. f.). *Ex.* : ·

Celui qui est content, est riche.

He who is contented is rich.

Je l'enverrai **à celle que** j'aime le mieux.

I will send it to her whom I love best.

Je parle de **celui que** nous avons vu chez le médecin allemand.

I speak of the one that we saw at the German physician's.

J'ai donné le livre **à celle qui** a trouvé la clef **avec laquelle** votre soeur a ouvert la porte.

I gave the book to that one who found the key with which your sister opened the door.

9. *That which* or *what*, meaning really '*that thing which*,' is rendered by **ce qui** for the Nominative, and **ce que** for the Accusative.—*All that* is rendered by **tout ce qui** for the Nominative, and **tout ce que** for the Accusative. *Ex.* :

Aimez *tout ce qui* est bon et beau.

Love all that (*or* everything which) is good and beautiful.

Faites *ce que* je vous dis.

Do what I tell you.

Ce qui est beau n'est pas toujours bon.

What is beautiful is not always good.

10. Proverbs and general statements usually commence with *Qui, whoever*. *Ex.* :

Qui sert les malheureux sert la divinité.

Whoever helps unhappy persons helps Providence.

Qui casse les verres, lés paie.

Who breaks (the glasses), pays (for them).

11. *Quoi, what*, is only used after prepositions referring to a whole sentence, or to *voilà, voici, ce, rien.*

Voilà *de quoi* il m'a entretenu.

That is what he entertained me with.

Je sais *à quoi* vous pensez.

I know what you are thinking of.

C'est *à quoi* je pense le moins.

This is a thing of which I think least.

À quoi vous vous fiez, est très incertain.

What you trust to is very uncertain.

Je ne sais **à quoi** il s'occupe.

I do not know what he is engaged in.

Quoi! n'est-ce que cela?

What! is that all?

De **quoi** s'agit-il là?

What is the matter there?

À quoi s'occupe-t-il?

What is he occupied with?

Il faut qu'il signe (*sēēn-yĕ*) le contrat; **sans quoi** il
sera nul.

He must sign this contract; otherwise it will be void.

Avez-vous de **quoi** payer ces factures?

Have you enough to pay for these bills?

Il n'a pas **de quoi** vivre.

He has not wherewith to live.

À quoi bon de sortir par ce temps?

What is the good of going out in such weather?

Après quoi after which.—*Sans quoi,* without which,
therwise.

Exercise.

You have apartments to let (*à louer*)?—Yes, sir, I have two; one furnished, the other unfurnished. Which of the two do you desire to see?—I do not know yet whether I shall buy furniture or not (*si je me mettrai dans mes meubles ou non*).—In that case, see them both (*les deux*). The unfurnished apartment is on the first floor, the other is on the second.—What is the rent (*le prix du loyer*)?— That is very dear.—Please to remember (*veuillez remarquer*) that the apartment is newly decorated (*fraîchement décoré*), and that there are looking-glasses over (*sur*) every mantel-piece.—Will you have the goodness to show me the second floor?—Here is the room; *will you please* (*donnez-vous la peine*) step in?—It is not large, but it is very neat (*propre*) and light.—The furniture is mahogany (*en acajou*), sir.—The paper is simple, but quite new (*frais*). —What do you ask for this room?—That depends (*cela dépend*). Will you take it *by the day* (*au jour*) or by the month (*au mois*)?—As I don't know yet *how long* (*combien de temps*) I shall stay (*je resterai*) in Paris, I prefer to hire it by the day.—That would be (*then, alors*) four francs per day (*par jour*). That seems (*semble*) to me rather (*assez*) dear.—Oh no, sir, you know that *everything* (*tout*) *has grown dear* (*a renchéri*) in Paris.—The price of rents (*des loyers*) has *about* (*à peu près*) doubled.—Take this room by the month and *I will let you have it* (*je vous la laisserai*) for one hundred francs.—That is quite a reduction (= a considerable reduction, *une diminution* [or *un rabais*] *considérable*) which I am offering you. — Very well, I'll take the room.

COMPANION TO THE
Revised Version of the New Testament.

Explaining the Reasons for the Changes Made on the Authorized Version.

BY ALEXANDER ROBERTS, D.D.,
Member of the English Revision Committee.

WITH SUPPLEMENT BY A MEMBER OF THE AMERICAN COMMITTEE.

Containing a Brief History of the Revision of the Work and Co-operation of the New Testament Companies, of the Points of Agreement and Difference, and an Explanation of the Appendix to the Revised New Testament.

ALSO, A FULL TEXTUAL INDEX,

Being a Key to Passages in which Important Changes have been Made.

This book, having been carefully prepared by Members of both Revision Committees, carries official weight. It shows what changes have been made, and also the reasons which influenced the revisers in making them. It will be difficult to judge of the merits of the revision without the aid of this Companion volume. Our edition is printed by special arrangement with the English publishers. It is well known that, by an arrangement between the two Committees of Revision, the changes suggested by the American Committee, but which were not adopted by the English Revisers, are published as an Appendix to the Revised New Testament. The *Companion* volume is an explanation of *all* the changes adopted by both committees, and of those suggested by the American Committee, but not assented to by the English Committee, in their final revision. The book will be indispensable to a right understanding of the revision. This cheap edition of the combined books, although authorized and copyrighted, will be sold for 25 cents in paper, and 75 cents in cloth—sent postage free.

TESTIMONIALS.

T. W. CHAMBERS, D.D., a Member of the American Committee of Revision, says of this book: "Many persons have expressed a desire that, simultaneously with the issue of the Revised New Testament, there should appear an authentic explanation of the reasons for such changes as will be found in its pages. The work of Dr. Roberts is exactly fitted to meet this desire.... Nowhere else in print can be found a statement so full and exact. It gives all needed information, and does it in an unexceptional way."

C. F. DEEMS, D.D., Pastor of the Church of the Strangers, New York, writes: "The Companion to the Revised Version seems to me almost indispensable. Even scholars who were not at the meeting of the Revisers would have a wearisome work in seeking to discover all the changes made, and to ordinary readers very much of the labor would be lost. .... All this is set forth by Dr. Roberts with admirable perspicuity. Those who have any intelligent interest in the Holy Scriptures, will find this little book absorbingly interesting. I shall urge every member of the church of which I am pastor to give it a careful reading, and purpose to introduce it as a text-book in our Bible-classes."

"So valuable, interesting and useful is this publication, that we advise every one who wishes to know the why and wherefore of the revision, to obtain it immediately."—*New York Observer.*

Paper, 8vo size, 25 cents; Cloth, 16mo, 75 cents.

.*.* For Sale by Booksellers and Newsdealers, or sent postage-paid, on receipt of price, by

I. K. FUNK & CO., Publishers, 10 & 12 Dey St., N. Y.

THE TEACHER'S EDITION

OF THE

REVISED NEW TESTAMENT

With New Concordance and Index, Harmony of the Gospels, Maps,
Historical and Chronological Tables, Parallel Passages printed
in full, Blank Pages Interleaved for manuscript notes, and
many other New and Indispensable Helps to the Study
of the Revised Version.

After the excitement connected with the sale of the first copies of the new revision, which lack the usual indexing headlines and marginal references to parallel passages, and also the appendixes of tables, maps, etc.—all of which helps preachers, teachers and Bible students have come to consider as absolutely essential to a working copy of the Bible—there arises an imperative demand for an edition of the Revised New Testament, containing all the marginal and appendix helps of former TEACHERS' AND REFERENCE BIBLES, adapted carefully and accurately to the Revised Version. We are, therefore, preparing, as rapidly as is consistent with accuracy, such an edition of the Revised New Testament. The work is under the supervision of well-known Bible scholars, with numerous helpers, and will be issued as early as it can be done with thoroughness. In style and size the book will resemble the Bagster Bible, "Fac-simile large edition," known as "the Moody Bible," being the same width and length and size of type. It will be supplied at prices *within the reach of all.*

This "Teachers' Edition of the Revised New Testament" will be an exact, *certified reproduction* of the entire Oxford and Cambridge Edition, including the Preface and all the marginal readings and explanations. It will contain the appendix notes of the American Revisers, printed in the margin of each page by the side of the passages referred to. The parallel passages, to which reference is made in the "Bagster Bibles," with numerous others, so far as appropriate, will be PRINTED IN FULL in the margin. The running headings, usually printed at the tops of pages of the King James version, will be here supplied. A small black mark will be inserted below the last letter of each verse to facilitate reference, and aid in RESPONSIVE READING of the Revised Version. The second half of the volume will consist of the most carefully prepared HELPS TO THE STUDY OF THE REVISED NEW TESTAMENT, gleaned from the best Teachers' Editions of the authorized version, and supplied from various original sources—all being revised and adapted to harmonize with the Revised Version. We shall introduce many other important features, making this the most valuable edition of the New Testament ever issued.

Popular Cloth Edition—Ready in July—Price, Postage Free, $1.00.

Send for prospectus giving full description and prices of finer Bindings.

I. K. FUNK & CO., Publishers, 10 and 12 Dey St., New York.

THE

𝕸𝖊𝖎𝖘𝖙𝖊𝖗𝖘𝖈𝖍𝖆𝖋𝖙 𝕾𝖞𝖘𝖙𝖊𝖒.

A SIMPLE AND PRACTICAL METHOD,

ENABLING

ANY ONE TO LEARN, WITH SLIGHT EFFORT, TO SPEAK FLUENTLY AND CORRECTLY

𝕱𝖗𝖊𝖓𝖈𝖍, 𝕲𝖊𝖗𝖒𝖆𝖓, 𝕾𝖕𝖆𝖓𝖎𝖘𝖍, 𝖆𝖓𝖉 𝕴𝖙𝖆𝖑𝖎𝖆𝖓.

BY

DR. RICHARD S. ROSENTHAL,

Late Director of the "Akademie für fremde Sprachen" in Berlin and Leipzig, of the "Meisterschaft College" in London, and Principal of the "Meisterschaft School of Practical Linguistry" in New York.

FRENCH.

IN FIFTEEN PARTS, EACH CONTAINING THREE LESSONS.

PART XIV.

NEW YORK:

I. K. FUNK & CO., Publishers,

10 AND 12 Dey Street.

TERMS.

We have arranged with Dr. ROSENTHAL, the author of the "Meisterschaft System," for its introduction in America under his own supervision, and he has opened

The Meisterschaft School of Practical Linguistry

FOR NON-RESIDENTS.

The student does not need to leave his home. The lessons of each language are prepared by the Professor, and printed and sent in pamphlet shape to each member of the School wherever he may reside.

The course of study for each language—German, French, Italian, or Spanish—makes fifteen pamphlets of three lessons each.

All members of the School have

THE PRIVILEGE

of asking, by letter, questions concerning each lesson, or consulting on any difficulty which may have occurred to them. All exercises corrected and all questions answered by return post by Dr. ROSENTHAL or one of his assistants.

TERMS OF MEMBERSHIP.

Five Dollars is the price for membership in the school for each language. This amount ($5.) entitles the member to receive the fifteen books or pamphlets containing the lessons, also answers to his questions. Return postage for the answer must accompany the question.

State distinctly which language, or languages, you desire to study There are *no extra charges*. The price, **Five Dollars,** pays for one language ; **Ten Dollars** for two languages, etc. All exercise. and questions must be written on a separate sheet of paper, and must state full address of the pupil.

Remittances must be made in Post-Office Order or registered letter addressed to

I. K. FUNK & CO.,

10 and 12 Dey Street, New York.

The Meisterschaft-System.

FRENCH.

PART XIV.

XIV.

(*Continuation.*)

1.

1. Where is Mr. B. ?
2. He has just gone out (*Il vient de*[1] *sortir*[2]), but for a moment only; he will be back (*il va rentrer*) imme-diately.
3. The postman has just brought a letter for you.
4. I have just observed (*Je viens de m'apercevoir*[3]) that there is no blind to my window.
5. I have just invited Mr. N. to dinner.

6. I have just received[3] this telegram, and I hope its contents will be satisfactory to you.
7. I have just received a letter from Mme. de N. an-nouncing (*qui m'annonce*) the death of her father.
8. My brother has just sold his furniture. Did I tell you that he is going to live in the country?

9. My sisters have just taken their places in the mail-coach; they are going to leave (*partir*[4]) to-morrow evening at six o'clock.

---

1) *Venir de*, with an Infinitive, corresponds to the English *to have just*, as : *Je viens* d'arriver, *I have just* arrived.—*Nous venons de* le voir, *We have just* seen him. In order that the student may get thoroughly familiar with the different constructions of *venir*, I repeat here the examples of *venir de* as given in a former lesson.

2) *Sortir*, to go out.—Is conjugated in the same manner as *servir ;* compare page 304, Note I.—*Part. pr.:* sortant. — *Part. p.:* sorti.— *Pres.:* Je sors (*sôr*), tu sors, il sort, nous sortons, vous sortez, ils sor-tent.—*Pret. :* Je sortis (*sor-tëë*).—*Fut. :* Je sortirai.—*Subj. :* Que je sorte.

XIV.

(Continuation.)

1.

1. Où est monsieur B. ?

2. Il *vient de*[1] sortir,[2] mais pour un moment seulement ; il va rentrer tout-à-l'heure.

3. Le facteur vient d'apporter une lettre pour vous.

4. Je viens de m'apercevoir[3] qu'il n'y a pas de store à ma croisée (*krō-āh-zay*).

5. Je viens d'inviter (*daing-vēē-tēh*) monsieur N. à dîner (*dēē-nēh*).

6. Je viens de recevoir[3] ce télégramme et j'espère que son contenu (*kong-tĕ-nü*) vous satisfera.

7. Je viens de recevoir une lettre de Mme. de N. qui m'annonce la mort (*mān-nongs lā mōr*) de son père.

8. Mon frère vient de vendre son mobilier (*vǎng-dr song mō-bēē-lyēh*). Vous ai-je dit qu'il va demeurer à la campagne (*kǎng-pān-yĕ*) ?

9. Mes soeurs viennent (*vyĕn*) d'arrêter leurs places à la diligence (*plāhs āh lāh dēē-lēē-jǎngs*) ; elles vont partir[4] demain soir à six heures.

---

3) *Apercevoir*, to perceive, is conjugated = *recevoir*, to receive. — *Part. pr.* : recevant. — *Part. p.* : reçu.— *Pres.* : Je reçois (*rĕ-swoǎh*), tu reçois, il reçoit, nous recevons, vous recevez, ils reçoivent (*rĕ-swoǎhv*).—*Pret.:* Je reçus, tu reçus, il reçut, nous reçûmes, vous reçûtes, ils reçurent.—*Fut.* : Je recevrai, tu recevras, il recevra, &c. —Thus also : *Concevoir*, to conceive ; *décevoir*, to deceive.

4) *Partir pour*, to set out, to leave for.—*Part. pr.*: partant.—*Part. p.*: parti (*pār-tēē*).—*Pres.*: Je pars (*pār*), tu pars, il part, nous partons, vous partez, &c., as *servir*. Comp. page 304.—*Perf.*: Je **suis** *parti*.

10. It has just struck nine.

11. It is just going to strike nine.

12. May I offer [1] you something to drink, madame?

13. I thank you very much, I have just had something.

14. Is it long since you saw Mr. D.?

15. I have just met him.

16. Is Mrs. L. at home?—No, madam, she has just gone out.

17. Then (*en ce cas*) I'll come back in an hour.

18. I have just seen Mr. T.

19. Does he get on well in his business?

20. Yes, his business goes very well.

21. Have you called on Mrs. B.?

22. I have been to her house, but did not find her in; she had just gone out.

23. Do you know that this poor C. has just lost his wife?

24. I come to pay you my debts (= what I owe you).

25. You need not have come expressly for that.

26. { Waiter, did you order a cab?
{ Have you got me a cab?

27. Let him come.

28. Has any one called here?

29. That happens very opportunely (*fort à propos*).

30. I have come expressly for that.

31. I shall be back at ten o'clock at the latest.

32. When did you return from the country?

---

1) *Offrir*, to offer.—*Part. pr.*: offrant.—*Part. p.*: offert. —*Pres.*: J'offre, tu offres, il offre, nous offrons, vous offrez, ils offrent (*sugar*).

10. Neuf‿heures *viennent de sonner.*

11. Neuf‿heures *vont sonner.*

12. Mademoiselle, vous‿offrirai-je [1] à boire ?

13. Je vous remercie bien, monsieur ; je viens de boire tout-à-l'heure.

14. Y a-t-il longtemps que vous n'avez-vu monsieur D. ?

15. Je viens de le rencontrer (*rāng-kong-trĕh*).

16. Madame L. est-elle chez‿elle ? Non madame, elle vient de sortir.

17. En ce cas je reviendrai dans‿une heure.

18. Je viens de voir tout-à-l'heure monsieur T.

19. Fait-il bien ses‿affaires ?

20. Oui, son commerce va très-bien.

21. Avez-vous‿été voir Mme. B. ?

22. Je suis‿allé chez‿elle, mais je ne l'ai pas trouvée ; elle venait de sortir.

23. Savez-vous que ce pauvre C. (*say*) vient de perdre sa femme (*făm*)?

24. Je viens vous payer ce que je vous dois (*d'woāh*).

25. Il ne fallait pas venir exprès.

26. { 'Garçon, avez-vous fait venir un fiacre (*fēē-ākr*) ?
    { Etes-vous‿allé chercher un fiacre ?

27. Faites-le venir.

28. Est-il venu quelqu'un ici (*kĕl-keŭng ēē-sēē*).?

29. Cela vient fort‿à propos (*prō-pōh*).

30. Je suis venu exprès pour cela.

31. Je reviendrai à dix‿heures au plus tard.

32. Quand êtes-vous revenu de la campagne ?

— *Pret. :* J'offris. — *Fut. :* J'offrirai, — *Imperat. :* Offre, offrons, offrez.

33. Please get out, gentlemen; we have just passed the frontier.

34. The train will soon be here.

35. Please hurry, gentlemen; the train from Brussels has just been signaled.

36. Shall I carry your trunk, sir, and get you a cab?

37. Would you allow me, sir, to put this little package under your seat (*banc*)?

38. Yes, please. (*Faites, je vous en prie.*)

39. Is it not in your way (*ne vous gêne-t-il pas*) as I have placed it just now?

40. Not the least in the world; I am quite comfortable.

41. The train starts at seven o'clock in the morning. I have just ordered (*retenir*) a cab for half past seven.

42. Do you know this gentleman? He has just addressed me in the street.

43. The carriage which has just passed has spattered me (*m'a éclaboussé*) from head to foot (*du haut en bas*).

---

1) *Tarder à* signifies *to delay*, as: *Ne tardez pas à* lui envoyer ces échantillons, Do not delay sending him these samples, *or* Hasten to send him these samples.—*Tarder de*, as an *impersonal verb*, means *to long*, as: *Il me tarde de*, I long to. — *Qu'il me tarde de* vous revoir, How I long to see you again.

Venir à means *to happen*, as: *S'il venait à* apprendre que vous êtes ici, If he happened to know that you are here. — Pendant que nous parlions de monsieur C., *il vint à* passer dans la rue, While we were talking of Mr. C. he happened to pass by in the street.

2) The *Subjunctive mood* must be employed after verbs of *commanding, ordering, wishing, permitting*, &c. Such are:

commander to command.	permettre, to permit.
demander, to ask.	prier, to beg, to ask.
désirer, to desire, to wish.	recommander, to recommand.
défendre, to forbid.	souhaiter, to wish.
exiger, to require, to demand.	souffrir, to suffer.
ordonner to order.	supplier, to beg, to request.
aimer mieux, to like better.	vouloir, to be willing.

33. Veuillez descendre, messieurs ; nous venons de passer la frontière (*frong-tyair*).

34. Le train ne tardera [1] pas à venir.

35. Dépêchez-vous, messieurs, le train de Bruxelles vient d'être signalé (*sĭn-yāh-lēh*).

36. Monsieur, voulez-vous que je vous porte [2] votre malle et que je vous aille [2] chercher un fiacre ?

37. Me permettriez-vous, [3] monsieur, de mettre [3] ce petit paquet sous votre banc ?

38. Faites, [4] monsieur, je vous en prie.

39. Ne vous gêne-t-il pas, comme je viens de le placer ?

40. Pas le moins du monde. Je suis tout à mon aise.

41. Le train part à sept heures du matin. Je viens de retenir [5] un fiacre pour six heures et demie.

42. Connaissez-vous ce monsieur ? Il est venu de m'accoster (*or* m'aborder) dans la rue.

43. La voiture qui vient de passer m'a éclaboussé du haut en bas (*dü ō-tāng-bāh*).

Examples : *J'ordonne* qu'il le *fasse.—J'aime* qu'il *soit* courageux.
— Il *souffrait* que je lui *disse* la vérité. — *Je supplie* qu'on me *permette* de partir.

3) *Permettre* and *mettre*, see page 352, No. 1.

4) *Faites*, meaning *yes*, is often used in this manner.

5) *Tenir*, to hold.—*Part. pr.* : tenant.—*Part. p.* : tenu.—*Pres.* : Je tiens (*tyaing*), tu tiens, il tient, nous tenons, vous tenez, ils tiennent (*tyĕn*). — *Imperf.* : Je tenais. — *Pret.* : Je tins (*taing*), tu tins, il tint, nous tînmes, vous tîntes, ils tinrent (*taingr'*). — *Fut.* : Je tiendrai (*tyaing-drēh*).—*Pres. Subj.* : Que je tienne (*tyĕn*), que tu tiennes, qu'il tienne, &c.—*Imperf. Subj.* : Que je tinsse, &c.—*Imperat.* : Tiens, tenons, tenez.

Thus also : *Appartenir*, to belong ; *s'abstenir*, to abstain ; *contenir*, to contain : *détenir*, to detain ; *entretenir* (*āng-tr'-tĕ-nēēr*), to keep up, to entertain ; *maintenir* (*maing-tĕ-nēēr*), to maintain ; *obtenir*, to obtain ; *retenir*, to retain ; *soutenir*, to sustain, to uphold, to support.

44. I am too warm; I must take off my hat.

45. You will take cold if you stand bare-headed (*nu-tête*).

46. I would not do that for all the money (*tout* l'**or**) in the world (**du** *monde*).

47. I must ask your permission to go away; I have several business errands (*courses*) to do.

48. I have just seen in the advertisements (*les affiches*) that there is a house to be sold in St. Martin's Street, inquiries to be made at your place (*s'adresser chez vous*)? Would you do me the favor to tell me what it consists of?

2.

1. Where are you going?

2. I intended to go to you (= I went to you).

3. Where do you come from?

4. I come from my brother's.

5. And I come from church (= from the church).

6. Will you come with me?

7. Where do you want to go?

8. We are going to take a walk.

9. I'll gladly accompany you (= I will it gladly [*bien*]). Where (*par où*) shall we go?

10. Wherever you like (= We shall go where [*par où*] you will like).

44. J'ai trop chaud; il faut que j'ôte mon chapeau.
45. Vous⌒allez vous⌒enrhumer, si vous restez nu-tête.

46. Je ne voudrais pas faire cela pour tout l'or du monde (*du mongd*).
47. Il faut que je vous demande la permission de m'en⌒aller; j'ai plusieurs courses à faire.
48. Je viens de voir dans les⌒affiches (*lay zāf-fëësh*) une maison à vendre rue St. Martin (*mār-taing*), s'adresser chez vous. Voudriez-vous me faire le plaisir de me dire en quoi elle consiste (*cong-sĭst*).

2.

1. Où allez-vous?
2. J'allais chez vous.
3. D'où venez-vous?
4. Je viens de chez mon frère.
5. Et moi, je viens de l'église.
6. Voulez-vous venir avec moi?
7. Où voulez-vous aller?
8. { Nous irons (*noŭ zëë-rong*) nous promener.
   { Nous irons faire un tour.
9. Je le veux bien. *Par* où irons-nous (*ëë-rong noŭ*)?

10. Nous irons *par* où vous voudrez.

11. Let us go to the Park (*au parc*), and let us call for your brother on our way (= in passing [*en passant*]).

12. All right (= As it will please you, *or* As you will).

13. { Is Mr. D. in?
{ Is Mr. D. at home?

14. No, sir, he just went out.

15. Can you tell me where he has gone?

16. I really cannot tell you, sir. I think he went to his sister.'s (= that he has gone to see his sister).

17. Do you know when he will return?

18. No, he did not say anything when he went out (= in going out [*en s'en allant*]).

19. In case (*si*) any one inquires for me, porter, please say (= you will say) that I have gone to the exhibition (*à l'exposition*).

20. I shall not be back *the whole day* (*de la journée*).

21. Did any one call during my absence?

22. Yes, sir, two of your countrymen came to pay you a visit (= wanted to pay you a visit [*vous rendre visite*]).

23. I am curious (*curieux*) to know who can have called (= come) the very day (*le jour même*) of my arrival.

24. Upon my word (*ma foi*), sir, I do not remember any more (*je ne me rappelle plus*); I cannot keep (*retenir*) those English names *in my head*, [*In my head* is not to be translated.]

25. But the (= these) gentlemen said that they would call again to-morrow morning before 12 o'clock.

11. Allons au parc et prenons votre frère en passant (*āng pā-sāng*).

12. { Comme il vous plaira.
    { Comme vous voudrez.

13. { Monsieur D. est-il chez lui ?
    { Monsieur D. est-il à la maison (*may-zong*) ?

14. Non monsieur, il vient de sortir (*sŏr-tēēr*).

15. Pouvez-vous me dire où il est allé ?

16. Je ne saurais vous le dire exactement (*dēēr rĕk-zāg-tĕ-māng*), monsieur. Je crois qu'il est allé voir sa sœur.

17. Savez-vous quand il reviendra ?

18. Non ; il n'a rien dit en s'en allant.

19. Concierge, si l'on vient me demander, vous direz que je suis allé à l'exposition.

20. Je ne rentre pas (*rāng-tr' pāh*) *de la journée.*

21. Est-on venu me demander pendant mon absence ?

22. Oui, monsieur ; deux de vos compatriotes (*kong pā-trēē-ŏt*) voulaient vous rendre visite (*rāng-dr' vēē-zēēt*).

23. Je suis bien curieux (*kü-ryeū*) de savoir qui peut être venu le jour même de mon arrivée (*ār-rēē-vēh*).

24. Ma foi, monsieur, je ne me rappelle plus ; je ne peux pas retenir les noms anglais.

25. Mais ces messieurs ont dit qu'ils repasseraient demain matin avant midi.

26. If these gentlemen should call in (*en*) my absence, you will please request them to write their names and addresses (down).

27. I am going to the country. I shall not come home this night (*or*, I shall not stop at home [*découcherai*] this night).

3.

Idiomatic expressions with aller and venir.

1. How do you do?

2. How are you?

3. How is your health?

4. That will do.

5. That will not do (*or*, That won't do).

6. That's a matter of course (*or*, That is understood, *or*, Of course).

7. That suits me; done!

8. That does not suit me in the least (*or*, at all).

9. This trimming is very becoming to you.

10. This coat does not fit you well.

11. Do you think that this dress fits me well?

12. This trimming is too light; it does not match well.

13. That might do (*or*, That might answer).

14. This key does not fit this lock.

15. How old is he? He is about ten years old.

16. It is very nearly 10 o'clock.

17. Business is very dull nowadays.

26. Si ces messieurs revenaient‿en mon‿absence, vous les prierez d'écrire leurs noms et leurs‿adresses.

27. Je vais à la campagne, je ne rentrerai pas cette nuit (*or*, je découcherai cette nuit).

3.

Idiomatic expressions with aller and venir.

1. Comment‿allez-vous ?

2. { Comment cela va-t-il ?
   { Comment ça va-t-il ?

3. Comment va la santé ?

4. { Cela va.
   { Cela ira (*ēē-rā*).

5. Cela ne va pas.

6. Cela va sans dire.

7. Cela me va, j'en suis.

8. Cela ne me va pas du tout.

9. Cette garniture (*gār-nēē-tür*) vous va très-bien.

10. Cet‿habit ne vous va pas bien.

11. Croyez-vous que cette robe m'aille bien ?

12. Cette garniture est trop claire; ça ne va pas.

13. Cela pourrait‿aller.

14. Cette clef ne va pas à cette serrure (*sĕr-rür*).

15. Quel‿âge a-t-il donc ?   Il va sur ses dix‿ans

16. Il s'en va dix‿heures.

17. Le commerce va bien peu maintenant.

18. Has he brought it about?[1] (*or*, Has he succeeded?)[1]

19. You will never succeed with it (*or*, You will never accomplish it).

20. I doubt if he can bring it about (*or*, if he can accomplish it).

21. I do not think he will accomplish it.

22. I do not think you will succeed with it; the undertaking (*l'enterprise*) is too difficult.

23. *He spent all his money.*[2]

24. Did you read this book?

25. No, sir, it is so tedious (*ennuyeux*) that I have not been able to read it through.

26. He married her at last.

4.

to take them to the Post-Office.

in order to [3]

them

---

1) The pupil must study the following idioms :

. Venir à bout d'un dessein (*dĕ-saing*), or Venir à bout d'une enterprise (*dün näng-tĕr-prēēze*) means to bring about; to accomplish; to succeed.

2) Venir à bout d'une chose, to make an end of a thing; to bring a thing to an issue.

3) Pour is used before an *infinitive* to express an *intention* or *design*, answering to the English *in order to*; whenever therefore the English *to* before an infinitive can be changed into *in order to*,

18. Est-il venu à bout[1] (*bōō*)?

19. Vous n'en viendrez jamais à bout.

20. Je doute (*dōōt*) qu'il en vienne à bout.

21. Je ne crois pas qu'il en vienne à bout.

22. Je ne crois pas que vous en veniez à bout; l'enterprise (*lāng-tĕr-prēēze*) est trop difficile.

23. Il est venu *à bout de son argent*[2] (*sōn nār-jặng*).

24. Avez-vous lu ce livre?

25. Non monsieur, il est si ennuyeux (*āng-nü͡-ēē-yeū*) que je n'ai pu venir à bout de le lire en entier (*ān-nāng tyēh*).

26. Il est venu à bout de l'épouser (*lay-pōō-zēh*).

4.

pour les mettre à la poste.

poŭr   lay   mĕt   rāh lā   pŏst.

pour[3]

les (Acc. pl.)

---

pour must be used in French. *Ex.:* J'ai fait mon possible *pour* payer mes dettes, I have done my utmost *to* pay my debts. — J'ai fait tout ce que j'ai pu *pour* l'en empêcher, I did all I could *to* prevent him from it.—Je suis allé moi-même *pour* ne pas vous déranger, I went myself *in order* not *to* disturb you.

The preposition *pour* is also used before the infinitive after the words *assez*, *trop*, and *suffissant* (and after the verb *suffire*). *Ex.:* Elle est assez riche *pour* acheter cette maison, She is rich enough to buy this house. Il est trop jeune pour y aller, He is too young to go there.

to put, to place, to lay, to set

to the post-office.

———————

1. Will you send for some wine?
2. I will send for some.
3. That is what I am looking for.
4. Did you send for me?
5. Get this book, please.
6. Your sister is quite ill; I must get a physician.

7. What are you looking for so eagerly [= in such a hurry] (*avec tant d'empressement*)?
8. He is looking for difficulties where there are none.
9. You are searching in vain (= *beau*).
10. What are you doing? It is like looking for (*c'est chercher*) a needle in a bundle of hay (*une botte de foin*).
11. Take this letter to the post.
12. Till what hour can letters be put into the box which are to leave by the evening mails (*par les courriers du soir*)?

———————

1) *Mettre* irregularly conjugated; comp. p. 352, No. 1. Observe the following idiomatic expressions: *Mettre à la voile*, to set sail.— *Se mettre à crier, pleurer, rire*, to begin crying, weeping, laughing.— *Voulez-vous vous mettre avec moi*, Will you be on my side (at play)?— *Mettre à part (or de côté)*, to put aside.— *Mettez votre chapeau*, Put your hat on.—*Elle se met avec goût*, She dresses stylishly.— *Mettre à profit* (*fёё*), to profit.

2) *Plaire*, to please.—*Part. pr.*: plaisant (*zăng*).—*Part. p.*: plu.— *Pres.*: Je plais, tu plais, il plaît, nous plaisons, vous plaisez, ils plai-

mettre[1]

à la poste.

---

1. Voulez-vous‿envoyer chercher du vin ?
2. Je veux‿en‿envoyer chercher.
3. C'est ce que je cherche.
4. M'avez-vous‿envoyé chercher?
5. Allez chercher ce livre, s'il vous plait.[2]
6. Votre sœur est bien malade; il faut que j'aille chercher un médecin.
7. Que cherchez-vous avec tant d'empressement (*tăng-dăng-près-sĕ-māng*) ?
8. Il cherche des difficultés où il n'y‿en a pas.
9. Vous‿avez *beau* chercher.
10. Qu'est-ce que vous faites? C'est chercher une aiguille (*ai-ghēē-yĕ*) dans‿une botte de foin (*fŏ-aing*).

11. Allez mettre (*or* Allez jeter) cette lettre à la poste.
12. Jusqu'‿à (*jüs-kāh*) quelle‿heure peut-on jeter à la boite les lettres qui doivent partir par[3] les courriers du soir?

---

sent (*playz*).—*Pret.:* Je plus, tu plus, il plut, nous plûmes, vous plûtes, ils plurent (*plür*).—*Fut. :* Je plairai, tu plairas, il plaira, &c.— *Pres. Subj.:* Que je plaise, que tu plaises, qu'il plaise, &c.—Thus also : *Se complaire*, to delight in ; *déplaire*, to displease. — *S'il vous plaît*, if you please.

3) *By*—with the passive voice—is usually translated by *par ;* but it must be rendered by *de*, when the verb denotes a *sentiment* or an inward act of the mind, as : Il est estimé *de* tout le monde, He is esteemed by everybody.

GRAMMATICAL REMARKS.

Exercises and Words used in Common Conversation.

Of the Indefinite Pronouns.

On *or* l'on, one, they, people.

Tout le monde, everybody.

Chacun (*shāh-keūng*), f. chacune (*shāh-kün*), each, every one.

Aucun (*ōh-keūng*), f. aucune (*ōh-kün*), (*with* ne), none, not one.

Quelqu'un (*kĕl-keūng*), f. quelqu'une (*kĕl-kün*), some one, somebody, anybody.

pl. quelques-uns (*kĕl-kĕ-zeūng*), f. quelques-unes (*kĕl-kĕ-zün*), some.

Personne (*with* ne), nobody.

L'un, e, — l'autre, the one —, the other.

pl. les uns (les unes),— les autres, the one —, the others.

L'un (l'une) et l'autre, both.

L'un (l'une) ou l'autre, either.

Ni l'un (l'une) ni l'autre, neither.

L'un (l'une) l'autre, *Gen.* l'un de l'autre, ⎱ each other;

pl. les uns (les unes), les autres, ⎰ one another.

Un autre, f. une autre, another.

D'autres, *pl.* others, other people.

Autrui (*ŏh-trü̃-ēē*), (*Gen.* d'autruï, *Dat.* à autrui), others, another.

Tel, f. telle, many a (man).

Plusieurs, several.

La plupart, most (with a following **Genitive, as**: La plupart **des** hommes, most men).

Quiconque (*kēē-kong*), whoever.

Tout, f. toute, all, everything.

pl. tous, toutes, all.

Quelque chose, something, anything. ——

Rien (*with* **ne**), nothing.

Le même, la même, the same.

1. **On** and its use has been explained.

2. **Aucun, personne,** and **rien** are always used with *ne*, as: *Personne* n'a parlé, No one spoke. — Il *n*'a *rien* fait, He has done nothing.—Avez-vous toutes les boîtes ? Je *n*'en ai *aucune*, Have you all the boxes? I have none.

a) When, however, these three pronouns *serve to answer a question*—without repeating the verb used in the question—*they cannot take ne,* as: Qui est là ? *Personne,* Who is there ? No one.— Qu'avez-vous ? *Rien,* What is the matter with you ? Nothing.

b) In *interrogative sentences* or in *sentences expressing a doubt* and after words of a negative meaning, as *sans, jamais, nulle part, ni,* &c., *aucun, personne,* and *rien* are used without *ne; aucun* then stands for *any; personne* for *anybody;* and *rien* for *anything.* As: J'ai fait ce long voyage *sans* voir *aucune* de mes connaissances, I made this long journey *without* seeing *any* of my acquaintances. — Il *n'*y a *jamais personne* chez lui, There is *never any one* at his house.

c) These pronouns always require *de before any adjective following them*, as : Il n'y a *rien* de plus beau, There exists nothing more beautiful.

3. **Not one** or **none** are rendered by **aucun ne** or **pas un ne,** as : **Aucun** *de vous* **n'**y était, None of you were there. — *Voyez-vous ces personnes ? Je* **n'**en *aperçois* **aucune** (*or* **pas une**), Do you see these persons ? I see none.

4. *Somebody, some one, anybody,* and *any one* are expressed by **quelqu'un** singular and masculine ; *some,* pl. by **quelques-uns** or **quelques-unes.** Ex. :
Somebody told me so, **quelqu'un** me l'a dit.
Do you know any one here ? Connaissez-vous **quelqu'un** ici ?

5. **La plupart,** *most,* takes the Genitive plural after it. The predicate must also be put in the plural. Ex.:
La plupart **de** ces pommes ne **sont** pas encore mûres. Most of these apples are not yet ripe.

6. *Another* is usually expressed by **un autre,** and the plur. *others* (Nom. and Acc.) by **d'autres** or **les autres.** Ex. : *Un autre* vous servira, Another one will help you. — Donnez-moi *d'autres* raisons, Give me *some other* reasons.

7. *Of* or *from others* is rendered *d'autrui,* and *to others,* *à autrui,* as: *Par soi-même on peut juger* **d'autrui,** From one's own self one can judge *of others.*

8: **L'un et l'autre,** fem. *l'une et l'autre* (pl. *les uns et les autres*, pl. fem. *les unes et les autres*), **both.**—They agree with the noun they refer to, in gender and number. Ex. :

L'un et l'autre *sont* allés au concert, Both have gone to the concert.

When preceded by a preposition we have to repeat the same in French before each of them, as :

Je le ferai **pour** *l'une et* **pour** *l'autre*, I shall do it for both of them (*fem.*)

Ni l'un ni l'autre (fem. *ni l'une ni l'autre*) requires *ne* before the verb, as : *Je* **ne** *le ferai* **ni** *pour* **l'un, ni** *pour* **l'autre,** I shall do it for neither of them (*masc.*)

9. **L'un l'autre** (l'une lautre [fem.]) ; les uns les autres ; les unes les autres (fem.), **one another** or **each other.** *L'un, l'une, les uns, les unes* are always the subjects, *l'autre, les autres* the objects of the sentences. All *active verbs* must in such cases take the reflective pronouns *se, nous, vous,* although **no** reflective pronoun is used in English ; as : *Ces deux soeurs* **s'aiment l'une l'autre,** These two sisters love each other.—*Vous vous nuisez* **l'un à l'autre,** You are hurting one another.—*Elles parlent mal* **l'une de l'autre,** They speak ill of each other (fem.).

N.B.—Observe that the prepositions must be placed between l'un and l'autre.

10. *Tel* has two significations, *such* and *many a* (*man*). In the former it is an adjective and agrees with its noun ; in the latter it is used without a substantive. Ex. : *Telle*

était la difficulté, Such was the difficulty.—*Tel parle de choses qu'il n'entend pas*, Many a man speaks of things which he does not understand.

Note. **Un tel** has also the meaning of so *and* so, as: *Chez Monsieur un tel*, at Mr. So and So's. *Madame une telle*, Mrs. So and So.

11. Notice also the expression: **Il n'y a rien de tel que**.... or **il n'est rien tel que**...., There is nothing like. Ex.:

Il n'y a rien **de tel** *que d'avoir une bonne conscience* (*kong-syāngs*).

There is nothing like having a good conscience.

Words.

Division (f) du temps (dēē-vēē-z'yong dü tāng).	*Division of Time.*
Un siècle (*sēē-ay-kl'*),	A century.
Une année (*ān-nay*),	A year.
l'année passée.	last year.
l'année prochaine (*pro-shayn*),	next year.
Un mois (*m'woāh*),	A month.
Une semaine (*sĕ-mayn*),	A week.
Un jour, une journée,	A day.
Une heure (*ün neūr*),	An hour.
Une demi-heure (*dĕ-mēe eūr*),	Half an hour.

Un quart d'heure (*kăr deūr*),	A quarter of an hour.
Une heure et demie,	An hour and a half.
Une minute (*mēē-nüt*),	A minute.
Une seconde (*sē-gongd*),	A second.
Le matin,	The morning.
La matinée,	The forenoon.
Midi (*mēē-dēē*) (*m.*),	Noon.
L'après-midi, (*m.*)	The afternoon.
Le soir (*s'woār*),	The evening.
La soirée (*s'woā-ray*),	The evening.
La nuit (*nü-ēē*),	Night.
Minuit (*mēē-nü-ēē*) (*m.*),	Midnight.
Aujourd'hui,	To-day.
Hier (*ēē-ayr*),	Yesterday.
Avant-hier (*ā-vāng-tyair*),	The day before yesterday.
Demain,	To-morrow.
Après-demain,	The day after to-morrow.
Le lendemain (*lāng-dĕ-maing*),	The next day, the morrow.
Le commencement (*cŏm-māng-sĕ-māng*).	The beginning.
Le milieu (*mēē-lyeū*),	The middle.
La fin (*faing*),	The end.

Les saisons (*say-zong*) *f. pl.*	*Seasons.*
Le printemps (*praing-tāng*),	Spring.
L'été (*m.*).	Summer.
L'automne (*lō-tŏn*),	Autumn.
L'hiver (*lēē-vayr*) *m.*,	Winter.
La belle saison.	The fine season.
La mauvaise saison,	The bad season.

Exercise.

Omnibus.—Tramway.—Cab.[1]

Do you pass[2] through the 'rue de Richelieu'? Yes,
sir. — Please put me down[3] at the 'Palais-Royal.'—
Fares,[4] please. —Would you be kind enough to hand my
fare[5] to the conductor? Would you be so kind to move[6]
a little?—Take a seat in that corner.—Why do we stop[7]?
— The street seems to be blocked up with carriages.[8] —
Would you be kind enough to give[9] the conductor a
sign[9] to stop?—Let me get out first.[10]— Give me your[11]
hand.—Don't hurry, wait till the 'bus stands quite still.[12]
— Conductor, a connection-ticket[13] for Passy. — This is
too late, sir; you ought to have spoken when you got
in.[14] — Have you a connecting-ticket[15]? Then get out
and enter this office. The omnibus for Passy has not
yet come in, but it will be here in a minute.[16]— I am very
tired; let us take a cab.—Cabman, here[17]!—Stop, please,
and turn round.[18]—Drive us to the 'Bois.'—On time.[19]—
(You will) drive us[20] through the 'Boulevards, la place
de la Concorde and les Champs-Elysées.'—What is your
fare,[21] cabman?—Is the charge for the luggage included[22]?—That is very dear.—Cabman, drive me[23] to the
N...hotel, R..street. — Do you know the hotel?

---

1) fiacre. — 2) est-ce que vous passez? — 3) descendez-moi. —4)
Places.—5) ma place *or* mon argent. —6) reculer.—7) s'arrêter.—8)
It seems (il parait) *that the street is blocked up* (encombrée) *of carriages.*
—9) de faire signe.—10) *le* premier.—11) *la* main.—12) attendez que
la voiture *soit* tout à fait arrêtée.—13) une *correspondance* (need not be
paid for extra).—14) il fallait le dire en montant. — 15) une correspondance. — 16) il ne tardera pas à venir.—17) Cocher, par ici !—
18) tournez. — 19) à l'heure *or* nous vous prenons à l'heure. — 20)
Vous prendrez les Boulevards, &c. — 21) combien vous dois-je? —
22) le prix des bagages est-il compris?—23) conduisez-moi.

COMPANION TO THE
Revised Version of the New Testament.

Explaining the Reasons for the Changes Made on the Authorized Version.

BY ALEXANDER ROBERTS, D.D.,
Member of the English Revision Committee.

WITH SUPPLEMENT BY A MEMBER OF THE AMERICAN COMMITTEE.

Containing a Brief History of the Revision of the Work and Co-operation of the New Testament Companies, of the Points of Agreement and Difference, and an Explanation of the Appendix to the Revised New Testament.

ALSO, A FULL TEXTUAL INDEX,
Being a Key to Passages in which Important Changes have been Made.

This book, having been carefully prepared by Members of both Revision Committees, carries official weight. It shows what changes have been made, and also the reasons which influenced the revisers in making them. It will be difficult to judge of the merits of the revision without the aid of this Companion volume. Our edition is printed by special arrangement with the English publishers. It is well known that, by an arrangement between the two Committees of Revision, the changes suggested by the American Committee, but which were not adopted by the English Revisers, are published as an Appendix to the Revised New Testament. The *Companion* volume is an explanation of *all* the changes adopted by both committees, and of those suggested by the American Committee, but not assented to by the English Committee, in their final revision. The book will be indispensable to a right understanding of the revision. This cheap edition of the combined books, although authorized and copyrighted, will be sold for 25 cents in paper, and 75 cents in cloth—sent postage free.

TESTIMONIALS.

T. W. CHAMBERS, D.D., a Member of the American Committee of Revision, says of this book: "Many persons have expressed a desire that, simultaneously with the issue of the Revised New Testament, there should appear an authentic explanation of the reasons for such changes as will be found in its pages. The work of Dr. Roberts is exactly fitted to meet this desire....Nowhere else in print can be found a statement so full and exact. It gives all needed information, and does it in an unexceptional way."

C. F. DEEMS, D.D., Pastor of the Church of the Strangers, New York, writes: "The Companion to the Revised Version seems to me almost indispensable. Even scholars who were not at the meeting of the Revisers would have a wearisome work in seeking to discover all the changes made, and to ordinary readers very much of the labor would be lost. ....All this is set forth by Dr. Roberts with admirable perspicuity. Those who have any intelligent interest in the Holy Scriptures, will find this little book absorbingly interesting. I shall urge every member of the church of which I am pastor to give it a careful reading, and purpose to introduce it as a text-book in our Bible-classes."

"So valuable, interesting and useful is this publication, that we advise every one who wishes to know the why and wherefore of the revision, to obtain it immediately."—*New York Observer*.

Paper, 8vo size, 25 cents; Cloth, 16mo, 75 cents.

*** For Sale by Booksellers and Newsdealers, or sent postage-paid, on receipt of price, by

I. K. FUNK & CO., Publishers, 10 & 12 Dey St., N. Y.

NOTICE TO SUBSCRIBERS.

A SUPPLEMENT

CONTAINING

1. KEY TO THE EXERCISES.
2. A COMPLETE FRENCH VOCABULARY.
3. COMMERCIAL AND SOCIAL CORRESPONDENCE.
4. ADDITIONAL GRAMMATICAL PECULIARITIES.

&c., &c.

WILL BE PUBLISHED IMMEDIATELY.

PRICE, 75 CENTS.—CLOTH.

SUBSCRIBERS WISHING TO SECURE THE SUPPLEMENT WILL
PLEASE REMIT 75 CENTS TO

I. K. FUNK & CO.,
10 & 12 Dey Street.

THE

𝕸𝖊𝖎𝖘𝖙𝖊𝖗𝖘𝖈𝖍𝖆𝖋𝖙 𝕾𝖞𝖘𝖙𝖊𝖒.

A SIMPLE AND PRACTICAL METHOD,

ENABLING

ANY ONE TO LEARN, WITH SLIGHT EFFORT, TO SPEAK
FLUENTLY AND CORRECTLY

𝕱𝖗𝖊𝖓𝖈𝖍, 𝕲𝖊𝖗𝖒𝖆𝖓, 𝕾𝖕𝖆𝖓𝖎𝖘𝖍, 𝖆𝖓𝖉 𝕴𝖙𝖆𝖑𝖎𝖆𝖓.

BY

DR. RICHARD S. ROSENTHAL,

*Late Director of the " Akademie für fremde Sprachen" in Berlin and Leipzig,
of the "Meisterschaft College" in London, and Principal of the
"Meisterschaft School of Practical Linguistry" in New York.*

FRENCH.

IN FIFTEEN PARTS, EACH CONTAINING THREE LESSONS.

PART XV.

NEW YORK:
I. K. FUNK & CO., PUBLISHERS,
10 AND 12 DEY STREET.

TERMS.

WE have arranged with Dr. ROSENTHAL, the author of the "Meisterschaft System," for its introduction in America under his own supervision, and he has opened

The Meisterschaft School of Practical Linguistry

FOR NON-RESIDENTS.

The student does not need to leave his home. The lessons of each language are prepared by the Professor, and printed and sent in pamphlet shape to each member of the School wherever he may reside.

The course of study for each language—German, French, Italian, or Spanish—makes fifteen pamphlets of three lessons each.

All members of the School have

THE PRIVILEGE

of asking, by letter, questions concerning each lesson, or consulting on any difficulty which may have occurred to them. All exercises corrected and all questions answered by return post by Dr. ROSENTHAL or one of his assistants.

TERMS OF MEMBERSHIP.

Five Dollars is the price for membership in the school for each language. This amount ($5.) entitles the member to receive the fifteen books or pamphlets containing the lessons, also answers to his questions. Return postage for the answer must accompany the question.

State distinctly which language, or languages, you desire to study There are *no extra charges.* The price, **Five Dollars,** pays for one language; **Ten Dollars** for two languages, etc. All exercise. and questions must be written on a separate sheet of paper, and must state full address of the pupil.

Remittances must be made in Post-Office Order or registered letter addressed to

I. K. FUNK & CO.,

10 and 12 Dey Street, New York.

The Meisterschaft-System.

FRENCH.

PART XV.

XV.

(*Continuation.*)

13. I want to have (*faire charger*) this letter registered.

14. They are received at the office till four o'clock only.

15. What! my last letter has not been received? Did you forget (*auriez-vous oublié*) to post it, John?

16. Oh no, sir; I have put it into the box myself.

17. And I wrote the address correctly; it is impossible that it should have been miscarried.

18. I shall go and inquire (*je vais aller*) at once at the *office of information* (*bureau des réclamations*).

19. I have sent a letter to Marseilles, and it did not reach (*elle n'est point parvenue*) its destination (*adresse*).

---

1) The French verb *faire* is used for *to do, to make*, and *to get* or *to cause*, and *to have* ; it must always be followed in French by the *infinitive* (*active*) without a preposition, as :

Où voulez-vous le faire faire ? Where will you have it done?

Observe the following idioms :

faire savoir à quelqu'un, to let one know ; to send word.
il fait chaud, it is warm.
il fait froid, it is cold.
faire un tour de promenade, to take a walk.
ne faire que, to do nothing but.
vous feriez mieux de ne pas le faire, you had better not do so.

faire faire, to get made; to order.
se faire des amis, to get friends.
faire semblant de (*säng-bläng*), to pretend.
faire voile, to set sail.
faire de son mieux, to do one's best.
c'en est fait de moi, I am undone ; it is over with me.

XV.

(*Continuation.*)

13. Je voudrais faire[1] charger (*or* faire recommander (*rĕ-com-māng-dēh*) ceïte lettre.

14. On ne les reçoit[2] au bureau que jusqu'_à quatre‿heures.

15. Comment? on[3] n'a pas reçu ma dernière lettre? Jean (*jāng*), auriez-vous‿oublié de la mettre_à la boite?

16. Oh, que non, monsieur; je l'ai jetée moi-même à la boite.

17. J'avais cependant (*sĕ-pāng-dāng*) bien mis (*mēē*) l'adresse; il est_impossible qu'elle se *soit_égarée*.

18. *Je vais‿aller* tout de suite au bureau des réclamations (*rēh-klāh-mā-syong*).

19. J'ai envoyé une lettre à Marseilles, et elle n'est point[4] (*po‿aing*) parvenue à son‿adresse.

---

2) Compare page 372, Note 3.

3) The word *on* (derived from *homme*, *man*) serves to render all *general and vague reports* expressed in English by *they say*, *it is reported*, *people say*, &c. = **on dit.** The verb following *on* must always be in the third person singular. *Ex.:* *On* croit, People think.—*On* ne peut pas faire tout, One cannot do everything.

· When—which is frequently the case—*the passive voice* is used in *English*, the verb must be changed *in French into the active voice* with *on*, as :

It is said, on dit.	On me trompe, I am deceived.
I was told, on m'a dit.	On n'a pas reçu mes lettres, My letters were not received.

4) The negative *not* is expressed by *ne—pas*, or *ne—point*.

20. I am surprised at that.[1] — When did you send off your letter?

21. A week ago to-day.

22. How do you know it did not arrive?

23. By a letter I have just received.

24. We are just going to sit down to dinner.

25. Waiter, lay another cover, opposite to the other one.

26. Place the soupe-tureen in front of me and hand me the ladle.

Idiomatic expressions with faire.

1. I am having that engine repaired (*réparer*).

2. Have this coat repaired (*raccommoder*).

3. I am having a silk dress made at this dressmaker's.

---

1) Observe the difference between the French and the English idiom.

2) The following prepositions govern the Genitive:

à côté de, by, beside.
à cause de, on account of.
au travers de, through.
au milieu de (*ôh mēēl-yeŭ dĕ*), in the middle of.
au lieu de, instead of.
près de, } by, next to.
auprès de, } near, close to.
au-devant de, before.
au-dessus de, above, upon.
au-dessous de, below, under.
loin de, far from.
au moyen de (*ôh m'woā-yaing dĕ*), by means of.

en deçà de, on this side of.
au haut de, on the top of.
du haut de, from above.
hors de out of.
au dehors de, outside, without.
autour de, around, about.
par delà de, } on that side.
au delà de, } on that side.
vis-à-vis de, } opposite (to).
en face de, } opposite (to).
lelong de, along.
à l'égard de, with regard to.
faute de, for want of.
en vertu de, in consequence of.

3) The following *simple* prepositions govern the objective case:

à (before *le* = **au**; before *les* = **aux**), at, in, to.

avant (denoting time), before.
envers, to, towards.

20. Cela m'étonne.[1] Quand avez-vous fait partir votre lettre ?
21. Il y a aujourd'hui huit jours.
22. Comment savez-vous qu'elle n'est pas arrivée ?
23. Par une lettre que je viens de recevoir.
24. Nous allons nous mettre à la table.
25. Garçon, mettez encore un couvert (sur cette table), vis-à-vis de[2] l'autre.
26. Mettez la soupière devant[3] moi, et passez-moi la cuiller à soupe.

Idiomatic expressions with faire.

1. *Je fais réparer* cette machine (*mā-shēēn*).
2. *Faites raccommoder* cet habit.
3. *Je fais faire* une robe de soie (*s'woāh*) chez cette couturière (*kōō-tür-yair*).

---

avec, with.	*hors*, ⎱ except, besides.
chez, at, at the house of.	*hormis*, ⎰ save.
contre, against.	*outre*, besides.
dans, in, into.	*malgré*, in spite of.
de (before *le* = **du**; before *les* = **des**), of, from.	*moyennant* (*m'woā yĕn-nāng*), by means of.
depuis, since.	*par*, through, by.
derrière, behind.	*parmi* (*pār-mēē*), among.
dès, from.	*pour*, for.
devant (denoting place), before.	*sans*, without, but for.
pendant (*pāng-dāng*), ⎱ during.	*sous*, under.
durant, ⎰	*selon* (*sĕ-lōng*), ⎱ according
en, in, within, into, to.	*suivant* (*süēē-vāng*), ⎰ to.
entre (*āng-tr'*), between.	*sur*, on, upon.
après (denoting time), after.	*vers*, towards.

Devant is a *local* preposition, as : Nous étions *devant* la maison, We were *before* (*in front of*) the house.—**Avant**, on the other hand, denotes *priority of time* and *order*, as : Je suis arrivé *avant* vous, I arrived before you.

4. Have some fresh coffee made.

5. I had some beef-tea made for you.

6. I am having a silk dress made by the same tailor who made yours.

7. They are having some boots made at the French shoemaker's.

8. I shall let him know.

9. You kept my clerk waiting (= You have made my clerk wait).

10. Let him know that I shall call again to-morrow morning.

11. *Will you communicate* [1] that to your agent?

12. Why have you not informed them of the news?

13. He is a cringing fellow. (He cringes.)

14. I shall never lower myself (*je ne m'abaisserai jamais*) to toadying (*à faire des courbettes* = cringing to a person).

15. You have made (*or* committed) a great blunder (*un pas de clerc*).

16. By coming here he has committed a blunder.

17. You have made *a great deal of fuss* (*des embarras*).

18. This boy makes a great deal of fuss.

19. You pretend (*or* you make believe [*vous faites semblant*]) that you are pleased with it.

20. He pretends to be ill.

21. He pretended to be ignorant of it (= not to know anything about it).

22. I am going now *to pack my trunk* (*faire ma malle*).

---

1) **Faire part de quelque chose à quelqu'un means to commu-**

4. *Faites faire* du café frais.

5. *J'ai fait faire* du bouillon (*bŏō-yong*) pour vous.

6. *Je me fais faire* une robe de soie par le même tailleur qui a fait la vôtre.

7. *Elles se font faire* des bottines chez le cordonnier français.

8. *Je le lui ferai* savoir.

9. *Vous⁀avez fait⁀*attendre mon⁀employé.

10. *Faites-lui* savoir que je reviendrai demain matin.

11. *Ferez-vous part de cela* [1] à᾽votre⁀agent.

12. Pourquoi *ne leur avez-vous pas fait part* des nouvelles?

13. Il fait des courbettes.

14. Je ne m'abaisserai jamais *à faire des courbettes*.

15. *Vous⁀avez fait⁀un pas de clerc*. (But rarely used.)

16. Il a *fait⁀un pas de clerc* en venant ici.

17. Vous⁀avez *fait des embarras* (*day-zāng-bār-rāh*).

18. Ce⁀garçon *fait bien des⁀embarras*.

19. *Vous faites semblant* (*sāng-blāng*) que cela vous plait.

20. *Il fait semblant* d'être malade.

21. *Il faisait semblant* de n'en rien savoir.

22. Je vais *faire ma malle* à présent.

---

nicate **something to a person**; to inform him of a thing; to impart or to convey knowledge.

23. I must pack my trunk at once.

24. Why have you not *put my room in order* (*fait ma chambre*) ?

25. How many times must you be told to put my room in order (*or* to clean my room)?

26. He tells stories (*des contes*).

27. You told us a story.

28. You are telling me a story.

29. He plays the lord (*le grand seigneur*) in Paris.

30. This man is very shrewd (*rusé*) ; he acts the saint (= the good apostle [*apôtre*]).

31. He got himself into a scrape (*or* into a difficulty).

32. He got himself into a scrape when he was in Saratoga.

Idiomatic expressions with mettre.

1. I have placed him among my friends (*or* among the number of my friends [*au rang de mes amis*]).

2. I know him well. . He has placed me since a long time (*depuis longtemps*) among the number of his friends.

3. They turned him (*on l'a mis*) out of doors.

4. Mr. B. is a man who knows how to take advantage (*mettre à profit*) of everything (*or* who knows how to make the best of everything).

5. I shall endeavor to turn (*mettre*) my German to advantage (*à profit*).

6. I defy you (*je vous mets au défi*) to prove it.

7. He defied me.

23. *Il faut faire ma malle* tout de suite.
24. Pourquoi n'avez-vous pas *fait ma chambre ?*

25. Combien de fois faut-il vous dire de *faire ma chambre ?*
26. *Il fait des contes* (*kongt*).
27. C'est͡un conte que vous nous͡avez *fait.*
28. C'est͡un conte que vous me *faites là.*
29. *Il fait le grand seigneur* (*lĕ grāng sĕn-yeŭr*) à Paris.
30. Cet͡homme est bien rusé ; *il fait le bon͜apôtre.*

31. Il s'est *fait des͜affaires.*
32. Il s'est *fait des͜affaires* quand͡elle͡était͜à Saratoga.

Idiomatic expressions with mettre.

1. Je.l'ai *mis* (*mēē*) *au rang* de mes͡amis.

2. Je le connais bien. Depuis longtemps (*long-tāng*) il m'a *mis* au rang de ses͡amis.
3. On l'a *mis* à la porte.
4. Monsieur B. est͡un͡homme qui sait *mettre* tout͡à *profit* (*prō-fēē*).

5. Je tâcherai de *mettre* mon͡allemand *à profit.*

6. Je vous *mets* (*may*) au défi (*day-fēē*) de le prouver.
7. Il m'a *mis͜au* défi.

8. She made me acquainted with it.   (She imparted the knowledge of this fact to me.)
9. Your imprudence has long since acquainted him with it.
10. He will easily familiarize himself with (*or* see through) that matter.
11. He begins to (*Il se met à*) work at half past five.

12. Don't begin to work, tired as you are.

13. Set about it immediately, pray.
14. They began to laugh.
15. He goes through fire and water (*il se met en quatre*) for his friends.
16. She would do anything for her friends.
17. The poor girl is indefatigable in his behalf.

Idiomatic expressions with prendre.

1. Do not take it amiss.   (Don't be offended at it.)
2. Don't be offended at what I am telling you.
3. Instead of taking the affair as a joke (*en riant*), he was offended at it.
4. You must not always take his compliments literally (*au pied de la lettre*).
5. He is simpleton enough (*assez simple*) to take all these compliments literally.
6. She takes all this *for gospel* (*au pied de la lettre*).

8. Elle m'a *mis au fait de cela.*

9. Votre imprudence (*aing-prü-dāngs*) l'a *mis* depuis longtemps au fait de cela.

10. Il se *mettra* aisément (*ay-zay-mǎng*) au fait de cette affaire.

11. Il se *met à* travailler (*trā-vāh-yēh*) à cinq heures et demie.

12. *Ne mettez-vous pas à* travailler, fatigué comme vous êtes.

13. *Mettez-vous-y* tout de suite, je vous prie.

14. Elles se *mirent à* rire (*mēēr tāh rēēr*).

15. *Il se met en quatre* pour ses amis.

16. *Elle se mettrait en* quatre pour ses amis.

17. La pauvre fille *se met en quatre* pour lui.

Idiomatic expressions with prendre.

1. Ne le *prenez* pas en mauvaise part.

2. Ne *prenez* pas ce que je vous dis en mauvaise part.

3. Au lieu (*lyeǔ*) de *prendre* la chose en riant (*rēē-ǎng*), il la *prit* en mauvaise part.

4. Il ne faut pas toujours *prendre* ses compliments (*kong-plēē-mǎng*) *au pied de la lettre.*

5. Il est assez simple (*saing-pl*) pour *prendre* tous ces compliments *au pied de la lettre.*

6. Elle *prend* (*prǎng*) tout cela *au pied de la lettre.*

7. We have appointed a day (*nous avons pris jour*) to settle this affair.

8. He has appointed a day to meet you. .

9. You have no right to examine (*prendre connaissance de*) his conduct.

10. She would look into that affair.

11. How do you manage (*vous y prenez-vous*) to prepare your lessons without a dictionary ?

12. You do not set about it rightly.

13. They manage very well indeed.

14. They managed very badly.

15. How did you manage it ?

16. This is the way he managed.

17. They managed it somehow.

To Speak, to Chat; to be Silent.

1. Speak (*or* talk) to me ; speak to him (*or* to her)

2. Speak loud ; speak low (softly).

3 To whom are you talking ?

4. Of what are you talking ?

5. Are you talking to me ?

6. Why did you not speak before (sooner) ?

7. Don't talk to me of it.

8. I do not want to know anything about it.

9. Talk sensibly.

10. The matter speaks for itself.

11. Let us have a chat.

12. You do nothing but talk all day long.

7. *Nous avons pris jour* pour régler cette affaire.

8. *Il a pris jour* pour vous rencontrer.

9. Ce n'est pas à vous à *prendre connaissance de* ses actions.

10. Elle a voulu *prendre connaissance de* cette affaire.

11. Comment *vous y prenez-vous* pour préparer vos leçons sans dictionnaire?

12. *Vous ne vous y prenez pas* bien.

13. *Ils s'y prennent* comme il faut.

14. *Ils s'y prirent* très mal.

15. Comment *vous y êtes-vous pris ?*

16. Voici comme *il s'y prit.*

17. Ils s'y sont pris on ne sait comment.

Parler, Causer ; se Taire.

1. Parlez-moi ; parlez-lui.

2. Parlez haut ; parlez bas.

3. A qui parlez-vous ?

4. De quoi parlez-vous ?

5. Est-ce à moi que vous parlez ?

6. Pourquoi ne parliez-vous pas plus tôt ?

7. Ne m'en parlez pas.

8. Je ne veux pas en entendre parler.

9. Parlez raison.

10. La chose parle d'elle-même.

11. Causons un peu.

12. Vous ne faites que causer (*or* jaser) toute la journée.

13. Be silent!
14. Hush! Silence!

To Know, to Say.

1. Do you know anything new? (*or*, What is the news?)
2. I do not know of anything new.
3. What? you do not know what the whole town is talking of?
4. I have not heard anything.
5. You pretend (*vous faites semblant*) not to know it.
6. If I knew anything about it I would tell you.
7. This is a false report; otherwise (*sans quoi*) you ought to know it.
8. Who says so? Every one says so.
9. May I inquire (*savoir*) who told you?
10. A person worthy of confidence. I have it from Mr. N.

To Know; to Forget: to Remember.

1. Do you know me?
2. I have not the honor of knowing you.
3. What, don't you recognize me?
4. I cannot recall you. I cannot remember your name.

---

1) *Tair*, to conceal.—*Part. pres.* : taisant.—*Part. p.* : tû.—*Pres.* : Je tais, tu tais, il tait, nous taisons, vous taisez, ils taisent (*tai:*)—*Pret.* : Je tus, tu tus, il tut, nous tûmes, vous tûtes, ils turent (*tür*). — *Fut.* : Je tairai. — *Pres. Subj.* : Que je taise, que tu taises, qu'il

13. Taisez-vous![1]

15. Chut (*shüt*) ! Silence (*sēē-lăngs*) !

Savoir ; Dire.

1. Savez-vous quelque chose de nouveau (*or* Qu'y a-t-il de nouveau) ?
2. Je ne sais rien de nouveau.
3. Comment ? vous ne savez pas ce que l'on dit dans toute la ville ?
4. Je n'ai rien entendu dire.
5. Vous faites semblant (*săng-blăng*) de ne pas le savoir.
6. Si j'en savais quelque chose, je vous le dirais.
7. C'est donc un faux bruit, *sans quoi* vous devriez le savoir.
8. Qui le dit ? Tout le monde le dit.
9. Puis-je *savoir* qui vous l'a dit ?
10. Une personne digne (*dēēn-yĕ*) de foi. *Je* le **tiens** de monsieur N.

Connaitre ; Oublier ; se Souvenir.

1. Me connaissez-vous ?
2. Je n'ai pas l'honneur de vous connaître.
3. Comment, vous ne me reconnaissez pas ?
4. Je ne puis vous *remettre*. Votre nom ne me *revient* pas.

---

taise, etc. — Thus : *Se taire*, to be silent. — *Pres.* : Je me tais, I am silent. — *Pret.* Je me tus, I was silent. — *Perf.:* Je me suis tû, I have been silent. — *Imperat.:* Tais-toi ; taisez-vous, be silent.

5. I do not remember having had the honor of meeting you.

6. I beg your pardon; I remember having had the pleasure of seeing you last winter at a ball given by Mrs. B.

7. Do you remember it?

8. I remember it very well.

9. So do I; I shall never forget (=always remember) it.

10. I have not forgotten what you said to me at that time (*alors*).

11. I cannot recall it; I have a bad memory (*la mémoire ingrate*).

12. May I ask you to remind me of it?

FOUNDATION SENTENCE.

If the weather is just as cold to-morrow

morning as it is to-night, make a fire in my son's

room as I am afraid he is ill.

5. Je ne me rappelle pas‿avoir‿eu cet‿honneur.

6. Pardonnez-moi, je me souviens d'avoir eu le plaisir de vous voir l'hiver dernier au bal de Mme. B.

7. Vous‿en *souvient-il ?*
8. Je m'en souviens très-bien.
9 *Moi aussi,* je m'en souviendrai toujours.
10. Je n'ai pas‿oublié ce que vous me dites alors.

11. Je ne puis me le rappeler ; j'ai *la mémoire ingrate.*

12. Oserais-je vous prier de m'en faire resouvenir ?

FOUNDATION SENTENCE.

S'il fait demain matin aussi froid que ce soir,
seel   fay   dĕ-maing mā-taing ŏs-seē fro-āh   kĕ   sĕ swoāre,

faites du feu dans la chambre de mon fils parce
fait   dü   feū   dāng   lā   shāng-br' dĕ mong feēs pār-sĕ

que je crains qu'il ne soit malade.
kĕ jĕ kraing   keēl   nĕ swoāh mā-lad.

1.

If the weather is just as cold to-morrow morning as it is to-night.

___

If ; whether

it makes

if it makes

to-morrow

morning

to-morrow morning

also; too; likewise; as

cold

as

to-night; this evening.

___

1) *Si* belongs to the so-called *simple conjunctions.* Conjunctions are used to connect either words or sentences. They are either *simple* or *compound ;* the *simple* consist of *one* word for each clause, the *compound* are formed of two separate words.

Simple Conjunctions.

Et, and.	*car*, for.
et—et, both—and.	*mais*, but.
aussi, also, too.	*toutefois,* ⎱ however.
tantôt—tantôt, sometimes—some-	*cependant,* ⎰
times.	*pourtant,* yet, still.
ou, or,	*autrement,* ⎱ otherwise, else,
ou—ou, either—or.	*sans cela,* ⎰
plus—plus, the more—the more.	*néanmoins*, nevertheless.
plus—moins, the more—the less.	*d'ailleurs*, besides, moreover.
moins—moins, the less—the less.	*si*, if, whether.
autant—autant, as much as.	*sinon*, if not

1.

Ṡ'il fait demain matin aussi froid que ce soir.

sẹēl   fay   dĕ-maing   mã̈-taing   ŏs-sēē   fro-ãh   kĕ   sĕ   swoãre.

Si [1]

il fait [2]

s'il fait

demain

matin (m.)

demain matin

aussı [3]

froid

que [2]

ce soir.

---

soit—soit, be it—or.	*quand,* when?
ni—ni, neither—nor.	*où,* where?
comme, as.	*d'où,* whence?
comment, how?	*puisque,* since, as.
donc, consequently; then.	*lorsque,* when, as.
ainsi, thus, so.	*quoique* (with the Subj.), though.
puis ; alors, then.	*pourquoi,* why?
que, that.	*pour,* in order to.
que, than (after a comparative).	

2) *il fait, il faisait,* etc., is used in speaking of the weather ; as, *il fait beau,* it is beautiful weather.

3) *aussi—que* (just) as—as, is used in *comparisons,* as : Il est *aussi* heureux *que* son frère. He is just as happy as his brother. — In *negative* comparisons *aussi — que,* or *si — que* may be used : Nous ne sommes pas *si* riches (*or* aussi riches) *que* vous, We are not as rich as you.

1. What kind of weather is it?—It is fine weather (It is fine).
2. It is bad weather.
3. It is very fine weather.—The weather is splendid.

4. The weather is very bad (*or* awful; abominable).

5. The weather is nice (agreeable).
6. The weather is not pleasant. (The weather is disagreeable).
7. It is clear.
8. The sky (*le temps*) is cloudy (overcast).

9. { It is gloomy.
   It is dry.
   It is damp.

10. The weather is certain.
11. The weather is uncertain (*or* changeable).

12. It is pleasant (*or* mild).—It is stormy.
13. Will it be fine to-day? (Are we going to have fine weather to-day?)

14. It looks as if we were going to have fine weather.

15. It looks as if we were going to have bad weather.
16. The weather is growing (*or* turning) bad.
17. It is growing fine.
18. It does not look as if we were going to have fine weather.

---

1) *Couvrir*, to cover.—*Part. pr.*: couvrant.—*Part. p.*: couvert.—
See *ouvrir*.

1. Quel temps (*tāng*) fait-il ? — Il fait beau temps (*or*, Il fait beau).
2. Il fait mauvais temps (*or*, Il fait mauvais).
3. Il fait⌣un temps magnifique (superbe; splendide; delicieux).
4. { Il fait⌣un vilain temps (*vēē-laing-tāng*).
{ Il fait⌣abominable (*nāhbl'*).
5. Il fait bon (agréable).
6. Il ne fait pas bon (*or*, Il fait désagréable).

7. Il fait⌣un temps clair(serein [*sĕ-raing*]).
8. Le temps est couvert (*koō-vayr*).[1]
9. { Il fait sombre (*sōngbr'*).
{ Il fait sec.
{ Il fait⌣humide (*tümēēd*).
10. Le temps est constant (*kon-stāng*).
11. Le temps est variable (*or* inconstant [*vāh-ryābl'*, *aing-kong-stāng*]).
12. Il fait doux (*dōō*).—Il fait⌣orageux.
13. { Le temps se mettra-t-il au beau aujourd'hui ?
{ Fera-t-il beau aujourd'hui ?
14. { Le temps a l'air de vouloir se mettre⌣au beau.
{ On *dirait*[2] que le temps va se mettre⌣au beau.
15. { Il y a apparence (*ă-pā-rāngs*) de mauvais temps.
{ On *dirait* qu'il va faire mauvais.
16. Le temps se dérange (*or* se gâte [*gāht*]).
17. Le temps se remet⌣au beau.
18. Le temps n'a pas l'air de vouloir se mettre⌣au beau.

---

2) On *dirait*, one would think ; *on ne le dirait pas*, one would not believe it.

19. It is beginning to grow fine again.

20. The weather is clearing up.

21. That's a sign of fair weather.

22. What beautiful weather we are having nowadays.

23. What weather! [These expressions may be used in regard to good or bad weather.]

24. You want to go out in such weather (*or* in this weather)?

25. The barometer points to fair; to rain; to change.

26. The barometer has risen (has fallen).

27. The sky is overcast; we are certainly going to have rain (*de l'eau*).

28. So much the worse, for (*car*) I have to make some calls (*or* to pay some visits).

29. You can put them off (*remettre*) till to-morrow.

30. But to-morrow we have to go (*nous devons aller*) to the country with Mr. Godet. Don't you remember that he promised to fetch us provided the weather were fine?

31. Do you think it is going to rain to-day?

32. Yes, it is raining already. [Observe the French mode of expressing these phrases.)

33. It rains (*or*, It is raining).

34. It has been raining.

35. It will rain.

---

1) *commencer*, to begin, is generally followed by *à*, as : On a commencé *à* jouer, They have begun to play.—But if a certain time is stated, it is followed by *de*, so as to avoid the repetition of *à*, as : Il commença *de* parler *à cinq heures*, He began to talk at 5 o'clock.

2) *Tant*, so much, so many.—*tant que*, as long as.—*tant mieux*, so much the better.—*tant pis*, so much the worse.

3) After the verbs of *thinking, believing, saying*, etc., *the Indicative* follows, when the verbs are used *affirmatively;* but the *Subjunctive* must follow, when they are used *negatively, interrogatively,* or *condi-*

19. Il recommence[1] à faire beau.

20. Le temps s'éclaircit.

21. C'est signe (*sēēn-yĕ*) de beau temps.

22. Quel beau temps nous‿avons‿aujourd'hui.

23. { Quel temps !
     { Voilà un temps !

24. Vous voulez sortir *par* ce temps (*or* par un temps pareil [*pă-rĕ-yĕ*], *or* par le temps qu'il fait) ?

25. Le baromètre est‿au beau ; à la pluie ; au variable

26. Le baromètre est monté ; (tombé).

27. Le temps est couvert ; nous‿allons sûrement (*sü-rĕ-māng*) encore avoir de l'eau.

28. Tant pis[2] (*pēē*) ; car j'ai des visites à faire.

29. Vous pouvez les remettre‿à demain.

30. Mais demain, nous devons‿aller à la campagne avec monsieur Godet. Vous rappelez-vous qu'il a promis de venir nous chercher, s'il faisait beau ?

31. Croyez-vous que nous ayons[3] de l'eau aujourd'hui ?

32. Oui monsieur, il en tombe déjà.

33. Il pleut (*or*, Il tombe de l'eau).

34. Il a plu (*or*, Il est tombé de l'eau).

35. Il pleuvra (*or*, Il tombera de l'eau).

---

tionally, i.e., when they are preceded by the conjunction *si*. If I say, for instance : *Je crois* que son employé *est parti*, I represent the departure as *a fact*, I believe *he has* left. But in the sentence : **Je ne crois pas** que son employé **soit** parti, I speak of his departure as *something uncertain*, as something which *may* have happened, consequently the *Subjunctive* must be used. — *Pensez-vous qu'il* **puisse** *faire* tout cela ? Do you think he can do all that ? Sortons, *si vous pensez* qu'il **fasse** beau temps, Let us go out, if you think it will be fine weather.

36. It is going to rain.

37. It is raining very fast.

38. It is raining faster and faster (*de plus belle*).

39. It rains as fast as it can pour (*à verse*); let us get under cover (*à couvert*).

40. It looks like rain.

41. Do you think it is going to rain?

42. It does not rain so heavily (*a diminué*).—It has left off raining.

43. The rain has settled the dust.—All nature has been refreshed by the rain.

44. I am afraid I shall get wet (*mouillé*).

45. I am wet through and through. —I am wet through to the skin. (*Literally:* to the bones [*jusqu'aux os*]).

46. My clothing (*or* my dress [ladies']) is soaked through and through.

---

1) *Craindre*, to fear.—*Part. pr.* : craignant (*krĕn-yāng*). — *Part. p.*: craint (*kraing*).—*Pres.* : Je crains (*kraing*), tu crains, il craint, nous craignons (*krĕn-yong*), vous craignez, etc.—*Pret.* : Je craignis (*krĕn-yĕĕ*). — *Fut* : Je craindrai (*kraing-drai*). —Thus also : *Plaindre*, to pity ; *se plaindre*, to complain ; *contraindre*, to compel, to constrain.

2) After verbs of *permitting, allowing, promising, fearing, rejoicing*, etc., *the Infinitive* with *de* must follow, if 1) the *main sentence* and the *dependent clause* have *one and the same subject*, or if 2) the subject of the dependent clause is a *pronoun* which has been mentioned already in the main sentence, as : *I* am afraid *I* shall get wet, Je crains d'être mouillé.—Tell *him he* should write to my father, Dites-lui d'écrire à mon père.

I add a full list of these verbs :

Accuser, to accuse.	*conjurer*, to entreat.
achever, to finish.	*continuer*, to continue.
avertir, to inform.	*conseiller*, to advise.
s'aviser, to determine.	*craindre*, to fear.
blâmer, to blame.	*défendre*, to forbid.
charger, to commission.	*dépêcher (se)*, to hasten.
cesser, to cease.	*détourner*, to deter.
commander, to command.	*différer*, to differ.

36. Il va pleuvoir (*or*, Il va tomber de l'eau).

37. Il pleut bien fort.

38. La pluie tombe *de plus belle*.

39. Il pleut‿à verse ; mettons-nous‿à couvert.

40. Le temps *est‿à la pluie*.

41. Croyez-vous qu'il pleuve (*or* que nous‿ayons de l'eau)?

42. La pluie a diminué (La pluie a cessé).

43. La pluie a abattu la poussière.—La pluie a rafraîchi (*shēē*) toute la nature (*nā-tür*).

44. Je crains[1] d'être[2] mouillé (*mŏŏ-yēh*).

45. Je suis tout mouillé. — Je suis trempé jusqu'aux‿os (*jüs-kō-zō*).

46. Mes vêtements (*vay-tĕ-māng*) sont tout mouillés.

---

dire, to tell.	*persuader*, to persuade.
dispenser, to excuse.	*plaindre*, to pity.
désespérer, to lose hope.	*plaindre* (*se*), to complain.
dissuader, to dissuade.	*prescrire*, to prescribe.
écrire, to write.	*presser*, to urge.
empêcher, to hinder.	*prier*, to pray, to ask.
s'empresser, to hasten.	*promettre*, to promise.
entreprendre, to undertake.	*proposer*, to propose.
essayer, to try.	*recommander*, to recommend.
éviter, to avoid.	*refuser*, to refuse.
feindre, to feign.	*regretter*, to regret.
féliciter, to congratulate	*réjouir* (*se*), to rejoice.
hâter (*se*), to hasten.	*remercier*, to thank.
jurer, to swear.	*se repentir*, to repent.
menacer, to threaten.	*reprocher*, to reproach.
mériter, to deserve.	*résoudre*, to resolve.
négliger, to neglect.	*risquer*, to run risk.
nier, to deny.	*sommer*, to summon.
offrir, to offer.	*soupçonner*, to suspect.
omettre, to omit.	*supplier*, to beg, request.
ordonner, to order.	*tâcher*, to endeavor.
oublier, to forget.	*trembler*, to tremble.
permettre, to permit.	*vanter* (*se*), to boast.

47. My hat is in a terrible condition (in an awful state).

48. What an object you look!

49. I was surprised (*or* overtaken) by a sudden rainstorm (*une averse*).

50. And you had neither an umbrella nor an overcoat?

51. The sky looked so fine when I went out that I did not take any precaution.

52. Yes, but the weather was sultry (*lourd*) and the heat stifling (*la chaleur accablante*), and there were those little clouds on the horizon which foretell a storm.

53. I fancied they would blow off.

54. You counted without your host. [French proverb.]

55. I am afraid it is going to rain.

56. It looks like a thunderstorm.

57. How hot it is to-day! It has not been so warm all summer.

58. I am afraid we are going to have a thunderstorm; it is going to rain at once.

59. That is nothing. That will soon pass over.

60. The weather is clearing up. The sun is shining again. It is going to be fine.

61. The sun is shining.

---

1) *ni—ni* (*née*) must always be accompanied by ne.

2) The *present participle* with *en* denotes *a*) either a means, or *b*) a *simultaneous action*, i.e., an action during the transaction of which another one is acted by the same subject; it is always invariable, and corresponds to the English present Participle preceded by the prepositions *by, in, on,* or *while;* or it is sometimes rendered by the simple Participle without preposition. Ex.:

Il riait *en* me *regardant,* He was laughing while he looked at me. —On se forme l'esprit *en lisant* de bons livres, We form our minds by reading good books.

3) The verbs *avoir peur, craindre,* and *trembler* require the particle ne before the verb in the Subjunctive Mood, but only when these verbs themselves are *affirmative* or *negative-interrogative.* Ex.:

47. Mon chapeau est bien arrangé (*ār-rāng-jay*).

48. Comme vous voilà fait !

49. J'ai été surpris par une averse.

50. Vous n'aviez donc ni [1] parapluie ni paletot ?

51. Le ciel (*syĕl*) était si beau que je n'avais pris aucune précaution (*prēh-kō-syong*) en partant.[2]

52. Oui, mais le temps était lourd, la chaleur accablante, et il y avait au ciel de ces petits nuages (*nü-āhje*) qui annoncent l'orage (*ăn-nōngs lō-rāhje*).

53. Je croyais qu'ils se dissiperaient.

54. Vous avez compté (*kong-tēh*) sans votre hôte.

55. Je crains qu'il ne pleuve.[3]

56. Le temps est à l'orage.

57. Qu'il fait chaud aujourd'hui ! Il n'a pas encore fait si chaud *de l'été*.[4]

58. Je crains que nous n'ayons de l'orage ; il va pleuvoir tout-à-l'heure.

59. Ce n'est rien. Ça va être bientôt passé.

60. Le temps s'éclaircit. Voilà le soleil qui parait.[5] Il va faire beau.

61. Il fait du soleil (*sō-lĕ-yĕ*).

Je *crains* qu'il ne vienne.
Ne craignez-vous pas qu'il ne vienne ?
But if the sentence be simply *negative* or simply *interrogative*, ne is not used, as :
Je ne crains pas *qu'il vienne.*
Craignez-vous *qu'il vienne ?*

4) *de* l'été, the whole summer through ; *de* la nuit, the whole night.

5) *Paraître*, to appear.—*Part. pr.:* paraissant.— *Part. p.:* paru.— *Pres.:* Je parais, tu parais, il paraît, nous paraissons, vous paraissez, ils paraissent (*pā-rĕs*). — *Pret. :* Je parus, tu parus, il parut, etc.— *Fut. :* Je paraîtrai.—*Pres. Subj.:* Que je paraisse.—Thus also : *Apparaître*, to appear ; *disparaître*, to disappear ; *reparaître*, to re-appear.

62. There is every indication of hot weather.

63. I feel warm.—I feel very warm.

64. How warm it is!—The heat is fairly choking (*or* overpowering).

65. The air is parching (*brûlant*); I am dying with heat.

66. One can scarcely bear the heat. (*Literally:* One does not know what to do on account of the heat.)

67. It makes one perspire (*transpirer*).

68. Let us step into the shade (*à l'ombre*).

69. Let us go into the shade.—It is shady here.

70. It is windy.—It is very windy.—There is a cold wind.

71. From which quarter is the wind?

72. The wind has changed (*or* turned].

73. It is pleasant for walking to-day.

74. What do you think of the weather? A little rain would not be amiss (*ne ferait pas de mal*).

75. We need rain.

76. Don't you think it is very warm weather for the season of the year?

77. Yes, this is one of the warmest springs I can remember.

78. The sun is as hot as in the midst of summer.

79. I am afraid we are going to have a thunderstorm to-day.

80. What wind! It thunders already! Do you hear?

62. { Il y a apparence de chaleur (*shā-leŭr*).
{ On dirait qu'il va faire chaud.

63. J'ai chaud. — J'ai extrêmement (*or* excessivement) chaud.

64. Ah! qu'il fait chaud! — Il fait‿une chaleur étouffante!

65. L'air est brûlant; je meurs de chaleur (*or* de chaud).

66. On ne sait que faire de chaleur.

67. Cela vous fait transpirer (*trāngs-pēē-rēh*).

68. Mettons-nous à l'ombre (*long-br'*).

69. Marchons à l'ombre.—Ici il fait de l'ombre.

70. Il fait du vent (*vāng*).—Il fait beaucoup de vent.—Il fait‿un vent froid (*froāh*).

71. Quel vent fait il? (*or*, Quel vent‿avons-nous)?

72. Le vent‿a changé (*or* tourné).

73. Il fait‿un temps très-agréable pour se promener aujourd'hui.

74. Que dites-vous du temps? Un peu de pluie ne ferait pas de mal.

75. Nous‿avons besoin de pluie.

76. Ne trouvez-vous pas qu'il fait bien chaud pour la saison (*sai-zong*)?

77. Oui, ce printemps (*praing-tāng*) est‿un des plus chauds dont je me *souvienne*.

78. Le soleil est‿aussi chaud qu'au milieu (*mēē-lēē-eŭ*) de l'été.

79. Je crains que nous n'ayons aujourd'hui de l'orage.

80. Quel tourbillon (*tōōr-bēē-yong*)! Il tonne déjà. Entendez-vous?

81. I just saw a flash of lightning.

82. The thunder roars.

83. What clap of thunder! the lightning has struck. Now it begins to rain.

84. Let us escape as fast as possible into this house.

85. God be thanked! the storm is over!

86. After the rain follows the fine weather. [French proverb.]

87. There is a draught here.

88. It is dusty.

89. It hails.

90. The hail has broken the window-panes (*les vitres*).

91. It is foggy.

92. It is quite fresh.—It is cold.

93. I feel cold.

94. It is freezing.—It freezes hard.

95. We had a hard frost last night (*cette nuit*).

96. We'll have a cold winter.

97. I am trembling with the cold.

98. It is growing colder.—It is growing warmer.

99. How many degrees have we? We have 3 degrees below zero.

100. It snows.—It is snowing hard.

101. It is thawing. — The ice is broken. — The snow is melting.

102. It is dirty.

81. Je viens de voir un‿éclair.

82. Le tonnere gronde.

83. Quel éclat de tonnerre! la foudre est tombé. Voilà qu'il commence à pleuvoir!

84. Sauvons-nous bien vite (*vēēt*) dans cette maison.

85. Dieu merci! l'orage est passé.

86. Après la pluie le beau temps.

87. { Il y a un courant (*rāng*) d'air ici.
{ Nous sommes‿ici entre deux‿airs.

88. Il fait de la poussière.

89. Il grêle (*or*, Il tombe de la grêle).

90. La grêle a cassé les vitres (*vēē-tr'*).

91. Il fait du brouillard (*brŏŏ-yāre*).

92. Il fait frais.—Il fait froid.

93. J'ai froid.

94. Il gèle.—Il gèle forte (*or*, Il gèle tout de bon).

95. Nous‿avons‿eu une forte gelée cette nuit (*nü-êē*).

96. Nous‿aurons‿un froid‿hiver (*ēē-vayr*).

97. Je tremble (*trāng-bl'*) de froid.

98. Le froid augmente (*māngt*).—Le froid diminue.

99. Combien de degrés‿avons nous?—Nous‿avons trois degrés de froid (*or*, Nous‿avons trois degrés au-dessous de zéro (*zay-rō*).

100. Il neige.—Il neige à gros flocons (*flō-kŏng*).

101. Il dégèle.—La glace s'est rompue (*rong-pü*).—La neige fond (*fongd*).

102. Il fait sale (*sāhl*) (*or*, Il fait de la boue).

2.

But before doing so make a fire in my son's room, as I am afraid he is ill.

But

before (Adverb)

make (Imperat)

some fire

in

the room

of my son

because

I am afraid

that he is ill

---

1. Please make a fire before bringing me the warm water.
2. If there is no fire in our bed-room, make one.

3. I cannot act otherwise (*autrement*).
— 4. I shall do it one way or another.
5. I have done my best.

2.

Mais auparavant faites du feu dans la chambre
may zŏ-pă-ră-văng fate dü feũ dăng lă shăng-br'

de mon fils parce que je crains qu'il ne soit malade.
dĕ mong ʃēēs păr-sĕ-kĕ jĕ craing kēēl nĕ swŏăh măh-lăd.

Mais

auparavant

faites

du feu

dans

la chambre

de mon fils

parce que

je crains

qu'il **ne** soit malade.

---

1. Faites du feu, je vous prie, avant de m'apporter de
   l'eau chaude.
2. S'il n'y a pas de feu dans notre chambre-à-coucher,
   faites-en.
3. Je ne puis faire autrement (*oh-tr'măng*).
4. Je le ferai de manière ou d'autre.
5. J'ai fait pour le mieux (*or* de mon mieux).

- 6. Do unto others as you would they should do unto you.
7. You can do what you like. (You may act as you please.)
8. Have you anything to do ?
9. Do what you please.
10. He has done it on his own responsibility.

11. That shall be done (*or* will be done) at once.
12. He does it very clumsily.
13. That happens sometimes.
14. It is getting late.
15. How does it happen that . . . . ?
16. I am not afraid of his coming.
17. I am afraid he is not coming.
18. Is there anything to fear (*or* to be afraid of) ?
19. It is to be feared that this may happen (*que cela n'arrive*).
20. I am afraid he will not succeed.
21. I am afraid my brother will loose his suit (*procès*).

6. Faites‿aux‿autres ce que vous voudriez qu'on vous fît (*fēē*).

7. Vous ferez comme‿il vous plaira (*or* comme‿il vous semblera bon [*sāng-blĕ-rāh bōng*]).

8. Avez-vous quelque chose à faire?

9. Faites comme vous voudrez.

10. Il l'a fait de son chef (*or* de son‿autorité privée [*prēē-vay*]).

11. Cela va être fait (*or* achevé, *or* fini, *or* terminé).

12. Il le fait très-gauchement (*gōsh'māng*).

13. Cela se fait quelquefois.

14. Il se fait tard.

15. Comment se fait-il que....?

16. Je ne crains pas qu'il vienne.

17. Je crains qu'il ne vienne pas.

18. Y a-t-il quelque chose à craindre?

19. Il est à craindre que cela n'arrive (*nār-rēēv*).

20. J'ai peur qu'il ne réussisse pas (*kēēl nĕ ray-üs-sĭs pah*).

21. Je crains que mon frère **ne** perde son procès (*say*).

COMPANION TO THE
Revised Version of the New Testament.

Explaining the Reasons for the Changes Made on the Authorized Version.

BY ALEXANDER ROBERTS, D.D.,
Member of the English Revision Committee.

WITH SUPPLEMENT BY A MEMBER OF THE AMERICAN COMMITTEE.

Containing a Brief History of the Revision of the Work and Co-operation of the New Testament Companies, of the Points of Agreement and Difference, and an Explanation of the Appendix to the Revised New Testament.

ALSO, A FULL TEXTUAL INDEX,

Being a Key to Passages in which Important Changes have been Made.

This book, having been carefully prepared by Members of both Revision Committees, carries official weight. It shows what changes have been made, and also the reasons whi:h influenced the revisers in making them. It will be difficult to judge of the merits of the revision without the aid of this Companion volume. Our edition is printed by special arrangement with the English publishers. It is well known that, by an arrangement between the two Committees of Revision, the changes suggested by the American Committee, but which were not adopted by the English Revisers, are published as an Appendix to the Revised New Testament. The *Companion* volume is an explanation of *all* the changes adopted by both committees, and of those suggested by the American Committee, but not assented to by the English Committee, in their final revision. The book will be indispensable to a right understanding of the revision. This cheap edition of the combined books, although authorized and copyrighted, will be sold for 25·cents in paper, and 75 cents in cloth—sent postage free.

TESTIMONIALS.

T. W. CHAMBERS, D.D., a Member of the American Committee of Revision, says of this book: "Many persons have expressed a desire that, simultaneously with the issue of the Revised New Testament, there should appear an authentic explanation of the reasons for such changes as will be found in its pages. The work of Dr. Roberts is exactly fitted to meet this desire....Nowhere e'.e in print can be found a statement so full and exact. It gives all needed information, and does it in an unexceptional way."

C. F. DEEMS, D.D., Pastor of the Church of the Strangers. New York, writes: "The Companion to the Revised Version seems to me almost indispensable, Even scholars who were not at the meeting of the Revisers would have a wearisome work in seeking to dis- cover all the changes made, and to ordinary readers very much of the labor would be lost. ....All this is s t forth by Dr. Roberts with admirable perspicuity. Those who have any intelligent interest in the Holy Scriptures, will find this little book absorbingly interesting. I shall urge every member of the church of which I am pastor to give it a careful reading, and purpose to introduce it as a text-book in our Bible-classes."

"So valuable, interesting and useful is this publication, that we advise every one who wishes to know the why and wherefore of the revision, to obtain it immediately."—*New York Observer.*

Paper, 8vo size, 25 cents ; Cloth, 16mo, 75 cents.

** For Sale by Booksellers and Newsdealers, or sent postage-paid, on receipt of price, by

I. K. FUNK & CO., Publishers, 10 & 12 Dey St., N. Y.

NOTICE TO SUBSCRIBERS.

A SUPPLEMENT

CONTAINING

1. KEY TO THE EXERCISES.
2. A COMPLETE FRENCH VOCABULARY.
3. COMMERCIAL AND SOCIAL CORRESPONDENCE.
4. ADDITIONAL GRAMMATICAL PECULIARITIES.

&c., &c.

WILL BE PUBLISHED IMMEDIATELY.

PRICE, 75 CENTS.—CLOTH.

SUBSCRIBERS WISHING TO SECURE THE SUPPLEMENT WILL
PLEASE REMIT 75 CENTS TO

I. K. FUNK & CO.,
10 & 12 Dey Street.

Lightning Source UK Ltd.
Milton Keynes UK
UKOW05f0649180118
316339UK00015B/371/P